Background to Spain

Background to Spain

B J W Hill
Eton College

Longmans

LONGMANS, GREEN AND CO LTD
London and Harlow
Associated companies, branches and representatives throughout the world

© *Longmans, Green and Company Limited, 1969*

First published 1969

SBN 582 31230.2

Printed in Great Britain by J. W. Arrowsmith Ltd, Bristol 3

Preface

In recent years there has been a greatly increased interest in Spain and Spanish affairs largely because of the enormous influx of visitors on holiday, and yet the general misunderstandings and misconceptions about Spain have continued to abound. It has long been apparent that a book was needed which would present a summary of Spanish history and culture for students and the general public and to encourage them to seek further information on their own account. This is what I have tried to achieve in this book, which is intended primarily as an introduction to Spain; with this in mind I have included for each chapter a short list of further reading for those interested in specific aspects of Spain and its culture.

In this book I have not shrunk from expressing my personal opinions, many of them debatable, because I think a book that takes no definite line provides reading no more stimulating than that of a railway timetable. If I have dwelt at length on Spanish literature and have given a smaller place to art and architecture, it is partly because I believe the spirit of a nation tends to find its widest expression in literature, and partly because this is likely to be of greater interest to language students. In dealing with literature I have attempted to give an outline of the contents of most major works in the hope that it will encourage those interested to read the works themselves.

I have used a wide range of sources in compiling this book, but I should like to acknowledge my special indebtedness to the following: *The Literature of the Spanish People* by Gerald Brenan (Cambridge University Press, 1951), *Historia de la literatura española* by M. Romera-Navarro (D. C. Heath, 1928), *Breve historia de la pintura española* by Enrique Lafuente Ferrari (Editorial Tecnos, 1953), *The Music of Spain* by Gilbert Chase (Dover Publications, second edition 1959), *The Golden*

Century in Spain by the late R. Trevor Davies (Macmillan, fourth edition 1958), *A History of Spain and Portugal* by William C. Atkinson (Penguin Books, 1960), *Spain* edited by the late E. Allison Peers, 1948. These books have been my chief guides and I am most grateful to all the authors for information supplied. It is impossible here to acknowledge all the works which have helped me in my task, but they are all mentioned in the bibliographies to the chapters and I hope that some of my debts may be repaid in this way. Finally I should like to thank the staff at Longmans for their help, encouragement and acute revision of the text.

B. J. W. HILL

Eton College
April 1968

Note In general there has been no attempt in this book to anglicise Spanish proper names except for a few which have been well-known to English speakers over the years, e.g. Seville, Catalonia. For this reason I have left the English form *Philip* rather than use the unfamiliar *Felipe*. I trust that readers will not be irritated by these apparent inconsistencies.

Contents

Illustrations

Acknowledgements

We are grateful to the following for permission to reproduce illustrations:

The Dowager Lady Aberconway: p. 456; The Art Institute of Chicago: pp. 452, 453; Associated Press Photo: p. 197; Barnaby's Picture Agency (Gerald Clyde): p. 415; Biblioteca del Monasterio de El Escorial: p. 461; Biblioteca Nationale, Madrid: p. 206; Camera Press: p. 419 *bottom* and p. 312 (Baron); Cifra Grafica: p. 146; George G. Harrap & Co. Ltd.: pp. 395, 398, 340, 402; Hispanic Society of America: pp. 364, 450; Isabella Stewart Gardner Museum, Boston: p. 486 *bottom*; Mas: pp. 48, 59, 215, 226, 235, 265, 294, 299, 355, 358, 418, 430, 432, 479; Mazo: p. 270; Mansell Collection: pp. 39 *left*, 60, 66 *left*, 67, 76, 77, 93, 108, 130, 153, 154, 185, 212, 242, 258, 259, 301, 429, 434, 435, 446 and Alinari photographs, p. 39 *middle, right* and Anderson photographs, pp. 44, 72, 91, 143, 150, 412 *bottom*, 416, 419, 438 *bottom*; Ministerio de Informacion y Turismo: pp. 58, 210, 211, 348; The Museum of Modern Art, New York: p. 196; The Museo d'Arte, The Courtauld Institute of Art: p. 448; The Director, Museo Nationale de Arte Moderno, Madrid: p. 449; The Trustees of the National Gallery, London: p. 445; National Gallery of Art, Washington, D.C.: p. 443; Paul Popper Ltd: pp. 64, 135, 192, 360, 458, 488, 490 *bottom*, 497 *bottom*, 499; The Press Association Ltd.: p. 201; Radio Times Hulton Picture Library: pp. 54, 66 *right*, 79, 99, 103, 120, 131, 187, 188, 199 *bottom*, 283, 289, 423, 428, 438 *top*, 473, 486 *top*; Spanish National Tourist Office: pp. 104, 165, 406, 408, 412 *top*, 421, 481, 490 *top*, 491, 494 *top*; Director, Victoria & Albert Museum: pp. 427, 439; The Wadsworth Atheneum, Hartford Connecticut: pp. 452, 453. p. 199 *top* is a photograph by the late Robert Capa, Magnum. The photographs on pp. 61, 238, 420, 494 *bottom*, 497 *top* are by the author.

Part I
The land and its history

Chapter 1
The land

A feeling of isolation immediately strikes any visitor to Spain, especially on entering the country by the normal route through Behobia or Irún at the western end of the Pyrenees. At the eastern end the impression of entering quite another world is not so pronounced; indeed the customs house at Le Perthus seems but an unnecessary stop on almost the first stretch of straight road after winding laboriously through the Pyrenees. This is because Catalonia has long had close links with France, and at one time Provence itself was ruled by the lord of Catalonia. Large numbers of Catalans still annually cross the border to find work harvesting in France or as domestic servants in well-to-do seaside villas.

To the west everything is different. Bayonne, the last big French town before the frontier, is a fine city with elegant buildings and wide avenues gay with flowers. Though Spanish is frequently to be heard in its streets, it remains essentially French. The road beyond is hilly but open, with glimpses of the sea occasionally to the right and later an extensive view of the foothills of the Pyrenees to the left. There are shady trees on each side of the road and plenty of signs of holiday-makers enjoying the bright sunshine and the cool Atlantic breezes. The gleaming garages advertising the latest types of petrol, oil, greasing, tyre maintenance and general car petting give the motorist a cosy feeling of being wanted.

Shortly before the border every fork road has a signpost indicating *Espagne* and the newcomer is at a loss which to choose. Probably the choice will fall on Behobia, which is the most direct route. Here the motorist will no doubt fill the tank of his car for the last time with his favourite brand of petrol before venturing into the unknown. The customs facilities at Behobia have been greatly improved of late; it is

LEFT *The fifteenth century collegiate church of Santillana del Mar*

now possible to drive straight across the rusty iron bridge which spans
the Bidasoa and on the other side a French gendarme operating on
Spanish territory casts a cursory glance at the travellers' passports.
A few yards farther on is an imposing gateway in granite, surmounted
by the arms of Spain. Here it is not necessary to leave the car for the
driver can push his passports across to a desk where a rather bored
official will stamp them without more ado. Beyond the gateway is a
granite custom house with various bays for cars painted in white lines
on the macadam. Several *aduaneros* will be lounging about taking little
notice of the visitors, but customs inspection is not usually strict, and a
short parley with an official in olive green uniform will suffice to
obtain clearance for the normal law-abiding visitor.

This ease of entry is comparatively new because the Spanish government has realised in the last few years that tourists are desirable con-
veyers of much needed foreign currency. Up till 1959 it was an
irritatingly tedious business. First of all a visa had to be obtained from a
Spanish consulate where the traditional formula of *Vuelva Vd. mañana*
(Come back tomorrow) was all too frequently employed. The visa
cost about 30s as marked by lurid stamps in the passport, but even so
the visitor had to pay another 70 pesetas or so at the frontier post. The
difficulty also lay in persuading any official to pay any attention. It was
a chilly reception; there was no actual unkindness, but there was an
unmistakable lack of interest. It must be admitted that on the whole
Spanish officials are awkward people to have dealings with; they are
mostly miserably paid and are often sour and discourteous. It seems
that their sole method of preserving their self-respect is by making
the person whose business they are despatching feel as small as
possible. If delay can be caused, it will be done, however trivial the
reason.

If this all sounds alarming for an intending visitor to Spain, he may
prefer to avoid the main frontier posts and enter by a small customs
barrier along the range of the Pyrenees. Access to one of these is often
difficult because of the strenuous driving involved on the mountain
roads, though the surfaces on the French side are almost universally
excellent. Traffic is usually very light at these small posts; an example is
Dancharinea, which can be reached reasonably easily from Bayonne
through exquisite mountain scenery. Here one policeman will carry
out all the necessary formalities and he will be so surprised and delighted
to see a car from a distant land that he will talk in the most engaging
fashion for half an hour or more. When at last the tourist drives away,

he will doubtless be convinced that the visitor from abroad is a welcome and privileged person; to a large extent he will be right, for Spaniards generally are some of the most hospitable people in the world and display excellent manners towards strangers. It may, therefore, be something of a shock to find the car halted not far beyond the frontier by two armed *carabineros* (excisemen) who are always on a sharp lookout for smugglers on the Pyrenean frontier. After examination of passports the visitor will be allowed to continue, but he may well have an uneasy feeling that he is now in a police state, and this time he will be definitely right.

The police

The foreign tourist is not much worried by the police providing that he drives with care and behaves with discretion. Many of the police are extremely helpful and the roads are now patrolled by police in Land-rovers bearing the banner of *Auxilio en la Carretera* (assistance on the road). Sometimes they can be a positive embarrassment in their eager-ness to help, and a British motorist who has stopped for a quiet cup of tea by the wayside may find himself besieged by eager rescuers con-vinced that he has broken down. Less pleasant are the police motor-cyclists, who operate in pairs and have arbitrary powers to enforce the rule of the road. They have a tendency to lurk on the far side of a blind corner in order to leap on any motorist who puts a wheel across the solid yellow line. Often a British motorist will find it difficult to see the yellow line from his driving position on the right, often the road is so narrow that it is well nigh impossible not to transgress by a few milli-metres, or sometimes a driver will harmlessly overtake a mule and cart plodding uphill at a scarcely measurable pace. If detected by the motor-cycle police, he will be peremptorily halted and an abject apology is the only wise course.

There are far too many police in Spain, and the ordinary Spaniard when travelling has to endure endless irritating checks. The most famous corps of police is the *Guardia Civil* who wear the flat-backed hats. They were originally raised in the nineteenth century to deal with banditry on the high roads, which they did very effectively, even if brutally at times. The usual procedure was to shoot prisoners shortly after capture and later make a report of attempted escape; this was a quicker and surer way of thinning the ranks of the bandits than bringing them to trial. *Guardias Civiles*, always in pairs, can frequently

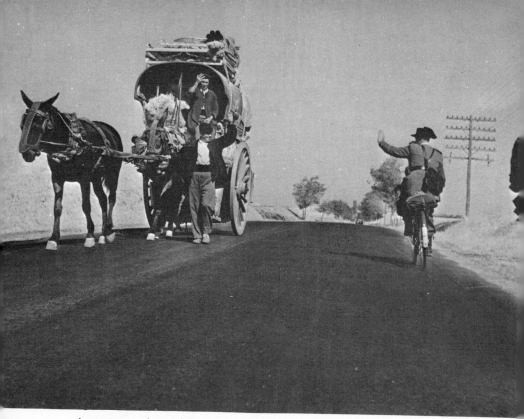

A greeting on the road from a Guardia Civil

be seen patrolling roads, each armed with a carbine and on separate sides of the highway to guard against surprise attack. The newly arrived visitor will feel apprehensive as he approaches them, for the *Guardias Civiles* may well make a motion as if to stop the car, but when it is seen to belong to a foreign tourist, they will invariably let it pass. Spanish cars and lorries are not so fortunate.

The *Guardias Civiles* are also to be found on railway trains and it is said that their hats were originally made flat to enable the wearers to lean back when travelling in a railway compartment. The *Guardia Civil* is organised on strict military lines and is housed in barracks which can readily be distinguished in every town by the motto displayed above the gateway: *Todo por la patria*. It is a general rule that no *guardia* serves on duty in or near his native district; in this way the police are aloof and distant in their dealings with the public, though it is quite possible to have long, amicable conversations with them when they are not on duty.

Another type of state police wear grey uniforms with red gorget patches. These are armed with pistols instead of carbines, and their function is the maintenance of public order in the towns and cities. They wear a normal service cap and lack the glamour of the picturesque and forbidding *Guardias Civiles*. There are also municipal police for traffic duties often called *guardias de porra*, from the truncheon which hangs from their belt. They have the right to fine traffic offenders on the spot, the culprit being stopped by a piercing blast on a referee's whistle. Here again the visitor is at an advantage and can generally escape a fine for crossing the street in Madrid against the traffic lights if he pleads ignorance and helplessness. For the most part the traffic police, from the smartest constable in Madrid to the seediest old officer in a remote country town, are invariably polite and helpful to strangers. Nevertheless it is highly advisable to avoid any kind of brush with the authorities in Spain. Several tourists have found that the police can be high-handed and unreasonable in their methods, especially after a road accident in which perhaps no blame can be attached to the visitor. Instances have been known of the car being confiscated and returned only after exhausting and expensive negotiations. The foreign motorist in Spain is well advised to take especial care when driving.

Roads and railways

Spanish roads have an evil reputation which is apt to scare away the nervous motorist. In this respect there is little need for apprehension. A vast amount of work is continually in progress to improve Spanish highways. On almost every road the motorist encounters the dreaded word: *Obras*; he will then know that for the next mile or more he will find the road a complete shambles. In Spain work is not done on one side of the road while the other is left free for traffic; the entire road is pulled to pieces and the motorist has to pick his way over a surface of loose stones which are still often laid by gangs of men carrying small baskets while others pack the stones down with hand rammers.

The result of all this labour has been to make the main roads reasonably good throughout the country, in spite of the great difficulties imposed by the physical and climatic conditions. Traffic is lighter than in many European countries, though nowadays the number of large lorries, mostly Leylands or Pegasus (Spain's own product), has increased greatly; these giants lumber through the villages in an alarming manner, scraping chunks of stone off the houses as they turn the corners of the narrow streets. The surface of the main roads, even where extensive improvements have been recently made, is mostly poor. Extremes of heat and cold, long periods of drought and sudden torrential downpours are bad for any surfaces, and those made without the help of modern heavy engineering equipment are unequal to the strain. Nevertheless, the *Peones Camineros*, whose lonely lodgings are to be seen at regular intervals of ten kilometres beside the main roads, cope manfully with the potholes on their beat, and the motorist need have no fear for his springs even though the constant jolting is at times trying.

The minor roads are more of a gamble. Often a secondary road may start in the most promising fashion, raising hopes of a spectacular short cut, only to peter out inexplicably in a mere mule track in the middle of a deserted countryside. At other times a signposted minor road may appear preposterously bad as it winds its way out of a village and yet improves vastly for no obvious reason in the wilderness. The only safe way is to make careful enquiries before branching off from the main road. The local inhabitants are normally voluble and eloquent on the subject of their roads, and are completely truthful. *Una carretera picada* is to be avoided.

Moreover, a trip along a side road, probably involving much work for the lower gears, may raise anxiety concerning petrol supplies. Garages are not nearly so plentiful in Spain as in France or England, nor are they so elegantly tempting. Like tobacco, petrol is a monopoly in Spain and like tobacco it is of poor quality. There are two kinds: *Super* or *Plomo* and plain *gasolina*. *Plomo* is the higher grade and therefore more expensive, but it is doubtful whether it functions better. A Spanish mechanic gave it as his considered opinion that '*Gasolina hace menos daño*' (ordinary petrol does less damage). Spanish petrol has improved in quality in recent years and is sufficiently combustible to propel most cars satisfactorily, though in mountain areas there is a notable lack of power.

There need be no real fear of a breakdown, even on lonely stretches of road. There are roadside telephones at fairly frequent intervals and peasants in any part of Spain readily help a motorist in distress. His car will be got to a garage even if it involves the indignity of being towed by a yoke of oxen. At almost any garage a first-class mechanic is to be found and he is likely to be an adaptable enthusiast. To keep their own ancient cars running without spares, and to tend the precious farm machinery, calls for considerable ingenuity on the part of local engineers. There is none of the helpless reliance on the maker's spares which characterises garages in highly mechanised countries and which causes such frustrating delays. A Spanish mechanic will work through the night to get the car ready for its owner to continue his journey the following day. Very likely he will himself make a special tool to undo some awkward nut, and himself fashion a new gudgeon pin or other exotic spare part to set the engine to rights. After a night's toil all will be ready and the mechanic will be grinning all over his face from the pride and pleasure of having achieved a difficult repair on an unfamiliar type of car. Usually too his charge will be extremely moderate, for the Spanish tend to spurn monetary rewards, preferring the satisfaction of a job well done.

Equally courteous service will usually be found on Spanish railways and most trains have clean and comfortable compartments, at least for first and second class passengers. Some of the comfort stems from a maddening piece of Spanish individuality, namely that the main lines have a gauge of 5 ft 6 in, as opposed to the European standard gauge of 4 ft 8½ in. The break in gauge at the frontier means that all passengers have to change trains, except on the latest luxury trains which have an adaptable gauge, but as compensation they find that Spanish compartments are more spacious and have some of the solid comfort, tasselled fringes included, of Victorian trains. On the whole Spanish trains are punctual, but then they normally leave themselves plenty of time for the journey, even allowing for the mountainous nature of the country. Many expresses average only 35 m.p.h. and even the crack train from the French frontier has managed no more than 45 m.p.h. over its whole journey. This is the TALGO (*tren articulado ligero*) for which a supplementary fare is charged and of which the Spaniards are very proud, for it is a Spanish invention by a Basque engineer, Señor Goicochea. It is a lightweight aluminium train, close coupled, with multiple diesel power units. Its low, silvery, snakelike shape gives it an odd appearance among the normally massive rolling stock, like a tube train that has escaped from its tunnels to the freedom of the main line.

It is inadvisable for the visitor to arrive at a Spanish railway station expecting to buy a ticket and step on a train. For one thing many Spanish expresses do not run daily, but only some three or four times a week. Moreover, frequently all places on certain trains will have been booked several days ahead, and though sometimes it is possible to acquire a ticket from profiteers in the station, it is unwise to take such a chance, which may prove expensive. The sensible course is to book the ticket for the journey well ahead at an office of the RENFE (*Red nacional de los ferrocarriles españoles*, National Network of Spanish Railways). Having taken this necessary precaution it often happens that the tourist finds his reserved seat already occupied, but this can be remedied by application to the ticket inspector who bears the eloquent name of the *interventor*. It is prudent to warn this official of any intention to travel in a higher class than one's ticket allows, because failure to do this may entail a charge of double the excess fare. Any argument, however righteous and justified, may lead to serious trouble with the *Guardias Civiles*, who are always on duty on trains.

A further snag about using Spanish railways is that most of the best trains run at night and, though there are comfortable sleeping compartments (*coches cama*), the traveller has little opportunity for seeing the countryside. To do this the visitor must use the slow trains (*trenes correo*, mail trains, or *trenes mixtos* for passengers and goods). These are definitely very slow indeed; the Irún–Madrid journey requires no less than twenty-three hours at an average speed of 17·2 m.p.h. These trains also tend to be crowded, but the journey is full of incident, and for those visitors who speak Spanish there is an excellent opportunity for striking up acquaintances, as the passengers are normally friendly and talkative. The train has a habit of stopping for about forty minutes between 2 p.m. and 3 p.m. to enable passengers to have lunch, which is often taken at one long table on the station platform while the locomotive hisses and gurgles gently at the head of the train. For any engine enthusiast Spain is a paradise, for besides powerful modern steam and diesel locomotives there are scores of period pieces, many dating from the 1880s, still loyally at work with steam leaking from every seam. If there is no definite halt for meals, passengers produce food of their own in the crowded compartments. Such snacks usually consist of *bocadillos* (literally, small mouthfuls); these are massive sandwiches made from a whole loaf of bread split in two with slices of salami sausage (*salchichón*) inserted. An exceptionally wide mouthspan is required to cope successfully with these delicacies. Spanish courtesy demands that when a passenger takes out his supply of food he should at once offer it to his companions, saying: '¿*Vd. gusta?*' (Would you like some?) Politeness also requires a refusal using the formula: '*Que le aproveche*' (May it do you good). Even so, Spanish hospitality is such that a famished foreigner with no stock of food would most certainly be induced to share with his companions.

The same friendly atmosphere pervades the buses that provide transport even to the most remote villages in Spain. There are indeed

luxurious motor-coaches for tourists provided by ATESA (*Autotrans-
porte turístico español S.A.*), but these are of less interest than the local
buses, which though often battered and rickety in appearance, faithfully
carry abnormal loads of passengers along roads with execrable surfaces
and terrifying bends, very much in the manner of stage coaches of old.
Any visitor who arrives at the boarding point will imagine that he has
no hope of a place because he will find some fifty or more people
waiting, but as often as not these will be well-wishers come to bid
goodbye to some couple leaving the village for the first time. At any
rate, all passengers are somehow fitted in, sitting, standing, squatting,
bumping against each other as the bus lurches and sways. There is
little comfort, but much friendliness and great comradeship, such as is
known only to those who have to make the best of a bad job. When
the visitor reaches his destination he will push his way out through a
gale of cheerful farewells. The driver, smiling and fresh after struggling
with capricious steering and suspect brakes, will leap with the agility
characteristic of the young Spanish male onto the roof to extract the
visitor's luggage from the amazing pile of assorted jumble assembled
there. For all this willing service no tip is sought or expected.

Hotels and restaurants

This indifference to purely financial gain is often noticeable in hotels
and provides a refreshing contrast to most European countries. In a
hotel or restaurant the meal is served quickly and efficiently by a
charming waitress or a genial waiter who is only too ready to discuss
the merits of football or bullfighting, or to remain discreetly silent if
the customer is not inclined to talk. At the end of the meal a tip is not
expected, but one will be courteously accepted, though never in an
unctuous fashion. An expression of satisfaction from the customer is
often appreciated as much or more than mere largess.

As in all countries the standard of hotels and restaurants varies
greatly, but in general hotels in Spain are clean and comfortable and
reasonable in price. The *Dirección General del Turismo* has taken great
trouble in regulating the prices charged according to the classification
of the hotel concerned. It is obligatory to display in every hotel bedroom
the charge made for the room and for each meal as well as *pensión*
terms. The classification specifies three types of hotels: A, B and C.
The B hotels are normally eminently suitable even for the most
fastidious tastes, while the C hotels provide a decent standard of

comfort. The least promising exterior may conceal a pleasant interior where an excellent meal and a comfortable bed can be obtained. One such hotel in Valdepeñas, just off the main road south from Madrid and a great centre for wine, had a ragged, but cheerful urchin wearing an antique commissionaire's cap stationed outside late in the evening actively soliciting custom. The hotel of which he seemed so proud was a tumbledown hovel, but a reluctant entry produced the surprising view of a spotlessly clean dining room where a first-class supper was served by a smiling waitress, who to reach the kitchen had to crawl through a low trapdoor like the entrance to a kennel. Her agility and dexterity must have been born of long practice and her willingness to plunge through the trap in search of additional refinements to the meal was remarkable. The bedrooms were as clean as the dining room and extremely comfortable. The bill for each person for supper, bed and breakfast came to no more than thirteen shillings (1959).

Unclassified *Pensiones*, and in rural areas the humble *Fondas*, can be comfortable and pleasant for short stays. The *Fondas* are particularly interesting because they are in essentials unchanged from those described by Cervantes in *Don Quixote*, though at times the possession of a somewhat reluctant electric light strikes an incongruous note. For anyone with a good knowledge of Spanish a stay in a remote *Fonda* is a worthwhile experience, for there is a splendid opportunity to talk at leisure with varied types of humble Spanish travellers. Providing the visitor does not require privacy, is not allergic to sleeping in fairly close proximity to asses and mules, and can eat food dripping with olive oil and reeking of garlic, a stay at a *Fonda* is fascinating. For those who cannot fulfil these conditions, and who have the money to spend, the *Dirección General del Turismo* organises a series of *Paradores* throughout the country. These are situated in beautiful surroundings and are created from ancient castles or monasteries, restored and fitted with all modern luxuries. Many of them are delightful, but some give the impression of being intended only for the richer type of tourist. Ordinary hotels are more hospitable and more typical of Spain.

The method of classifying hotels is curious. It is calculated by the number of bathrooms available. Since the higher grade hotels are able to charge considerably enhanced prices, it has been worthwhile for hotelkeepers to install enough baths to raise their classification status. In a hotel in Algeciras quite a modest room had a bathroom attached in which there were no less than fourteen taps, but as in so many hotels in Spain no attempt had been made to connect these luxurious fittings to a water supply.

This is not so illogical as it may seem at first sight. The Spaniards as a race, though scrupulously clean in almost every way, do not worship baths to the same extent as their forebears, the Romans, or as the Anglo-Saxons. But Spain paradoxically is clean compared with European industrial countries, for since there is practically no coal in Spain the air is not constantly charged with grime. Moreover, it is useless connecting elaborate bathroom equipment to a public water supply which does not itself function except fitfully. An Englishwoman entering her first hotel in Spain in the attractive seaside village of Zarauz on the Biscay coast jumped for joy on seeing a bath in a cubby-hole in her bedroom. Her darkest fears of Spain were at an end; after the exhausting journey she would have a bath and change her clothes before dinner. The bath itself was about a quarter filled with somewhat murky cold water. Gaily she pulled out the plug and swilled round the bath before fetching her towel. Subsequent enquiries elicited the fact that she had allowed the whole of the next day's water supply to drain away. The main was in operation each evening and then only for an hour.

Lack of water, or more precisely irregularity of supply, is one of Spain's chief problems. Rivers are often rushing torrents in the winter, sweeping away boulders and trees as they race towards the sea. In summer these same rivers are merely wide beds of bleached stones. Efforts are made to harness these rivers for useful purposes, and extensive lakes and dams provide water power to drive turbines for producing electricity. Great advances have been made in the last twenty years, but even the most ardent Hispanophile can scarcely call the supply of water or electricity anything but hesitant.

In the high arid central plateau water conservation is an acute problem, but in the north there is an abundant rainfall and the poor supply of water in towns and villages is the result of bad organisation. The Romans went to great lengths to maintain adequate supplies as the imposing aqueduct at Segovia proves. Spaniards, however, dislike being organised and though they are capable of intense effort over limited periods, they have no gift for steady, unspectacular routine tasks. They therefore prefer to rely on the village fountain, which is also a convenient social meeting place. Nevertheless it is irritating for a stranger to find that water is scarce amid plenty as he travels through the lush green countryside of the north.

The Basque provinces

The Basque provinces which lie closest to France at the western end of
the Pyrenees are a strange mixture of agriculture and industry, of things
ancient and modern. It is possible to drive along a good motor road
amid green mountains, occasionally meeting a Basque peasant dressed
in blue and wearing a beret, the regional headdress; he will probably
be leading two oxen yoked together with great woolly fringes to keep
the flies out of their eyes. They will be drawing a primitive cart of
crude design at a pace which would be scarcely measurable on a
speedometer. Just round the corner from this charming rustic scene the
traveller will be surprised to find a huge iron works or chemical factory
in full and furious operation, with heavy lorries emerging from the
gates and jostling another bullock cart out of the way. Similarly,
villages of immense antiquity, whose habits and customs have not
changed for centuries, will be found next to huge modern hydro hotels
built in these remote mountains to offer spa treatment in the sulphur
springs that gush from the rock.

Bilbao, the capital of the province of Vizcaya, is a thriving city, for
the Basques are good businessmen and possessed of bounding energy.
They are in fact never still for a moment and like their renowned tennis
player, Borotra, they leap and jump with unwearying zest. This
springiness is said to originate from the fact that they live in a mountainous district where no step is ever taken on level ground, but always
up or down. Whatever the origin, the national vigour is amazing and
when work is ended, surplus energy is expended in playing the regional
sport, *pelota*, which is considered by many the fastest game in the world.

It is a form of fives, but with only a front wall and (usually) a sidewall.
On a proper *pelota* court (*frontón*) this is of considerable size, but for
popular amusement in the villages any wall suffices, with a probable
preference for the wall of the church. The priest himself may well be
one of the most enthusiastic performers among the parishioners. In the
simpler form of the game the ball is struck with the bare hand and since
the ball is as hard as a fives ball but much larger, hands have to be
hardened by years of practice at the game. Even so, it is not uncommon
in a long match to see one of the players stoop down and tread firmly
on each hand in turn to press out the blood which internal bleeding
has brought into the palms and fingers. The more elaborate type of
pelota requires the players to wear a long curved basket (*cesta*) on one
hand. The ball is caught in the basket and swept back at lightning speed

LEFT *Roman aqueduct in Segovia*

ABOVE   *A game of pelota*

BELOW   *Iglesia Colegiata, Santillana del Mar*

to the front wall. The skill and quickness needed are astonishing and the matches between the leading professionals excite the keenest interest, not least because a row of bookmakers stationed in front of the crowd enables spectators to bet on the result, not only of the match, but of any rally in the game.

Betting is one of the national vices of Spain, and in this respect the Basques conform to type, but mostly they are fiercely individualistic. Throughout the history of Spain there has been a constant agitation for Basque separatism and independence. This is not surprising in view of the fact that the Basques are of completely distinct stock from the remainder of the Spanish race. Where they originated is a mystery; it is tempting to suppose they represent a last relic of the Celt–Iberian race that inhabited Spain before the Romans colonised it, but the Basque language bears no relation to any Celtic tongue. It has been vaguely identified with some central European dialects and the present theory is that the Basques are the result of the ancient migration of a tribe which has miraculously preserved its identity and language over thousands of years in a strange land. The Basque tongue is still spoken in isolated districts, and posters in Bilbao are often printed in both Spanish and Basque, but this mysterious and picturesque language is slowly losing ground before the civilising influence of state education and wireless programmes.

Asturias and Galicia

West of the Basque provinces lies the mountainous region of Asturias, whose inhabitants are likewise strongly independent in outlook. The Romans subdued them only after a long and bitter campaign, and Asturian peasants died under torture hurling defiance at their tormentors. Asturias too was the cradle of Christian resistance to the Moors, and in recent times Asturian miners have used their explosives with telling effect in civil strife. Asturias is one of the few regions in Spain where coal is found in any quantity, but the total output is a mere 14 million tons a year and the province remains like its more westerly neighbour, Galicia, a predominantly agricultural area. The rainfall is plentiful and the fine, persistent drizzle on the mountains produces excellent grazing for sheep, while in the valleys fruit grows abundantly, though the comparative lack of sunshine precludes the growing of grapes and other subtropical fruits. Cider is the wine of the country and

ABOVE *Threshing in Castile*

BELOW *Transport near Burgos*

has become a popular drink in other parts of Spain, the most famous brand widely advertised bearing the name of *El Gaitero* (the Bagpiper).

Bagpipes seem indigenous wherever Celtic races remain, and the Galicians display many of the characteristics of the Celts. They are sentimental, poetical, and passionately attached to their native land. Their dialect is indeed a language of its own, though it is of Latin origin; it has a fine literature and in fact cradled the Portuguese language. Like Basque it is still spoken extensively in country districts, but is receding before the advance of Castilian.

The Galicians are poor, for it is hard to wring a livelihood from the bare, dripping mountains, but they are an industrious and enterprising race and thousands emigrate to seek their fortune overseas. Galician maids are highly prized in wealthy households in Madrid and recently large numbers have come to find work in England, where they prove themselves at once intelligent, hard-working and adaptable, but also supremely obstinate. Every Galician emigrant, whether a humble domestic servant or a rich rancher in South America, plans eventually to return to the homeland. There, if means allow, he will found some charitable institution or acquire a country house (*casa solariega*) with a coat of arms carved in stone above the doorway. All over northern Spain massive stone houses can be found separately or huddled together in villages and all bear the blasons of their builders. One such village, now preserved as a national monument, is Santillana del Mar, not far from Santander and a fitting neighbour to one of Spain's earliest known places of habitation, the caves of Altamira. In these can be seen pictures, beautifully executed to conform to the configuration of the roof, of bison, wild boar, deer and other animals. Estimates of their age vary between 11,000 and 50,000 years.

Old and New Castile

South from Asturias lie the provinces of Old and New Castile, marking the gradual southward progress of the Christians reconquering Spain from the Moors. The Castiles are a barren tableland, though in spring the countryside in places looks green enough with the new corn growing. How the farmers till these scattered rocky fields is a miracle, and no one who sees the site of their labours can ever truthfully level the charge of idleness at the Spanish race, or at any rate at the Castilians. No less mysterious is how the labourers reach their fields, which often lie miles from the lonely villages. There are no isolated farms; all houses are clustered together in strong, forbidding villages whose centre of defence is a fortified church. From these villages peasants sally forth on donkeys, or in carts drawn by mules, and trudge the weary journey along stony tracks to reach their fields. There they plough the sandy, boulder-strewn soil with the most primitive implements and somehow conjure wheat, barley and oats from the reluctant earth.

In July the aspect of the countryside is entirely different. The yellow corn is harvested and the whole landscape is tawny with stubble. Everything is bare; no tree is in sight except some withered plane trees which an optimist has tried to grow beside the main road in imitation of the highways of France. The deep blue sky is dotted with humpy white clouds and a strong wind is blowing from the not far distant *sierra*, making the heat of the blazing sun bearable. This is the wind that forms an integral part of the threshing technique, which in its extreme simplicity evokes scenes from the Bible. Outside the crumbling villages is a communal threshing floor of cobbles over which the corn is spread. Two mules draw a sledge on which the children squat as grinning makeweights. The friction of the sledge loosens the chaff from the grain and the separation is finally achieved by tossing both into the air, where the steady wind blows the chaff into a more distant heap while the grain falls heavily into a nearby golden pile. Recently a few threshing machines have made a diffident entry into the Castilian landscape, just as the occasional tractor is to be seen apologetically competing with mules and donkeys. Many of the threshing machines are hand operated, and a Castilian peasant stained a rich mahogany hue by a combination of sun, wind and long matured dirt turns a large handle, looking for all the world like an organ grinder.

The cities of Castile are old and all bear signs of the long, heroic struggle with the infidel and the perpetual battle with the elements. Burgos with its noble cathedral is a bastion of the Christian faith, the city of the national hero, the *Cid Campeador*, who struggled for independence—his own mostly, but for Christian freedom when it suited his purpose—up to his death in 1099; even after he died, if legend be true, his embalmed body struck terror into the Moors. It is a pity that the modern statue erected in Burgos to his memory should make him look like some Wagnerian hero of the 1890s.

Segovia offers a splendid Roman aqueduct of granite, so accurately cut that no mortar or clamps are needed to support the stones of its arches, ninety-two feet high in the centre as it spans a valley partly consisting of drab houses. It brings water to the old city at whose western extremity the Alcázar (fortress), part Moorish, part Christian, is perched on a lofty rock like an illustration in a book of fairy tales.

Further south, high amid an upland wilderness, stands Ávila, completely surrounded by its eleventh-century granite walls, which look so new and clean that cynical tourists suspect a large-scale sham. But there is nothing new in Ávila; only the hideous railway station and sheds outside the walls jar the ancient solid bleakness of the city, where only heroes and the dynamic, practical mystic poetess, Santa Teresa, had the fortitude to endure the hardships of life in a wild outpost.

Southward still, in a warmer, sunnier position, Toledo towers on its hill above the deep channel of the Tagus spanned by a Roman bridge. Toledo has remained a medieval city which even hordes of tourists cannot jolt into modernity. The motorist drives agonised down streets of startling narrowness with a single, all-purpose gutter in the centre, and finds himself forced to stop while a file of donkeys laden with panniers unconcernedly claims right of way as the senior method of transport. It is a city full of surprises, with a Jewish synagogue as a Christian church, and Roman, Visigothic, Moorish and Christian architecture jumbled in amazingly harmonious accord. Through all its streets can be heard the tapping of hammers as craftsmen fashion knives and scissors and swords in Toledo steel with Arabic inlay work as decoration. Toledo has a charm and dignity that no combined onslaught from all the travel agents in Europe can destroy. As the seat of the primacy of Spain and former capital it is aloof and unspoilable.

Madrid alone of the towns of Castile is a modern, cosmopolitan city, growing, thriving and bustling on a site where no town has any right to exist. Though the court occasionally resided at the Alcázar that stood there until 1734, Madrid was not established as the capital until 1561, when Philip II chose it because it is almost the exact geographical centre of Spain, and because the keen mountain air soothed his gout. Madrid is the loftiest sited capital in Europe with an average altitude of 2,000 feet and its situation is desolate in the extreme. Its climate is exacting too, hot sunshine alternating with freezing winds; *la pulmonía fulminante* (thundering pneumonia) was in the days before sulphonamides a scourge of the population. To walk out of the blazing heat of the Gran Vía into the freezing temperature of a narrow, sunless side street was an uncomfortable and dangerous experience.

Despite all its natural handicaps Madrid flourishes. Since the Civil War (1936–39) it has more than doubled its population, resulting in rapid extension of suburbs, some of which contain miserable shanties made with flattened petrol tins. But the general aspect of Madrid is one of spaciousness, with fine avenues, pleasant parks and imposing rather than beautiful buildings. Very few of the buildings in the fashionable part of the city are old, in marked contrast with almost all other Spanish towns. The Plaza Mayor indeed dates from 1619, but its fine uniform plan now looks seedy and dreary, and scarcely lives up to the grandiose spectacles it witnessed three centuries ago, when plays by Lope de Vega were acted there, bullfights were held and the grisly ceremonies of *autos de fe* were performed. The royal palace is a handsome eighteenth-century building constructed in 1738 by the French-born king, Philip V, to replace the ancient Alcázar on the same site, which he had burnt to the ground as being too humble to house a grandson of Louis XIV.

Most of the city buildings are of nineteenth-century construction and somewhat florid, like the main post office in the Plaza de la Cibeles. Its spires and gothic excrescences have earned for it the nickname of *Nuestra Señora de las Comunicaciones*. Much of the life of Madrid is

BELOW   *Plaza Mayor, Madrid*   RIGHT   *Arco de Cuchilleros, Madrid*

redolent of the nineteenth century. The uniformed nursemaids with children dressed in frilly and spotlessly white clothes; the portly gentlemen unashamedly sitting in the window of their clubs watching the passers-by, especially the girls, who never walk singly, always in pairs; the well-to-do married women with time on their hands because servants are still plentiful, waiting for their husbands to leave their offices so that they can go to some place of amusement (for married women cannot go unaccompanied)—all these phenomena, besides many others such as trams, ornate lamp-posts, flamboyant fountains, florid decorations in hotels and restaurants, make Madrid a pleasant throw-back to a more leisured, luxurious age. Though there are indeed poor quarters of Madrid where families huddle in squalid poverty, the general atmosphere is gay, cheerful, well-mannered and contented. The beggars have gone from the streets and the church porticoes, and only the wailing cries of the aged or maimed lottery ticket sellers introduce a disturbing note into the prevailing theme of prosperity.

Extremadura

Very different is the region west of Madrid on the Portuguese border, Extremadura, which is poor and backward. Much of it is barren, dusty and sunbaked, but even some fertile parts such as the valley of Las Batuecas have become proverbial for their primitive conditions of living. With its scanty population, its unrelieved poverty and its intemperate climate, Extremadura is shunned by tourists, but there are places of interest for anyone bold enough to travel south from the glorious university city of Salamanca on the fringe of New Castile. Cáceres, a town of Roman origin but with an extensive Arab overlay, gives a reminder too, with its *casas solariegas*, of the adventurous Extremadurans who set out to explore and conquer the new world, such as Cortés in Mexico and Pizarro in Peru. Badajoz on the Portuguese frontier is a fortress town with a history of perpetual bloodshed, and its name is familiar because of the capture of the town by Wellington on 6 April 1812. Its subsequent brutal sack by British troops is a dark incident on which little light has been shed.

The most interesting town in Extremadura is undoubtedly Mérida, which boasts the best preserved Roman remains in Spain. The Roman bridge over the Guadiana is a noble piece of architecture of finely cut granite blocks with sixty arches extending over half a mile. Parts of two aqueducts survive and the piles of one named Los Milagros are topped with storks' nests which give them a picturesque untidy appearance. The Roman theatre is one of the most beautiful ancient monuments in Spain. Dating from 18 B.C. it has seven blocks of seats (hence its name *Las Siete Sillas*) with room enough for 5,000 spectators.

Andalusia

The road over the Sierra Morena leads to Seville, the chief town of Andalusia, the province which for foreigners typifies all Spain. The magnificent climate, the fertile plains with all the subtropical fruits, the picturesque costumes seen at festival times, the dancing and *flamenco* singing, the handsome horses and gaily decked mules, the passion for bullfighting, the ceaseless, effervescent gaiety of the Andalusians combined with an ability to neglect hard work, all make a composite picture which seems to the foreigner to be the image of the whole national character and way of life. In actual fact the Andalusian is

Casería del Conde, Alameda, a large Andalusian farm

profoundly different in character and habits from the majority of
Spaniards. His slurring speech, endless chatter, eagerness to cut a dash,
have made him a slightly comic figure in the eyes of the rest of the
Peninsula. But comic or not, he is an attractive person whose cheerful-
ness and vivacity have never been dulled by grinding poverty and
semi-starvation. Andalusia, which might well be the richest region of
Spain, has long suffered from agricultural neglect because the land has
been in the hands of absentee landlords who hire peasants to work only
at busy periods of the year, such as harvest or seed sowing times. The
peasants owning no land themselves are powerless to earn a living at
other seasons of the year. Many go north to Valencia to seek work or a
patch of ground to till. Others merely shrug their shoulders with oriental
resignation and stay and starve, knowing that the warm sun will soften
the pangs of hunger. Much has been done in the way of piecemeal
agrarian reforms and government sponsored schemes of agricultural
improvement, and poverty is not immediately apparent to the tourist
in the big towns or the holidaymakers along the Costa del Sol. But in
the less fertile parts of the province east of Motril and around Almería,
tumbledown villages thronged by nearly naked children make miserable sightseeing, and bands of wild gypsies cause the motorist to hasten
fearfully along the execrable surface of the picturesque coastal road,
beside which the bright blue Mediterranean seems to mock the
wretchedness of the landscape.

The main towns of Andalusia are unforgettable. Seville boasts the
largest cathedral in Europe, dominated by the lovely Moorish minaret,
La Giralda (the weathercock), from which in Muslim times the muezzin
used to call the faithful to prayer. The Alcázar, although built in 1364
by Pedro the Cruel, is Moorish in every detail, with its intricate
stalactite plasterwork in multitudinous colours. The gardens are completely subtropical, with palms and orange trees and many fountains,
and they provide a haven of peace amid a city whose inhabitants amply
testify that the Spaniards are the noisiest race on earth. The streets
are full of bustle and life except during the siesta period and their
extreme narrowness amplifies the shriek of tortured tyres, the ceaseless
hooting of cars, the ringing of the horses' hooves on the cobbles, and
the continuous conversation which even in the soft Andalusian dialect
resembles an argument to the death. The din continues far into the
night, for the Andalusian is at his most dynamic in the comparative
cool of the darkness. When the weary tourist, sweltering in his hotel
bedroom, eventually falls asleep, he finds his rest is brief because as like

RIGHT   *The Giralda Tower, Seville Cathedral*

as not, on the roof of the house opposite, a brood of hens with an eager cock will make the dawn hideous with noise again. Only the siesta (3 p.m. to 6 p.m.) provides peace: all life suddenly ceases after the late luncheon hour, and however ingrained one's northern habits of waking hours may be an afternoon sleep is a physical necessity in Seville.

Córdoba has the charm of quietness which Seville entirely lacks, though modern industrialisation in the north-west of the town may shake its calm a little. It is still possible to wander fascinated through the maze of narrow streets and peep into the cool *patios* with their bright flowers. The great mosque which has been appropriated as a cathedral must surely rank as one of the wonders of the world. Begun in 786 it offers a forest of marble, porphyry and jasper columns of varying patterns; there are in fact 850 of them, all exquisitely worked. In the centre of this forest stands a sixteenth-century Baroque choir and sanctuary (1523–99). When the plans for this incongruous centrepiece were first formulated, the Córdoba town council, like any worthwhile planning authority, rose in wrath, and with a forcefulness denied to modern authorities threatened with death any workman who should take a hand in demolishing any part of the mosque. Unfortunately the town council was overruled by the Royal Council and the work was put in hand, but Charles V, visiting Córdoba some years later, realised his mistake and said reprovingly to the Chapter: 'If I had known what you wished to do, you would not have done it, for what you are building here can be found everywhere and what you previously possessed exists nowhere.' There is no need to weep unduly over what was done because unbelievably the Gothic choir fits its Moorish surrounding like the jagged stone inside a peach.

To the south-east of Córdoba in a lofty position stands Granada, the last Moorish kingdom to fall to the Christians in 1492. Granada would be a fine town without the Alhambra and the Generalife, but these two Moorish palaces make it a city of enchantment. The Alhambra was a fortress as well as a palace and stands secure on a steep hill whose slopes were planted with elms by Wellington; visitors seem suddenly plunged into an English wood, green, leafy and cool, and quite unlike the usual somewhat prickly vegetation of southern Spain. The melting snows of the Sierra Nevada supply Granada with water in abundance, and the slopes up to the Alhambra are gurgling with brooks and fountains and tiny waterfalls which in the hours of darkness mingle their harmonious chatter with the clear shrill song of many nightingales.

The tinkle of fountains must have fascinated the Arabs, for the

RIGHT   *Córdoba, Callejón de las flores*

ABOVE *Granada showing the Alhambra against the background of the Sierra Nevada* RIGHT *The Gardens of Generalife, Granada* BELOW *Court of the Lions in the Alhambra in Granada*

La Dama de Elche

Alhambra is filled with leaping jets and ponds, and the halls and courtyards of the palace are deliciously cool even in the heat of August. The best known of the courtyards is the *Patio de los Leones* with its battery of a dozen squat animals round the central fountain. Allowing for the fact that Arabian lions were not as large as the Kenya variety these curious beasts could never be described as lifelike, but their very strangeness is the reason for their fame. The delicacy of the columns in the arcades and the stalactite stucco work inside the halls is unsurpassed in Europe. It dates mostly from the fourteenth century when Yussuf I took up residence in Granada. Such fragile work needed constant repair and the palace was well maintained until about 1700, but after that it was allowed to decay miserably until its romance was triumphantly rediscovered by Washington Irving, and extensive repairs were effected between 1830 and 1862.

The Generalife or the High Garden (Jennat-el-Arif in Arabic) was a summer residence of the sultans of Granada and was redecorated as early as 1319, its date of origin being unknown. The buildings have mostly decayed, but the gardens and the views are a marvel. Roses in full bloom in April and all kinds of sweet smelling shrubs and flowers in among lines of stately fountains make the visitor long to dwell for ever in Granada. No wonder the last Moorish king, expelled in 1492, turned and wept at the last sight of the city on his way to exile.

A narrow road with a surface suspect in places leads through the mountains east of Granada to Guadix, a cathedral city whose chief curiosity is the series of caves inhabited by gypsies and looking like a gleaming white honeycomb. Cave life is a feature of Spain and cave dwellers appear by no means discontented with their homes. Most of them are neat, clean and reasonably well appointed; some indeed in the Sacro Monte in Granada have electric light, and also telephones by means of which hotel proprietors and couriers keep the gypsies informed about parties of tourists eager to witness and photograph what they fondly imagine to be spontaneous gypsy dancing.

Beyond Murcia and not far from the Mediterranean is Elche which contains the only commercial date forest in Europe. The lofty palms waving their plumes against an almost coppery blue sky are a magnificent spectacle. At Elche in 1892 was found a superbly sculptured bust of a woman dating from the Phoenician period of occupation in the third century B.C. *La Dama de Elche* is now to be seen in the Prado Museum in Madrid, and the repose and dignity of her expression seem symbolical of the Spanish character.

Gypsies at the roadside

The Mediterranean coast

The Mediterranean coast of Spain is well known to tourists who love the white, sunbaked beaches with the perpetual blue sky and the grey mountains to landward. As far as Valencia the coastline is hilly and in places rocky, but then the mountains recede further inland, leaving a huge flat plain amply watered by melted snow and rain from the hills. It was in the plain of Valencia that the Arabs organised the complex irrigation system with thousands of ditches (*acequias*) which water the smallholdings. Moorish in origin also is the Water Court controlling the system, and unique as a law court in that it has functioned outside the Cathedral every Thursday since 960 without using any document or paper of any kind.

Date Forest at Elche

The *huerta* (market garden) of Valencia is some of the most fertile land in the world and cultivation is intense, thanks to the unremitting toil of the small farmers, who rent their gardens and live in *barracas* beside their precious crops. The abundant water, rich alluvial soil and constant sunshine make it possible to grow as many as eleven different crops a year; the sight of summer vegetables growing briskly at Christmas is always a puzzle to northern visitors. Rice is grown extensively south of Valencia and a staple of regional cookery is *paella*, a delicious and filling rice dish cooked in olive oil, with meat or fish added. North of Valencia are miles of orange groves which seem to bloom and fruit in turns throughout the year. Some trees are in full flower, others have green fruit, while yet others are a mass of golden ripe oranges. Everywhere throughout the whole countryside lingers the sweet, intoxicating scent of orange blossom.

Above Valencia lies Catalonia, whose inhabitants have long considered themselves independent of Spain and who cherish their own dialect and literature akin to that of Provençal French. The Catalans are the best business folk in Spain, and Barcelona with its teeming population has more bustle and activity, and a greater air of efficiency, than any other city in Spain, including Madrid. But it is by no means merely an industrial seaport; it is a lively, gay capital city, with the tree-lined avenues known as Las Ramblas as its lifeline and the Plaza de Cataluña as its nerve centre.

North of Barcelona is the rugged coastline, the Costa Brava, which foreign tourists in recent years have claimed as their own, so that at every turn in the glorious corkscrew mountain road that connects the charming fishing villages can be seen discarded cigarette packets, empty tins of baked beans and other litter. Despite the foreign invasion this coastline is as beautiful as any in Europe, and its inhabitants remain strongly independent, unaltered and unalterable, like everybody and everything in Spain.

Chapter 2
Invasion and reconquest

The early history of the Peninsula is concerned with a series of foreign invasions starting with the arrival of Phoenician and Greek traders in the coastal areas followed by colonisation by the Romans. It was the Romans who finally conquered the whole country after a long and bitter struggle against the Carthaginians who had established extensive settlements and the native Iberians whose fighting qualities and obstinate endurance are characteristics transmitted to their descendants in modern Spain. The decay of Roman power left Spain at the mercy of nomadic tribes from Germany and the Visigoths succeeded in establishing a kingdom with its capital at Toledo in the fifth century A.D. Though their conquest was complete, they left only a veneer (apart from the introduction of Christianity) on the solid Roman civilisation beneath. Next came the Moors in 711. They swept through the country, checked only in the mountains of the north-west, from which in the course of the following seven centuries the Christians gradually fought back and conquered despite innumerable setbacks and interminable internecine squabbles.

The original inhabitants of Spain are a matter of historical conjecture. The Iberians seem to have been an African race closely related to the Berbers; they spread northwards and fused with the Celtic tribes who in the fifth century B.C. had crossed the Pyrenees and settled in the west of the Peninsula. Matthew Arnold, in his poem *The Scholar Gypsy*, gives a somewhat idealised portrait of the Iberians as 'shy traffickers' meeting the Phoenician traders, who as early as the eleventh century B.C. had crossed the Mediterranean from Syria to set up trading posts on the coasts of Spain. The Phoenicians were merely merchants and attempted no form of colonisation, although they may well have founded the city of Cádiz. Their town of Tartissus, now disappeared, at the mouth of the Guadalquivir may have been the Tarshish of the Bible. What they most certainly did was to establish the use of money among the Iberians.

Greek traders began to appear on the eastern coast of Spain about 630 B.C., and their interests were more definitely colonial. Saguntum was a Greek settlement, but they penetrated far inland and Grecian relics scattered from Málaga to the Pyrenees attest their presence in most of the eastern half of the Peninsula.

The next settlers in Spain were the Carthaginians, whose aid the Phoenicians invited in local struggles against the native Iberians. The new guests liked their environment so much that they decided to settle and drove out their hosts. The Carthaginians like the Greeks were colonisers, and after the first Punic War, which ended in 242 B.C., Hamilcar instituted a policy of conquest in Spain so as to rival the power of Rome in Italy and Sicily. Spain was also to provide a base from which Rome itself could be attacked and Carthaginian supremacy in the Mediterranean restored. Hamilcar's son Hannibal continued this policy, and in 219 B.C. laid siege to Saguntum, the Greek colony near Valencia and an ally of Rome. Livy vividly describes the siege which lasted for eight months; it ended only when the defenders built a huge brazier into which they flung all their possessions and finally themselves, preferring self-destruction to surrender.

The Roman conquest

Hannibal set out from Spain on his great expedition across the Alps to Italy, where he won many victories but, lacking a siege train, could not take a city. He was too great a general for the Romans to venture to attack him and their strategy was directed to assaulting his bases in Spain. In 209 B.C. Scipio Africanus arrived in Spain and Roman domination of the Peninsula began. The Carthaginians were defeated and driven out, but the subjugation of the whole Peninsula was a slow and laborious operation, for the Celtiberians, the *Hispani*, were tough fighters, skilled like their descendants in the art of guerrilla warfare. The Romans suffered many defeats and often resorted to terrorisation to reduce their tenacious adversaries, the tribes of the Cantabrian mountains holding out for three centuries. Numantia, a fortified town on a plateau (in the modern province of Soria), defied Roman troops for twenty years and only capitulated in 133 B.C. after a fifteen months

Hadrian   *Trajan*   *Theodosius*

siege. The Iberian women, according to legend, sacrificed their long hair to make bowstrings when the supply of normal material was exhausted.

If the Roman conquest of Spain was slow and difficult, it was complete and definite, thanks to the policy of pacification pursued by Augustus Caesar, whose work is remembered in such place names as Badajoz (*Pax Augusta*) and Zaragoza (*Caesarea Augusta*). Roman civilisation was firmly implanted in all parts of the Peninsula and Vulgar Latin, the language of the Roman legionaries, became the normal tongue everywhere except in the Basque provinces. Spain became perhaps the most important of the Roman provinces. Three of the emperors, Hadrian, Trajan and Theodosius, were Spanish born, and the philosopher, Marcus Aurelius, the last pagan emperor, was of Spanish descent. Many of the greatest writers of the Silver Age of Latin literature were Spaniards; the two Senecas and Lucan, the epic poet, came from Córdoba; Martial, the satirist, was born in Calatayud in the uplands of Aragon and returned there to die in A.D. 121, Quintilian, the great orator, lived in Calahorra near Logroño in Navarre; Pomponius Mela, the geographer, was a native of Algeciras. Such was the fame of Latin literature by Spanish writers that even so severe a critic as Cicero could find no greater fault than that their style was *pingue quiddam atque peregrinum* (somewhat coarse and foreign).

All Spain was pacified; the Roman system of urban life was fully established and has never been relinquished. In every part of the country great architectural and engineering works were undertaken. Spanish soldiers justly acquired fame in the Roman legions for their bravery and dash, and for their ability to suffer hardship in dignified silence. Spanish legionaries were spread to the farthest limits of the empire; they guarded the wall built by their compatriot, Hadrian, in north Britain against the raids of the Picts; they watched the shores of the Danube provinces, where their particular form of Vulgar Latin still survives in the Roumanian language, an outpost of latinity surrounded by Slavonic or Magyar tongues.

Conquest by Visigoths

It was because Spain's best troops were on service overseas, and because life in the Peninsula was so highly organised, with a huge slave population, that so little resistance was shown when wandering Germanic tribes of Suevians, Alans and Vandals arrived in A.D. 409 to ravage the country. The invaders themselves were quickly subdued by fresh hordes of Visigoths who crossed the Pyrenees in 414, and a Visigothic kingdom was soon established in Spain. But if the conquest was easy, it was the conquerors who in fact succumbed to the civilisation of the conquered. The victors learned the language and adopted the customs of the Romanised Spaniards, and though Visigothic rule lasted for three hundred years it left remarkably little trace on the country, except perhaps in lawgiving. The great *Lex Visigothorum* in 649 promulgated a code of laws and usages (Gothic and Roman mingled) which was to last for many centuries to come.

The Visigoths had arrived in Spain not as mere armies, but as communities with women and children. Intermarriage with the Romanised Spaniards was forbidden until 672; the ban was not rigidly enforced, but even so there was little fusion between the two races. The Gothic nobility lived apart, delighting in country life and quite separate from the urban Roman population. The kingship was elective and was a constant source of weakness, since any succession involved the bitterest rivalry. Several attempts to make the monarchy hereditary failed, and the tenure of a Gothic king was insecure in the extreme. In the three hundred years of Gothic rule there were thirty-five kings, of whom thirteen died violent deaths. It was small wonder that kings sought support against the turbulent nobility and it was in the Church that they found the stabilising influence needed to keep them on the throne, for even so short a time as ten years.

Christian communities

Christianity had taken root early in Spain. Tradition has it that St Paul and St James both preached in Spain, and by the second and third centuries many Christian communities were established. They suffered numerous persecutions until Constantine instituted a policy of tolerance in 506 and Theodosius, himself a Spaniard, made Christianity the official religion of the Roman Empire. A Church synod had met at Elvira near Granada in 313, twelve years before the great council at Nicaea in Asia Minor had promulgated the Nicene Creed.

The Visigoths, too, were Christians, but adhered to the Arian heresy which denied the Trinity in so far as Christ was not recognised as being of one substance with the Father. The Spaniards were orthodox catholics and there ensued discord for over a century between the Spanish Christian Church, which was steadily growing in power, and the Visigothic kings. At length in 589 King Reccared summoned a council of catholic and Arian bishops to debate the issue. The catholics won the day and henceforth the Church was allied with the kings and bolstered the insecure monarchy. The secular power of the Church was thus created in Spain, and it early showed its zeal for persecuting any kind of heretic, in particular Jews, large numbers of whom had settled in Spain. Compulsory baptism was forced on them and they were forbidden to hold any office. Their children were brought up either in Christian families or in convents; all Jewish festivals were prohibited and the evidence of Jewish witnesses was inadmissible in courts of law. It would have been easy therefore to have excused the Jews if they had conspired with Arabs in Africa, fellow Semites, to free them from the tyranny of Visigothic rule. Such is the age-long accusation against the Jews in Spain, but the truth of the charge is largely vitiated by the fact that the Arab invasion occurred soon after the reign of King Witiza, who had initiated a more tolerant policy towards the Jews and whose reputation in Christian annals has suffered precisely for this reason.

The Moorish invasion

The collapse of the Visigothic monarchy was occasioned by internal dissension. Witiza died in 710, having attempted to share the throne with his son Achila in order to secure his succession. This device had been used by Witiza's own father, but now in 710 the nobles insisted on their right of election. They appointed one of their number, Roderic, as king, and civil war immediately broke out. Tradition has it that Count Julian, Visigothic governor of Ceuta in North Africa, enlisted an Arab mercenary force to cross to Spain to fight on behalf of Achila. The instigation for this move is said to have come from Achila's uncle, Oppa, Bishop of Seville. Whatever the truth of this may be, an Arab army of some 7,000 men, mostly fierce Berber warriors under the command of Tarik, landed near Gibraltar (*Gebel-Tarik*, Tarik's rock) on 30 April 711.

King Roderic was engaged on one of the innumerable revolts in the north, but he hurried south, collecting the largest army possible, numbering 90,000. The Arabs had by now been reinforced, but even so they mustered only some 12,000 men when the two forces met near Jerez de la Frontera, on the banks of the river now known as the Guadalete (Arabic, *Wad-el-leded*, the river of delight). The battle according to the chronicles, lasted seven days. The Christian army consisted mostly of foot soldiers, presumably serfs who had little enthusiasm for battle since their lot was slavery no matter who won the day. Tarik on the other hand was strong in cavalry and his Berbers, recently converted to Mohammedanism, were fanatic apostles of their faith besides being skilled trained soldiers. Nevertheless, superior numbers were beginning to tell when the two wings of Roderic's army, one commanded by the treacherous Oppa, defected and Tarik achieved a decisive victory. Roderic's fate is uncertain, but the remnants of his army fled eastwards and northwards leaving the Peninsula wide open to the Arabs.

It would be wrong to suggest, as so many catholic historians have, that the Arabs were mere hordes of savages. From the beginning, it seems, they were prepared to treat the conquered with some tolerance, for in 713 Theodomir, who claimed to be Roderic's rightful successor, was able to make a treaty with the Arabs in a document which is still extant. Upon a promise to pay tribute to the Caliph, Theodomir was allowed to reign independently over large tracts of territory near Granada and in Murcia, and the right of continuing in the Christian faith was conceded.

Perhaps this nominal independence was won by putting up a show of resistance, which the other remnants of the Gothic armies failed to do. These retreated hastily northwards, abandoning Toledo, their capital, though it is said that some of the holy relics were salvaged. In seven years the Arabs overran the entire Peninsula with the exception of the extreme north-west, where in the mountains of Asturias the Christians were at last able to stand. Under the energetic Pelayo, whom they had elected leader, a small band joined battle with the Muslims at Cova-donga. The Christians were holding a position in the mountains around a cave and were able to shower rocks and boulders onto the infidels as they advanced up a narrow defile. With the Moors thrown into con-fusion, the Christians charged down the mountainside and caused havoc among their foes. The statistics of the battle as gravely set forth in the chronicle of Sebastian, Bishop of Salamanca (866–910), are illuminating. Pelayo's force numbered a mere thirty men who in their charge slaughtered 124,000 Moors and a further 63,000 pagans were drowned in the tiny Río Bueno nearby. The remainder took refuge in France, where 375,000 more perished.

Exaggeration apart, Covadonga (718) was one of the world's decisive battles because henceforth the Moors abandoned the attempt to dislodge the Christians from the Asturian mountains and poured north-east-wards into France where they progressed as far as Tours before being defeated and hurled back by Charles Martel (the Hammer) in 732.

The beginning of the reconquest

The Christians were thus given precious time in which to reorganise, and under Alfonso I (739–757), Pelayo's successor, large tracts of terri-tory were retaken as far south as Salamanca. Unfortunately it was again dissension among the Christians as much as prowess on the part of the Moors that hindered the progress of the Reconquest and caused so many hard won gains to be lost times out of number. The strength of the Christians depended on the leader, and as with all dictators the problem of succession was an insoluble one. The newly elected king (chieftain would be the more accurate designation) always had to deal with a host of rival claimants at the outset of his reign. The usual method was large-scale murder or else blinding and incarceration. Kinship was no inducement to mercy, and only after this initial carnage was a king able to turn his attention to battling with the Moors. Confusion was made worse by the practice of a king dividing his kingdom among his children just before his death; thus after years of slow unification the Christian territory in Spain would again be split into a series of petty kingdoms each jealous of the other and bitterly quarrelsome.

Fortunately the Muslims were equally divided, composed as they were of many races, Berbers, Syrians, Arabs, Moors, with only their

religion as a unifying force. All these were disputing the spoils taken in Spain, and though at first they were nominally subject to the Caliph of Damascus, the forces of disruption were too great. In 756 Abd-al-Rahman I established himself as independent emir at Córdoba with a *wali* or governor at Zaragoza linked by only the slenderest thread of allegiance. But the Moors avoided the chief weakness of Visigothic rule by establishing the principle that a dying emir should choose the ablest of his sons (not necessarily the eldest) as his successor. This gave some stability to the Moorish monarchy and under al-Haquem I (796–822) some signs of intellectual activity became apparent. This activity was intensified under Abd-al-Rahman II (822–852) who pursued a policy of peace and even concluded a ten year truce with the Christians of the north. Moreover, in his search for an ally against the Caliph of Damascus who still had pretentions to dominion in Spain, Abd-al-Rahman established diplomatic relations with Byzantium and thus introduced the culture of the eastern empire into Andalusia.

The splendour of Moorish civilization

When war is the normal condition of life, any period of peace brings prosperity, and Córdoba quickly grew and attracted trade from all over the Mediterranean. Abd-al-Rahman II was a great builder and extended and adorned the mosque at Córdoba founded in 786. The city rose to its greatest height of magnificence and culture during the long reign of Abd-al-Rahman III (912–961) who was powerful enough to assume the title of Caliph. It was under his rule that Córdoba became the centre of enlightenment with splendid buildings and schools in which Greek and Arabic learning flourished side by side. Arab medicine was the most advanced in a world in which superstition played a larger part than science. It was to Córdoba that the Christian King Sancho I came in 957 after he had been deposed not only for his incompetence, but also for his excessive obesity. Arab doctors were able to prescribe the juices of certain herbs which effected an admirable slimming cure and Sancho was restored to slenderness and princely grace. He was thus enabled to return to León and win back his throne with the help of a Moorish army.

This was only one of the countless incidents that prove that the Christians and Moors were never divided one from another by an impenetrable barrier. Dissatisfied Christian leaders frequently sought aid from the Moors or served with them against Christian princes.

Interior of the Mosque at Córdoba

Charlemagne himself was induced to enter Spain in 778 to help the Moorish governor of Zaragoza, Suleiman-el-Arabi, against Abd-al-Rahman I, who had lately scandalised orthodox Muslims by assuming the title of Caliph of Córdoba. Charlemagne was at that time an ally of Haroun-el-Rashid, the Caliph of Bagdad who claimed suzerainty over Moorish Spain. Charlemagne's first action was to besiege and take the Christian city of Pamplona. It was not surprising therefore that the Basques and Navarrese attacked his rearguard in the pass of Ronces-valles when the Emperor's army was returning to France. Contrary to all the legends and *Chansons de Geste*, Charlemagne's campaign was never a crusade against the infidel.

Thousands of Christians lived in the Moorish states in Spain and for the most part they were allowed to live in peace, their only disability being the compulsory payment of a poll tax. Many of them embraced Mohammedanism to evade this tax, although it was not heavy; these were known as *renegados* or *muladíes*. The majority, however, remained true to the Christian faith and were allowed to worship in their own churches, where they used a special ritual, simpler than the Roman one and devoid of the practice of confession. This Mozarabic ritual (Christians living among the Moors were called *Mozárabes*, almost Moors) survived in Spain until about 1067, when the Roman ritual was intro-duced under the influence of the first Archbishop of Toledo, a French-man named Bernard.

Though the *Mozárabes* were usually tolerated in the Moorish states, there were periodic persecutions, and at times there arose Arab leaders with a fiery zeal for conquest and conversion. The greatest of these was al-Mansur who started his career as a letter writer at the palace gate and who from 981 until his death in 1002 ('and buried in hell' so the Chris-tian chronicles state) dominated the Caliphate of Córdoba and struck terror into the hearts of the Christians as far as Barcelona in the north-east and Santiago in the extreme north-west. Santiago de Compostela contained the tomb of St James the Great, who was reputed to have preached in Spain and to have been buried there after his martyrdom. His place of burial had been forgotten, but was, so the legend runs, miraculously revealed to a Galician peasant working in the fields by a star shining on the spot where the body lay. Hence the name Com-postela (Latin, *Campus Stellae*). A cathedral had recently been built over the precious tomb when al-Mansur arrived and razed the building to the ground; the tomb, it is said, escaped destruction because a divine splendour shone from it and dazzled the Muslim iconoclasts. St James had frequently exerted his power on behalf of the Christians whose war cry invoked his aid: *Cierra España y Santiago* (Spain and St James, close in on the enemy!). He appeared in person on a white horse bearing a standard with a red cross at the battle of Clavijo in 846 and directed the slaughter of the Moors. Since no writer, Christian or Moorish, mentions such a battle until the thirteenth century, it is likely that the history of Clavijo was invented to boost the reputation of the shrine of Santiago, established as a place of pilgrimage in 1120.

It was all the more humiliating, therefore, that al-Mansur should take away the doors and bells from Santiago's cathedral and carry them in triumph to Córdoba. Fortunately for the Christians he himself perished five years later, out of grief, it is said, for having lost the battle of Calatañazor when the three Christian kingdoms of León, Castile and Navarre united for the first time. Again the authenticity of this union and this battle is highly questionable; it may be yet another propaganda invention of historians writing some two hundred years later. A contemporary chronicler, the monk of Silos, states that a demon carried off al-Mansur and that dysentery annihilated the Moorish army. It is understandable enough to wish to substitute martial glory for medical misery in Christian annals, but the monk's version seems the more probable.

The decline of Islam

Al-Mansur's death marked the beginning of the decline of Islam in Spain. His forceful personality had dominated the caliphs and no one was found fit to replace him. After 1031 the Caliphate broke up into a series of petty states called *taifas*. This left the way open for the Christians to make substantial inroads into Moorish territory and though the Christians were by no means united, the two great kingdoms of Castile and Aragon were definitely established; various marriages between the reigning families at times induced the kingdoms to act in unity. The weakened Muslim powers resorted to the expedient of inviting aid from Africa, and the *Almorávides* (religious fanatics), under a vigorous leader named Yussuf, crossed from Morocco and in 1086 defeated Alfonso VI of Castile, who had but lately taken Toledo from the Moors by dubious diplomatic methods. Yussuf suffered heavy losses in the battle and withdrew to Africa, but next year he returned with a fresh army, proclaiming a *jihad* or holy war. He found the Muslims of Andalusia lukewarm supporters and returned to Africa. However, he came a third time to Spain and quickly made himself master of almost all the former Muslim territories, establishing Córdoba as his capital and capturing Valencia in 1102.

The Cid

Valencia had been since 1094 an independent state under the rule of Don Rodrigo Diaz de Bivar, the Cid, and after his death in 1099 his wife Jimena had continued to rule in his stead. Beset by the Almorávides and despairing of help from Christian princes, the gallant Jimena made a sortie from Valencia with, it is said, her husband's embalmed body in full accoutrements, his sword Tizona by his side and mounted on his charger Babieca, leading the army. Believing that the mighty Cid had come to life again, the Almorávides fled in dismay. Whatever the truth of this romantic story, Jimena and her army with her husband's body reached Christian territory safely, but the Moors were not so dismayed

Statue of the Cid at Burgos

as to be unable to take immediate possession of Valencia and the fertile land around it.

The Cid is the national hero of Spain and is the central figure of the first great epic poem of Spanish literature, *el Poema de mío Cid*, composed about 1140. His career was really that of an independent free-booter, but his arrogant, swashbuckling methods and his refusal to submit to arbitrary authority endear him to Spaniards, who are by nature profoundly anarchical. Born in a village named Bivar near Burgos, about 1040, Rodrigo grew up in stirring but troubled times. Fernando I, King of both León and Castile, had by his efforts united most of Christian Spain and had made valuable conquests from the Moors, but on his death in 1065 committed the usual fatal folly of dividing his dominions among his children. Civil war soon broke out between Alfonso, King of León and Sancho, King of Castile. Alfonso, after gaining a partial victory, was treacherously attacked at night by Rodrigo, and after suffering imprisonment for a time was obliged to take refuge with the Moorish King at Toledo. Sancho turned to attack his other brother and after defeating him turned his attention to his two sisters. Elvira surrendered her town of Toro quickly, but Doña Urraca was made of sterner fibre and put up a resolute defence in Zamora where the siege lasted so long that it has created a proverb: *No se tomó Zamora en una hora.* During the siege Sancho was murdered by a traitor named Bellido Dolfus and it was suspected that the crime was inspired by Alfonso.

The Castilian nobles for want of a better candidate felt obliged to elect Alfonso King of Castile as well as of León, but the Cid, who had witnessed Sancho's death, made Alfonso swear that he had taken no part in the murder. Such an act was not calculated to endear Rodrigo to the new King, who in 1081 found a pretext for banishing his troublesome vassal. The Cid took service with the Moorish ruler of Zaragoza; he fought and defeated on several occasions the Catalans as well as the King of Aragon who attacked his Muslim master. Reconciled with Alfonso in 1087, he was exiled again in the following year and now allied himself with the Count of Barcelona, who had been touched by Rodrigo's generosity to him after defeat in battle. It was now Rodrigo's turn to dominate the Moorish provinces in the north-east and the culminating achievement was the capture of Valencia and its subsequent defence against the Almorávides. Feared and admired by the Moors and Christians alike, Rodrigo worthily earned his double title of Cid (Arabic *Sidi*, chieftain) and *Campeador*, champion, but in Spanish legend his virtues have been magnified and his treachery, cruelty and greed for booty have been conveniently forgotten.

The end of Muslim power

After the Cid's death, the power of the Almorávides gradually declined and small independent Muslim states again appeared, giving the Christians the chance of making further conquests. Their progress was, however, halted once more by a fresh invasion from North Africa when a Berber tribe, the Almohades, entered Spain in 1146 and quickly gained control of almost all the Muslim states. It was they who inflicted the disastrous defeat on the Christians at Alarcos near Badajoz in 1195. By then the struggle against the Mohammedans had assumed the form of a crusade and Castile, Navarre and Aragon united to face the fresh threat of complete Muslim conquest. The Pope, Innocent III, gave the campaign his support, and the Archbishop of Toledo persuaded several European courts to send troops to help the Spanish Christians. An English contingent took the field among the foreign allies, some of whom returned home disgusted at the scant opportunities for plunder.

On 16 July 1212 the united army met the Moors at Las Navas de Tolosa, a small upland valley near Jaén. The Christians won an overwhelming victory, but any account of it is made more difficult by the soaring imaginations and general unreliability of the Christian chroniclers. King Alfonso VIII himself, in his letter to the Pope relating the fortunes of the day, gives the Moorish losses at 100,000 slain, whereas the Christians, so he says, lost only twenty or thirty men. Such figures are scarcely credible in themselves and are difficult to reconcile with the confirmed report that the Christians were at one time on the brink of disaster and were rallied only by the outstanding leadership and fighting qualities of the Archbishop of Toledo, Rodrigo Ximénez. Once again, according to later chroniclers, divine intervention had a hand in the victory, a great red cross appearing in the sky at the crisis of the battle. Earlier in the day, it is said, the Castilian vanguard had been guided through the mountains to an advantageous position between the two main bodies of the Moorish army by a shepherd lad sent by God and later known as Isidro. His image in stone is to be seen in Toledo cathedral, and after his canonisation in the seventeenth century he was adopted as the patron saint of Madrid.

Uncertain as the details of the battle are, its effect, even though the victory was not followed up, was such that the power of the Moors in Spain was broken for ever. By 1284 all Spain was reconquered for the Christians save for the kingdom of Granada, which paradoxically held out for another two hundred years. This was because after the death of Fernando III of Castile (1217–52) the crusading spirit died among the Christians, who enjoyed the benefits of a great revival of learning under Alfonso X *el Sabio*, but then relapsed into internal squabbles with only spasmodic raids into Moorish territories either in Spain or across the straits in Africa.

Part of the reason why Granada was able to continue as an independent Arab kingdom was that its ruler, Mohammed-ibn-Alhamar, had sought and been granted an alliance with the King of Castile, Fernando III (canonised in 1671 for his conquests and the pious severities practised on himself). The Arab monarch helped the Christian ally to conquer his Muslim brethren in Seville, which was captured in 1248. Fernando treated the Moorish defenders magnanimously, but many preferred to take refuge in the kingdom of Granada, whose forces had helped to reduce their city. To the modern reader who tries to discern a clear-cut division between Christians and Mohammedans, the history of medieval Spain is baffling in the extreme.

Foundation of Castilian culture

The capture of Seville with its navigable river and fertile land was of great importance to the Christians, and with King Jaime of Aragon making triumphant gains in the east, including the capture of Valencia in 1239, they were able to indulge in a brief respite from war and turn their thoughts momentarily to culture, and to participation in the affairs of the rest of Europe. Alfonso X *el Sabio* (1252–84) was a poet of distinction, though he wrote in the Galician dialect. Among other works which were produced in Spanish as opposed to Latin, hitherto used for all documents of importance, was the *Crónica General*, the first history of Spain. Alfonso also drew up a digest of Roman and Visigothic laws called the *Siete Partidas*, which reveals a great advance over the old *Fuero Juzgo* in the conception of a civilised community. Legal process is substituted for trial by ordeal and a comprehensive survey is made not only of delinquency, but also of morality and religion. The king's authority is exalted as of divine origin, but there is an attempt to limit the power of the nobles by enhancing the prestige of the clergy and commons. The towns had been gradually acquiring increased influence in government because by supplying money and munitions they had won in exchange a number of privileges (*fueros*), which in some instances amounted to semi-independence. In various assemblies of the *Cortes* in the thirteenth century the *comunidades* are found to be concerning themselves with public morals; they even lectured Alfonso X on his personal extravagance, charging him to reduce his expenses by moderating his excessive appetite.

Alfonso X was ambitious to the point of folly in schemes for self-aggrandisement abroad. He attempted to acquire Gascony, then held by Simon de Montfort for Henry III of England. Alfonso shortly withdrew and agreed to a compromise, marrying his daughter, Eleanor to Prince Edward; the marriage was celebrated with great pomp in the monastery of Las Huelgas at Burgos.

Alfonso next made strenuous efforts to secure election as Holy Roman Emperor, but his claims were opposed and eventually Pope Gregory I, wearying of being so constantly importuned, refused further correspondence with Alfonso and excommunicated any who might support his claim. Alfonso, who had in fact been proclaimed emperor in 1257, was at length induced to renounce the title in 1275.

These enterprises impoverished Castile, and Alfonso's reign, which might have been glorious, ended with dynastic quarrels. His eldest son, *el Infante de la Cerda* (so called because of a hairy mole on his face) died in 1275 and Alfonso in accordance with Castilian custom declared his second son, Sancho, to be his heir instead of his grandson. Such a situation inevitably led to civil strife after Alfonso's death, especially as the King had allotted his grandsons certain territories to be held during his lifetime only. The war dragged on until near the end of the century, when an uneasy peace was made leaving Sancho's son, Fernando IV, in possession of the throne of Castile, and the King of Aragon fortunately distracted by a war in Sicily. The peace was not long lasting for Fernando died in 1312, leaving his infant son Alfonso as his successor. An immediate squabble broke out over who should be the young King's guardian. This fresh disturbance was settled only in 1324 when Alfonso XI summoned the *Cortes* at Valladolid and assumed power himself at the age of thirteen.

The youthful monarch proved to be an administrator of genius as well as a valiant soldier. He secured the support of the towns against the turbulent nobility and rendered the kingdom so peaceful that he was able to institute reforms in local administration and justice. He also found the strength to make an onslaught on the Moors, who had taken advantage of the troubles in Castile to attack frontier towns. They had, moreover, received from Africa large reinforcements commanded by the Emperor of Morocco himself. Alfonso, badly outnumbered, called on the aid of the kings of Portugal and Aragon, both of whom he had recently been fighting. With the forces of Portugal to help him on land and an Aragonese fleet patrolling sulkily and unhelpfully off the coast, Alfonso XI advanced against the Moors near Tarifa and decisively defeated their army on 8 October 1340, slaughtering thousands of infidels and capturing the whole of the emperor's harem.

The victory could not be exploited because the Aragonese fleet refused to cut off the retreat of the Moors, and the substantial reinforcements that Alfonso received from many parts of Europe were more of a problem than a help since they brought no provisions. However, two years later the King was able to lay siege to the key port of Algeciras. It was strongly fortified and valiantly defended, and it took Alfonso's tatterdemalion army almost two years to reduce it, the besiegers suffering from starvation almost as severely as the defenders. Adventurers from all over Europe joined in the siege, including two English nobles, named by the chronicle *el Conde de Arbi y el Conde de Soluster*, identifiable as the Earls of Derby and Salisbury. A quasi-fictitious personage at the siege was Chaucer's 'verray parfit, gentle knyght';

> In Gernade at the seege eek hadde he be
> Of Algezir . . .

Presumably he was a member of the English force accompanying the two noblemen.

After the capture of Algeciras a truce was made with the Moors, but Alfonso broke it on a flimsy excuse and proceeded to lay siege in 1350 to Gibraltar, the importance of which as a secure base had only just been realised. Unfortunately plague broke out in the Castilian camp and the King died, leaving his crown to his only legitimate son, Pedro. Christian conquests against the Moors ceased for almost a century and a half.

Civil war

Pedro I *el Cruel*, though only fifteen at the time of his accession, was soon involved in family feuds. It is understandable that there should have been enmity between him and his five illegitimate brothers, but his treatment of his queen, Blanche de Bourbon, niece of the French King, was monstrous. He married her with great ceremony at Valladolid, but after two days deserted her to return to his mistress, María de Padilla. Blanche was imprisoned shortly afterwards in the fortress of

Murder of Pedro the Cruel at Montiel 1369

Arévalo. Pedro then had the effrontery to declare the marriage void and married a beautiful widow, Juana de Castro, whom he soon abandoned in turn. The bishops of Salamanca and Ávila were too terrified to protest. Later when Queen Blanche was moved to the Alcázar in Toledo there was an immense popular demonstration in her favour and a rebellion broke out which Pedro found too strong to crush. He therefore resorted to lying and falsely promised to take Blanche back as his Queen. For this purpose he was allowed to enter Toledo, but once in possession of the city he sent Blanche a prisoner to Sigüenza and set about slaughtering the principal citizens of Toledo and other rebel leaders.

His eldest half-brother, Enrique de Trastamara, fled to France and induced the famous warrior knight, Bertrand du Guesclin, to fight in Spain on his behalf. The White Companies thus organised fought with such success that Pedro was driven out of Castile and after vainly seeking aid from Portugal persuaded the Black Prince, then governor of the English province of Gascony, to intervene in his favour, offering him among other inducements the great ruby (now in the royal crown of England); Pedro had seized it from a friendly Arab prince whom he had treacherously murdered.

The Black Prince, eager to test his prowess against so renowned a foe as du Guesclin, agreed to Pedro's proposals and foolishly believed his promises of rewards. He crossed the Pyrenees through the pass of Roncesvalles and defeated and captured du Guesclin in the battle of Nájera. Pedro was thus dramatically restored to his throne and immediately sought vengeance on his enemies, offering to buy the Black Prince's captives in order to slaughter them. The Black Prince, however, refused to behave in so unchivalrous a fashion, being also enraged at Pedro's refusal to honour his promises of rewards for services. He released du Guesclin to the French for a small ransom and returned disillusioned to Bordeaux. The disheartening expression 'castles in Spain' was added to the English language as a result of this expedition.

With the departure of the English the civil war in Spain was renewed, and this time Pedro was cornered in a castle in Montiel in La Mancha in 1369. He was treacherously induced to come to a parley with du Guesclin and Enrique de Trastamara and was stabbed to death, according to Froissart, in a hand to hand scuffle with his half-brother. It was a fitting end for a miscreant who had revolted all his contemporaries by his senseless brutalities. It was later maintained that he was merely upholding the common people against the nobility, and it is true that the towns supported him almost to the end, but this may have been because Enrique de Trastamara was scarcely more acceptable than Pedro and was surrounded by foreign mercenaries. In any event, history has rightly adhered to the title of Pedro el Cruel and has rejected Philip II's attempt to have him remembered as el Justiciero (the Dispenser of Justice). Such a title scarcely suits a homicidal maniac.

The triumph of Enrique de Trastamara did not bring peace to Castile, for his right to the throne was challenged first by the King of Portugal and then by John of Gaunt, both of whom had married daughters of Pedro by his mistress, María de Padilla (the daughters of this union had been declared legitimate by a cowed Cortes). Both claimants withdrew in the face of difficulties, but they renewed their claims after Enrique's death in 1379. The quarrel with Portugal was patched up by the marriage of the Portuguese King's daughter to Juan I, King of Castile, but a royal marriage did not prevent the Castilians from invading Portugal in strength, assisted by French troops. A small Portuguese army accompanied by a tiny English force of bowmen and men at arms utterly defeated them at the battle of Aljubarrota on 14 August 1385. Once again John of Gaunt landed at Corunna, this time with his wife and daughters, and was crowned at Santiago, King of Castile and

León. His eldest daughter, Philippa, was given in marriage to King Fernando of Portugal and plans were made for an invasion of Castile. After some skirmishing, however, plague decimated the Anglo-Portuguese force and John of Gaunt was content to end the struggle with yet another marriage pact; this time his second daughter, Catherine aged ten, was betrothed to Juan I's eldest son, Enrique, aged eight.

John of Gaunt retired to England well pleased with his expedition; he had received 600,000 francs in gold for his pains and left two daughters, one as queen of Portugal and the other wedded to the heir apparent to the throne of Castile and León. Juan I was likewise satisfied because he was now related by marriage to both his rival claimants to the throne, and the Trastamara dynasty was thereby greatly strengthened.

Meanwhile, the Moors had not been slow to take advantage of the dissensions among the Christians. Algeciras had been recaptured and other gains had been secured in Andalusia. The Christians had to be content with containing as best they could the Moors within the extensive kingdom of Granada. Many towns still bear the honourable title *de la Frontera*, among them Jerez, commemorating their post of danger confronting the infidel, for which they received certain privileges. An uneasy truce was established with the King of Granada and this enabled the Christians during the reign of Enrique III (1390–1406) to turn their attention to more distant lands. The Canary Islands were secured for Castile and embassies were sent east as far as Constantinople and Samarkand.

The court of Juan II

The first half of the fifteenth century saw a period of comparative peace during the reign of Juan II (1406–54), not because of any competent administration on his part for he was weak and vacillating, though generally amiable, but because his reign began with a Regent of great ability, Fernando de Antequera, who was elected King of Aragon in 1411. Later Juan left matters of government to his favourite, Don Álvaro de Luna, who, though ambitious and supremely acquisitive, was a firm and just administrator; over a period of thirty-five years he established a rule of law and order such as Castile had scarcely known before. Though sections of the nobility were constantly intriguing against him, he managed to keep his position secure, defeating the malcontents at Olmedo in 1445. The result of his firm policy was that in Castile the arts of peace at last began to emerge; wealth increased,

learning was extended and literature flourished. The nobility were perhaps kept from war by the growing cult of the ideal of chivalry which
had spread from France in the previous century. A courtly society was
established in which women were idolised and men sought to perform
deeds of knightly valour in order to please their ladies. Jousting became
a regular occupation for young and gallant noblemen, and Don Álvaro
de Luna himself excelled in the lists.

It was a sad day for Spain when Juan II began to listen to the urgings
of Don Álvaro's enemies and decreed his arrest and execution, which
took place on a vast and richly decorated scaffold at Valladolid in 1453.
The King had been angered with his favourite, who had forced him to
take as his second wife a princess from Portugal. He did, however,
regret his decision to execute Don Álvaro and sent messengers to stay
the execution, but these, it is said, were intercepted by order of the
Queen, now a bitter enemy of the man who had arranged her marriage.

The killing of Don Álvaro de Luna was a piece of folly whose results
Juan II did not live to see, but in the reign of his son by his first marriage
to María of Aragon, Enrique IV (1454–74), the royal authority became
an object of mockery, and Castile sank to a state of lawlessness and
misery worse than at almost any time in her troubled history. Like his
father he was governed by favourites, but of far inferior mettle to Don
Álvaro. The first was Juan de Pacheco, who was given the title of
Marqués de Villena and remained a constant source of trouble. The
second was Beltrán de la Cueva whose relations with Enrique's queen
were such that the daughter she bore was nicknamed throughout the
kingdom la Beltraneja, and was declared illegitimate by the *Cortes*
despite the King's protests.

Such was the disaffection of the nobility and the common people
that at Ávila in 1465 an effigy of Enrique was cast down from a dais
in the main square in the presence of the Archbishop of Toledo, and
the young prince Alfonso was placed on the throne of state. Alfonso
was the son of Juan II by his second wife, Isabel of Portugal, and was
recognised as king in many cities of Castile. The three years of civil war
which ensued were ended in July 1468 by Alfonso's death in circumstances which suggested poison, since apparently his death was proclaimed publicly throughout Castile three days before it occurred. The
confederation of rebellious nobles then turned to Isabel, Juan II's
daughter by Isabel of Portugal, and urged her to proclaim herself queen.
She, however, was as prudent as she was beautiful, and from the safety
of a convent in Ávila pleaded with the malcontent nobles to come to an

Ávila, bulls at Guisando

understanding with the King. A truce was arranged and Enrique and Isabel met in 1468 near a place named Toros de Guisando, so called because of some sculptured monsters of pre-Roman origin. There Enrique acknowledged Isabel as his heir and gave her the right to marry whom she pleased providing his consent to her choice were first obtained.

The union of Castile and Aragon

There were many suitors for Isabel's hand, including the Duke of Clarence, brother of Edward IV of England. Isabel secretly sent a representative to inspect the various suitors in France and in Aragon and chose the most handsome, who was also the most eligible, Fernando, heir to the crown of Aragon. There was widespread opposition to her choice for the nobles feared that a union with Aragon, which had lately greatly extended her power by conquests in Italy, would threaten the independence of Castile. Enrique himself even revived the claims of la Beltraneja. The Marqués de Villena made an attempt to capture Isabel, but she was saved by the Archbishop of Toledo, who at the head of a body of horsemen carried her off to Valladolid. Fernando, in order to reach his betrothed, was forced to disguise himself and undergo adventures that were as romantic as they were perilous and uncomfortable. However, all ended happily and Fernando and Isabel were married on 19 October 1469 amid popular rejoicing.

Enrique spent five more years intriguing against Isabel's succession to the throne; on his death in 1474 she was crowned Queen of Castile, with Fernando in the awkward and somewhat humiliating position of prince Consort. He made one attempt to be recognised as king, but thereafter behaved with great moderation, discreetly and ably supporting his wife's energetic efforts to restore order. She indeed had troubles enough, for some disaffected nobles persuaded the King of Portugal to marry la Beltraneja and claim Castile as his own. Five years passed in intermittent warfare before peace was made with Portugal and the unhappy Beltraneja retired to a convent.

When reasonably secure on her throne Isabel once more turned her attention to the problem of enforcing law and order in the land. Acting

Entry of Fernando and Isabel into Granada

Fernando of Aragon at dinner

with great vigour she achieved an almost miraculous change in the internal situation in Castile in a very short space of time. Whereas in her brother's reign authority had been openly flouted and the country-side tyrannised by bands of robbers, Isabel secured respect for the law by reviving an old institution, the *Santa Hermandad* (Holy Brotherhood), which had previously been a kind of vigilance committee, often operating against the Crown's authority. Isabel made it a potent weapon to enforce the royal commands, and the harsh but effective methods of the *Santa Hermandad* struck such terror into the hearts of evildoers that they troubled the land no more. Even a hundred years later Sancho Panza, when engaged in an exploit of doubtful legality with his master Don Quijote, went in dread of the *Santa Hermandad*. Their method when a criminal was taken in the act was to put him to death on the spot by shooting arrows into his body.

As well as these punitive measures against lawbreakers Isabel drew up a revision of the *Siete Partidas* and established new courts of law with the object of making it possible for all citizens to obtain swift and impartial justice, so that the strong and rich could no longer oppress the weak and needy. In order to institute these reforms it was essential that the central authority of the Crown should be strong, and the added royal prestige led to a weakening of the influence of the nobles and the

Cortes, thus paving the way for the absolutism of Philip II and his successors.

The Holy Inquisition

Isabel's piety made her an easy prey for religious fanatics and she was induced to accept the institution of the Holy Inquisition. It was indeed arguable that a need existed to protect Castile against potential traitors since there were Moors and Jews in almost every community in the land. The Holy Office had been operating in Aragon since the thirteenth century, and perhaps Fernando sided with the priests in urging his wife to adopt it in Castile, seeing in it a method of diverting some of the wealth of the Jewish community into the royal coffers. The Inquisition was formally established in Castile on 2 January 1481, and in the following year a Dominican monk Tomás de Torquemada, was appointed chief inquisitor. It would be a mistake to believe all the Protestant exaggerations regarding the policy and methods of the Inquisition, but that the

Tomb of the Catholic Kings, Granada

result was a cruel persecution of the Jews is beyond doubt. In the ten years to 1492, when the Jews were finally expelled, no less than 2,000 of them were burnt at the stake in Andalusia and 17,000 were 'reconciled', suffering a lesser penalty, such as imprisonment or banishment; in every case their property was confiscated.

The conquest of Granada

The treasure thus plundered from the Jews was employed on the great project for subduing the Moorish kingdom of Granada. It was a formidable task, for Granada was now at the height of its splendour and wealth, and could muster quickly an army of 50,000 men, all highly trained and especially skilful as light horsemen and archers. In 1479, however, Fernando succeeded his father as King of Aragon, and Christian Spain, truly united for the first time for seven centuries, was strong enough to challenge the Moors, who were enervated by luxurious living and torn by family feuds.

It was a palace revolution of a typically oriental pattern in Granada that enabled the Christians to continue the campaign after some bungling generalship by Fernando in 1482 had placed the Spanish forces in jeopardy. King Abul Hassan was forced to leave Granada and set up his government in Málaga because of a palace revolt fermented by Queen Zoraya who was jealous of the King's preference for one of his younger wives. His son, Abu Abdullah or Boabdil, known by the Spaniards as *el Rey Chico*, assumed power in Granada in his stead. Boabdil was defeated and captured by the Christians, but when it was seen that his absence enabled his father to regain the entire kingdom, Fernando had the good sense to release *el Rey Chico* so that he could continue to cause dissension in the Moorish camp. The Moors grew weary of this internal strife and chose yet another king, a younger brother of Abul Hassan, one Abdallah called Ez-Zagal (the Valiant). He lived up to his name and managed to inflict a heavy defeat on the Christians in a narrow pass at Axarquia. But the fame of the crusade against the last bastion of Mohammedanism in Spain had spread throughout Europe and volunteers swarmed to join the Christian forces, including once again an English detachment under Earl Rivers and Lord Scales. The combined army totalled more than 50,000 men, with a great train of artillery for siege work.

Made wary by recent defeats the Christians moved slowly into Muslim territory and settled down to besiege Málaga, which was taken in 1487. The Christian host, now doubled in size, moved on to capture Baeza where Ez-Zagal had established his capital, his rival, Boabdil, being at this time supreme in Granada itself. Had the Moors been united, they might well have withstood the Christian invasion, but while Baeza was under siege, the Moors in Granada did nothing to help. Even so it was only the courageous persistence of Queen Isabel that inspired the Christians to continue in spite of pestilence and frustrating defeats. Eventually Baeza surrendered and Granada itself was invested from April 1491 onwards.

Again the Christians made no attempt to take the city by storm, but merely waited for famine and disease to take their toll of the population, now greatly increased by the influx of refugees from the surrounding countryside. Meanwhile skirmishes took place in the plain outside the city and individual Christian and Muslim champions battled in single combat. At length on 2 January 1492 Boabdil, realising that he could not hope for relief from outside and encouraged by the generous terms which the Christians were offering, agreed to capitulate and set forth from the palace of the Alhambra to meet the glittering cavalcade of Christian conquerors. A great silver cross was raised on one of the towers of the Alhambra as were also the banners of the kingdoms of Castile and Aragon. At the sight of these symbols of victory the whole Christian host, so the chronicle states, fell on their knees and gave thanks to Almighty God for the final deliverance of the Peninsula from the infidels after a struggle of close on eight centuries.

Chapter 3
The great century

The final victory of the Christians over the Moors gave Spaniards confidence in their ability as a warring nation and with the political unity which the marriage of Fernando and Isabel had established the scene was now set for the full development of the national spirit. The remarkable expansion of the Spanish Empire in the sixteenth century was directed by the Habsburg dynasty which came to rule Spain in 1516. Charles I, the first Habsburg monarch, not being a native born Spaniard, was a man of European outlook and quickly extended Spanish interests outside the Peninsula. His son, Philip II, was a talented administrator who concentrated political power entirely in the hands of the monarchy and miraculously controlled a worldwide empire from his austere apartments in the Escorial.

Among those who saw (or professed to have seen) the Christian banners flying over Granada was a visionary of Genoese origin, Christopher Columbus, who for several years had been pestering the courts of Europe with a wild plan for reaching India by sailing westward. The scheme had been laid before the Kings of Portugal, England and France who had all rejected it, either on grounds of impracticability or because, in Portugal's case, of commitments elsewhere, notably on the west coast of Africa. Columbus was received coldly at the Spanish court, and the commission ordered to enquire into the project with typical Spanish tardiness took five years to reach a decision, which was unfavourable. Columbus in despair was about to depart from the Court of Castile, but some influential and enlightened persons had been convinced by his arguments and Isabel was persuaded to authorise the equipping of an expedition.

The small port of Palos near Cádiz was ordered to supply three ships

LEFT   *Columbus departing for America*

RIGHT   *Discovery of the Antilles by Columbus, from a drawing attributed to him in the Epistola Christofori Columbi (1494?)*

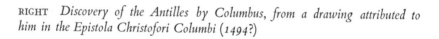

or caravels, none of which was of more than a hundred tons displacement. On 3 August 1492 Columbus in the flagship *Santa María* sailed with his little fleet from Palos. After putting in for repairs at the Canary Islands (already in Spanish possession), the fleet sailed almost due west out into unknown seas and against unfavourable winds. It was only Columbus's firmness of purpose and belief in the correctness of his theories that enabled the expedition to head westward for week after week. Bad weather, compass variations and the seemingly boundless extent of deserted ocean raised many a clamour for return among the crews, but Columbus kept on. At last the presence of floating wreckage of trees and flights of shore birds raised the hopes of all, and on the night of 12 October land was sighted. The following morning Columbus and his followers went ashore with as much ceremony as they could muster after so arduous a voyage, and took possession of the land in the name of Isabel of Castile. Columbus had hoped that he had discovered a land mass, but in fact he had gone ashore on a tiny Bahaman island, named by him San Salvador and now known as Watlings Island. The natives were friendly and unwarlike people, but their nakedness and

Natives of Hispaniola

lack of any form of civilisation scarcely suggested the wealthy races of whom Columbus had dreamed.

Columbus discovers America

Other islands were found in the vicinity, but the mainland was not reached before Columbus returned to Spain, leaving a small garrison on San Salvador in a fortress built from the remains of one of the expedition's ships, which had become unseaworthy. Columbus had kidnapped a few natives for exhibition purposes and had collected some small gold ornaments. Or reaching Spain he paraded his specimens throughout the country on his way to the court, which was then at Valladolid. He was everywhere received with acclamation and his exaggerated accounts of the wealth and beauty of the new lands he had discovered were eagerly heard. The enthusiasm so engendered enabled him to set out again in 1494 with a band of fifteen hundred adventurers, but not until his third voyage did he find the mainland at the mouth of the Orinoco. The natives here were considerably more hostile and only a brief landing was possible.

If Columbus's four voyages between 1492 and 1504 produced little material wealth either for himself or for Spain, they showed the way for other adventurers, and in less than a hundred years a few thousand Spaniards had explored, conquered and exploited a vast new continent which throughout they continued erroneously to call the Indies.

The Catholic Monarchs

Meanwhile in Spain the conquest of Granada had seen the country nominally united in one Christian community, although in fact there were still so many local variations and *fueros* or special privileges that unity was far from being an established fact. The Catholic Monarchs (*los Reyes Católicos*), a title conferred on Fernando and Isabel in 1494 by the Spanish Pope Alexander IV, were joined in marriage, but their kingdoms of Aragon and Castile were entirely separate.

In Aragon, which comprised also the provinces of Catalonia and Valencia, the King was anything but secure, for both the nobles and the towns claimed a host of exemptions and privileges. The kingship was not still an elective office, but at his coronation he knelt before the *Justicia Mayor* who crowned him with a haughtily independent formula: 'We who are as good as you swear to you who are no better than we, to accept you as our king and sovereign lord provided you accept all our laws and liberties, but if not, not.' The nobles claimed exemption from the jurisdiction of the courts of law and from taxation, and asserted that they had the right to indulge in private warfare. The nobles too had the advantage of forming two sections of the *Cortes* of Aragon, the greater nobles being known as the *Brazo de los Ricos Hombres* and the minor nobility the *Brazo de Caballeros;* below them were the representatives of the clergy and the towns. In theory the decisions of the *Cortes* had to be unanimous, which involved interminable delays, and there was a well-established principle that no grant of money was made to the king without previous redress of grievances. In addition to these limitations on the royal power in Aragon, Catalonia and Valencia each had its own *Cortes* equally insistent on their rights and liberties. It is small wonder that Fernando sought a diversion for his turbulent subjects in foreign conquests in Italy.

In Castile the situation was very different. Isabel had terrified the nobility and demolished most of their castles, except in strategic positions. She omitted the nobles from the *Cortes* which in any case she summoned but rarely. In place of the former rebellious and inefficient rulers she established a form of Civil Service selected from the educated middle classes (*los letrados*), whose offices depended solely on the queen's pleasure and whose loyalty to the Crown was therefore assured. Isabel likewise tamed the towns by inserting a royal official with wide powers in each municipal council; this was the *Corregidor* who sat with and dominated the local *regidores* (town councillors).

In a country like Spain where many districts are thinly populated and extremely isolated the problem of central control was acute. To overcome these difficulties Isabel had created an efficient police force in the *Santa Hermandad* and she also sought an alliance with the great guild of sheep farmers known as the *Mesta*, which had been formed in the thirteenth century. This powerful society controlled flocks of some two or three million sheep which migrated south in the winter along the traditional sheep tracks (*las Cañadas Reales*), grazing where they could. Such migrations naturally led to many disputes, not only among the shepherds and flock owners, but also with farmers whose crops had been eaten by voracious Spanish sheep. To deal with these disputes the *Mesta* had special judges (*alcaldes entregadores*); Isabel was able to secure the right to appoint these numerous officials and thus extend royal authority to the remotest rural areas.

An even more powerful weapon in the hands of the Crown was the Church. Spain had always been a fervently catholic country and the crusade against the Muslims had made religious feeling even more intense. But Spain is a land of paradox and this nation of ardent Roman Catholics was also strongly opposed to any interference by the Pope. Hence the Crown was able to appropriate the patronage of almost all the more important ecclesiastical offices, and the clergy as a result were perforce royalist in outlook. The appointment of any foreigner to a benefice in Castile was forbidden, and in 1514 the Crown felt strong enough to prevent the publication of any Papal Bull without prior approval of the Royal Council. This measure caused the utmost resentment in Rome, but it remained permanently in force, and in 1567 Philip II was able to disregard an edict of Pope Pius V banning bullfighting in all catholic countries.

The power of the Inquisition

The most potent force of all in the unification of the land and the submission of all subjects to the Crown was undoubtedly the Inquisition, since its jurisdiction extended to high and low alike. Such was its power that in 1559 the Inquisition arrested secretly as he lay in bed the Primate of all Spain, the Archbishop of Toledo. Secret action was the most terrifying aspect of the functioning of the Inquisition; suspects just disappeared, and often nothing more was heard of them until they were produced at an *auto de fe* where sentences against heretics were publicly pronounced and which was a credible representation of what the day of judgment might be like. The proceedings of the Inquisition were more humane than is popularly supposed in Protestant countries; torture was used sparingly and in a form which would leave no permanent injury, prisons were regularly inspected and prisoners awaiting trial were better cared for than in normal prisons. The accused could object to any judge on the grounds of partiality and a conviction could be secured only on the evidence of seven witnesses.

Nevertheless the Inquisition was an instrument of ruthless oppression because pardon for any offence could be obtained on one condition only, the denunciation of accomplices. Thus the secret arrest of one individual often led to a series of further arrests and no one was safe, though it is true that there were severe penalties for wrongful accusation. Trials lasted an interminable time (that of the Archbishop of Toledo took seventeen years), so thorough was the investigation. Penalties on convicted persons varied from a warning or a public flogging, to release to the civil power for burning, which was reserved for the most stubborn cases or for relapsed heretics. One of the commoner forms of punishment was the wearing for a prescribed period of distinctive clothing, usually of a vivid yellow embroidered with a red St Andrew's cross and known as a *San Benito*. To wear this garment in public places exposed the wearer to violence from the mob, for the sympathies of the public were normally strongly in favour of the Inquisition. Moreover, when the prescribed period ended the *San Benito* was permanently displayed with a suitable inscription on the walls of the parish church, exposing the wearer and his descendants to public derision and scorn.

Any conviction by the Inquisition in the family would be fatal for prospects of advancement in a profession; certificates of purity of religious views were sought as eagerly in the sixteenth century in Spain as were certificates of purity from Jewish blood in Nazi Germany. The Inquisition had the same intentions as the Nazi rulers, namely the unification of national thought and the preservation of a single national aim in a community of widely conflicting interests. Its management was in the hands of officials nominated by the Crown and thus the Crown was enabled to exercise a direct influence over not only the bodies of all subjects, but over their minds as well. Moreover, the Inquisition operated alike in Castile and Aragon, thus preparing the way for the complete unification of the Peninsula achieved by Philip II.

The coming of the Habsburgs

The move towards unity was temporarily halted by an accident of royal succession. Queen Isabel died in 1504 leaving as her heir her third child, Juana *la Loca*, who had married in 1496, despite increasing signs of madness, Philip the Fair of Flanders, son of an Austrian Archduke of the Habsburg dynasty. Isabel in 1503, observing her daughter's insanity, had ordained in her will that Fernando should act as regent, but on her death Philip the Fair claimed the throne of Castile in the name of his wife. All the latent forces of anarchy so recently repressed by Isabel rallied to Philip's support, leaving Fernando so weak that he retired to his wars in Italy, where he sought to consolidate the newly won Aragonese possession, the kingdom of Naples. He also married Germaine de Foix, daughter of the French king, who stipulated that the kingdom of Aragon should pass to any child of this marriage. It seemed that the life's work of Isabel and Fernando was to be undone and that Spain would once again be split into entirely separate kingdoms; but Germaine's only child died in 1508 and in the meantime Philip the Fair had also died, after making himself thoroughly unpopular by his greed and rapacity. Fernando thus regained the regency of Castile, which he held successfully until his death in 1516. To keep peace at home he employed the same method which had succeeded in Aragon, namely war abroad, mainly directed against France, in the course of which he annexed to Spain the kingdom of Navarre.

From 1509 poor Queen Juana had been living in strict seclusion at Tordesillas, where she remained until her death in 1555. On Fernando's death Juana's eldest son, Charles, was proclaimed King throughout Spain, thanks largely to the energy and foresight of the aged Cardinal Cisneros who had played a great part in the purging of the Spanish Church of many of the abuses which in other countries led to the Protestant revolt. The Habsburg Charles, half-Flemish, had been brought up in Flanders and was ignorant alike of Spanish customs and of the Spanish language; any kind of foreign invasion is the one factor which will cause Spaniards to unite and the scene was set for rebellion now that the nobles were seeking an alliance with their ancient enemies the towns. Charles's arrival in 1517 only served to fan the flames of revolt, for he brought with him a retinue of rapacious Flemish companions

who received numerous favours, offices and pensions, the Archbishopric of Toledo, the richest benefice in Europe, being conferred on a Flemish boy of sixteen, Guillaume de Croy.

The *Cortes* of Castile meeting at Valladolid in 1518 protested against the appointment of numerous foreigners, but the deputies were won over by bribery and made Charles a grant of money (*servicio*), largely because payment for their own services had to be made out of such a grant. The *Cortes* of Aragon were stubbornly independent, but were likewise won over by liberal bribery and pronounced themselves satisfied when Charles was crowned in the traditional fashion on his knees. The *Cortes* of Catalonia were likewise obedient, and all Spain might well have been won without struggle had not Charles's attention suddenly been focused on gaining the crown of the Holy Roman Empire, which fell vacant on the death of his grandfather, the Emperor Maximilian, in 1519.

His success in winning the election against such rivals as Francis I of France and Henry VIII of England was due to bribery on a colossal scale with money borrowed from German bankers, notably the Fuggers, to whom he pledged much of the property of the crown of Castile. Such an action caused the deepest resentment in Castile, and the *Cortes* meeting in Santiago in the spring of 1520 were in a thoroughly hostile mood. The King was conciliatory and promised that offices should be allotted only to native born Spaniards, that the export of Spanish bullion should be stopped, and that his absence from Spain to look after his imperial interests would not last more than three years. These promises made little impression on the deputies (*procuradores*), but bribery was more effective and eventually the usual *servicio* was granted, whereupon it was announced that the Governor of Spain during Charles's absence was to be his old tutor, Adrian of Utrecht, 'a native of these realms by reason of the length of time he has been here'. With this Parthian shot, Charles I of Spain left the Peninsula to become the Emperor Charles V, assuming for the first time the title of *Majestad*, a dignity which other European monarchs immediately copied.

Rebellion had broken out even before Charles left on 20 May 1520. It was a popular movement in the towns, but at first it also had the support of noble families still disgruntled at the loss of privileges which they had suffered under Isabel. Nevertheless it was the townsfolk who were the driving force of the rebellion, which accordingly bears the name of the revolt of the *Comuneros*. Toledo was the scene of the first rebel success under the leadership of two noblemen, Juan de Padilla

LEFT   *Carlos V by Titian, in the Prado*

and Pedrolaso de la Vega, brother of the great lyric poet, Garcilaso. The citizens formed a commune on democratic lines, and their example was quickly followed by many other important towns in the valley of the Duero, including Zamora, Salamanca, Ávila, and Segovia. It was against this last that the governor of Castile, Adrian of Utrecht, directed the slender forces at his disposal, but the inhabitants resisted stoutly and the royalist commander sent to Medina del Campo, north west of Segovia, to fetch artillery from the royal arsenal. The town council, sympathising with the *Comuneros* in Segovia, refused to relinquish the artillery, and there were clashes in the narrow streets with the royalist troops who, in order to create a diversion, set fire to some buildings. The fire spread so quickly that most of the town was soon ablaze and, since Medina del Campo was the warehouse of Spain, large quantities of merchandise from many parts of western Europe were destroyed.

This wanton destruction roused the rebel towns, who were already seeking means of concerting their actions and had formed at Ávila a committee of delegates known as the *Santa Junta*. Padilla, with the help of the artillery which had survived the fire at Medina del Campo, seized Tordesillas, and the rebels were able to lay their grievances before Queen Juana *la Loca* and to beg her to assume her rightful place on the throne. Her speech from the throne, however, was vague and rambling, and in no circumstances could she be induced to sign any document which would give a semblance of legality to the revolt. Nevertheless, the *Comuneros* were in a strong position since a rising in Valladolid had dispersed the Royal Council there, some of whose members were arrested.

The rebellion was becoming increasingly popular in outlook, and the natural target for any reformers was the nobility who, though shorn of ancient privileges, were still wealthy and possessed of enormous estates whose vassals could form a sizeable army. The nobles, alarmed at the increasingly egalitarian doctrines of the *Comuneros*, sided with the Crown, greatly strengthening the royal forces. Padilla was defeated in April 1521 and was captured and hanged, whereupon the whole revolt collapsed, except that Toledo held out until 25 October under the leadership of Antonio de Acuña, Bishop of Zamora, the last of the fierce episcopal warriors of Spain.

Almost at the same time as the revolt of the *Comuneros* in Castile, a popular rising had taken place in Valencia. The cause of it was a typical piece of Spanish incongruity: the populace took up arms in August 1519 in protest against the leniency of the Inquisition in dealing with some persons found guilty of moral offences. Charles, eager to leave Spain to claim his imperial title, granted the petitions of the Valencian populace, who had formed themselves into a brotherhood (*Germanía*), and this action infuriated the Valencian *Cortes*, who withdrew support from the Crown. The *Germanía* was able to beat the royal troops in a battle near Gandia (23 July 1521), and thereafter they attacked the Moorish vassals who worked on the estates of the nobility, slaughtering many and forcibly baptising others, thereby bringing them within the jurisdiction of the Inquisition. But three months later the *Germanía* was defeated outside the walls of Valencia and the revolt was at an end, apart from certain isolated districts where it was kept alive until May 1522 under the leadership of *El Rey Encubierto*, said to be an illegitimate grandson of Fernando and Isabel.

The comparatively simple suppression of these two rebellions greatly strengthened Charles's position, particularly because the nobility were ranged on his side. Not only did the wealthy landed nobility rally to his cause, but the gentry in the towns, the *Hidalgos*,* alarmed by proposals made by the *Germanía* to abolish all private incomes, seized control of most of the town councils and ensured that *procuradores* to the *Cortes* should be royalist in sympathies. The King thus had the support of all three estates, the nobles, the clergy and the towns, and the *Cortes* showed itself less unwilling than formerly to grant substantial *servicios*. Moreover, the attitude of the King towards Spain had greatly changed; he had learned Spanish, albeit with a lisp which is said to be responsible for the Castilian pronunciation of *z* and *c* (before *e* or *i*) as a *th* sound, for the King-Emperor was now greatly admired in Spain and his idiosyncrasies were quickly copied.

So loyal and friendly to the King did the *Cortes* become that they gradually abandoned their powers, and by 1544 they were petitioning that they should not be summoned more often than once every three years because of the great expense involved in an assembly of the *procuradores*. The way was then open to royal absolutism and rule by decree, which was perfected in the following reign and which has persisted in Spain with relatively short intervals up to the present day.

The Conquistadores

Such peaceful conditions as existed within Spain during Charles V's reign were due to a sudden rise in prosperity. The influx of bullion

---

* From *Hijo de algo*, son of something.

Magellan

from America (£126,000 a year between 1511 and 1520 rising to £5,672,000 a year between 1551 and 1555) caused a sharp increase in prices, which acted as a stimulus to trade. Moreover Spain had a complete monopoly in America which then had no factories and would pay any price for manufactured goods. In fact it was reckoned at the *Casa de Contratación* (the Board of Trade for the Indies) at Seville that the average profit on manufactured goods exported to America was 166 per cent. It is not surprising that industry flourished all over Castile. Spanish goods won a reputation for high quality, and such articles as Spanish gloves and swords were eagerly sought everywhere in western Europe. Julián del Rei, a Morisco craftsman in Toledo, gained such a reputation with his swords and daggers that his trademark was well known in England. It consisted of a small dog that was frequently mistaken for a fox; hence it was that Bardolph was able to exclaim to his French prisoner: 'O Signieur Dew, thou diest on the point of fox' (*Henry V*, Act IV, Scene 9).

The source of supply of all the bullion which gave rise to this prosperity was the gold and, more especially, the silver mines in South America, the conquest of which was a feat of remarkable courage, resource and endurance by a handful of Spanish conquistadores. After the re-establishment of Española (the first town had been in a fever-ridden area) adventurers set forth to explore the mainland, journeying

Cortés   Francisco Pizarro

ever further south, but never finding the end of the land mass. Among the navigators was an Italian, Amerigo Vespucci, serving with the Spaniards and for some reason it is his name that was settled on the new continent,* though officially the new territories were known as *Las Indias* and every adventurer was still seeking Cipango (Japan), mentioned by Marco Polo. Settlements were made on the Isthmus of Panama, and in 1513 Núñez de Balboa made his way across the narrow neck of land from Darien and set eyes on another ocean, which they called the southern sea.

It was a Portuguese navigator Fernando de Magallanes (in Spanish) or Magellan (in English) who gave this ocean its modern name. He had sailed to India by way of the Cape of Good Hope with the Portuguese but he had quarrelled with the King of Portugal, and he proposed to Charles V that he would sail to the spice islands by the westerly route and thus capture a share of the lucrative spice trade without infringing the Treaty of Tordesillas (1494), whereby all land discovered west of a line a hundred (later revised to 375) leagues west of the Cape Verde Islands should belong to Castile, and all new territory to the east of the line should be Portugal's. Sailing with five ships from Sanlúcar, near Cádiz, in September 1519, Magellan explored the east coast of South America, sounding every inlet on his way south, but finding no channel

* Probably because he became the first *Piloto Mayor* in the school of navigation established at Seville.

through to the other ocean. The expedition wintered off Patagonia, so called because the natives wearing primitive moccasins seemed to have such large feet (*patagones*). Then after quelling a serious mutiny Magellan resumed his southward quest until he reached the straits that bear his name. His ships sailed laboriously through the narrow channel between towering cliffs and against winds that blew in sudden fierce squalls. For six weeks they toiled on until at last they emerged upon a calm sunlit sea, which after their ordeal they named *el mar pacífico*.

Their trials were by no means at an end; for ninety days they sailed on a north-westerly course without sighting land. Their provisions were almost exhausted and the crews were decimated by scurvy. At last after a profitless call at some islands where the natives were expert pilferers, Magellan landed in the Philippines, where he met his death aiding the local king in a skirmish against rebellious natives. His Basque pilot, Juan Sebastián de Elcano, took over command of the remnants of the expedition; Borneo was visited and a cargo of spice was loaded in the Moluccas. Eventually one ship reached Seville, by way of the Cape of Good Hope, in 1523 with a few exhausted seamen as crew. The cargo of spice when sold more than paid the expenses of the whole expedition, and Elcano was awarded by Charles V the arms of a globe and the motto *Primus me circumdedisti*.

Conquest of Mexico

Meanwhile the discoveries on land in the new world had brought but little profit. In 1517, however, Hernández de Córdoba reached the peninsula of Yucatán and discovered the relatively high civilisation of the Mayas, then declining in power, being subject to the Aztecs who dwelt inland. Hopes of rich spoil induced Hernán Cortés to set out to conquer all the territory inhabited by these tribes, and in 1519 he sailed from Cuba with the governor's leave, having collected eleven ships, six hundred men, sixteen horses (a type of animal unknown in the new world) and a few small cannon. After landing near Tabasco he defeated and then pacified the local tribe of Tlaxcalans, who were subject to the Aztecs and who bitterly resented their overlords. From this tribe Cortés took to himself a mistress, the faithful Doña Marina, from whom he learned of the great capital city inland. Cortés determined to make the conquest himself and renounced the superior authority of the Governor of Cuba. Like all conquistadores he founded a city, Vera Cruz, on the Spanish model with a mayor (*alcalde*), town councillors (*regidores*) and

Cortés meeting Montezuma

magistrates (*jueces*). He then made the bold stroke of burning his ships
(most of them were no longer seaworthy) so that no fainthearts should
wish to sail back to Cuba.

Luck was indeed on his side because the Aztec religion preached a
doctrine that a great white god (the first emperor returned to life)
would come from over the sea to put an end to the Aztec empire. The
reigning emperor, Montezuma, was undecided what to do with the
white invader and merely sent ambassadors begging him to depart.
This made Cortés the more determined and he entered Mexico city on
8 November 1519, marching with his tiny force of Spaniards and native
auxiliaries across a causeway to a city built in the middle of a great lake.
It was a city of fine stone buildings with magnificent gardens, and the
palace in which the Spaniards were hospitably lodged by Montezuma
was filled with gold ornaments that made them gape with wonder
and greed.

Their position was indeed precarious, for their retreat could easily be
cut off and the local population was clearly hostile. It was only Montezuma who prevented his subjects from attacking and seizing the Spaniards in order to drag them to the top of a great mound where blood-

stained priests regularly indulged in human sacrifice. Once again
Cortés took a bold course and arrested Montezuma as a hostage,
demanding that he should embrace the Christian religion and acknowledge Charles V as his overlord. Montezuma was resigned and agreed
to accept the second condition, but would not abandon his ancestral
gods.

Shortly afterwards Cortés received news that the governor of Cuba
had sent an expedition of 1,400 to bring him to obedience. Accordingly
he left a garrison in Mexico city to guard Montezuma and marched
out to meet the threat from his fellow countrymen. Cortés caught his
would-be captors by surprise in a short skirmish and induced most of
them to join him in entering Mexico city. This was done in ill-omened
circumstances, for the inhabitants were more hostile than ever. Soon
after his arrival crowds of Aztecs besieged the palace in which the
Spaniards lodged; Cortés obliged Montezuma to attempt to pacify
them, but the Aztec's former godlike authority had gone and he was
struck on the head by a stone and died three days later.

In this dire predicament Cortés decided to fight his way out along
the shortest causeway. On the night of 21 July 1520, the *Noche Triste*,
the Spanish force sallied forth, but met with fierce assaults all along the
causeway, whose bridges were all cut. Only the most determined
Spaniards and those who were carrying least booty managed to escape.
Cortés rallied his troops at Otumba and at once began preparations for
a final assault on Mexico city.

Aided by some Spanish reinforcements from the coast and the
warriors of a neighbouring tribe, formerly subject to the Aztecs (their
supply problems being eased by the fact that they usually ate their
prisoners), Cortés cautiously returned to attack Mexico. He was taking
no chances this time and even constructed twelve brigantines for
warfare on the lake. However, the Aztecs defended their city with the
heroism of despair and all attacks were repulsed, with considerable
losses, made harder to bear because Spanish prisoners could be seen
being driven up the temple mound to be sacrificed on the concave
stone, where the victim's heart was cut out by the priest while the great
snakeskin drum boomed incessantly.

At last Cortés decided on the reduction of the city by starvation
since the Aztecs, though willing to eat their prisoners, refused to touch
their own dead. The water supply to the city was cut and the brigantines on the lake kept ceaseless vigil to prevent relief supplies of food
and water being smuggled in by night. Eventually the city surrendered

with its buildings blazing and its streets littered with corpses. Montezuma's great store of treasure was never found. Presumably it lay beneath the waters of the lake.

The remainder of the empire of the Aztecs was quickly conquered
and pacified, for Cortés, though ruthless and implacable in war, was a
humane and skilful colonizer. The conquest of so great an empire made
a profound impression in Spain, where Aztec chiefs clad in brightly
coloured feathers were paraded in the great towns, to the amazement
of the people. But if the conquest of Mexico excited the wonder and
pride of the Spaniards, it was the conquest of Peru with its Inca empire
that brought Spain its chief source of wealth from the new world.

The conquest of Peru

Rumours had reached Panama before 1520 that a vast and wealthy
empire existed far down the Southern Sea, and in 1524 Francisco
Pizarro, Diego de Almagro and Hernando de Luque, a priest in Panama,
entered into a partnership to explore and conquer this empire. The
priest supplied the money and the other two set out with high hopes.
Their early efforts met with little success apart from confirming the
existence of the Inca empire, and it was clear that their resources were
insufficient for such an enterprise. Pizarro returned to Spain and in 1529
at Toledo he successfully enlisted Charles V's support, being granted
the title of Captain-General of any lands he might discover and receiving 500,000 maravedíes (about £650).

In 1531 Pizarro and Almagro once more sailed south and landed at
Túmbez, which they had discovered on previous expeditions. From
there 168 Spaniards sallied forth to conquer an empire which extended
over most of the western part of central South America. If the Inca
empire cannot exactly be described as civilisation, it achieved at least
a 'magnificent barbarism'. The capital, Cuzco, was a town of splendid
stone buildings, and throughout the empire there radiated a system of
roads, along which were stores of food placed at convenient intervals
so that armies could be marched swiftly from one area to another. The
wheel was unknown, but in a country whose capital was high in the
Andes it would have been an unnecessary luxury. Llamas provided a
surer, if limited, means of transport up the steep mountain paths.

Luck again favoured the Spaniards for at the time of the conquest
the Inca empire had been rent by civil war between Huascar, the heir
to the old kingdom of Cuzco, and Atahualpa, the ruler of the northern

part of the empire, who had emerged victorious. It was against the northern capital Tomebamba that the Spaniards marched and they encountered Atahualpa near Cajamarca. Pizarro, following the example of Cortés, was determined to seize the Inca ruler and in a battle in which the few Spanish horsemen struck terror into the hearts of thousands of Inca warriors, Atahualpa was captured. As a condition of his release he undertook to fill with gold and silver the room in which he was imprisoned. When his promise had almost been fulfilled, news was received of an impending attempt by the Incas to rescue Atahualpa. In August 1533 Pizarro produced a trumped up charge against Atahualpa of murdering Pizarro's half-brother, and after first baptising him in the Christian religion had him garrotted.

Pizarro then set up a puppet Inca as emperor and sent Almagro on to capture Cuzco, which was successfully accomplished. But Cuzco was far distant and Almagro, like most conquistadores, had ambitions for independent rule. Civil war broke out among the Spaniards, during which the Incas rebelled and both Cuzco and Pizarro's newly founded capital of Lima were almost lost. Almagro was eventually defeated, tried and executed by Pizarro's brother, Hernando, but Almagro's son continued the struggle, and in 1541 assassinated Francisco Pizarro. Charles V now had to intervene, and a royal army defeated the younger Almagro, but it was a long time before disgruntled conquistadores were finally pacified and order was established under the viceroy, Don Francisco de Toledo.

All the early conquistadores from Columbus onwards attempted to maintain for themselves and their heirs an independent rule in the lands they had discovered, but the Crown dealt firmly with them and usually sent out viceroys to govern in their stead. Several conquistadores, including Columbus and Cortés, returned to Spain to die in comparative obscurity. The intentions of the Crown in the Indies were of the highest, and both Isabel and Charles V issued strict instructions regarding the treatment of the native population. The main purpose was to bring the inhabitants of the newly discovered lands into the fold of the Catholic Church, and conquistadores constantly employed a priest to make a harangue (with or without an interpreter) on the subject of the Holy Trinity to puzzled Indians, after which force of arms was normally employed as being more persuasive.

The Crown was genuinely concerned about the welfare of the natives, and Isabel had issued an edict that Indians were not to be enslaved, though this rule was later relaxed in the case of cannibals and prisoners of war. The lands were shared out to Spanish settlers in what were called *encomiendas* (trusts); on these *encomiendas* the natives were bound to work for a certain period for their overlord, but any excess work was to be paid for and the overlord was bound to protect and care for the physical and spiritual welfare of his *encomendados*. It was comparatively easy to define these conditions in Burgos where the laws of the Indies were issued in 1512, but to enforce them in distant wild regions was another matter. There is no doubt that the *encomienda* system was greatly abused and nameless cruelties were often practised on the natives. The original inhabitants of the Antilles died out almost completely, due to war, forced labour, starvation and the introduction of European diseases such as smallpox. Negro slaves from Africa were early introduced as being hardier and more suitable for rigorous work in a hot climate, and this experiment was extended to the mainland. Bartolomé de las Casas, the first Spaniard to be ordained a priest in the New World, campaigned vigorously for the welfare of the natives and induced the Crown to issue new laws for the Indians limiting the *encomienda* system, but these had to be suspended because of opposition from Spanish settlers. Las Casas returned to Spain and continued to publish a series of tracts on the abuses practised against the Indians. With the best of intentions he probably overstated the case, and the dark picture he painted was eagerly seized upon by the enemies of Spain. The fact remains that Spanish civilisation was quickly established and has remained in being ever since in spite of the independence of all the colonies gained in the nineteenth century, and of countless revolutions and changes of government since.

Charles V's empire in the New World was therefore permanent, and it was certainly profitable. All told the amount of bullion imported into Spain from the Indies between 1503 and 1660 amounted to £257,488,418, excluding any which might have been smuggled into the country. This enormous influx of gold and silver was responsible for the early prosperity of Spain, and also in great measure for her rapid economic decline which began about 1560. The rise in prices was an early stimulus to the home trade, but it made exports to other European countries too costly and Spain's external trade dwindled, though the monopoly in the Indies continued long enough to mask the effects of this shrinkage. But by late in the sixteenth century the Spanish settlers in the Indies had built up their own industries and commerce with America tended to contract. Moreover, a large class of *hidalgos* had grown up nurtured in the belief that it was ungentle-

manly to work and soil one's hands with trade and these combined with
the vast army of monks, priests, soldiers and beggars formed an excessive proportion of the population which was totally unproductive.

The Wars of Charles V

The most obvious and immediate reason for loss of bullion was the
ceaseless warfare in which Charles V engaged throughout his reign.
His election to the crown of the Holy Roman Empire inevitably involved Spain in all the quarrels of Europe. The King of France, Francis I,
was bitterly jealous of Charles, having himself been an unsuccessful
candidate for the Empire. The French attacked Navarre in 1521, taking
advantage of the revolt of the *Comuneros* in Spain. They captured
Pamplona after a long siege during which a young Basque gentleman,
Ignacio Loyola, had his leg broken; he was afterwards inspired to
found the Society of Jesus. The French were successfully expelled from
Navarre, but there was fighting on the Netherlands frontier and more
especially in Italy, where possession of Milan was the cause of dispute.
For Charles control of Milan was essential in order to maintain communications between Spain and his Austrian possessions, since the sea
route to the Netherlands depended on the friendliness of England.
Charles had visited Henry VIII in 1520, and Wolsey's good offices had
been secured in exchange for the Bishopric of Badajoz, worth 5,000
ducats a year (about £2,500), together with some 2,000 ducats a year
from the ecclesiastical revenues of Palencia. But England's good will
could in no way be depended upon, and Milan must be held. Francis I
realised that if he could win Milan he would hold the key to
Europe.

At first the French made considerable headway in northern Italy,
capturing Milan, and in October 1524 they laid siege to the fortified
city of Pavia. An imperial force was collected to relieve the city, but
it was inferior in numbers to the French army; moreover, since pay
was as always grossly in arrears, the imperial troops, consisting of
Germans, Italians and Spaniards, were near to mutiny. They demanded
an immediate battle, hoping for plunder; had Francis held off, the
imperial army would assuredly have dispersed in search of pillage.
Pride forbade this course because Francis had sworn to take Pavia or to
die in the attempt. The Imperial troops attacked during the night of
24–25 February 1525, with Spanish battalions leading. The beleaguered
forces in Pavia, under the shrewd and courageous Spanish general de

Leyva, made a timely sortie and almost the whole French army was destroyed. Francis himself was taken prisoner.

This resounding triumph not only gave Charles effective control over northern Italy, but also afforded an opportunity to crush France completely. If he had had the strength to march on Paris, it must have fallen, but Charles had to resort to diplomatic measures to obtain a favourable peace treaty. But his terms were harsh and would have involved the virtual destruction of the monarchy in France. As a condition of the release of the captive French King, now lodged in a tower of the Alcázar in Madrid, he demanded the Dukedom of Burgundy with all its dependencies, the renunciation of all French claims to Milan and Naples, and the restoration of the estates of the Constable of France, the Prince de Bourbon, who had deserted to the imperial cause. The French stubbornly refused such terms and Francis at one stage renounced the crown of France in favour of his son, in the determination to remain a prisoner forever rather than submit to such terms. Unwilling to have Francis as a permanent guest Charles modified his demands, only to find that Francis suddenly gave way and signed the treaty of Madrid (14 January 1526), though with no intention of observing the terms of it.

As soon as he was out of Spain Francis obtained leave from the anti-Spanish Pope Clement VII to break his oath, in spite of the fact that he had left his two sons as hostages in Madrid. A few months later he formed an alliance, the Holy League of Cognac, with the Pope and other Italian princes against Charles. Enraged at this betrayal Charles despatched reinforcements to Italy from Germany and Spain. The army mustered at Piacenza, but it was unpaid, starving and mutinous. It soon became completely uncontrollable and marched southward, bent on plunder. The two generals, the Duke of Bourbon and General Frundsberg, went with it—whether willingly or forcibly is uncertain. Frundsberg died of apoplexy at Bologna and the mutinous army attacked Rome, where Bourbon was killed in the first assault by a shot from an arquebus aimed by Benvenuto Cellini, the great silversmith and even greater romancer. The Pope in terror shut himself with the cardinals in the Castle of St Angelo, which was not taken by the attackers, thanks, Cellini claims, to stupendous efforts by himself in charge of the artillery. The rest of Rome was put to the most brutal sack for days on end in May 1527.

The story of the plunder of the Eternal City shocked the whole of Catholic Christendom, and the effect produced on devout catholics in Spain was profound, although Charles, after withholding the news for

as long as possible, disclaimed any responsibility for an attack on the
Holy See. The French, roused to a fever pitch of religious fervour,
invaded Italy, capturing Milan and laying siege to Naples. When
things seemed blackest, Charles had the good fortune to receive the aid
of the Genoese fleet under Admiral Andrea Doria, who abandoned the
Holy League. This enabled him to ship troops from Spain to Italy and
raise the siege of Naples; and, aided by an outbreak of plague in the
French army, he managed to retake Milan. Another French invasion
of Italy was decisively defeated by de Leyva at Landriano (21 June 1529).
The French were exhausted and Spain was able to make peace with the
Pope, and a month later with France by the treaty of Cambrai. Charles
abandoned his claim to Burgundy and released his hostages, Francis's
two sons, in exchange for two million crowns. The domination of
Charles V over Europe was now complete and he was able to receive
the Imperial crown from the Pope amid scenes of great splendour at
Bologna (22–24 February 1530).

There was, however, no respite from war. Spain was particularly
sensitive to the Mohammedan menace, both for historical and for practical reasons. Moorish pirates from Africa harried Spanish shipping in
the Mediterranean, and raided the Valencian coast, often with the connivance of the Moriscos, but the real menace to Christendom was the
Turkish Empire, which was expanding in power and territory under
Suleiman the Magnificent (1520–66). Belgrade had fallen to the Turks
in 1521, and in 1526 the disastrous battle of Mohačs field in Hungary
had opened up the Danube Valley, leaving Vienna in the greatest peril.
It was a move by Charles six years later that relieved the city; he sent
Admiral Andrea Doria with a fleet of forty-four galleys and 10,000
men to raid various fortresses in the Peloponese. This expedition
achieved considerable success and before returning to Genoa loaded
with booty Doria had so threatened the Turkish bases that the Muslims
withdrew from the Danube Valley.

As a counterstroke, the Turks sent Barbarossa, a renegade Christian
and a fearsome pirate, to capture Tunis, then held by the Moors in
allegiance to Charles. This was accomplished in August 1534, and
Spanish sea routes in the Mediterranean were now seriously menaced.
In the following June, Charles assembled a fleet of 400 ships in Sardinia
and sailed across the narrow seas, anchoring on 15 June off the ruins of
Carthage. He then captured La Goletta, the fortress guarding Tunis,
and advanced against the city itself, having captured almost the whole
of Barbarossa's fleet as well as much spoil. Inside Tunis was a large

number of Christian slaves, whom Barbarossa intended to massacre. He was dissuaded by the slaves' owners, who disliked seeing valuable property go to waste. The slaves, hearing of the approach of their fellow Christians, rose up, killed their guards and seizing weapons did such execution that by 21 July 1535 Tunis lay defenceless, and Charles entered without striking a blow. Unfortunately while the Christians were engrossed in plundering Tunis, Barbarossa escaped to Bone and thence to Algiers, whence he was still able to harry Spanish shipping.

Meanwhile the French were again on the move and were even in secret communication with the Turks. Indeed, some of the guns captured at La Goletta bore a lily, showing that they had been cast in the arsenals of France. Charles, anxious to avoid war, offered the Duchy of Milan to Charles of Angoulême, Francis's second son, on condition that he married the widow of the late Duke, or else Charles's daughter Margaret. This offer was refused, and Charles then made a dramatic gesture inspired by the ideals of medieval chivalry. He pronounced a great harangue in Spanish (17 April 1536) to the Pope, cardinals and ambassadors of Europe, proclaiming the justice of his cause and offering to fight Francis in single combat, the gages being Milan and Burgundy. This fresh offer was again refused, no doubt because it was an outmoded form of warfare and the French continued their advance into Italy. Spain retaliated by entering Provence. Neither side made much progress, both being exhausted; they were equally glad to accept the Pope's mediation, by which a ten year truce was signed at Nice (1 June 1538). Francis and Charles met in the fortress town of Aigues Mortes with a display of the utmost friendliness, and later the Emperor travelled all across France, being entertained everywhere in great splendour.

The truce was something of a reverse for Charles, but it was desperately needed since the Muslim menace was once more serious. The possession of Algiers by the Muslims made shipments of Spanish troops to Italy a perilous undertaking, and in October 1541 Charles set out with a large force to capture the pirates' headquarters. An expedition at such time of year was completely contrary to the advice of all his commanders, because the season was the stormiest in the Mediterranean, but Charles felt secure in the knowledge that he was already in secret communication with Hassan Aga, Barbarossa's lieutenant governor at Algiers, who had signified his willingness to surrender the city. All went well at first, and troops were safely landed close to Algiers, one of the leaders being Hernán Cortés, the hero of Mexico. It was then learned that Hassan Aga had no intention of surrendering Algiers; this would have mattered little since the strong imperialist army would almost certainly have taken the city, but at a fatal moment an appalling gale burst, soaking all the powder in Charles's army and smashing his fleet to pieces as it lay at anchor in the bay. Andrea Doria withdrew the remnants to a safer anchorage, where Charles's battered and decimated army rejoined them three days later, after much toil and suffering. Hernán Cortés, who in Mexico had often been in worse situations, was in favour of renewing the attack, but Charles decided to cut his losses (150 ships and 12,000 men) and withdraw, after suffering the first major defeat of his reign.

No attempt at revenge was possible for the French were again on the warpath, this time in open alliance with the Turks, whose fleet spent the winter of 1541 at Toulon, the ships filled with Christian slaves. The French tried to invade Spain, but Perpignan, then a Spanish fortress, held out stubbornly, and a diversion was created by the Imperial army marching on Paris from the Netherlands. It got as far as Landrécies, with light cavalry reconnoitring even further towards Meaux, before it was turned back. The French also won a sweeping victory at Cérisoles (Easter Monday 1544) near the Italian border. It became clear, however, that neither side was achieving any substantial progress, and peace was signed at Crespy in the following September.

This peace enabled Charles to turn his attention to the suppression of a revolt by the Lutheran princes in his German territories. He defeated their army completely on the Elbe at Mühleberg (24 April 1547), where some dauntless Spanish soldiers swam the river, sword in mouth, and captured a number of pontoons, thus enabling the main body to cross and fall on the Lutherans, who were encamped feeling falsely secure. A patchwork peace was made by the Interim of Augsburg (1548), which, though Catholic in tone, made all possible concessions to Lutheranism. Like most religious compromises it was a failure.

It had indeed been the valour and splendid discipline of the Spanish troops which had made so many of Charles's victories possible. The Spanish army had been welded into a formidable fighting machine early in the century by Gonzalo de Córdoba, *el Gran Capitán*, who organised the infantry into *coronelias* of 6,000 men, subsequently divided into the famous *tercios* of half that number. Half the *tercio* was armed with long pikes, a third used short swords and javelins, and the remainder were armed with arquebuses. But it was the spirit of the Spanish soldiers that gave them their superiority. They had been brought up on stories of the prowess of their forefathers against the Moors, and a crusading ardour still blazed within them. Born and reared in a barren, bleak land, they were hardy and tough, and were able to exist on an incredibly frugal diet and still be fit to march and fight. For over a century Spanish troops were unmatched in Europe.

Philip II

Charles was weary of war and weary of the burden of empire, and he began actively to consider his successor. After much consideration he abandoned the attempt to make his son, Philip (born 1527) emperor, and relinquished the succession of his German territories to his brother, Ferdinand. He concentrated on uniting Spain and the Netherlands, a union which economically was advantageous, since Spain was predominantly a producer of raw materials and the Netherlands were a manufacturing and trading community. The difficulty was communications, because Milan and the German route were no longer practicable. The French were still actively hostile, even after the death of Francis I in 1546, and friendship with England was therefore essential to keep open the sea route to the Netherlands.

The divorce of Catherine of Aragon by Henry VIII and his desertion to Protestantism had alienated Spain and England. Fortunately for Charles the death of Edward VI (6 July 1553) and the accession of Mary, Catherine of Aragon's daughter, opened up the possibility of an alliance. Mary was willing to marry Philip, who had been left a widower at the age of eighteen. To secure this union Charles made every kind of concession to placate English detestation of a Spanish marriage. Philip was to be known as King of England only during Mary's lifetime; any heir of the marriage would inherit the Netherlands and the Franche Comté; if Philip's son by his first marriage, Don Carlos, should die without an heir the whole Spanish inheritance would go to the child of Philip and Mary. In addition to all this he brought with him a dowry of £60,000; moreover he was careful not to offend English Protestant leanings. Though Mary had persuaded Parliament to restore Catholicism as the official religion, Philip exerted considerable influence to prevent persecution of the Protestants.

The couple were married in Winchester Cathedral on 25 July 1554, and Philip's bearing and considerate behaviour made a favourable impression. All that was now needed to complete Charles's plans was a child, but this was not to be and Philip, to whom his English marriage had always been merely a painful duty, left England on 28 August 1555.

Charles, though disappointed, continued with his plans for abdication, a complicated matter which took several years to complete. The Spanish part had been made easier by the death in 1555 of his mother, Juana *la Loca*, who in law had been Queen of Spain all this time. Eventually on 17 September 1556 Charles left Ghent, his native town, for Spain; there he retired to a monastery in Yuste where he lived another two years in peaceful retirement after a life in which his health had been ruined by his ceaseless activity and by his gluttony at table.

Philip was left with a vast empire, but also another French war and royal debts amounting to £9,700,000, excluding many millions worth of *juros* or annuities bearing interest of $7\frac{1}{2}$ to 10 per cent, which had been purchased by countless Spanish investors. The menace of France was soon dealt with, for Philip's polygot army in Flanders (including some English), under command of Emmanuel-Philibert of Savoy, won an overwhelming victory at St Quentin (2 August 1557) in which almost the whole French army was captured or annihilated. Though this crushing defeat was never followed up, the truce of Cateau-Cambrésis (3 April 1559) marked at last the end of Franco-Spanish wars in the sixteenth century.

The burden of debt·was not easily shaken off, though in 1557 Philip attempted to solve his problems by a partial renunciation of his obligations. This merely had the effect of lowering royal credit, and the many further loans which Philip was forced to negotiate in his reign could be obtained only at more exorbitant rates of interest. A second decree in 1575 attempted to lower interest rates, but had the effect of halving the capital value of *juros* as well as increasing the already crippling taxation. So great were the repercussions that in Seville two banks stopped withdrawals and the fleet bound for America could not be loaded for lack of ready money; the great trade fair at Medina del Campo was suspended.

Almost all Philip's actions contributed directly or indirectly to hastening Spain's decline, yet for most of his reign the Spanish people were solidly behind him and he was and still is known by Spaniards as Philip the Wise (*Felipe el Prudente*). The Protestant view is quite different, for he is described as a tyrant and a fanatic who took a delight in torturing and burning any who wavered in adherence to the Catholic faith. This was the picture painted by William the Silent, Prince of Orange, in his *Apologia* (1581), designed as an anti-Spanish manifesto; the same theme recurs in the *Relaciones* by Antonio Pérez, Philip's renegade secretary, published in London in 1594. Perhaps Spaniards

RIGHT   *Philip II by Titian, the Prado*

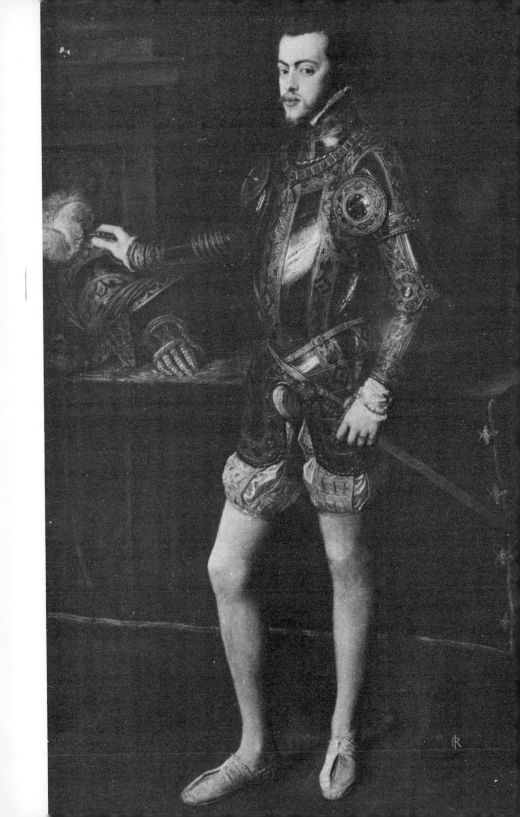

took his virtues for granted and felt that no apology for Philip was needed. Certainly much evidence exists for assuming that the general view of Philip is a prejudiced one. His letters to his two daughters, Isabel and Catherine, reveal fatherly affection and a humorous interest in their childish doings. He was respected and loved by his servants, whose welfare was his personal care. He was a man of devout and strictly moral life, and was frugal and austere in his tastes, though he maintained a splendid court with the most rigid rules of etiquette in order to keep his nobles in their places. He was a man of learning, skilled in Latin, French and Italian; he was a great collector of books, a talented musician and a patron of the arts. In his leisure moments he was a good enough chess player to oppose the great Ruy López, whose name is still familiar as the inventor of an opening move. If Philip did vigorously pursue a policy of enforcing orthodox Catholicism in Spain and the Netherlands, it was because the doctrine of one state, one religion was then universally adopted and was no more unusual than the enforcement of the strict party line in Nazi Germany or Communist Russia. His policy was dictated solely by the need to maintain the unity of his wide dominions. To this end he supported Elizabeth when her position on the throne of England was anything but secure, and his reason was that a successful Catholic revolt would place Mary Queen of Scots on the throne and unite England and France.

His real weakness lay in the rigidity of his personal rule, for he so centralised the government of the whole Spanish Empire that he made it impossible for anyone to succeed him except a born civil servant like himself. Of the many instructions that Charles V had left for his son, the one that impressed him most was: 'Depend on none but yourself.' Under Philip II there were no less than twelve councils by the end of his reign, dealing with various matters ranging from the Treasury (*Hacienda*) to the Indies. Chief of these councils was the Council of State (*Consejo de Estado*), but this was purely an advisory body, all of whose members were appointed by the King. He was in no wise bound to abide by their advice for he was answerable to no one but God.

Philip was careful to split his council into two sections of sharply opposed opinions and roughly equal strength, with the result that their advice would rarely be unanimous. He could listen to both sides of any question and make his own decision. The leader of one faction on the Council of State was the Duke of Alba, an able general eager to suppress ruthlessly any hint of disorder or revolt. The more conciliatory party was led by Ruy Gómez, Prince of Éboli, who was charming and

L'AUTO-DA-FE, ou l'Acte de Foi.

An 18th century Auto de Fe

courteous, and an adept at dealing with foreign ambassadors in the most soothing manner.

Philip employed this system of maintaining equilibrium in his Council of State all his reign, long after Alba and Éboli had left the scene. But it was Philip himself who insisted on making every decision, even on trivial points, and before long he acquired a truly bureaucratic love of paperwork, so that the advice of the council would be submitted to him in writing; he would annotate this document copiously and possibly send it back for further advice before he issued any decision. Often secretaries working in adjoining rooms received from the King written communications, to which they likewise had to reply in writing.

Philip was enormously industrious and the system he created was immensely thorough, but it was also unbelievably slow. Everything had to be dealt with in rotation, and momentous matters such as the Revolt in the Netherlands had to wait while minor problems of court etiquette were laboriously solved. Philip never caught up with his ever increasing mass of documents and the delays in Spanish governmental decisions became notorious throughout the world. 'If death came from Spain, we should live to a great age', was the despairing comment of the Spanish Viceroy of Naples.

The first threat to the unity of Spain came at the very beginning of Philip's reign, before he had returned from the triumphant campaign in northern France. Protestantism shyly raised its head in Spain, but was at once suppressed by the Inquisition, first in Andalusia and then in Valladolid where its leaders were more stouthearted, for two resolutely refused to recant and were burnt without first having been strangled. Philip himself was present at the *auto de fe* in Valladolid on Trinity Sunday (21 May) 1559; there Don Carlos de Seso was burnt alive and is said to have remonstrated with Philip who replied: 'If my son were to oppose the Catholic Church, I myself would carry the faggots to burn him.'

This story is almost certainly apocryphal and may have originated from the tragedy which befell Philip in the death of his son by his first marriage, Don Carlos. He was a sickly, misshapen youth, who early showed signs of sadistic tendencies that proved him quite unbalanced. He was later seriously hurt at the University of Alcalá after a fall down a flight of stairs while pursuing a girl. His life was saved only by an operation removing a triangular piece of bone from his skull. Thereafter he became even more unbalanced, developing a fierce hatred of his father. Eventually he began plotting secretly to leave Spain, but revealed his plans to his uncle Don John of Austria on 23 December 1567. For once Philip acted promptly, since the heir to the Spanish Empire wandering abroad would be an admirable weapon in the hands of Spain's enemies; immediately after the Christmas festivities Philip personally arrested his son and cast him into prison where the poor lunatic several times attempted to commit suicide, and finally died in July 1568. Philip was grieved beyond measure, and his grief increased his natural reserve so that the whole affair was shrouded in mystery, giving place to the wildest rumours that Don Carlos was beheaded, poisoned, smothered or strangled by negro slaves. It seems likely that he died from natural causes, aided by the medical remedies of the day, for the doctors made him sleep naked on a bed strewn with ice.

Revolt in the Netherlands

Meanwhile, revolt was brewing in the Spanish Netherlands, which consisted of seventeen separate provinces in what is now Holland and

Belgium. The Netherlanders were a great trading and manufacturing race and the provinces were at the height of their prosperity, with Antwerp as their greatest port, and the money market of Europe. There were, however, many causes of discontent with Spanish suzerainty. In the first place there was mutual detestation between the Netherlanders and the Spanish garrisons. The Netherlanders were essentially tradesmen, indifferent to religion and inclined to gluttony and drunkenness; the Spaniards considered themselves *hidalgos* and were fervent Catholics, austere and moderate in their habits. Moreover, taxes were heavy and had recently been increased, and the Netherlanders resented subsidising the idle Spanish from the fruits of their own thrift.

Worst of all was the religious problem, for the Netherlands were wide open to Protestant influences from England, to Lutheran preaching from Germany and to the Calvinist doctrine then gaining headway in France. Charles V had attempted to repress heresy in the Netherlands by a series of decrees known as Placards, the last of which (25 September 1550) made even the most trivial offence against the Catholic religion punishable by death. Philip had maintained all these measures against heresy and kept the Inquisition vigilant in the Netherlands, though it never worked as methodically or as ruthlessly as in Spain.

Philip's policy in the Netherlands had on the whole been conciliatory, for he had placed the whole government of the country under natives, with William of Orange and Count Egmont appointed to the Council of State and Knights of the Golden Fleece. The regent was Margaret of Parma, daughter of Charles V by a Flemish woman; she was an energetic person with a bass voice and moustache, and considerably skilled as a governor. But Philip put greatest trust in Granvelle, a son of Charles V's chancellor, an able administrator and scholar who, it is said, could dictate despatches to secretaries in five different languages at the same time. Associated with him were Viglius, a Netherlander and a learned jurist, and the Count of Berlaimont, a loyal nobleman from the southern Netherland provinces.

The great lords on the Council took offence at the trust placed in this trio and began to stir up trouble among the lesser nobility. All the Netherland nobility were in debt to a greater or less extent, mainly because of their extravagant households (William of Orange had so large a kitchen staff that he dismissed twenty-eight cooks in one day in an effort at economy). The main hope of many of the Dutch lords lay in rebellion and possible plunder. They therefore petitioned Philip for Granvelle's dismissal, which was unexpectedly granted. Emboldened by this success they demanded an end to religious persecution, but this Philip refused. The malcontents then drew up a solemn Request (December 1565) which they presented to the Regent in Brussels, reiterating the demand for an end to persecution and calling on her to suspend the Inquisition pending receipt of the King's reply. It was then that Berlaimont contemptuously referred to the petitioners as *les Gueux* (the Beggars), a name soon to become famous.

The Regent innocently granted the request for temporary religious toleration, whereupon Calvinists poured into the Netherlands from France, Germany, Geneva, and even England, and in August 1566 they looted monasteries, wrecked churches and almost destroyed the great cathedral at Antwerp. Such an outburst of 'Calvinist fury' enraged the Netherlanders, most of whom were Catholics, and there was a swing of opinion in favour of the Spaniards. Unfortunately Philip was determined to stamp out heresy and sent the Duke of Alba with 10,000 seasoned Spanish troops to restore order. After his arrival in Brussels (22 August 1567), he set up a Court of Tumults, which tried and executed all suspected of rebellion, no matter what their rank; Count Egmont was included among the victims, though he had trusted in his privileges as a Knight of the Golden Fleece. How many were executed is unknown, but Alba is said to have boasted that he put 18,000 persons to death, and the tribunal came to be known as the Council of Blood.

Alba was desperate for money, since bullion destined for him had been seized in the Channel by English seamen. He therefore proposed new taxation, similar to the *alcabala*, or sales tax in Spain. A once for all capital levy of one per cent was to be raised on all property, while a sales tax of 10 per cent on the value of movable goods and 20 per cent on immovable goods was to be imposed. Such a tax was useful because it affected all classes alike, and had been an excellent weapon against the nobles in Spain, but in a great trading country it would be crippling commercially. After some postponement it was finally enforced in 1572. Wholesale executions had left the Netherlanders comparatively unmoved, but this blow at their economy roused everyone to rebellion.

On Alba's arrival *les Gueux* had taken refuge in eighteen ships, and had ranged the channel in search of prizes, having been given letters of marque by William by virtue of his sovereign title of Prince of Orange in the Rhone Valley. The Sea Beggars were at first given facilities in English ports and they thrived greatly. In 1572, however, Elizabeth changed her policy and expelled them; by great good fortune they found the port of Brill, near Flushing, empty of its Spanish garrison. They seized the town (1 April 1572) and fortified it, and soon a whole series of harbours and islands in the western Netherlands were in the hands of *les Gueux*, reinforced by the return of many of their country-men who had fled abroad. Here, amid the estuaries, canals and dykes, they were safe from the Spanish *tercios* and formed a secure base from which to carry on the war against Spain for the next forty years, long after the death of Philip II.

The rebellion of the Moriscos

During this time rebellion had broken out in Spain itself; the Moriscos of Granada had been goaded into a revolt which might have turned into another full scale Mohammedan war. At the end of the Reconquest the Moors had been given generous terms, including freedom of worship, but this pledge had been broken in 1502 and all Moors who chose to remain in the province of Granada had been obliged to accept Christianity. A similar step had been taken in Aragon after the troubles of the *Germanía*, so that the whole Moorish population of Spain was nominally Christian. Charles V in 1525 had attempted to suppress Arabic as a language in Spain, and also Moorish dress and customs, but the Moriscos, who were industrious tradesmen, had bought him off by accepting a special tax (*farda*) in exchange for the right to speak Arabic and wear Moorish costume.

In Granada a large part of the population was Morisco and they practised their own religion behind closed doors, though they outwardly observed the obligations of the Catholic Church, such as making their confession at Easter, for example, when they said the same things as the previous year. They worked behind closed doors on Sundays and on feast days, and they took baths even in December, accompanying them with Mohammedan ceremonial and ritual. Such a state of affairs horrified the Archbishop of Granada, who took his tale of woe to the Pope. Philip was easily prevailed upon to take action and in 1567 issued a *Pragmática*, forbidding the use of Arabic after a three-year period in which all Moriscos were to learn Spanish, banning all forms of artificial baths, and requiring the doors of all Morisco houses to be left open on all holy days, Christian or Mohammedan, so that covert Muslim practices could easily be detected.

This decree was persisted with even though the Captain-General of

Granada, the Marqués de Mondéjar, who really understood the Moriscos, warned that it would lead to civil war and pointed out the inadequate resources of the Spaniards in Granada to meet such an emergency. The rebellion actually began on 23 December 1568, and though the city of Granada itself did not revolt the district to the south was completely overrun by the rebels, who slaughtered priests and monks, and sold large numbers of Christian men, women and children into slavery on the Barbary coast. The Marqués de Mondéjar, acting with the greatest energy, managed virtually to quell the revolt by promising an amnesty to all who surrendered, and by meting out the utmost severity to those who did not. Unfortunately the Captain-General of the neighbouring province of Murcia, the Marqués de los Vélez, jealous of Mondéjar, invaded Granada with his undisciplined militia, attacked the Moriscos who had laid down their arms trusting in Mondéjar's promise, and plundered and slaughtered in the most wanton fashion. The rebellion immediately flared up again and became more widespread than ever.

Philip determined on energetic measures and appointed as commander of the Spanish troops in Granada his half-brother, Don John of Austria, son of Charles V by a German woman, Barbara Blomberg. After some months of hesitation, during which Philip tried to make all the decisions himself, Don John was given a free hand and with reinforcements of veteran Spanish troops from Italy managed by the end of 1570 to reduce to submission the whole province of Granada. The entire Morisco population of the province was sent to live among the old Christians of other parts of Castile, where they were carefully supervised; their children were compulsorily sent to school, their homes were regularly visited and their poor and sick were cared for. Such indeed was the intention of Philip, who was far more humane than history has ever declared; in practice, however, these humane instructions were indifferently carried out and the cancer of Morisco discontent was spread all over Castile instead of being confined to Granada. This rich province now lay waste, and over 60,000 Spanish lives had been lost in the civil war.

The Battle of Lepanto

The real danger of the Morisco revolt had lain in the possibility of the Turks invading southern Spain in support of their fellow Muslims. This they could have easily done, for they had in 1565 inflicted a

ABOVE *The Battle of Lepanto* *War in the Netherlands* BELOW

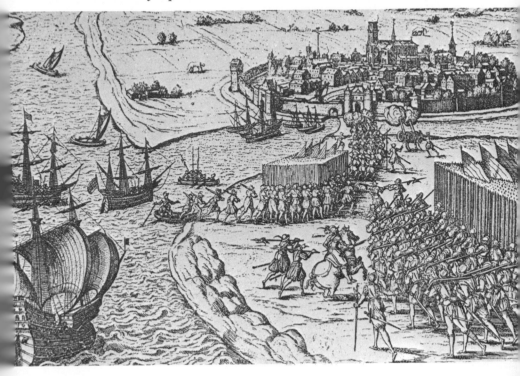

disastrous defeat on the Spaniards at the island of Los Gelves (Djerba) near Tripoli and now had almost complete command of the Mediterranean. The Turkish Emperor, Selim II, decided, however, to attack Cyprus, a Christian outpost belonging to Venice, and Spain was saved from another Muslim invasion. But the threat made Philip sink his differences with the Venetian Republic and join a Holy League against the Turks.

In September 1571 a combined fleet under the command of Don John of Austria set sail to strike a decisive blow at the Turks, whose fleet was sighted on 7 October in the bay of Lepanto, at the narrow part of the gulf of Corinth. The ensuing naval battle was the last in which the traditional methods of grappling and boarding were used to any large extent; nevertheless it was the superior fire power of the Christian fleet that won the day. Not only were there six galleasses with heavy guns ahead of the main line, but also the galleys had been shorn of their sharp forepeaks in order to improve the field of fire of their forward guns. The whole Turkish force was almost annihilated, except for a squadron under Uluch Ali, the Governor of Algiers, whose experience in Mediterranean piracy enabled him to escape. Some 16,000 Turks were either killed or captured, and 10,000 Christian slaves were freed from Turkish galleys. The Christian losses were also heavy and the victory was not exploited, although Don John, intoxicated with success, dreamed of establishing a Christian empire in the east, with Constantinople as its capital. Nevertheless, Muslim naval power in the Mediterranean was destroyed for ever and Cervantes, who was wounded in the hand during the battle, had some cause to describe Lepanto as 'the noblest occasion that past or present ages have seen or future ones may hope to see' (Prologue to *Don Quijote*, Part 2).

The war in the Netherlands had been going badly for Spain in spite of many brilliant victories by Requesens, Alba's successor. Much difficulty was caused by Philip's virtual bankruptcy in 1575, for Spanish troops were unpaid and in a state of mutiny; on 4 November 1576 they sacked and plundered Antwerp with almost unparalleled ferocity and this 'Spanish Fury' had the effect of uniting all the Netherland provinces in a determined effort to drive out the Spaniards. In vain was Don John of Austria sent there to restore order; his resources were inadequate and he was forced to come to terms with the Netherland States-General (1 February 1577), promising to remove all Spanish troops and to maintain the liberties of the Netherlands in return for recognition as governor. Bitter and angry he seized Namur and defied the States-General, thereby increasing the detestation of all Netherlanders, even the Catholics, for the Spaniards. In September 1577 William the Silent entered Brussels in triumph with almost all the Netherland provinces under his control.

Union with Portugal

If the war in the Netherlands was a perpetual source of trouble and disappointment to Philip, he had the consolation of achieving a splendid and unexpected success in the Peninsula itself. In 1578 King Sebastian of Portugal had been killed at the battle of Alcazarquivir during his mad expedition to Africa against the Emperor of Morocco. He was succeeded by an aged and infirm great uncle, Cardinal Henry, for whom there was no direct successor. Philip claimed to be heir to the Portuguese monarchy through his mother Isabel, daughter of Manuel *el Afortunado*. Philip immediately set about measures for supporting his claim; his first act was to ransom the Portuguese prisoners taken in Morocco, thus giving himself a lead over the numerous other claimants who came forward. After much heated debate and disagreement King Henry accepted Philip as his heir, and died shortly afterwards (31 January 1580). Popular feeling was intensely hostile to accepting a foreigner as king and the nationalist party raised an army of peasants, declaring Antonio, Prior of Crato, an illegitimate descendant of King Manuel, to be the rightful monarch. Philip, acting with unusual speed, put the Duke of Alba, who had lately been in semi-disgrace, in charge of a powerful army which marched into Portugal and easily defeated Antonio's raw levies at the bridge of Alcántara near Lisbon. Philip entered Portugal from Badajoz and received the oath of allegiance from the Portuguese Cortes on 3 April 1581. He behaved in the most circumspect and conciliatory manner, swearing to maintain the liberties of the Portuguese people, to reserve trade with their dominions overseas solely for Portuguese nationals, and finally to appoint no Spaniards to offices in Portugal. This promise was observed scrupulously by Philip, but in spite of this virtual independence the annexation of Portugal brought immense benefits to Spain, including a series of safe Atlantic harbours and easy access to the rich trade in spice, pearls, precious carpets and other luxuries from Persia and the Far East. France indeed became alarmed at the growth of Spain's power and sent a fleet to the Azores to enable Don

Antonio to set up a rival base there, but the French were intercepted by a Spanish fleet inferior in numbers under the command of the Marqués de Santa Cruz who gained an overwhelming victory (26 July 1582).

This success gave Spain the reputation for being invincible at sea as well as on land. It was only the English who seemed capable of making such an assertion appear exaggerated. Elizabeth had been allowing her seamen to prey on Spanish shipping, not only in the West Indies but also in the English Channel. Philip had been compelled to swallow every insult from the English, since any alliance between England and France would be fatal to his sea communications with the Netherlands. But the situation began to change because Henry III of France was showing increasing friendliness towards the Huguenots, and it seemed certain that he would accept as his successor the Huguenot, Henry of Navarre. The Catholic League in France was therefore driven to an understanding with Philip. Its leader was the Duc de Guise, uncle of Mary Queen of Scots. Keeping Mary alive had long been Elizabeth's most effectual counter to any Spanish attempt to invade England, but now that Philip and the Guises were allied the unhappy Queen of Scots became a positive danger to Elizabeth, who had her executed on 18 February 1587.

Moreover England had intervened in the Netherlands and had supported the rebels just when victory seemed within grasp of the Spaniards. Alexander Farnese, son of the former Regent Margaret of Parma, had been conducting a masterly campaign, capturing Antwerp and subduing almost all the southern Netherlands. William of Orange, on whose head Philip had long set a price, had been assassinated by a Burgundian fanatic Balthazar Gérard (9 July 1584). At this crisis it was only the English force bunglingly led by the Earl of Leicester that kept the revolt alive until William's son, Maurice of Saxony, effectively took charge of operations.

The Invincible Armada

Philip had already been seeking Elizabeth's downfall, aiding the Irish rebels (1580) and being a party to the Throgmorton plot to kill the Queen (1584). This latter event caused diplomatic relations to be broken off and open war was inevitable, reluctant though both sovereigns were to embark on hostilities. Philip's plan of campaign was to transport Farnese's army from Flanders to England, accompanied by a naval force sufficient to keep control of the Channel, and thus secure the communications of the invading troops. In Lisbon, Cádiz and almost all the peninsular ports ships were fitted out and stores amassed for the *Armada Invencible*. But there were great difficulties apart from the perpetual lack of ready money; much of the equipment had to be bought abroad, some of it from Protestant contractors in Germany and Denmark. Drake's daring raids on Cádiz and Lisbon in 1587 caused the postponement of the expedition for a whole year, during which Farnese's army in Flanders deteriorated considerably and Spain's most experienced admiral, the Marqués de Santa Cruz, died. His successor, the Duque de Medina Sidonia, was a most reluctant commander, and Philip's meticulous instructions to him showed that the King was equally anxious about the expedition. The story of overweening Spanish pride in the invincibility of the Armada is a myth of English historians.

Eventually the fleet of 130 miscellaneous ships (total tonnage 57,868) with 30,000 soldiers on board set out from Lisbon on 29–30 May 1588. A storm compelled it to put into Corunna for a refit, and as a result

Adam's Map of the Spanish Armada

The Escorial near Madrid

its arrival in the English Channel was delayed until 29 July. The Duke's orders were to sail direct to Calais and not to attempt to engage the English fleet in its south-western ports; a more resolute commander might have disregarded these instructions and fought another Lepanto in Plymouth Sound, where the English fleet lay trapped by an adverse wind. Medina Sidonia obeyed his orders implicitly and struggled up the Channel with his fleet in a great crescent formation seven miles long. The running fight with the smaller English ships was indecisive, and on 6 August the Armada anchored in the Calais roadstead; it had by now lost several ships, including the flagship of the Andalusian squadron with 50,000 ducats in gold on board.

Once at Calais Medina Sidonia requested Farnese to embark his troops in his fleet of flat-bottomed boats and invade the English coast forthwith. Unfortunately, Elizabeth had called the Dutch to her aid and their fleet was blockading Farnese in Dunkirk and Nieuport. On the night of 7 August Drake sent eight fire ships in among the anchored Spanish fleet; the fire ships actually did no damage, but the Spanish captains were so alarmed that they cut their cables and put to sea in rough weather, scattering along the Flemish coast. The following day they formed up again off Gravelines and from morning to night fought a fierce battle with the English, who kept to windward and whose more manoeuvrable ships poured a series of deadly broadsides into the unwieldy Spanish galleons until their ammunition was exhausted.

On 9 August a violent wind was driving the Spanish ships onto the lee shore, and at one time there was no more than six fathoms of water beneath them. At the last moment the wind changed and they were blown to the comparative safety of the North Sea. Nevertheless, the Armada was in dire peril because a return through the Channel was unthinkable with the English fleet barring the way; the sole escape route was round the north of Scotland and so back to Spain, keeping to the west of Ireland. The difficulties were enormous; the weather was stormy, the pilots were totally unfamiliar with the route, the ships were clumsy in a rough sea and many were heavily damaged, the stores were inadequate and there was a grave lack of fresh water. Several ships were wrecked on the Scottish and Irish coasts. At length some fifty-three ships limped back to Spain; 9,000 men had perished in this disastrous venture.

Philip received the news with unruffled calm and the loyal Castilians at once pledged their support for a further expedition against England, but plans for this came to nothing. The English tried to follow up their success by landing a force at Peniche, near Lisbon, to attempt to place Antonio on the throne of Portugal, but this venture found no support from the Portuguese and sickness caused the English to abandon it. A more successful expedition was carried out seven years later when in 1596 the Earl of Essex captured Cádiz and held the city to ransom.

Meanwhile Philip's attention had been concentrated on other schemes. The first was the unification of Aragon after his treacherous secretary Antonio Pérez had sought refuge there. The Aragonese mob had rioted in support of Pérez after he had been imprisoned at Zaragoza; they claimed that their *fueros* (privileges) had been flouted. Eventually he was able to make good his escape to France where he spent his time disseminating calumnies against Philip. This whole incident provided Philip with an excuse to invade Aragon with Castilian troops and severely limit the extent of Aragonese privileges.

His other scheme was ambitious in the extreme, namely to secure the crown of France, and it came within a short distance of succeeding.

Henry III of France had caused the leader of the Catholic League, the Duc de Guise, to be assassinated in his presence at the Château de Blois (23 December 1588). This had roused the Catholics in France to such a fury that the people of Paris declared Henry deposed, and shortly afterwards he was in fact assassinated (1 August 1589), leaving no male heir. At this stage the Catholics in France would have been willing to accept Philip as king, for his third wife had been Isabel de Valois, daughter of Francis I. The League, however, dared not put a Spaniard on the throne and moreover the Guise family themselves entertained vague hopes of kingship. In the meantime Henry of Navarre, the distant Protestant cousin of the late king, had gained a great victory at Ivry (14 March 1590) and was besieging Paris. A brilliant campaign by Spanish troops under the Duke of Parma invading from the Netherlands temporarily relieved the city. Philip was now pressing the claims of his elder daughter by Isabel de Valois, the Infanta Clara Eugenia; his ambassador in Paris was busy wooing the Parisians by distributing 120 crowns' worth of bread daily. When the *Etats-Généraux* met in the Louvre (26 January 1593) to elect a king, the Spanish case was badly argued and the *Parlement de Paris* invoked the Salic law, which forbade the crown to pass to a female or even through the female line. Moreover, Henry of Navarre, remarking with practical cynicism that '*Paris vaut bien une messe*', had become a Catholic and was now generally accepted as the future king, thanks to his tact and charm. His accession as Henry IV in 1594 meant war with Spain, but it was clear that Philip was now fighting against a united France, and he decided to cut his losses, signing the treaty of Vervins in May 1598. He had failed to win the French crown, but he had at least succeeded in keeping France Catholic.

Last years of Philip II

In the last years of his life Philip attempted to make peace everywhere for the very good reason that he was bankrupt. He came to terms with England, leaving the capture of Cádiz unavenged and he sought to disengage himself from the Netherlands by assigning them to his cousin, the Archduke Albert, who was to wed the unfortunate marriage pawn, Doña Clara Eugenia. This attempted settlement proved a hopeless failure because the Dutch ignored it, and the war continued as a legacy for Philip's successor.

This was not the only unpleasant legacy that Philip was to bequeath, for his total debts amounted to 100,000,000 ducats (approximately £50 million). In 1596 his bankers had refused him further credit and Philip had been obliged to suspend the payment of all interest in order to force his creditors to come to terms with him. An agreement was finally made in 1598 shortly before Philip's death, but when at last he expired in his austere apartments in the Escorial at the end of a long and revolting illness bravely borne, Spain was left crippled with taxes and in full financial decay. But if Philip's policy had pointed the way to Spain's destitution, at least during his reign the Spanish spirit had flourished abundantly. Though his empire has crumbled away, the fruits of the Spanish spirit in literature, religious thought and mysticism, architecture and painting are still among the glories of the world.

Chapter 4
Habsburgs and Bourbons

Philip II's heirs were weak and degenerate and Spain, ineptly ruled by palace favourites and corrupted by the influx of gold and silver from the Indies, declined lamentably in the seventeenth century. The Habsburg dynasty collapsed on the death of the epileptic Charles II in 1700 and Louis XIV's powerful diplomacy succeeded in establishing the Bourbons on the throne of Spain. Their enlightened attempts to introduce French civilisation and culture to Spain made little impression on the native conservatism of Spaniards who were blinded by memories of past glory, but this native obstinacy saved Spain from subjugation by Napoleon who found ferocity aided by British military tenacity impossible to conquer.

All absolute rulers are confronted with the problem of finding a suitable successor, but the only candidate open to Philip II was totally unfitted to continue the enormous labour of personal government which had been established by years of patient toil in the Escorial. Philip III was the sole survivor of the five children born to the late King by his third marriage to his cousin Anne of Austria; on his accession in 1598 he was a sickly youth of twenty and had no taste for work. His father when dying is said to have remarked to his loyal Portuguese adviser, Don Cristóbal de Moura: 'God who has given me so many kingdoms has not granted me a son fit to govern them.' When a few hours after the old King's death Moura brought a load of despatches for the new King to study, they were left on a sideboard unread.

Somebody had to govern and Philip III assigned the task to his old friend the Marqués de Denia, who was soon afterwards created the Duque de Lerma. So began a long period of rule by favourites (*validos*)

LEFT *Conde-Duque de Olivares by Velázquez*

who governed on behalf of the King, and at the same time enormously enriched themselves and their families. The Duque de Lerma was a man of some fifty years when he came to power and was possessed of great personal charm, entirely lacking in the traditional Spanish arrogance so that foreign diplomats found it a pleasure to deal with him. Such a conciliatory manner was a valuable asset at this particular moment because the bankrupt state of Spain demanded a cessation of all warlike activity in the shortest possible time. Peace with England while Elizabeth was still on the throne was impossible because not only were the English flushed with success after the defeat of the Armada, but since rich prizes from the Spanish Indies could legally be taken they also found war more profitable than peace. The accession of the peace-loving James I in 1603 enabled negotiations to be opened, and the Treaty of London (19 August 1604) saw the beginning of a period of almost cordial relations between England and Spain, whose able ambassador in London, Don Diego Sarmiento de Acuña, exercised considerable influence over James I; among other things he secured the execution of Sir Walter Raleigh as a punishment for his piratical acts around the mouth of the Orinoco.

Peace with England made the perpetual problem of the revolt in the Netherlands less acute because in the past the rebels had received much assistance and encouragement from the English. The French, though nominally at peace with Spain, continued secretly to aid the rebellious Dutch, but though Spain suffered heavily from attacks by the Dutch fleets both in the Channel and the Mediterranean, her armies in the Low Countries gained a series of victories under the energetic leadership of Ambrosio Spinola, who with his brother (killed in a naval battle) had put new life into the Spanish troops by ensuring that they were regularly paid, something which only a wealthy Milanese could have achieved. These victories enabled the Spaniards to arrange a truce of twelve years with the Dutch, and this was ratified by the signing of the Treaty of Antwerp on 9 April 1609.

Freed from the war with the English and the Dutch, Spain was left with only minor troubles to settle in Italy, but the endless battle against Turkish and Barbary pirates continued. Spanish diplomacy induced the Shah of Persia to make war on the Ottoman Empire, and this stroke at the enemy's rear enabled the Marqués de Santa Cruz, with galleys from Naples, to destroy pirate strongholds among the islands of Greece. Though Spain was in full political and financial decay, she was still the mightiest naval and military power.

The expulsion of the Moriscos

The danger from the Turks and Barbary pirates was increased by the presence in Spain of large and ever growing numbers of Moriscos, especially in the district of Valencia where they probably almost equalled the Christians. Throughout the sixteenth century it had been the aim of the government to provide proper instruction for the Moriscos in Christian doctrines, but all schemes had foundered for lack of money, in spite of great efforts by Juan de Ribera, who became Archbishop of Valencia in 1568 and who devoted a tenth of his personal revenues to this cause. There is little doubt that the majority had no desire for instruction; they would infinitely have preferred to have been left to the exercise of the Mohammedan religion, which they practised in secret, but they had been forcibly converted to the Catholic faith as a condition of being allowed to remain in their homes. Their overlords frequently encouraged covert Mohammedan practices because they were then able to blackmail the Moriscos into paying the dues required from non-believers, which they should have escaped on conversion. As suspect Christians the Moriscos dwelt in constant dread of the Inquisition, for any relapse would almost certainly be punished with burning at the stake.

All might still have been well if the most obdurate and disaffected Moriscos had been allowed to emigrate, but this the law forbade under pain of severe penalties; the reason for this is obscure, but the ban was probably due to the fact that the Church could not bear to see even the most dubious Christian convert emigrate to a Muslim country, and that Morisco overlords were loath to part with industrious tenants. Though the numbers of Christians were constantly depleted by losses in war, by emigration to the colonies, and by the enforced celibacy of the religious orders, the Moriscos, who were denied the right to bear arms, to emigrate or to enter the priesthood, multiplied rapidly.

Some Moriscos escaped from Spain with the aid of raids by Muslim pirates, as when in 1584 a fleet from Algiers bore off 2,300 of them. Other hotheaded Moriscos saw visions of all Spain once more under Arab domination, and used their local knowledge to direct the Turkish and Barbary pirates on predatory expeditions. Not content with conspiracies with their fellow Mohammedans, the Moriscos also turned to the Christian enemies of Spain for help in possible insurrections. Morisco emissaries handed to the Duc de la Force the sum of 120,000 ducats (about £60,000) as a pledge of their willingness to raise a force of 80,000 men in support of a French invasion of Spain. Henry IV of France did not consider the moment opportune, but he bore in mind the possibility of a blow at Spain and was in fact discussing the project in his coach with the Duc de la Force when Ravaillac stabbed him to death (14 May 1610).

Even Archbishop Ribera, hard though he had striven to improve the lot of the Moriscos, finally agreed that the only solution to the problem was wholesale expulsion. This remedy had long been under discussion, as well as more violent and bloodier methods such as enslavement, mass slaughter or mutilation. It was suggested that the Morisco population should be transported to Newfoundland to avoid adding to the number of hostile infidels in North Africa. Eventually, however, the government decided on what it considered the most humane course, namely compulsory transhipment to Africa, and measures were taken to prevent the Moriscos being ill-treated on their way into exile. Indeed in the Valencia region, where the expulsion was first put into operation in 1609, many of the Spanish nobility accompanied their Morisco vassals to the port of embarkation, Alicante, to ensure that no exploitation or molestation took place. The expulsion was effected with very little resistance except in the Val de Ayora, where veteran troops brought on purpose from Italy crushed an attempted rebellion, slaughtering several thousand Moriscos.

The ease with which the first expulsion had been achieved encouraged the government to order immediate deportation of Moriscos from other areas; Castile and Extremadura on 28 December 1609, Granada and Andalusia on 12 January 1610, Aragon and Catalonia on 29 May 1610. By 1614 the process was completed and only a few exceptions had been permitted, such as certain craftsmen of proved Catholic reliability, or Morisco women married to old Christian husbands. Attempts to evade the expulsion orders were treated with the utmost severity, and such were the efforts to comb out the Moriscos that many truly devout Catholics were deported to North Africa, where several died as Christian martyrs. Nevertheless, hundreds must have managed to conceal themselves sufficiently to escape detection, and even to continue Moorish practices. As late as 1769 the Inquisition discovered a mosque in full operation in Cartagena, and this was not an isolated occurrence. Estimates of the numbers expelled vary wildly; even Spanish historians have given the figure as high as a million, but later research would suggest that the true total may not have been more that 150,000.

The expulsion of the Moriscos has been described as the final act of financial suicide committed by the Spanish government, since the Moriscos were undoubtedly skilled, industrious and productive workers. Various writers have described the rich agricultural area of Valencia as a desert after the expulsion, but the study of the price of wine and rice (the latter produced almost exclusively in this district) between the years 1610 and 1620 shows no famine increase such as would have occurred had production suddenly ceased. In fact large numbers of Spanish workers arrived in the neighbourhood of Valencia from the mountain areas of the north and other barren parts of Spain. It is true that this migration caused still further depopulation of the less fertile areas and contributed to the general poverty and decay of Spain as a whole, but the expulsion of the Moriscos was a factor that hastened Spanish financial ruin without being the basic cause of it.

Accounts of the cruelty of the expulsion have likewise been exaggerated. It was indeed carried out as humanely as possible, but a wholesale uprooting such as this inevitably caused widespread suffering, misery and personal loss. The Moriscos were allowed to take all their movable belongings into exile (with certain exceptions), but their fixed property was generally forfeited to the state and persons in high places made large fortunes from these confiscations. Lerma himself is said to have received 250,000 ducats, his son the Duque de Uceda 100,000 and his daughter and son-in-law 150,000 between them.

Social problems

It was corruption in every walk of Spanish life that was the ugliest feature of the reign of Philip III, and as Spain became more and more poverty-stricken, extravagance and ostentation in and around the court increased to unimaginable proportions in comparison with the austere days of Philip II. Attempts were made from time to time to reduce expenditure, as for example when in 1601 the court moved from Madrid to Valladolid, where it was claimed that goods were cheaper. The move of course brought destitution to thousands of Madrid tradespeople, and it was rumoured that Lerma, who owned much property in and around Valladolid, had been paid a large sum by its citizens to secure the court's migration. After five years the citizens of Madrid found themselves obliged to pay him an even higher price for the court to return to the capital.

With such an avaricious minister at the head of affairs popular discontent was widespread, and Lerma's favourites, on whom he showered titles, offices and benefits, were especially hated. Chief among these was Rodrigo Calderón, son of a Spanish captain by a German woman and Lerma's favourite page, who was accused of murdering Francisco Jaura, an obscure member of the Madrid underworld. The opposition to Calderón, both in the court and in the town, was such that Lerma was powerless to protect him and foresaw his own imminent fall from favour. Lerma took the precaution of persuading the Pope to make him a cardinal so that his person and property might be protected by ecclesiastical dignity, and on 14 October 1618 he retired from the Court to Valladolid with all his ill-gotten gains.

He was succeeded in royal favour by his son, the Duque de Uceda, who had been foremost among the party at court plotting his father's downfall. For Spain this change meant that a less intelligent but equally grasping man, surrounded by equally greedy adherents, was in charge of all affairs of state. Rodrigo Calderón was brought to trial, facing no less than 244 charges; in spite of his privileges as a nobleman (he had been created a marquis) he was put to the torture, but was finally acquitted on all counts. Just as he was about to be released from prison Philip III died (31 March 1621) and Calderón is said to have exclaimed: 'The King is dead and I am a dead man too.' His prophecy proved true, for the new King's favourite, the Conde de Olivares allowed his case to be tried anew; he was condemned, and was executed on 21 October 1621. His gallant demeanour on the scaffold in the Plaza Mayor in Madrid gave rise to the proverb: *Tienes más orgullo que Don Rodrigo en la horca* (You are prouder than Don Rodrigo on the gallows).

Philip IV was sixteen years old when he came to the throne and was no more inclined to govern than his father, being given to profligacy and debauchery. He was dominated by one of the gentlemen of his household, Don Gaspar de Guzmán (later the Conde-Duque de Olivares), whom he appointed as head of the government in place of the Duque de Uceda. Olivares differed from the two previous *validos* in that he was ambitious for power not wealth. His first act was an attempt to curb extravagance, corruption and luxury, and to restore the traditional Spanish virtues of frugality and simple living. To achieve this he immediately brought to trial many of those who had held high office during the previous reign. First among these was the Duque de Lerma who, in spite of being a cardinal, was first imprisoned and then condemned to pay 72,000 ducats a year to the treasury for twenty years to make up for past peculation. His son, the Duque de Uceda, was likewise prosecuted, but he escaped with a modest fine of 20,000 ducats and eight years exile from the court. Even noblemen who had rendered great service to the state were not spared, as for example the Duque de Osuna, who had proved himself a brilliant viceroy of Sicily and Naples. He was charged with enriching himself at the expense of the state and was cast into prison. It is true that his ostentatious manner of living on his return from Italy was absurd, even for an extravagant age. His coach in Madrid was followed by twenty others filled with Spanish and Neapolitan members of his suite, and when he attended a joust or a bullfight in the Plaza Mayor he was accompanied by a hundred lackeys in blue and silver livery.

The King himself was induced to set an example in economy, and at one stroke halved the expenditure of the royal household by reducing by a third the number of offices on the various councils. Noblemen were ordered to retire from the court and live on their estates, where they were to turn their attention to improving agriculture. Stern edicts were issued to curb extravagance in dress, and officials visited the shops to burn forbidden luxuries such as ruffles and ruffs. The latter were a source of great expense since they cost 200 reales apiece (more than £8) and six reales for each dressing, an operation that might be necessary sixty or seventy times a year, if the ruff should last that long. Surprisingly enough the elimination of the ruff succeeded because Philip IV adopted a new fashion with a high collar, and such was still the prestige of Spain that his example was followed everywhere in Europe.

Other plans for financial reforms met with greater resistance from interested parties. An attempt was made to prevent peculation by obliging all persons appointed to high office to make an inventory upon oath of all their possessions; subsequent inventories were to be demanded on promotion or retirement and any increase in wealth was deemed to have been acquired illicitly. This well-intentioned scheme soon foundered on the non-cooperation of office holders. Efforts to reduce the number of officials engaged in the administration of the law and to prevent bribery were scarcely more successful. Proposed reforms in methods of tax collection failed because of vested interests. So cluttered with officials was the machinery of tax gathering that often the expense of collection was greater than the sum collected. The *alcabala* (sales tax) was crippling to industry and trade; the tax farmers were able to appoint their own judges to hear any disputes, so that judge and plaintiff were virtually the same person. Hence any litigation in connection with taxation inevitably meant ruin, and probably one more addition to the growing ranks of beggars and vagrants.

The Catalan rebellion

Olivares was not slow to realise that the true weakness of Spain lay in lack of unity, for the provinces, despite constant efforts by Charles V and Philip II, continued to demand and enjoy a large measure of independence. He therefore attempted to suppress the privileges of the provinces, particularly of eastern Spain, by weakening the power of their *Cortes*, hoping doubtless to replace all these bodies by one single assembly subservient to the King's will. With this in mind the *Cortes* of Valencia and Aragon were bullied into making grants of money and men needed for war in 1626. The *Cortes* of Catalonia, however, had to be treated more circumspectly, because the province was one of the richest in Spain. The King wrote in his own hand an affectionate letter explaining his need for money. He had reckoned without the obstinacy of the Catalans, who turned a deaf ear to these blandishments, and the session of the *Cortes* had to be suspended without any grant being made. Its resumption six years later (1632) under the presidency of the King's brother was marked with equal obstinacy, and much bitterness was engendered over trifling matters such as the traditional right of the councillors of Barcelona to remain with their heads covered in the presence of the King or his deputy.

Such attempts to interfere with the independent *Cortes* of Catalonia caused bitter resentment in the province, and occasion for revolt came in 1639 when Castilian troops were quartered there after a successful campaign against the French in Roussillon, a campaign in which the Catalans had played a prominent part without receiving, in their view, adequate recognition. The Castilian soldiery, with their pay as usual in arrears, behaved brutally and constant brawls arose. One of these on the feast of Corpus Christi (7 June 1639) became so violent that the mob set on the Viceroy and stabbed him to death. Order was restored only after three days of looting and pillaging, but the government in Madrid showed moderation by sending as the next viceroy a native of Catalonia, the Duque de Cardona. He was successful in pacifying Barcelona, and paid serious attention to the grievances of the Catalans, imprisoning many Castilians guilty of crimes of violence. Olivares unwisely refused to allow the Castilian soldiers to be punished and at this moment of crisis Cardona died with the result that a fresh revolt broke out.

It was in essence a popular revolt in which the Catalan nobility took little part, but it also had a tinge of religious fanaticism because the local priests were urging their congregations to avenge alleged acts of sacrilege committed by the Castilian troops. This religious fervour made the revolt difficult to crush and Olivares at length determined on really stern measures. A force of 23,000 infantry and 3,000 cavalry was mustered under the command of the Marqués de los Vélez, and Catalonia was invaded on 8 October 1640. At first all went well and the Castilians made such progress that the Catalans appealed to Richelieu for help. With the aid of French forces they drove Vélez back from Tarragona and at the same time recognised Louis XIII as Count of Barcelona. Catalonia then became one of the main theatres of war between France and Spain, and it was only after lengthy operations that the Castilians secured the surrender of Barcelona at the end of a siege of fifteen months. Even so Philip had to agree to the retention of Catalan liberties and privileges. In truth the defenders of Barcelona were finding the French more odious than the Castilians.

The revolt in Catalonia, and another more serious one in Portugal, led to the downfall of Olivares. He had never lacked enemies and among them was the Queen, Isabel de Bourbon, whom he had grievously insulted by remarking, when she gave an opinion on state affairs, that monks should be kept for praying and women for child-bearing. In January 1643, shortly after Philip had returned from a discouraging visit to the fighting in Catalonia, Isabel persuaded him that it was owing to the policy of Olivares that the territories of the Spanish crown were slipping away. Philip had been depressed by the lack of success of Castilian troops in the autumn campaign, and the news of the revolt in Portugal was a further blow which the enemies of Olivares used to great advantage. On 17 January 1643 Philip dismissed his favourite, and refused to change his decision in spite of all the efforts of Olivares to persuade him. Henceforth the King would dispense with favourites and rule personally as his grandfather had done.

Portuguese secession

It was a disastrous period at which to take on the burden of government, for Spain was involved in the Thirty Years War and faced with revolts in the Peninsula. Portugal had long been simmering with indignation against rule by Spaniards who had largely disregarded the promises made by Philip II at Thomar in 1580 on becoming king. Moreover they had felt obliged not to help in the defence of the Portuguese empire, although it had by the act of union inherited all Spain's enemies. The Dutch had captured much of the Portuguese East Indies, and the English had preyed upon the trade with Brazil. In Portugal itself the *Cortes* had been summoned only once (1619) since the death of Philip II and this was regarded as part of Olivares's plan to unify the whole Peninsula under Castilian control.

None of these grievances caused as much bitterness as the favour shown by the Spanish government to Portuguese Jews. Portugal had never come under the searching scrutiny of the Spanish Inquisition, and though its own native Inquisition persecuted heretics with intermittent zeal, a Jewish colony, professedly Christian, had prospered. Since the Portuguese for all their far-flung empire were now for the most part poverty-stricken, the blame for the economic decline of the nation was laid on the Jews. The bankruptcy of Spain had several times induced Lerma to show favour to the Portuguese Jews in return for large sums of money. Olivares likewise in 1627 granted certain privileges to the Jews on payment of 1,500,000 *cruzados* (about £750,000). Such deals incensed Portuguese Christians, who claimed that Christ was being sold again, with Spain in the role of Judas. Popular discontent in Portugal was nourished by a remarkable and widely believed legend that King Sebastian had in reality survived the battle of Alcazarquivir (1587) and would one day return as the rightful king. So strong was this belief that the return of Sebastian was still awaited in 1763, when his age would have been well over two hundred. In the meantime many impostors arose claiming to be King Sebastian; one of these was a Calabrian peasant, Marco Tullio, who was widely accepted in Venice even though he could not speak a word of Portuguese.

The upper classes in Portugal were as ready as the common people to throw off the Spanish yoke, but with greater realism they looked for their leader to John, Duke of Braganza, whose grandfather had been lured into renouncing his claims to the throne by the promise of full sovereignty in Brazil. The Duke himself had little desire to be king, preferring music and hunting, but his Spanish wife, daughter of the Duque de Medina Sidonia, was determined, like Lady Macbeth, that her husband should wear the crown. Olivares was aware that some conspiracy was in the wind and tried to remove the Duke of Braganza by offering him the governorship of Milan, a post usually given to a royal prince. The Duke refused on the grounds that he could not speak Italian, and thereafter avoided a series of traps laid for him by Olivares, who finally ordered him to come to Madrid with the entire Portuguese army to join in the struggle in Catalonia.

The time for rebellion had arrived and on 1 December 1640 the blow was struck swiftly and efficiently. Two days later the Duke of Braganza entered Lisbon as John IV, and in a very short space of time nearly all the fortresses throughout the land fell into the hands of the rebels without resistance. Olivares tried to laugh off this reverse by telling Philip that he would be able now to occupy all Portugal without caring for its ancient liberties and at the same time confiscate the extensive personal possessions of the Duke of Braganza. In fact Spain could find no effective counter to the Portuguese revolt. Both the French and Dutch were actively aiding the Portuguese, and the only commander of a large force stationed near Portugal at the outbreak of the rebellion was the new King's brother-in-law, the Duque de Medina Sidonia, who, instead of suppressing the rising, initiated one of his own to make himself king of Andalusia. He was arrested and brought to Madrid where he confessed his treason; in view of his exalted rank he was pardoned on payment of a large fine, and on condition that he challenged his brother-in-law to single combat. This he did with all the pomp of medieval chivalry, but his challenge remained unanswered.

Spain was showing signs of disintegration abroad as well as in the Peninsula. Sicily and Naples both revolted in 1647 and though the risings were suppressed, Spanish power in Italy was decidedly on the wane. The bitterest blow of all came from the Netherlands. A Spanish army of 26,000 men under the command strangely enough of a loyal Portuguese Francisco Melo was besieging the town of Rocroi (some hundred miles north-east of Rheims) with the object of marching on Paris afterwards. A French Army under the Duc d'Enghien, later known as the Great Condé, arrived to relieve the town and a decisive battle was fought on 19 May 1643. At first the French left and centre were compelled to withdraw, but Enghien leading the right wing with great dash routed a force of German and Walloon infantry and was then able to attack the closely packed squares of veteran Spanish infantry in the centre. The Spaniards fought with great tenacity and hurled back three assaults, but at length they could not withstand the concentrated attacks and the heavy artillery fire. In all they lost some 14,000 men killed, wounded and prisoners. It was clear that their fighting methods were out of date and the reputation of the Spanish *tercios* for invincibility was gone for ever.

The Battle of Rocroi

Such was the situation that faced Philip IV when he decided to govern on his own. He was a much more able and intelligent man than his father, being a patron of the arts and passionately interested in drama. He indulged with eagerness in theatricals which were staged in the Queen's apartments and it was claimed that he was the author of three of the plays performed, one of which was entitled *El Conde de Essex*. As a rider, hunter and jouster he excelled, and he showed the greatest affection and kindness to his family and his entire household. He even managed to continue friendly relations with his Queen, Isabel de Bourbon, in spite of his constant love affairs with various mistresses, by whom he had numerous illegitimate children. This promiscuity revealed a fundamental weakness of character, but more dangerous for Spain was his reluctance to express an opinion for himself. Diligently as he attended to the business of state after the fall of Olivares, he almost invariably accepted the advice of his councillors and showed little ability as a leader himself.

In one respect, however, Philip insisted on having his way in spite of much advice to the contrary and that was in visiting the scene of the fighting with the French forces and the Catalan rebels who were now threatening the centre of Aragon. On his way he passed through Agreda (10 July 1643) and visited the monastery, where he met the abbess, Sor María Jesus. He immediately fell under the spell of her forceful character. For twenty years he corresponded with her, confiding all his troubles, doubts and sorrows and receiving in return much wise counsel, which exercised a profound influence on him.

The Treaty of Westphalia

This influence, however, was not so strong as to prevent Philip from falling back into his old habits of promiscuity and idleness: in spite of his resolution to govern by himself he resorted to another favourite, Don Luis de Haro, a nephew of Olivares. Though he never attained the same dominance over the King, Sor María resented his influence and spoke of him as el malo dedo (the wicked finger) in Spain's affairs which indeed continued to go from bad to worse. In the Netherlands another heavy defeat at the hands of the Great Condé made Spain eager to negotiate a peace, and eventually by the Treaty of Westphalia (1648) she reluctantly recognised the independence of the northern Netherlands, known as the United Provinces. The war with France continued largely because Mazarin's terms were too harsh and Spain hoped to take advantage of the sporadic revolt of the French nobility known as the Fronde (1648–53). In this the Spanish government judged correctly, and for a time the Great Condé was actually fighting for Spain. After the rebellion faded out, Marshal Turenne defeated the Spaniards at Arras (1655) and though there were minor Spanish successes in 1658 exhaustion compelled her to sue for peace, especially as Cromwell had intervened powerfully on the side of France in 1657.

Hope of a settlement was buoyed up by the prospect of a marriage between Louis XIV and the Infanta María Teresa. Such a union had previously been impossible since the Infanta was the heiress apparent to the throne of Spain, Philip's only legitimate son having died in 1646, two years after the death of Queen Isabel de Bourbon. But in 1649 Philip had taken as his second wife his niece Mariana of Austria, who bore him a son, Philip Prosper, in 1657, and this scrofulous infant was now heir to the Spanish empire. María Teresa was free to marry the young French king and a settlement was negotiated on this basis. The discussions took place on the Isle of Pheasants in the middle of the river Bidasoa. The island belonged half to Spain and half to France and a large marquee was erected exactly over the boundary line so that the delegations faced each other across a table with their seats planted on national soil. At length on 17 November 1659 peace was signed and provision was made for María Teresa to marry Louis XIV bringing a dowry of 500,000 gold ducats. On payment of this dowry she would renounce all claim to inheritance from Spain or succession to the Spanish throne. The dowry was in fact never paid.

Freed from war with France Philip roused himself to another attempt to win back Portugal. There war had continued in a desultory fashion since 1643, but Philip now sought to intensify the activities of his armies. For a while no success was achieved, but in 1663 Évora, a hundred miles south-east of Lisbon, was captured. By now French help (in defiance of the Treaty of the Pyrenees) had reached Portugal and Marshal Schomberg drove the Spanish forces back to Badajoz. With Charles II of England now allied to the house of Braganza Spain's hopes of reconquest became even more slender. No advantage was taken of the opportunity offered by a palace revolution in Portugal whereby Don Pedro exiled his profligate brother Alexander VI and seized power himself. The danger from France was growing graver. Louis XIV had invaded the remaining Spanish territories in Flanders in May 1667. Peace was therefore hurriedly made with Portugal whose independence was recognised by the Treaty of Lisbon (13 February 1668) negotiated through the mediation of Charles II of England. An indication of how the proud spirit of Spain had decayed was shown by the great jubilation with which this settlement was received in Madrid.

Carlos II and the Queen Mother

Philip IV did not live to see this humiliation; he died on 17 September 1665, full of remorse for his many misdeeds and of gloomy forebodings for the future of his empire. His son Philip Prosper had died in 1661, but only five days after this calamity his wife had born him another son, Carlos; it was to this epileptic child that Philip left his crown, explicitly excluding in his will María Teresa or her issue. The Queen Mother was nominated as tutor to the infant King and Regent of the realm; she was devoted to the interests of Austria and was dominated by her Austrian confessor, Father Nithard, to whom she entrusted the most powerful positions in the government of Spain. She secured his appointment not only to the Royal Council but also to the office of Inquisitor-General. Father Nithard was no politician, but he was frugal, upright and by no means avaricious. As a foreigner, however, he was bitterly resented by the Spaniards, nobility and common people alike. There were endless intrigues against him, fomented mainly by Don Juan José, a handsome bastard son of Philip IV by an actress. He had won himself a reputation as a general in Sicily and Naples as well as in the Netherlands and Portugal, though his operations had not been uniformly successful. Doubtless he had an eye to succeeding to the throne himself; the wretched Carlos II was not expected to live long. At the height of his quarrel with the Queen Mother Don Juan José travelled down from Barcelona to Madrid with a force of cavalry and infantry and reviewed his troops ostentatiously three miles from the capital (24 February 1669). He was thus in a position to oblige the Queen Mother to dismiss her confessor, who departed the next day, refusing a large sum of money offered to him and taking nothing out of Spain but his habit and his breviary.

Popular rejoicing at his departure was immense and Don Juan José was emboldened to threaten and bully the Queen Mother still further, thereby losing much support from the public. Mariana was therefore able to get rid of him by making him viceroy of Aragon, and to install as virtual ruler of Spain another favourite named Valenzuela, who kept contact with the exiled Father Nithard. Valenzuela became so indispensable to the Queen Mother that he was allowed to occupy a royal suite in the palace and visited Mariana at late hours of the night to give her secret information, thus acquiring the nickname of El Duende del Palacio (the Palace Elf). Valenzuela made strenuous efforts to gain popularity by wholesale distribution of honours and favours, and by providing supplies of free food for the Madrid populace as well as entertaining them to an endless series of bullfights and theatrical performances. The young King was passionately addicted to bullfights and approved of the policy of Valenzuela, who also used to accompany him on hunting expeditions; on one of these the inept King wounded his minister in the thigh when aiming at a stag.

For all his liberality Valenzuela received nothing but hatred in return; the great nobles were especially jealous of the titles showered on a man they considered an upstart. Meanwhile Don Juan José had returned to the court on 27 December 1677, his term of office as viceroy having expired. He appeared once again surrounded by a formidable bodyguard and was able to demand that the Queen Mother should leave the court and that Valenzuela should be imprisoned. These terms were reluctantly agreed and Mariana departed to live in exile at Toledo, barely fifty miles away. Valenzuela sought refuge with the monks at the Escorial, but this sanctuary was of no avail and he was exiled to the Philippines; he eventually died in Mexico as a result of being kicked by a colt which he was breaking in.

Great hopes were now set on Don Juan José fulfilling the role of chief minister, but these hopes were doomed to bitter disappointment since he squandered his energies in disputing trivial items of court etiquette with the intention of emphasising his own dignity. In the meantime Spain had suffered more heavy defeats in the war which Louis XIV had forced on her and the Peace of Nimeguen in September 1678 came as a relief, even though it deprived Spain of more territory in Flanders and the whole of the Franche-Comté on the Italian border. At least the French agreed to evacuate Puigcerdá in the Pyrenees. As the Spanish plenipotentiary, Don Pedro Ronquillo, remarked at Nimeguen: 'Better be thrown out of the window than from the top of the roof.'

Don Juan José sought to retrieve this disaster to some extent by arranging a French marriage for Carlos II who obligingly fell in love with the portrait of the lady suggested, Marie-Louise, eldest daughter of the Duc d'Orléans. If, as was constantly suggested, Don Juan José hoped to succeed the sickly Carlos, it is strange that he should have engineered a marriage that might well dash these hopes. But he was losing his influence with the King and moreover he may well have had forebodings of his own approaching end. He died on 17 September 1679, a month before the French bride arrived at the Spanish frontier.

The marriage was not destined to last long for the Queen died in 1689, without having borne an heir. Carlos married again, this time a German princess, Maria Anne, daughter of the Elector Palatine. This second marriage was also childless. It has been asserted that Louis XIV received private information from his niece that Carlos was impotent and that he laid plans accordingly to secure the Spanish succession. Certainly the terms Louis offered to end yet another war with Spain in 1697 were oddly generous considering the defeats he had inflicted. By the Treaty of Ryswick (29 September 1697) he returned nearly all his conquests in Spanish Flanders as well as territory occupied in Catalonia including Barcelona. It was clearly pointless to denude an empire which he was reserving for his own family. He then entrusted the task of building up a pro-French party in Spain to an able diplomat, the Marquis d'Harcourt who was so successful that he almost won over the German born Queen from the Imperial faction. He was helped in his work by the tactlessness of the Imperial ambassador, who kept on reminding Carlos of the imminence of his death and the urgent need to settle the succession.

The poor bewildered epileptic was a victim of every ambassador, minister and person of influence at the court; they all pressed their views on him. He was anxious that his dominions should not be partitioned at his death and when he fell gravely ill in September 1700 he was persuaded by Cardinal Portocarrero that the best chance of preserving his empire intact lay in nominating a French successor. Carlos drew up a will on 3 October naming the Dauphin as his successor. 'God alone', he said, 'is He who gives kingdoms, for to Him alone they belong. Now I am nothing.' Relief at making this decision caused the King's health to improve so much that he embarked on a round of pleasures. Meanwhile, the contents of the will, which were supposed to be secret, had been communicated to Louis XIV, but at the same time the Austrian party assumed that they were to be favoured since on a recent occasion the Queen and other members of the Imperial faction had secured a promise from the ailing King.

News of the decision was not long in being announced for the poor King after a brief bout of enjoyment took sick again and died on 1 November 1700. His will was opened at once and its contents were read to a crowded gathering of ambassadors and noblemen. The Duque de Abrantes charged with delivering the news is said to have remarked to the Austrian ambassador after an exchange of honeyed compliments: 'I have the greatest pleasure, my dear friend, and the most genuine satisfaction of taking leave for ever of the illustrious House of Austria.' Whether or not this offensive jest is authentic, it reflects the feelings of the Spanish nobility, who regarded the Habsburgs as responsible for the present calamitous state of Spain. Nevertheless, the courier who was sent to offer the crown to Louis XIV's grandson, Philip, Duc d'Anjou, had orders in case of refusal to go on to Vienna to beg the Archduke Charles to accept.

Spain in decay

The poverty and degradation of life in Spain had reached unimaginable proportions. Since the shipments of treasure from the Indies had declined steeply after about 1630, recourse had constantly been made to debasement of the coinage as a regular means of raising money for the government. Private individuals thereby lost most of their savings and trade shrank to minimal proportions since goods of any kind were beyond the means of all but the wealthy. As an example of this, it was stated that Seville at the end of the sixteenth century operated 16,000 looms for weaving silk and woollen cloth, but that the number had fallen to 300 at the time of the death of Carlos II, and the city contained only a quarter of its former population. Manufacturers were indeed strangled by the *alcabala* which by the end of the seventeenth century had increased to 14 per cent of the value of an article each time it changed hands. Spaniards were forced to sell raw materials cheaply abroad in order to import manufactured goods which were unobtainable in Spain. Hence America, which required manufactured articles and not raw materials, no longer traded extensively with the mother country and bullion imports were reduced to a mere trickle. At the same time foreigners, particularly Frenchmen, abounded in Spanish towns (there were said to be more than 40,000 of them in Madrid alone) because they as foreigners were better able to evade the many restrictions and imposts on trade. Moreover, thousands of French artisans and labourers crossed the Pyrenees to do the menial tasks for which the Spaniards considered themselves too exalted. The love of ostentation and the fierce feeling of family pride characteristic of the nobility had penetrated to the lowest classes; it is said that even the labourers in the fields worked with swords buckled to their sides to demonstrate their claims to be *hidalgos*. In the midst of poverty public festivals of preposterous extravagance took place in Madrid; every bullfight cost 60,000 *reales* (about £3,000) and the celebrations for the birth of the short-lived Philip Prosper lasted for days, involving the expenditure of 800,000 *pesos* (about £800,000). Even today in the poorest of Spanish towns no expense is ever spared in organising gorgeous fiestas.

The desire to be more than a mere labourer reached such a pitch that it led to what was called *empleomanía* (post-seeking frenzy) and much of the blame was attached to the fact that grammar schools were so numerous in the early seventeenth century. Peasants' sons acquired a smattering of education and then sought employment in some more exalted position than productive cultivation. The civil service became bloated with surplus officials creating nothing but restrictive regulations. It is estimated that there may have been as many as 150,000 civil servants to administer a country whose population had shrunk from eight million to five million. The universities swarmed with students of no great intellectual attainments; the professions of law and medicine became swamped with mediocre practitioners, and indeed have largely remained so.

The priesthood and the religious orders claimed a large share of the surplus population; even as early as 1623 it was stated that there were 9,083 monasteries in Spain, not counting nunneries. All this vast priestly class was entirely non-productive and funds for its maintenance were extracted by a complex system of tithes and first-fruits levied on the ever shrinking producing classes. One of these extractions was the *luctuosa*, the right to the best head of cattle on the death of a peasant; this meant that whenever a peasant's family suffered a bereavement it also lost its foremost means of earning a living from the land. Small wonder that many peasants joined the throngs of vagrants and beggars in the towns or lived as gypsies on what they could steal. To remedy this flight from labour several panic expedients were tried, such as the *pragmática* of 1633 which threatened a punishment of two hundred lashes and six years in the galleys for anyone, not a gypsy by birth, who should adopt gypsy ways. Another ordinance of 1627 had severely restricted the publication of books 'because they are already abundant enough. . . . The hand should be restrained from engaging in superfluous pursuits that yield no profit to the community.'

Later in the century (1680) there were further restrictions on the production of books and printed matter unless approved by the appropriate tribunal of the Inquisition. Yet while the Church limited freedom of expression its own institutions had become hopelessly corrupt. Scandals in religious houses were by no means infrequent; the affair of the nunnery of San Plácido in 1628 caused a widespread stir when it was found that the nuns were guilty of immorality and of practising black magic and demonology. The nobleman, Villanueva, whose benefaction had founded the nunnery, was a frequent visitor at night and was found sitting in the abbess's lap while she picked insects out of his hair. Olivares himself, it is said, had recourse to the spells of the nuns in an effort to become the father of a male heir. At the very end of the century (1698) the Inquisitor-General, Tomás de Rocaberti, Archbishop of Valencia, endeavoured to obtain information from nuns at Cangas who were reputed to be possessed of a demon, in order to discover whether the King's illness was due to witchcraft. The demon speaking through these nuns revealed that the Queen Mother had cast a spell over her son on 3 April 1675 by giving him a cup of chocolate containing a potion concocted from the limbs of a dead man. The remedies for this spell were anointing with holy oil, purging and separation from the Queen; these remedies were vigorously applied and the King's illness grew worse.

In both these instances the Inquisition intervened with sharp censure for such conduct and through its vigilance Spain largely escaped the witch mania that beset the rest of Europe. But the Inquisition remained a vast instrument of repression, and though it contained men of the highest integrity, who earnestly sought to maintain strict religious and moral standards in Spain, the proceedings of the Inquisition were as a whole utterly repellent, with *autos de fe* regularly staged on days of special rejoicing. These included an occasion in 1680 which celebrated the marriage of Carlos II with Marie-Louise, when 118 accused persons were punished.

All through the century attempts were made to remedy the chaotic state of Spain. Indeed in the reign of Carlos II there is evidence of a gradual rise in population, though some towns like Cádiz, Murcia and Corunna are said to have thrived solely because of the flourishing activities of smuggling. The various *Cortes* at their meetings continually petitioned the King to remedy abuses and the language of their complaints is often so vivid that an exaggerated picture of Spain's plight is conveyed. The *Cortes* often made the King grants of *servicios* on condition that he would not further debase the currency, only to find that such promises were almost immediately broken. If the methods of the head of the state were so fraudulent, it is impossible to expect that the subservient assemblies should remain uncorrupted. In any case they were summoned less and less frequently as the century went by; in fact the *Cortes* of Castile were not assembled at all after the death of Philip IV, and in 1700 the grandson of such an absolute monarch as Louis XIV would be unlikely to revive an already decayed parliamentary system.

The War of the Spanish Succession

Philip V, a lively youth of seventeen, did not deem it necessary to summon the *Cortes* of Castile to take the traditional oath of allegiance, but from the start he was faced with the need to fight for his throne. The Holy Roman Emperor immediately declared war in favour of the Archduke Charles, the Habsburg Pretender. He was soon joined (September 1701) by England and Holland, who were alarmed at the thought that the whole Spanish Empire, including Flanders, would be virtually controlled from Versailles, for Louis XIV had declared that the Pyrenees no longer existed and had directed that the French ambassador in Madrid should permanently have a seat on the Spanish Royal Council. Philip at first left for Italy to deal with the threat to his possessions of Naples and Milan, but after achieving only partial success hastened back to Spain (January 1703) to face the dangerous situation at home where the Castilian nobles, resenting the presence of Frenchmen in high positions, were plotting with the Austrian party. The problems confronting Philip were more than a young foreigner of no great ability could possibly solve and he early became a prey to melancholia, from which only his spirited fifteen-year-old queen, Marie Louise of Savoy, could stir him.

Meanwhile, in 1702, a British fleet under the command of Sir George Rooke had sailed into Cádiz bay with 12,000 troops on board and had demanded the surrender of the city, which was defended by a garrison of only 300 men with rusty cannon. Fortunately for Spain the British commanders wasted time wrangling about plans of attack while all Andalusia lay at their mercy, and in the meantime the Queen stung the Spaniards to action by offering her jewels to raise money for equipping a force in the south. The English hurriedly left Cádiz when they heard the news that a Spanish treasure fleet had taken refuge at Vigo. There the harbour was stormed and most of the galleons were sunk or captured along with a large portion of the treasure.

Portugal now ranged herself on the side of the Archduke Charles, and Philip had to raise an army, largely French and equipped and trained in the French style, which he hurried to the Portuguese frontier. That he had been able to gather this force in a bankrupt country was due in no small measure to the reforms made by his French finance minister Orry, who in a brief space of time reorganised the collection of taxes so that most of the money came to the Treasury instead of clinging to the hands of the tax gatherers and other officials. His reductions in the number of sinecures and pensions caused further discontent among the Spanish nobles at court, who leaned even more towards the Austrian party. Archduke Charles landed at Lisbon (4 May 1704) from an English ship, and was received with royal honours as Carlos III. Before the Portuguese army could take the field, the Spanish forces commanded by the Duke of Berwick, a bastard son of James II of England, invaded Portugal and quickly overran a large part of the country. To create a diversion Admiral Rooke left Lisbon to attack Barcelona, but was driven off by the Catalans who for the moment

Carlos III by Goya

ABOVE *Cádiz*   *Admiral Rooke captures Gibraltar*   BELOW

were loyal to Philip. Rooke, on his way back from Barcelona, seized Gibraltar (23 July 1704) which was ill-defended, as its importance as the key to the Mediterranean had never been fully understood by the Spaniards.

English reinforcements in Lisbon enabled the Portuguese to counter-attack in 1705, and landings in Valencia and Barcelona, both of which were now ready for revolt, brought war on two fronts. Barcelona surrendered to the English commander, Lord Peterborough, who had a hard task to prevent the Catalans and Germans from plundering and massacring the Castilian and Neapolitan garrison. The Archduke was now proclaimed as Carlos III in Catalonia (5 November 1705) and by the end of the year much of Aragon and Valencia had also declared for him. Philip hurried with troops from the Portuguese frontier through hostile Aragon and attacked the Archduke in Barcelona (April 1706). His assault was hampered by savage *guerrillero* activities by Catalans in his rear and also by reinforcements landed by the English fleet. Philip was obliged to abandon all his stores and baggage and to flee igno-miniously to France, whence he returned by way of Navarre to Madrid (6 June 1706). There he found that the Portuguese forces under the Earl of Galway were marching on the city; once more he was compelled to flee, this time to Burgos, and Carlos III was proclaimed king of Spain in the capital. If the Castilians resented Philip and his French ministers, they detested even more the presence of an occupying force of upstart Portuguese and heretic English. Carlos III received a chilly welcome from the inhabitants of Madrid.

In the meantime Berwick was able to threaten Galway's communi-cations through the mountainous country west of Madrid, and even-tually forced him to retreat. Philip returned to the capital in October 1706 amid the plaudits of the populace. His troubles were by no means at an end. The Marqués de Santa Cruz, admiral of the Spanish galleys, handed over the naval arsenal at Cartagena to the Austrian faction, and the Archduke was secure in eastern Spain with the Balearic islands and Naples also in his possession. In the spring of 1707 events turned in favour of Philip. Berwick was attacked by Galway's forces at Almansa about sixty miles south-west of Valencia, but in spite of inferior numbers he completely routed the English and Germans. Before long Aragon capitulated to Berwick, who had now been joined by the French forces from Italy under the command of the Duc d'Orléans. All Spain with the exception of Catalonia was now solidly in the hands of Philip's armies.

If events were favouring Philip at home, the situation abroad was disastrous. Naples and Milan were in Austrian possession and the resounding victories of Marlborough in Flanders had brought France almost to her knees. Louis XIV therefore advised Philip to make it appear that Spain was now entirely independent of France, and indeed the bitter hostility between the French and Spanish troops in Catalonia lent colour to this deception. Nevertheless, Louis XIV's overtures for peace were rejected and the war continued, though by now the pride of the Castilians had been roused and in the spring of 1710 Philip found himself with a sizeable army in Catalonia. His military adviser, Villadarias, who had vainly attempted to recapture Gibraltar, was incompetent; Philip's army was quickly routed and fled in disorder to Madrid. The Archduke was once more able to advance on the capital, which he entered on 28 September 1710 with mixed forces of English, Dutch and Germans. The citizens of Madrid could perhaps have borne the oppressive rule of the Archduke, but they were outraged by the sacrilegious plundering of churches performed by heretical mercenaries. Philip had meanwhile reorganised his troops in the north, and a French army under the Duc de Vendôme arrived in Spain, enabling Philip to march on Madrid. The Archduke withdrew hastily to Barcelona while the English contingent of 5,000 under Lord Stanhope retreated towards Portugal pursued by Vendôme who forced them to surrender at Brihuega. Philip advanced into Aragon which capitulated and soon only Barcelona still held out against him.

At this stage an unexpected event transformed the whole aspect of the War of Spanish Succession. The Emperor Joseph I died (17 April 1711) and his brother the Archduke Charles succeeded him. Neither England nor Holland had any desire to see Spain and all its possessions once more united with the Empire, and they opened peace negotiations at Utrecht in January 1712. The following year a treaty was concluded, although Austria continued the war for another year. Spain suffered severe losses: all the remaining Spanish Netherlands, Naples, Milan, Sardinia and Sicily (ceded to Savoy), also Gibraltar and Minorca, which were to remain in English hands. But Spain retained all her possessions in the Indies and since under the terms of the treaty the crowns of France and Spain were never to be united, she was now freed from involvement in Europe, a policy which had brought her utter ruin in the past hundred years.

The Emperor remained sulkily at war with Spain, at least nominally, and the Catalans were equally obstinate and more active. In Barcelona they declared that they would rather die than submit to a Bourbon king, and Berwick's assaulting troops were resisted street by street. It was only after he had set the town on fire that the citizens at length surrendered. Catalonia, Aragon and Valencia were deprived of their privileges and assimilated into the central authority. The *Cortes* were summoned very rarely under Philip's rule, but when they were assembled, deputies from the eastern provinces were obliged to travel to Madrid. Only Navarre and the Basque provinces retained their ancient liberties as a reward for their constant loyalty.

Cardinal Alberoni

Philip well deserved the title accorded to him by the people of *El Animoso* (the Spirited), but his activity was sustained almost entirely by his wife's energy, and she in her turn was dominated by an aged and crafty Frenchwoman, the Princesse des Ursins. In February 1714 Queen Marie Louise died and Philip came to rely entirely on Mme des Ursins, who was in effect the real ruler of Spain. Since Philip was the most uxorious of men, it was clearly necessary to find him another wife as soon as possible, and Mme des Ursins was trapped by an obscure Italian priest, Father Alberoni, into suggesting as a bride Elizabeth Farnese, daughter of the Duke of Parma. By this means it was hoped that Spain would begin to regain her lost territories in Italy. Alberoni assured Mme des Ursins that Elizabeth Farnese was a sweet and tractable girl and the old princess, wily as she was, came to greet the king's new bride totally unprepared. She made some trite remark about the slowness of Elizabeth's journey to Spain whereupon the new Queen shouted: 'Take away this old fool who dares to insult me.' The old princess was hustled into a waiting carriage and was driven at once, still in her court dress, over the Pyrenees in mid-winter into France. The whole incident had been contrived by Alberoni who now became the Queen's chief adviser.

Alberoni, a mellifluous, plausible priest with a taste for complicated intrigue, first trained the new Queen to gain mastery over her husband by devoting herself to his passion for hunting. When her influence was firmly established, Alberoni was emboldened to begin building up Spain's naval strength and to foster plots in almost every country in Europe. Elizabeth Farnese's ambition was to provide her children with an inheritance in Italy, and she induced Alberoni to send a well-equipped Spanish expedition to capture Sicily in June 1718. The attack on Sicily was largely successful, but this flagrant breach of the Treaty of

La Granja, the Royal Palace

Utrecht roused other European powers, already exacerbated by Alberoni's intrigues against them. An English fleet under Admiral Byng attacked the Spanish squadrons off Syracuse (11 August 1718) and completely routed them. Later that year war was declared between England and Spain; Alberoni attempted to aid the Old Pretender by sending an expedition to Scotland, but this failed ignominiously. In April 1719 the French sent a force, commanded oddly enough by the Duke of Berwick, to invade the northern provinces of Spain after Alberoni had assisted a Breton revolt against the Duc d'Orléans, the Regent for the young Louis XV. In October of the same year an English squadron captured Vigo and did great damage along the north coast of Spain. Such disasters caused the Duke of Parma to urge Philip to dismiss Alberoni who was hustled out of Spain into France amid numerous hostile demonstrations. Though Alberoni had been made the scapegoat for all that had occurred, he had in truth done much in Spain to reorganise the finances, trade and the navy, and had certainly given Spain the means to make her presence felt once more in the councils of Europe.

Philip was suffering more and more from melancholia and planned to shut himself up in the new palace he had built for himself at La Granja, between Madrid and Segovia. So deep was he sunk in lethargy that in 1724 he issued a decree abdicating in favour of his son Luis, a youth of seventeen, bright, cheerful and affable. Luis was well received by the Spanish people who were deeply resentful of the Queen's ambitions in Italy and who therefore dubbed the new King *El Querido* (the Beloved). Their pleasure was shortlived because it was found that Luis received all his instructions from La Granja, and it was suggested that Philip had abdicated in the hope of succeeding to the crown of France if the sickly Louis XV should die soon as predicted. Speculation on this point was abruptly ended by the sudden death from smallpox of the luckless Luis after a reign of only seven months (August 1724).

Baron Ripperdá

Since the next heir to the throne, Fernando, was only eleven years old, the Council of Castile earnestly pleaded with Philip to resume the crown which he had sworn to renounce for ever. Spurred on by his ambitious wife Philip agreed, and returned as king more gloomy and more dependent on his wife than before. French influence in Spain had been weakened by the resentment caused by Louis XV's marriage to Maria Leczinska instead of Philip's daughter as planned in 1722. This rift in the Bourbon family gave a chance to a remarkable Dutch adventurer, Baron Ripperdá, to become the chief minister in Spain. This flamboyant character had settled in Spain after successfully establishing a Dutch cloth factory near Segovia. With lavish promises that were not fulfilled he lured Austria into an alliance with Spain, but England, France and Prussia quickly joined forces to counter this dangerous union and Ripperdá's fall followed swiftly. In May 1726 he left Spain with a generous, though unpaid pension and settled in Morocco where he adopted the Mohammedan religion and where his name is still revered.

In 1727 the Spaniards made an effort to recover Gibraltar, but the Emperor refused to help and repeated attacks from the land were useless while the English commanded the sea. Peace negotiations were therefore opened with England and were concluded by the Treaty of Seville (1729) between England, France, Holland and Spain, leaving the Emperor isolated. One of the provisions of the treaty was the recognition of the right of Philip's son by Elizabeth Farnese to succeed in

due course to the Duchy of Parma. In fact the Duke of Parma died in
1731 and the Infante Carlos was received enthusiastically by his Italian
subjects. Such an easy success caused Spain to become more ambitious
in the Mediterranean, and in 1732 a large expedition sailed from Alicante with the ostensible purpose of retaking Oran, which capitulated
almost without a struggle. In the following year Spain turned her
attention to seizing once again the kingdoms of Naples and Sicily and
the campaign ended successfully in July 1735. The Emperor was too
heavily embroiled in disputing the Polish succession to counter this
move, and in 1736 he reluctantly signed the Treaty of Vienna, ceding
Naples and Sicily to Carlos in return for Parma and Milan. This was a
solid gain for Spain, but Elizabeth Farnese was far from satisfied. Parma
was her native land and she had two other sons for whom to provide.
With such an ambitious mother all powerful in the council chamber,
Spain could never escape from war.

The War of Jenkins's ear

The next struggle was no fault of the Queen's, but was caused by a clash
of trading interests between Spain and England in America. Under the
enlightened policy of the minister who succeeded Ripperdá Spanish
commerce had expanded greatly, while the English monopoly (known
as the *asiento*), granted by the Treaty of Utrecht, to supply 4,800 negro
slaves each year to South America, gave opportunities for trading in
other goods. Attempts by Spain to curb this illicit trading led to
frequent disputes culminating in 1739 in the quarrel of Captain Jenkins's
ear, which England claimed had been brutally cut off eight years earlier
and which now was produced as evidence preserved in a box. The
Spaniards countered this accusation by asserting that an English captain
had cut off the ears and nose of a Spanish prisoner and had destroyed
evidence of this barbarity by forcing the victim to eat them. The
English public was incensed, and much against Walpole's will war
was declared on Spain. Neither side met with much success, but
Spanish privateers were especially active against English merchantmen,
who paid a heavy price for avenging the loss of Jenkins's ear.

The Austrian Succession

More serious for both nations was the general European war which
broke out in 1740 to decide the Austrian succession after the Emperor

Charles VI had died leaving his crown to his daughter Maria Theresa. Philip V seized this opportunity to attempt to win back Milan and Parma by landing troops at Genoa. The English sought to prevent this extension of the power of Spain in the Mediterranean. After early successes the Spaniards were heavily defeated and Elizabeth Farnese's plans for her second son's inheritance in Italy came to nothing.

On 9 July 1746 Philip V died of apoplexy, having for several years suffered from prolonged attacks of insanity. He was succeeded by Fernando, the surviving son by his first wife; though the new King treated his stepmother with due consideration, she was no longer able to exercise much influence in state affairs and she retired to La Granja still scheming on behalf of her own sons. Fernando was married to a Portuguese princess to whom he was devoted, and who shared his passion for music. Both of them were determined to keep Spain out of war so that she could recover financially and cultivate the arts of peace. The Treaty of Aix in 1748 put an end to the war of Austrian succession and Elizabeth Farnese had the satisfaction of seeing her second son, Philip, recognised as Duke of Parma.

Attempted reforms

A Spanish nobleman, the Marqués de la Ensenada, had taken charge in 1743 of the finances of the nation and in a short time had achieved far-reaching reforms. Up to now the same hated taxes, the *alcabala* and *millones* (tax on food) had been in force although their incidence had been lightened by better methods of collecting and various exemptions and bounties. In 1717 an experiment had been made in Valencia whereby nearly all the taxes had been replaced by a single duty on salt, and the sudden increase in trade and industry in the area was remarkable. This experiment, with certain modifications, was now imitated in Castile, with the result that between 1742 and 1750 the revenue increased annually by five million ducats whereas under the Habsburgs an additional tax often meant a fall in revenue. Ensenada also encouraged the reopening of silver mining and once again allowed the export of metal, imposing a royalty for the benefit of the Treasury. This enlightened economist was disgraced in 1754 after being accused of secretly negotiating a treaty with France, and Spain lost an able minister whose efforts left the Treasury with a surplus of 300 million *reales* (possibly £14 million) by the time Fernando VI died in 1759.

Being childless Fernando was succeeded by his half-brother Carlos, King of Naples, who continued his enlightened policy. It was indeed uphill work that these two Bourbon kings had to face. The Spaniards clung to their old habits of sloth and ignorance with ridiculous tenacity, and reforms almost always had to be contrived by foreigners. For thirty years after the death of Philip V most of the leading figures in Spanish political life were foreigners: Wall, an expatriate Irishman who succeeded Ensenada in 1754; Grimaldi, a native of Genoa who ruled Spain from 1763 to 1777; Squillaci, from Sicily, who administered the finances from the beginning of the reign of Carlos III. Earlier another Irishman, Bowles, had been summoned to investigate the diminishing output of a valuable mercury mine in Almadén in La Mancha. He found that the miners were sinking vertical shafts instead of following the vein. He suggested that an oblique shaft would remedy the trouble, but the Spanish miners ignored his advice and continued in the fashion of their fathers. The government intervened and dismissed the traditionalist miners, but to reopen the workings miners had to be obtained from Germany.

Yet another Irishman, Higgins, had been physician to Philip V, who did not dare entrust himself to the Spanish doctors, whose sole healing methods were bleeding and purging. As late as 1787 most Spanish doctors had no knowledge of the system of the circulation of the blood, more than 150 years after Harvey had proved the theory correct. Spanish surgeons bled patients for two days from the right arm and then for two days from the left arm so as to equalize the quantity of blood. In 1760 Squillaci made a determined effort to cleanse the streets of Madrid from the filth that cluttered them, but there were objections from every side and the doctors protested that as the mountain air of the capital was so thin the vapours given off by the accumulated filth were necessary to thicken it sufficiently for healthy existence. Even in minor matters of dress Spaniards were blindly conservative and obstinately continued to wear the broadbrimmed hats and cloaks that their fathers and grandfathers had worn. Grimaldi and Squillaci unwisely sought to force a change of fashion by obtaining the issue of an edict in January 1776 forbidding the wearing of the round *chambergo* hat and long cape by public officials. In March this arbitrary ban was extended to the general populace, who in the eyes of foreigners all looked like bandits muffled up ready for a robbery. Officers were stationed in the streets armed with shears to clip off pieces of the offending garments. On Palm Sunday these officers were defied by a mob dressed in traditional garb and soon all Madrid was in an uproar. The Walloon guards fired on the crowd whose fury was then roused. Any Walloon who could be seized was murdered and his head covered with a broadbrimmed hat was thrust on a pole and paraded before the royal palace. Carlos III himself retired disgusted to Aranjuez, but he agreed to dismiss Squillaci, who fled from Madrid while his house was being sacked. He was replaced by a Spanish minister, the Conde de Aranda, who had the sense to drive the *chambergo* hat and long cloak out of fashion by making it the official costume of the public executioner.

Aranda was not a traditionalist in spite of being a Spanish aristocrat, and after suppressing more riots in Madrid with great severity he turned his attention to clerical problems. The Bourbon kings had always sought to limit the power of the Church in Spain; as early as 1707 the clergy had been made subject to taxation, though at first it was disguised as a loan. Ten years later Alberoni, himself a priest, abandoned the subterfuge of a loan, and despite papal protests threatened imprisonment or exile for those priests who refused to pay or obstinately claimed the privileges of their order. Now in 1767 it was determined to rid Spain of the Jesuits (following France's example) because it was maintained that they had stirred up the recent riots with the object of restoring the supremacy of the Church. About 6,000 members of the order were hustled out of Spain in circumstances of great personal hardship, and all the wealth of the Jesuits was confiscated. The Pope protested violently, saying that it was 'the last drop in the cup of our affliction'. His protests were merely brushed aside with the reply that it was 'simply an indispensable economic measure'. Such was the fear in which Aranda was held that no one in Spain dared to raise a revolt, and the Inquisition trembled for its very existence. It is significant that between 1746 and 1781 only fourteen persons were burnt as heretics. The last victim, an old woman accused of sorcery, was burnt in Seville 7 November 1781, and after that no one else in Spain ever suffered at the stake for religious opinions.

The Seven Years War

Carlos III was not so adroit at avoiding war as his predecessor Fernando VI; he unwisely allowed himself to be involved in the Seven Years War just as France was losing it and as a result Spain had to surrender Florida to England. He was more wary of French entreaties to intervene in the American War of Independence, but when it was clear that

England was in dire trouble the temptation to retrieve Gibraltar and Minorca was too strong to resist. Minorca was indeed taken in February 1782 after a lengthy struggle against a tiny British force, but Gibraltar stood firm against all assaults until it was relieved by Rodney, who routed and captured the blockading fleet. Spain's intervention on behalf of the North American colonists gave rise to serious disturbances in her own possessions in South America, and when finally peace was signed at Versailles in 1783 all that Spain had to show for a long and costly war was the recovery of Minorca and Florida. Henceforth until his death in 1788 Carlos III was at pains to keep out of further military engagements.

It would be difficult to overestimate the benefits conferred on Spain by Carlos III who carried on the work initiated by his two Bourbon predecessors. In every sphere of public welfare energetic measures were taken. Schools, hospitals, asylums, almshouses were built in many parts of Spain; savings banks were opened and new industries were established and fostered by the Government, for example the glass factory at La Granja, the porcelain potteries of the Buen Retiro and the leather crafts of Seville and Córdoba. Learned societies had been founded to encourage the study of science and letters and the kings had shown themselves eager patrons of the arts. Philip V in particular, when building the new Royal Palace at Madrid (1735), had scoured Europe to amass a splendid collection of artistic treasures. Madrid had been largely rebuilt with wide, paved streets and magnificent avenues, and a system of good roads was constructed all over Spain to replace the miserable mule tracks which for so long had been the sole means of communication by land. Rivers were made navigable and canals were dug not only to improve communications but also to bring into cultivation large tracts of arid countryside as for example in Catalonia where a canal was constructed between Amposta and Alfaques. By numerous reforms in taxation and a more equitable distribution of its incidence, trade was freed from its previous crippling burden and expanded rapidly. By the end of the reign of Carlos III the population of Spain had risen to more than 10 million, thus doubling in size in about a century.

Some of this rise in population was due to the very large influx of foreigners into Spain, and they occupied all the leading positions in every form of enterprise. This was the weakest feature of all the improvements that the early Bourbon kings achieved. They imposed an alien façade of culture and progress on Spain, and there was no native backing to embody it solidly in the Spanish nation. In the eighteenth century there was almost no Spanish writer or painter worthy of notice: most artistic works were mere imitations of French styles. Hence the reaction to the advances made by the Bourbons was quick to materialise, and its effects have not been thrown off even yet.

Reaction set in on the succession to the throne of Carlos IV who, though amiable, was weak, ignorant and narrowly devout. The outbreak of revolution in France in 1789 no doubt underlined the dangers of democracy to the ruling classes of Spain and as a precaution all newspapers except the official gazette were banned in Spain lest contagion might spread across the frontier from France. At the same time impractical and ineffectual efforts were made to help Louis XVI against the revolutionaries who, full of confidence after their defeat of the Austrian and Prussian invasion, declared war on Spain in 1793 and in just over a year had advanced as far as the river Ebro threatening an advance on the capital itself.

Napoleon's demands

Meanwhile in Spain a new *valido* had arisen, the first for nearly a century. He was Manuel Godoy, a guards officer of twenty-five, who was created a grandee of Spain and subsequently became Commander-in-Chief of the Army and the Navy, as well as chief minister on the Royal Council. It was said that he owed this preferment to the fact that his mistress was none other than the Queen, María Luisa of Parma; she dominated her mild and unprotesting husband who was deeply immersed in the study of the art of clock-making and embroidery. Godoy was an arrant coward and in 1795 sued for peace with the French revolutionaries. The following year the Spanish fleet was placed at their disposal for use against the British navy, which soon defeated it at Cape St Vincent (February 1797) and captured Trinidad in the West Indies. Spain wanted to withdraw from this disastrous alliance, but Napoleon on his rise to power kept up the pressure and forced her to send an army supported by French troops to oblige Portugal to close her ports to British ships. In 1803, when France resumed war with England, he made further demands on Godoy for men, but a nebulous neutrality was bought at the price of a tribute of six million francs a month. This sacrifice availed him little for England regarded it as a warlike act and in 1804 seized the Spanish treasure fleet.

Godoy now had no alternative but to enter the war. The results were immediately disastrous, for the combined French and Spanish fleets, in

Carlos IV and family by Goya, the Prado

attempting to break the blockade of Brest by making a sortie
to the West Indies, were caught on their return by Nelson off Cape
Trafalgar near Cádiz and utterly routed (21 October 1805). Godoy now
foolishly thought that he could outwit Napoleon; while he sent a
Spanish contingent to fight with the French Army at Jena, he secretly
began to organise forces for the defence of Spain against the French.
In 1806, however, he was compelled to pay Napoleon 24 million francs
which Spain could ill afford, and at the same time he eagerly entered
into a pact with the Emperor for partitioning Portugal; the southern
portion was to go to Godoy, while the northern part would be at the
disposal of Napoleon. This was doubtless a bluff on the Emperor's part

to lure Godoy to his destruction, for news of his attempted double-cross had reached Fontainebleau.

Godoy's supine behaviour and the many disasters it had entailed had roused Spain against him, and against the King who tolerated him. A faction arose which sought to put his son Fernando on the throne in place of Carlos, for at the time Fernando was the idol of the public. How unworthy he was of their adoration was clear when in 1806 he wrote a fulsome letter to Napoleon, begging to be allowed to marry a lady of the imperial family, his Neapolitan wife María Antonia having lately died. Napoleon was inclined to encourage Fernando, whose hatred of his dominating mother and her creature weakened still further Spanish national unity. This suffered even more harm when Carlos IV arrested his son for treason in corresponding with the French, although he quickly forgave him.

Napoleon had by this time decided upon the destruction of the Bourbons in Spain, but his most pressing problem was to deal with Portugal, whose ports enabled the British navy to maintain a strangling blockade of France. On 27 October 1807 the treaty of Fontainebleau was signed with Spain, giving Napoleon the right to march 26,000 French troops through Spain (with 40,000 more to follow) in order to conquer Portugal. Spain's national integrity was of course fully guaranteed by the treaty, but how effective the guarantee was may be gauged from the fact that a French army under Junot had already entered Spain before the agreement was made. Junot marched straight across Spain with great speed, and by the end of November reached Lisbon without opposition, but the Portuguese royal family had left for Brazil aboard British ships, taking with them a large amount of treasure.

The French now made no pretence of guaranteeing Spanish independence; French troops poured across the Pyrenees and Murat entered Burgos. This further series of calamities was blamed on Godoy; the mob sacked his residence at Aranjuez and would doubtless have killed him, had not Murat saved him and sent him to Bayonne. Carlos IV now tardily agreed to abdicate in favour of Fernando, for he continued to enjoy the favour of the people, who were unaware of his correspondence with Napoleon about a possible marriage. Napoleon summoned Fernando to a conference at Bayonne. Unsuspectingly he went there in April 1808 and was confronted with his parents and Godoy. A long wrangle ensued and in the end Fernando was persuaded to recognise his father once more as king. Immediately this was achieved

Napoleon easily prevailed upon Carlos to relinquish the crown anew, and in June 1808 the Emperor proclaimed his brother Joseph Bonaparte King of Spain. The Spanish royal family was interned.

This ingenious plot, which had apparently delivered Spain into the hands of France almost without a shot being fired, was the work of Napoleon's wiliest diplomat, Talleyrand, who at first marvelled delightedly at the success of it. He realised sooner than his master, the Emperor, what a fatal mistake it was. He had reckoned without the spirit of the Spanish people, and had forgotten that they are proud, obstinate and violent. Even if they were too weak to fight, they were strong enough to murder.

Chapter 5

The failure of the struggle for democracy

The French Revolution had spread ideas of liberalism throughout Europe, but it was during the struggle against French invaders that Spaniards began to turn their thoughts to democratic government. The *Guerra de la Independencia* was basically a popular movement, since the royal family and many of the nobility were to a greater or less extent collaborators with the French. Inspired by noble ideals a democratic Constitution was drawn up at Cádiz in 1812, but such was the fervent loyalty of Spaniards to the monarchy that Fernando VII on his return from France in 1814 easily succeeded in restoring absolute rule. But the desire for democracy was still strong and the mid-nineteenth century saw Spain torn by rival factions of Liberals and Conservatives. After endless political upheavals and two bloody civil wars some sort of stability was established only by blatant manipulation of political elections which brought both democracy and the monarchy into disrepute and the latent anarchy in the Spanish character was afforded a reason for coming to the surface. Spasmodic unrest was temporarily suppressed by a military dictatorship in the 1920s, but this was immediately followed by a brief Republican period in which well-intentioned Liberal intellectuals entirely failed to control extremists. A military revolt expanded into a protracted civil war in which foreign Fascist and Communist elements fought on opposite sides. The right wing was ultimately victorious and since 1939 Spain has once more been ruled by a military dictatorship which has given the nation some stability and a measure of prosperity, but which has stifled all hopes of training Spaniards for democracy.

LEFT *Fernando VII by Goya*

The first outbreak of violence against the French occurred in Madrid on 2 May 1808, when the populace saw the weeping younger brother of Fernando being led out of the royal palace to a waiting carriage. It was immediately assumed that the remaining members of the royal family were being removed to Bayonne for internment, though it has since been postulated that they were in fact going for an airing. The Madrid mob rushed on the coaches and cut the traces; they then carried the royal prince back to the balcony of the palace amid demonstrations of enthusiastic loyalty. Murat's troops tried to restore order, but in a short time arms were distributed to the populace from the artillery park which had been opened by two Spanish officers, and cannon were wheeled out onto the streets. The rest of the Spanish army remained in barracks and it was left to the citizens to struggle with the French troops, who put down the insurrection, though not without some loss to themselves. The following day the French had their revenge and hundreds of townsfolk were summarily executed by French firing squads, as Goya has gruesomely depicted.

El Dos de Mayo is still celebrated in Madrid as an example of national heroism, but perhaps its success has been somewhat extravagantly praised by a horde of minor poets. French severity cowed the inhabitants of Madrid. The *Junta* left to govern the country in Fernando's absence was wholly subservient to the French and Murat was able to report that the pill had been swallowed. But the self-sacrifice of the Madrid townsfolk released the springs of national pride throughout the rest of the country. With typical Spanish individualism and separatism *Juntas* (committees) for the organisation of defence sprang up everywhere, and on 18 July 1808 at Bailén a Spanish army was able to inflict on the French army a defeat that made Joseph Bonaparte hastily leave Madrid and return to Bayonne, since the northern provinces were also in a state of ferment.

At the same time Sir Arthur Wellesley landed in Portugal with a British force of over 10,000 men, who ironically enough had been mustered at Cork ready for an attack on Spanish American possessions. Almost at once Wellesley won two victories, at Rolica and Vimiero, which forced Junot to surrender his troops in Portugal on condition that British vessels shipped them back to France. It was a cheap price to pay for clearing the country of the French.

In October a force under Sir John Moore advanced from Portugal into Spain with a view to meeting with other British troops at Burgos, where they were to join Spanish units, now wildly optimistic after

Bailén. The onset of winter in such difficult terrain made Moore's position hopeless, and early in December he decided to retreat to Corunna without having fought a battle, a decision which was greeted by voluble protests from the Spaniards. Madrid was now gravely threatened by Napoleon himself and Moore at infinite risk of losing his entire force reversed his decision and pressed on towards Burgos. Meanwhile Napoleon had entered Madrid, had issued rapid orders for the abolition of the Council of Castile and the Inquisition, for the suppression of many monasteries and also for fiscal reforms, and had then turned north-west to destroy the British.

Moore had accurate information about the enemy's activities and avoided a large pincer movement by Soult and Napoleon, who had crossed the Sierra de Guadarrama on 22 December leading his horse through drifts of snow shoulder high. Moore might have fought at Astorga, but he considered it too risky and continued to retreat through cold drenching rain, with his troops becoming progressively more dispirited and disorderly. Disturbed by news from Austria, Napoleon handed over the pursuit to Soult and departed hastily from Spain. The British force reached Corunna on 11 January 1809 and embarked safely, though Moore himself was killed in the final rearguard action. It was a disastrous retreat and losses in men and material, not to mention prestige, were heavy; but at least the operation had drawn large French forces away from southern Spain, giving time for Spanish resistance to be organised.

In the event Spanish resistance in the south proved ineffectual. Joseph Bonaparte had returned to Madrid and undertook the conquest of Andalusia himself. He was delighted to find his campaign turn into an almost bloodless victory as the supreme *Junta* retired to a marshy stronghold in Cádiz and the remainder of Andalusia had shown itself docile. Wellesley, soon after his return to Portugal, thrust Soult from Oporto and then, turning east, moved on Madrid. But, after winning a brilliant victory at Talavera (less than a hundred miles from Madrid) had been forced by lack of supplies and Spanish failure to cooperate, to retire to the fortified lines of Torres Vedras on the coast above Lisbon. Two large and over-confident Spanish armies suffered disastrous defeats in November 1809 at Ocaña and Alba de Tormes. In spite of these victories the French position in Spain was by no means secure because *guerrillero* bands were by now active everywhere, often led by dispossessed priests or monks. Their ability to fall unexpectedly on French supply columns with devastating effect was unequalled, and the glory

ABOVE 'El dos de mayo' by Goya, the Prado

BELOW 'El tres de mayo' by Goya, the Prado

of these exploits, real and imaginary, gave the Spanish provincial masses a new feeling of power and importance.

Dreams of democracy

While Masséna fought Wellesley at Busaco and fruitlessly attacked the lines of Torres Vedras in the autumn and winter of 1810, and hunger was hampering the French in Portugal in 1811, the supreme *Junta* at Cádiz was dreaming of a democratic Spain united with overseas terri-tories, and was busy drawing up a constitution. This was a long and tedious business because there was a grave lack of agreement among the members of the *Junta*. Some were impressed by the bravery shown by monks and priests in resisting the French and were in favour of a return to traditional clericalism, since democracy in France had withered under Napoleon; others wished to follow the example of England and establish a parliamentary system. The latter gained the ascendancy and assembled a token *Cortes* from representatives who were able to reach Cádiz; the theory of representation was that there should be one deputy for every 50,000 head of population in Spain and for every 100,000 in the colonies.

This assembly in the security of their marshy fortress hammered out the Constitution of 1812 which was to play so large a part in the remain-der of nineteenth-century political history. National sovereignty was henceforth to reside in the *Cortes* which were to consist of a single chamber elected by manhood suffrage; the monarchy was to be limited in power and the king could only defer and not veto laws made by the *Cortes*. The *Cortes*, besides being the legislative body, would also control taxation and expenditure, and the size of the armed forces, and would supervise the responsibility of ministers and civil servants as well as guard the freedom of the press. The *Cortes* would assemble for three months each year, but a permanent deputation would watch over affairs of state while the *Cortes* were not in session. The king was answerable for public order and safety, declaring war and making peace, appointing magistrates and bishops and choosing his ministers. Under no circumstances might he suspend, prevent or dissolve any meeting of the *Cortes* which were also to nominate a council of state to advise the king; of this council only four members might be grandees of Spain and four ecclesiastics. This was the sole concession to the traditional role of the nobility and clergy.

The Constitution with its 384 articles was proclaimed with as much state as Cádiz afforded on 19 March 1812. The opportunity was taken

to list the causes of Spain's past ills and to put forward the ideal conception of a nation in which the subject was inviolable and there were
the same laws and the same taxation for everyone. It was a brave
declaration, but it made three assumptions all of which were to prove
false. First, it assumed that the mass of the population understood the
functions, responsibilities and discipline which democracy involves;
secondly, it assumed that all would be tolerant of the views of others;
thirdly, it assumed that the king would willingly accept the limitations
of his power by a constitution on which he had never been consulted.
It was not then known that Fernando in captivity at Valençay was
fawning on Napoleon like the most unctuous *afrancesados*, and that the
stirring letters circulated among the *guerrilleros* and purporting to come
from Fernando were mere forgeries. In Spain he was Fernando *el
Deseado* who would return in triumph to set all to rights when the
Guerra de la Independencia was won.

Hopes were running high because in 1812 Wellington was at last
able to take the offensive against French forces depleted by the require-
ments of the fateful Russian venture. In January Ciudad Rodrigo was
taken, and two months later the key fortress in the south, Badajoz,
was also stormed after the bloodiest of assaults. A victory at Salamanca
left the road to Madrid clear, and British troops entered the capital in
the blazing heat of August amid scenes of great rejoicing. Wellington
pushed on to Burgos, but the French brought up large reinforcements
and, with his flanks also insecure, he decided on a retreat which was not
definitely halted until Ciudad Rodrigo was reached. It was bitterly
disappointing for the Spaniards and for the British public that Madrid
had been won and lost so quickly, but Wellington and his army knew
that the next campaign would be decisive.

The final offensive began on 20 May 1813, and so quickly did it
progress that Madrid was entered on 26 May and on 21 June the
French under Jourdan and Joseph Bonaparte were routed at Vitoria,
with the loss of 8,000 men and vast quantities of baggage, including
Joseph's coach. In exactly one month Wellington had advanced 300
miles over some of the roughest country in Europe, and by the beginning of October he was across the Bidasoa and into France.

British history books are inclined to treat the success of the Peninsular
War as purely a British affair, whereas Spanish historians in dealing
with the *Guerra de la Independencia* scarcely mention the presence of
British forces. A true assessment is difficult to make, but it is certain
that the main credit must go to Wellington, who overcame insuperable

Wellington on horseback by Goya, Apsley House

difficulties with great skill. It is true too that the Spanish troops generally failed badly, mostly through incompetence, not lack of courage; they showed a fatal tendency to give battle in the plains where French superiority in cavalry and in the art of manoeuvre was able to rout Spanish forces which had the advantage in numbers. The work of the *guerrilleros*, however, was of immense value to Wellington because they tied down huge numbers of French troops in frustrating escort and security duties. Portuguese troops who had been trained by English officers made an excellent showing in the field as a part of the Allied Army, which included efficient detachments of the King's German Legion.

Storming of Badajoz

Return to absolutism

The ardent members of the Constituent *Cortes* realised the danger that
Fernando would not tolerate the constitutional changes made in his
absence and proclaimed in his name, and attempted to safeguard themselves by seeking to forbid his return to Spain unless he accepted the
Constitution. They were deceived by Fernando's vague words into
believing that acceptance was complete. He stated that 'as for the re-
establishment of the *Cortes*, and all measures useful to the kingdom
which have been taken in my absence, they shall have my approval in
so far as they conform to my royal purpose'. Still cautious, the Liberals
in the *Cortes* tried to prescribe a fixed route for the King's return to
Madrid, but the rapturous welcome given to him as soon as he set foot
in Spain assured Fernando that he had nothing to fear from the apostles
of liberty. He turned aside from his set route, and the loyal support of
an army in Valencia enabled him in May 1814 to issue a proclamation
renouncing the Constitution and declaring his intention of 'bringing
back all things into the state in which they were in 1808'. Simultaneously persecution of the Liberals began; the leaders of the party were
arrested and sentenced to banishment, imprisonment or death. So

repressive and vindictive were Fernando's measures that one man was actually executed for having led the applause during the public sessions of the *Cortes*. The King was a man of sullen and uncertain temper and none of his favourites or officials enjoyed any semblance of security; they vied with one another in harshness towards those with Liberal sympathies in an attempt to retain Fernando's favour. Such brutal repression was greeted with applause by the mob who tore down the stone commemorating the Constitution and ran through the streets screaming: '¡*Viva el rey absoluto; viva la Inquisición*! ¡*Mueran los masones*!'

A return to the traditional ways of Spanish life was welcomed by the great majority of the country who cared nothing for politics and who were at a loss to understand the complex mechanism of a constitutional parliament. But the *Guerra de la Independencia* had by necessity forced many areas of Spain to organise its own local forms of government by means of *Juntas*, and the seaboard towns in particular had seen the benefits of localised government. Many famous *guerrillero* leaders had sprung from the humblest origins, and their sympathies were entirely with the ordinary folk, who had resisted French invaders while the King had prostrated himself before Napoleon. Many of the nobility too had fought with the *guerrilleros*, thus coming into contact with the common people, and had in the process assimilated more democratic ideas. In spite of the persecution and exile of nearly all the Liberal leaders, who included many of the ablest and most intelligent men in Spain, the new libertarian spirit was very much alive in the Peninsula and numerous abortive revolts flared up in various parts of the country. The colonies were now in open rebellion and Fernando made efforts to reinforce the viceregal troops in America. For this purpose he spent some of the sorely needed Spanish finances in purchasing from his sole European supporter, the Tsar, eight warships with which to convey to America the army he was collecting in southern ports, but when the ships arrived, they were found to be rotten and unseaworthy.

The morale of the army was equally poor, the troops being as usual in arrears with their pay. General Castaños appeared before the king in midwinter wearing the white duck trousers of his summer uniform; when asked the reason, he replied: 'Sire, I have just got my July pay and my July clothes.' It was not surprising then that in January 1820 the most serious revolt originated among the army gathered at Cádiz waiting to embark for the colonies. It was led by Major Riego, commanding an Asturian battalion, and Antonio Quiroga, a colonel in the Royal Regiment. The Constitution of 1812 was reaffirmed at Cádiz and after some initial hesitation the movement was endorsed by garrisons at Corunna, El Ferrol, Zaragoza and Barcelona.

Fernando, who was by nature as cowardly in adversity as he was tyrannical in prosperity, became alarmed for his safety, and in March he agreed to accept the Constitution, uttering the nauseatingly insincere statement: *Marchemos francamente, y yo el primero, por la senda consti-tucional* (Let us walk boldly, I in the lead, along the constitutional path). Once again the fickle Madrid mob applauded its faithless monarch, and this time blessed him for giving liberty to the nation. At first the Liberal revolution seemed to promise political improvement because govern-ment was in the hands of the *Doceañistas*, the men who had drawn up the constitution of 1812 and who were moderate in outlook. But the more violent faction, the *exaltados*, was not to be denied, and the capital seethed with political clubs and masonic lodges which poured forth a mass of revolutionary doctrine. Fernando, who was not without a certain sardonic humour, summed up the situation when he declared: 'Spain is a bottle of beer; I am the cork. Without me it would all go off in froth.'

The Liberal government found itself in the embarrassing position of having to restrain its own supporters and to be accused of being reactionary in outlook. Meanwhile, a genuinely reactionary party had been formed, the *Junta Apostólica*, which quickly established agencies throughout Spain with the avowed intent of saving Church and King from the Liberal revolutionaries. Events in Spain had provoked rebel-lions in Naples, Portugal and Piedmont, and the monarchies of Europe became alarmed. England remained aloof, but Russia, Prussia and Austria at the Congress of Verona (October 1822) insisted that action should be taken to restore Fernando VII to his rightful position. France was reluctant to intervene for fear of offending England, but the proposal that Russia should send an army through France to Spain convinced Louis XVIII that he must act. Accordingly a well-equipped French army under the Duc d'Angoulême was despatched to the Pyrenees on the excuse of establishing a *cordon sanitaire* to prevent a yellow fever epidemic spreading into France from Catalonia.

In Spain the news of likely foreign intervention had spurred on the *exaltados* who had won a majority in the *Cortes* at the elections in the spring of 1822 and who had chosen the fiery, but unintelligent Riego as their President. The *Junta Apostólica* was especially active in the north of Spain and a victory over the Liberal troops at Brihuega (24 January 1823) showed Louis XVIII that the way was clear for a successful invasion of Spain and on 7 April the French army (*los cien mil hijos de San Luis*) crossed the Bidasoa and advanced on Madrid with scarcely any opposition. The Liberal government moved to Seville, taking the King with it in spite of his protestations and pleas of illness. The first action of the French on reaching Madrid in May was to post guards over the houses of well-known Liberals to prevent reprisals from the extreme royalists. Having summoned a Council of Castile to establish a Regency, the Duc d'Angoulême marched southward to rescue the King, who was moved forcibly by the Liberals from Seville to Cádiz on 16 August. A brief siege was followed by the release of the King, though only after a promise had been extracted from him not to victimise those holding Liberal opinions.

Once Fernando joined his French cousin at Puerto de Santa María on 1 October 1823, he forgot all about his promise made a few hours earlier, and gave full rein to his vengeful nature. The Duc d'Angoulême, who was conciliatory and fair-minded, left Spain in disgust, though not before he had secured the escape of several of the Liberal leaders. The unfortunate Riego, who had been no more than a puppet, was hunted down and captured. In vain did he make a full recantation of all his crimes against the King; he was executed in November shortly before Fernando's triumphant return to Madrid. It was then that the real purge began, and courts martial hastily condemned to death anyone accused of Liberal leanings, even if the charge were no more than possessing a portrait of Riego. In eighteen days 112 executions took place. The Russian and French ambassadors at length protested against these ruthless reprisals, and on 10 May 1824 Fernando was graciously pleased to issue what he termed an amnesty, which, however, excluded fifteen classes of offenders from its benefits. The exclusions were enough to embrace the entire Liberal party, and anyone suspected of Liberal sympathies and anyone seeking or holding public office was obliged to undergo scrutiny by *Juntas de Purificación*. Political clubs were closed, and in some cases universities too since they were regarded as breeding grounds for subversive plots. Some seats of learning, however, were entirely submissive, like the Universidad de Cervera, whose loyal address had begun with the words *Lejos de nosotros la funesta manía de pensar* (Far from us the pernicious habit of thinking).

Nevertheless, the proclamation of the so-called amnesty caused widespread dissatisfaction among the extreme royalists, and Fernando's refusal to re-establish the Inquisition was received with horror by the Church party. Both of these groups now tended to turn to the King's brother, Don Carlos, as the real upholder of traditional Spanish government. Fernando found himself in the farcical situation of repressing both ultra-royalist and Liberal revolts. In Catalonia a rebellion provoked by churchmen in 1827 was put down with ruthless severity by the sadistic Conde de España, an ardent royalist who nonetheless delighted in executing large numbers of ultra-conservative rebels. In 1831 an attempted Liberal revolt by General Torrijos, who was lured into landing at Málaga from Gibraltar, ended in the death of himself and his fifty-two supporters. Shortly after this the inoffensive Mariana Pineda was executed in Granada for complicity in minor Liberal plots, and for embroidering a banner with the words *Ley, Libertad, Egalidad*.

Thus Fernando maintained his precarious position on his throne. His real problem was to find a successor. He had been married three times, but was still childless, and his heir was his brother, Don Carlos, who had been clearly implicated in the Catalan revolt of 1827. It was not difficult therefore for Doña Carlota, the wife of Fernando's brother Francisco, to persuade the King in 1830 to marry her sister Cristina of Naples. The new Queen was a sprightly and intelligent woman of twenty-three who enlivened the whole Spanish court with her gaiety. It was rumoured that she had liberal sympathies and the progressive party was greatly encouraged by her arrival. The Carlists were correspondingly depressed and later alarmed when it was known that Queen Cristina was pregnant. A son would have been fatal to Carlist aspirations and Queen Cristina and her ambitious sister were soon busy persuading Fernando that even if the unborn child should be a daughter, her succession was both feasible and desirable. Traditionally succession through the female line in Spain was perfectly legal and Isabel *la Católica* was a shining example of its successful application; indeed in Spain women had and still have greater rights in this respect than women in England, for females inherit titles ahead of collateral males more distantly related. The only difficulty was that Philip V in 1713 had instituted by decree the Salic Law, which was the rule with the Bourbon dynasty in France. But Carlos IV for reasons unknown had set aside this decree in 1789 although he had four sons living; his renunciation of the Salic Law had gone through the formality of approval by the *Cortes* (Philip V had not bothered with such a triviality), but Carlos mysteriously had then omitted to publish the decree. Fernando made up for this omission in March 1830, thereby raising a storm of protest from the Carlists which in turn caused him to veer towards the side of the Liberals.

The first Carlist war

In November 1830 Queen Cristina gave birth to a daughter, and the news made the danger of a Carlist revolt even more imminent. It was only prevented by the orders of Don Carlos himself, who, though obstinate to a degree, was frank and honourable in his dealings with his brother. Nevertheless, Fernando continued to dread a Carlist rebellion and when in 1832 he fell gravely ill, his ministers, who were Carlist in sympathy, easily persuaded him to revoke his decision to leave his crown to his daughter, Isabel. The *Pragmática* was issued on 18 September 1832, but its effective life was short. The story goes that the spirited Doña Carlota arrived post-haste at La Granja where the King lay ill, boxed the ears of Calomarde, the hated Minister of Justice, rated Fernando for his weakness and tore up the decree. It is impossible to know whether this story is true; there were other powerful reasons for this change of mind, for there was a strong Liberal reaction. In any event the King publicly revoked his recent decree on 31 December 1832, and Calomarde was banished from court amid general rejoicing.

Fernando recovered sufficiently to resume the reins of government and on 20 June 1833 a solemn ceremony was held in Madrid at which the nobles and clergy were invited to take an oath of allegiance to Isabel as heir to the throne. Don Carlos civilly refused this invitation and with his brother's leave retired to Portugal, where strangely enough an almost identical problem of succession existed. The irony of the situation was that Fernando was supporting the absolutist claimant in Portugal while making concessions to the Liberals in Spain in order to secure the crown for his daughter. Spain was seething and Fernando's death on 29 September 1833 effectively removed the cork from the bottle. Within four days Don Carlos was proclaimed King by the provincial postmaster in Talavera, and though this minor revolt was quickly crushed, the Basque Provinces, Catalonia and Valencia took up arms in answer to the summons from Don Carlos issued on 4 November.

In Madrid Fernando's Conservative Prime Minister, Zea Bermúdez, gave way in 1834 to Martínez de la Rosa, a veteran of the Constitution of 1812 and a romantic writer whose drama, *La Conjuración de Venecia*, achieved a notable success that same year. His Liberalism had cooled with age and possibly it was for this reason that the Regent, Queen María Cristina, chose him and entrusted him with the formulation of a new Constitution which was entitled the *Estatuto*. This established two-chamber government consisting of the upper *Estamento*, composed of *Próceres* (Peers) and an unlimited number of clergy, soldiers, magistrates and other officials nominated by the Crown. The lower *Estamento* consisted of *Procuradores* elected under a system which was inevitably complex in such a scattered and disorganised country. No act was valid without the agreement of both chambers and the Crown, and since debate was limited to subjects chosen by the Crown, the powers of the lower *Estamento* were severely limited. Such an unbalanced constitution was scarcely likely to please the more advanced Liberals who formed the majority of the *Cristinos* and it was not surprising that military operations to suppress Carlist activities were not conducted with much vigour.

The supporters of Don Carlos consisted mainly of the nobility, clergy and the Basque peasants who were passionately devoted to the Church and to their traditional *fueros*. The large towns in the north, such as Bilbao and San Sebastián remained aloof, but the French border was wide open to the Carlists who obtained large quantities of supplies from sympathisers in France and were at first better equipped than the *Cristino* armies. The early Carlist successes were due almost entirely to the energy and ability of their leader Tomás Zumalacárregui, who as well as being a brilliant military commander organised an efficient system of collecting money to pay for the war. His army was highly trained but essentially local and civilian; it could assemble quickly, move with great rapidity over the most difficult mountain country, fight a battle and disappear as if by magic should larger enemy forces come on the scene. The *Cristino* armies lacked the same unified command and all that a succession of generals could achieve was to blockade the Carlists north of the river Ebro. An attempt was made to invade the Basque provinces by way of the valley of Amescoa, but Zumalacárregui withdrew taking all supplies with him; the *Cristinos*, suffering great privations, were forced to abandon the operation. They resorted instead to the use of flying columns to hunt down and capture Don Carlos, but they were no match for the Carlists, who were nearly all experienced mountaineers. One particularly strong peasant known as *El Burro del Rey* (the King's Donkey), carried Don Carlos on his back to inaccessible hiding places when danger was at hand. Frustrated everywhere the *Cristino* general Rodil gave way to terrorism, decreeing death for all Carlists and their abettors (August 1834), and set about a systematic attempt to starve the Basques into submission. This merely enraged the Carlists who fought all the more stubbornly, winning two battles in Álava and matching their opponents in ruthless extermination of prisoners. Such was the ferocity and inhumanity shown by both sides that foreign powers protested, and a commission from England led by Lord Elliot arrived in Spain to arrange a treaty between the two sides for more humane conduct of the war. This was successfully concluded on 27 April 1835.

The signing of this unexceptionable agreement was immediately seized upon by the more advanced Liberals in Madrid as evidence that Martínez de la Rosa was attempting to come to terms with the Carlists. Faced with stormy debates in the lower *Estamento* and outbreaks of mob violence in Madrid, Martínez de la Rosa resigned and was succeeded by his finance minister, Toreno. The bickering of the Liberal politicians was equalled by the ineptitude of the *Cristino* generals, though to be fair it must be said that they were kept miserably supplied and instant success was always demanded of them. The Carlists were clearly in the ascendant and occupied all the north-west of Spain except Pamplona, San Sebastián and Bilbao, which General Espartero could hold but from which he utterly failed to break out. The Carlists held the main road south and at any moment they could have begun an advance on Madrid with fair hopes of success. Instead Don Carlos chose, against the advice of Zumalacárregui, to besiege Bilbao in the hope that possession of such an important port would open the way to supplies from Austria, Prussia and Russia, who were thought to be in sympathy with his cause. It proved a fatal move for on the fifth day of the siege Zumalacárregui was wounded in the leg, and nine days later he died because of, rather than in spite of, the ministrations of a local physician. With his death the Carlists lost their precious unity of command; not only was the siege of Bilbao abandoned, but the *Cristinos* inflicted a crushing defeat at Mendigorría (16 July 1835) on the Carlists who were now commanded by General Moreno, a man especially hated by the Liberals because he had treacherously lured Torrijos to his death in 1831. England and France now began to demonstrate more active support for the Liberal cause. The French cut off supplies from the Carlists and a detachment of the Foreign Legion operated with success against Carlist forces in Catalonia, while a British naval squadron blockaded the northern coast and a British Volunteer Legion from their base at San Sebastián kept the Carlists at bay in the Basque provinces.

The war continued largely as stalemate, with both sides showing the utmost ferocity to helpless captives. Nogueras, the *Cristino* commander, brutally shot the mother of Cabrera, the leader of the Carlist troops in the north-east; he in retaliation shot six women held as hostages. The only hope that prisoners of war had of saving their lives was of enlisting in the forces of their captors, but even this could not be relied upon, especially with volunteer forces. At Rubielos in September 1838 seventy *Cristino* volunteers were stripped naked by Carlist troops and then ridden down by lancers for sport. Such brutality was encouraged by the commanders on both sides, who carried on a hideous rivalry in cruelty.

Lack of supplies drove the Carlists to more desperate tactics than they had hitherto employed. They organised a series of raids deep into *Cristino* territory in the hope of impressing foreign powers with the strength of their forces, as well as collecting much needed stores and recruits. Perhaps, too, Don Carlos thought that the appearance of his troops in more distant provinces would rouse the rest of Spain to his cause, but in this he was utterly disappointed. General Gómez with a raiding party slipped through the *Cristino* blockade and penetrated Galicia as far as Santiago de Compostela, but though he gained a few recruits there was no general rising. Finding his return route blocked, he turned southward, roved through Extremadura and reached Córdoba. He encountered little opposition because the whole country was almost stripped of troops, but he collected wagon loads of booty and firearms which he took from the local national guards. On his way back north he joined another band of Carlists under Cabrera, the *guerrillero* leader of the War of Independence, and together they threatened Madrid. However, one of the few competent *Cristino* generals, Narváez, caught up with them and defeated them at Maja-ceite, near Los Arcos (25 November 1836); one of his own brigades chose this moment to mutiny and he was prevented from annihilating the Carlist forces, who had quickly scattered. Gómez returned safely to the Carlist lines at Orduña in December having marched 2,500 miles in six months, but though he came back with a force larger that that with which he set out, and with a sizeable quantity of booty, he had achieved nothing decisive save that he had revealed the utter weakness of the *Cristino* government.

In fact while Gómez had been on his travels a namesake of his, a sergeant in the palace guard at La Granja, had carried out an extraordinary revolution. The whole country was sickened by the ineptitude of a string of ministers who though professedly Liberal were in reality little more than court politicians since their hands were tied by the

Estatuto Real of 1834. There was a universal clamour for a return to the Constitution of 1812, but the Queen Mother, misled by her ministers, refused to call the *progresista* party to power and on 4 August 1836 issued from La Granja a proclamation condemning the mutterings for revolt as anarchical. The palace guard at La Granja consisted of only eight companies of foot and two squadrons of cavalry, and the sergeants were almost all of radical political convictions; they harangued the men and persuaded them to mutiny. Having assembled them under arms in the courtyard, Sergeant Gómez, accompanied by another N.C.O. and a private soldier, insisted on seeing the Queen Regent to whom he explained the need for accepting the clear demands of the provinces for a return to the Constitution of 1812. A wrangle ensued over the meaning of the word liberty, but the sergeant who was something of an orator stuck to his point. Queen Cristina gave a somewhat evasive promise to refer the matter to the *Cortes* when it next assembled, but since the audience had now lasted for three hours, the troops outside became restive and started howling threats and insulting remarks about the Queen Mother's private affairs. Faced with a dangerous and undignified situation Cristina gave way and signed a *Pragmática* of three lines, ordering the observation of the Constitution of 1812.

The result of this extraordinary revolution was that a more radical ministry came to power under Calatrava, the previous Minister for War. The Constitution of 1812 was found unworkable and a committee was appointed to revise it; its report, approved by the *Cortes* on 27 April 1837, produced a compromise arrangement. As a constitution it was superior to that of 1812; not only was it briefer (77 articles compared with 384), it was also more practical. It was, however, a moderate document leaving much power still vested in the Crown. In any country with a democratic tradition it would have been readily acceptable, but with Spaniards, who are fundamentally anarchical and intensely individualistic, it found little favour. The *progresistas* felt defrauded because the new constitution was insufficiently radical, the Catholics hated it because it allowed freedom of worship, the Conservatives deplored any attempt at democratic government, the poorer classes were indignant at the property qualification which excluded them from voting, the provinces rejected it because it was pledged to the abolition of the local *fueros*, and the Queen Regent was sulking after the undignified treatment she had received when she had been compelled to enter Madrid a prisoner of her own guards. In fact no one was satisfied with the new constitution except the tamest of Liberals, such as Martínez de la Rosa, who praised it fervently.

It was at this point Don Carlos decided at last to invade Castile, and for this purpose he marched eastward to Catalonia to join forces with Cabrera (June 1837). The eastern provinces received Don Carlos coolly for the most part, but with fresh supplies he gained a substantial victory over the *Cristinos* at Herrera on the borders of New Castile, and when on 12 September 1837 he was joined by another raiding party, which had advanced through Valladolid, Segovia and La Granja, the Carlists were able to reach the village of Arganda del Rey, only ten miles from Madrid.

The capital was in a fever of anxiety. The ministry promptly resigned and evaded their responsibilities, all except General Espartero who as well as being Minister of War commanded the army covering Madrid. He had led it out to meet the Carlist raiders to the north-west, but they had evaded him. Madrid was defended only by the militia, and no one knew how many would-be Carlists were in its ranks. Don Carlos tried to win the capital, not by force, but by issuing a conciliatory proclamation in which he offered to cede the crown to his son, who would marry his cousin, Queen Isabel. 'The august widow' (Queen Cristina) was to be sent back to Italy, and the Liberals were reassured with the comforting words, 'the days of the Inquisition and despotism are gone forever'. Madrid did not rise to this bait and with Espartero and his army hurrying back to do battle, Don Carlos took fright. He retreated after spending only one day at Arganda and his shoddy army melted away while his generals quarrelled. His last opportunity of victory was gone.

Espartero pursued the Carlists northwards, but discipline in the *Cristino* army was as bad as among their enemy forces. General Escalera had been murdered on 16 August 1837 at Miranda by his own troops, and General Sarsfield had suffered similarly at Pamplona. Espartero was a strong-willed commander and not afraid of severity. He shot every tenth man (chosen by lot) from the guilty battalion at Miranda and dealt out similar punishment to Sarsfield's murderers. Such stern methods restored discipline and Espartero had the gift of compelling loyalty from his troops. Unfortunately he was dictatorial and conceited, and his rise to power provoked the Carlists into continuing a stubborn resistance, with Cabrera organising raids as far south as La Mancha. This new danger near the capital led the government to commission General Narváez to raise and train a reserve army of 40,000 men.

RIGHT   *Church of San Pablo, Valladolid*

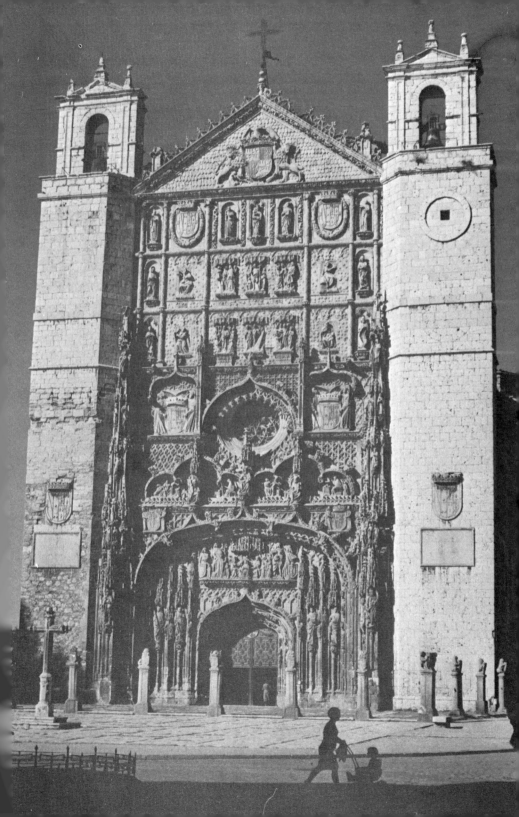

Immediately Espartero feared for his own military supremacy from such a dangerous rival and induced the government to disperse Narváez's army (31 October 1838). Narváez was foolish enough to lend his name to a plot to overthrow the government, and Espartero was able to demand his trial by court martial for treason. Narváez prudently took refuge in France. Espartero for the time being was rid of his rival, but an excellent chance of finishing the war had been lost because of the inability of Spaniards to cooperate with each other.

Political rivalries

Rivalry and dissension in the Carlist camp were equally rife and caused the collapse of resistance in the Basque Provinces. By January 1839 General Maroto, commanding the Carlist forces, was negotiating with Espartero, nominally concerning exchange of prisoners. Against the express desires of Don Carlos, who by now seemed to have lost interest in the struggle, Maroto agreed to the Convention of Vergara, which ended the war in the Basque Provinces. On the whole the terms were generous and the sole remaining difficulty was the vexed question of Basque *fueros*, but Espartero promised to use his influence with the government to ensure that these were maintained. Don Carlos departed to France fulminating against Maroto's treachery and the 'betrayal of Vergara'.

Cabrera continued the war in Catalonia for another year, ruthlessly and successfully, but pointlessly, until the arrival of Espartero with overwhelming forces obliged him to seek refuge in France (2 June 1840). Such was the strange compelling power of this veteran *guerrillero* that his farewell to his troops gave rise to several suicides among his followers; two Aragonese soldiers refused to be separated and fought each other to the death with bayonets in token of their friendship.

Espartero was the hero of the hour. This son of a carter from La Mancha was loaded with titles, Duque de la Victoria, Príncipe de Vergara, Conde de Luchana, and everyone sought his advice and opinion. He was reluctant to commit himself, but agreed to become Prime Minister as soon as he could return from ending the campaign against Cabrera in Catalonia. Meanwhile the Queen Regent, accompanied by her daughter, journeyed to Catalonia, ostensibly to take the waters at Caldas, but her real purpose was to visit Espartero and enlist his support. The first meeting was affable enough, but a clash soon came. The government, which had Conservative leanings even though it was officially Liberal, had just formulated a controversial law imposing a property qualification for voters in local council elections. The purpose of this enactment was to give the middle and upper classes control of the municipal councils, which were mostly staunchly progressive and readily formed themselves into revolutionary *juntas* at the slightest hint of disaffection. The enactment approved by the *Cortes* was sent to Barcelona for Cristina's signature. Espartero pronounced against it, but the Queen Regent, hitherto submissively seeking his aid, suddenly turned stubborn and signed the new law.

Espartero countered by resigning all his titles, though he allowed himself to be persuaded to change his mind. He had also resigned his command, but he never relaxed control of his army and his chief of staff is reputed to have stirred up the Barcelona mob against Cristina so that Espartero could appear in the streets and appeal for patience. Cristina found herself relying on Espartero for personal protection. Her position was made all the more insecure because of the guilty secret of her private life, which was known to only a few people, one of whom was Espartero. A few months after the death of Fernando VII she had married a handsome corporal in the Bodyguard, Fernando Muñoz, whose prompt action had saved her from a carriage accident. By this marriage Cristina forfeited the legal claim to the Regency and to the income that went with it. Since she loved both power and money, the marriage was kept secret for seven years although several children were born of it.

In spite of her doubly precarious position Cristina had no intention of meekly submitting to Espartero; she betook herself to Valencia and the protection of the loyal Conservative general, O'Donnell. Madrid, however, decided in favour of Espartero; the National Militia took over the city and a radical *junta* was formed. Similar *juntas* sprang up all over the country and demanded that the new law should immediately be repealed and that the Queen Regent should publicly denounce the 'perfidious counsellors' who had advised her to sign the act. This she refused to do, especially as Espartero had written to her peremptorily urging her to appoint a new ministry of six 'patriots' and flatly refusing to obey her order to march against the rebels in Madrid. She confirmed new ministers in their posts and then announced her intention of abdicating. No amount of persuasion would make her change her mind and she sailed to Marseilles on 17 October 1840.

A new Regent had to be found and Espartero, the most popular figure in Spain, was clearly the man for the task, but some members of the *Cortes* were reluctant to leave so much power in the hands of a man of such overweening conceit, and suggested that he as Regent should have two assessors. At this Espartero flew into a rage and threatened to retire into private life. The *Cortes*, bowing to this threat, confirmed him as the sole Regent (18 May 1841), but his high-handed action created a determined opposition right at the outset of his term of office. He had another bitter opponent in Cristina, who from Paris never ceased to stir up trouble, protesting as a loving mother about the persons appointed to supervise her daughter Queen Isabel. The Radical ministry had chosen persons who had never been open to the corrupting influence of court life; Argüelles, President of the Council and nicknamed *el Santón* (the Puritan) was her guardian, the aged poet and *doceañista* Quintana her tutor; her Lady of the Bedchamber was an austere female named the Marquesa de la Belgida, and her governess was the widow of the democratic *guerrillero* Mina. All these worthy people found that their authority was continually flouted by the warmhearted, but self-willed Queen, aged eleven, who made fun of her mentors and associated with members of the old court aristocracy when the opportunity arose. There was even a plot to abduct Isabel. Two generals, Concha and León, marched a regiment into the Royal Palace at night (7 October 1841), but the Corps of Halberdiers, eighteen old soldiers in all, held the palace staircase until help arrived in the form of the National Militia. Concha escaped, but León was caught and later executed by a firing squad, a penalty which seemed not unreasonable, but which was hailed by Espartero's opponents as an example of cold-blooded brutality.

Espartero's immense popularity declined rapidly, especially in the northern provinces where his promise to retain the Basque *fueros* was flagrantly broken. Barcelona, which was ever separatist in outlook, revolted and demanded independence. The rebellion was confined to the city itself and did not spread to the rest of Catalonia. It could easily have been dealt with locally, but Espartero hurried up from Madrid and bombarded the city with artillery destroying more than four hundred houses (3 December 1842). The city surrendered and was fined £12,000 for the insurrection. Such violent measures against the chief industrial city of Spain were naturally a target for bitter criticism by Espartero's opponents and an insistent demand was made for an amnesty for all political offenders. This would have meant the return of General Narváez who was in exile in France. Espartero fought hard to suppress the clamour, but in May 1843 rebellions broke out in Andalusia and Catalonia. Espartero in a mood of black despair set out southward to quell the revolt in Andalusia. During his absence Generals Narváez, Prim and Serrano advanced from Catalonia and Valencia, entering Madrid on 23 July and setting up a new ministry to govern in the name of the Queen and Liberty. They called on Espartero to surrender, and General Concha who had a score to settle with him pursued him into Andalusia, where he was preparing to bombard Seville. Almost all Espartero's troops deserted him, Cádiz rebelled at his approach, and it was left to a British man-of-war to take him off at Puerto de Santa María and convey him to London, where he was received with applause and for a time lodged at the Mansion House.

Spain entered a period of Conservative government, at first under civilians, Olózaga and González Bravo. The first fell quickly, accused by the thirteen-year-old Queen of forcing her against her will to sign a decree to dissolve Parliament. The second showed repressive reactionary tendencies and amongst other acts created *la Guardia Civil*, for which on the whole Spain must be profoundly thankful. He also restored to Queen Cristina her generous pension, with arrears, and created her ex-corporal husband a Duke and *Grande de España*. Queen Cristina had to delay her return from Paris in order to give birth to yet another Muñoz Borbón, but when she did return to Spain (2 May 1844) she used her powerful influence to get rid of her benefactor González Bravo, who was replaced by General Narváez, a man of infinitely greater authority.

Narváez was a stern disciplinarian who made insurrection and rebellion unprofitable. Even Espartero was deterred from attempting a rising in view of the severity with which rebels were punished; in a little over a year in office Narváez had 214 persons shot for political offences. So ready was he with the firing squad that years later the story was told that Narváez on his deathbed when asked if he forgave his enemies replied: 'I have none; I have shot them all.' A new constitution was introduced in 1845, but it differed little from preceding Conservative efforts in this direction, though the muzzling of the press and the property qualification for electors made any democratic swing to the left less easy to engineer. Any rigorous disciplinarian is bound to be unpopular and Narváez fell from power in January 1846, but mostly for reasons of disagreement with the Court. He was, however, recalled some eighteen months later when Queen Isabel and the Court became alarmed at the rising tide of revolution throughout Europe.

Dynastic negotiations

Isabel had been officially declared of age on her fourteenth birthday, although throughout her life her conduct was never that of a responsible adult. Half Europe was seeking her hand in marriage and it was clear that she, although of age, was to have no say in the choice of a husband. Prussia and Austria were pressing for her marriage with the Conde de Montemolín, now styling himself Carlos VI since his father Don Carlos had in 1845 retired from the fray. Such a union, it was hoped, would end dynastic quarrels in Spain for good and all. Great Britain hankered after a marriage with the Saxe-Coburg family, but in deference to the alliance with France this project was abandoned. When Queen Victoria met King Louis-Philippe in 1843 at the Château d'Eu it was agreed that Isabel should marry a Bourbon descendant of Philip V, and that when an heir to the throne had been born, her sister María Luisa should be free to marry a prince of the House of Orléans. The Bourbon descendant presented a problem, and for a time the only likely candidate was the Count of Trapani of Parma, Isabel's uncle. The Spanish nation was in favour of the Queen taking a native-born husband, and her aunt, Doña Carlota, seized this opportunity to press the claims of her son, the Duque de Sevilla. This young, handsome naval officer impressed Isabel by his dashing ways, but in his desire for popularity he rashly associated himself with wild Liberal schemes, including an abortive rising in Galicia, and his royal cousin was obliged to banish him instead of marrying him.

Thereafter a cruel plot was concocted by Queen Cristina and Louis-Philippe, that Isabel should marry the Duque de Cádiz, the younger brother of the Duque de Sevilla, and at the same time María Luisa should marry the Duc de Montpensier, Louis Philippe's third son. The Duque de Cádiz was a weak and effeminate youth who was believed to be impotent, so there was little likelihood of issue by the marriage. The throne of Spain would thereby devolve in all probability on the Orléans family. Despite protests from Great Britain and from the Carlists the double marriage took place in Madrid with great ceremony on 10 October 1846. When a mother arranges such a match for her sixteen-year-old daughter, it is hard to blame the bride if the marriage is not a success. Within a year the royal couple were estranged; Isabel's name was scandalously connected with the handsome young general Serrano, and her husband was believed to be plotting to make himself king.

Louis-Philippe did not enjoy his success long for the violent revolution in Paris in 1848 toppled him from the throne and sent him to exile in England, itself torn with Chartist demonstrations. Spain did not escape unrest including an attempted revolt by the Duque de Sevilla and a Carlist rising led by Cabrera now far more liberal in outlook after years of exile and marriage to an English wife. Both risings were easily suppressed and Narváez gained considerable popularity in Spain by dismissing the British ambassador suspected of having stirred up trouble in Madrid and Andalusia.

Reaction and revolt

Narváez resigned in January 1851, after the Queen Mother, who owed him much, had been scheming against him. Civilian government under Bravo Murillo attempted reforms, but achieved little except the signing of a Concordat with the Pope, which had been under negotiation for several years. Successive Liberal governments had shown strong anti-clerical policies and had regularly seized Church lands in order to raise desperately needed cash by their sale. By the Concordat the Church was once more empowered to own property and the Catholic religion was acknowledged in Spain to the exclusion of any other. All education, public and private, was to conform to the doctrines of the Church which should have powers to suppress harmful books. The Concordat represented a surrender to the Papacy and the forces of reaction. Bravo Murillo, either emboldened or frightened, became even more reactionary and attempted to rule by decree. Even the court was alarmed and he was dismissed, but his successor took little heed of this warning, and clamour for a more liberal administration grew loudly insistent. The newspapers were gagged and some used to print a blank sheet in protest against not being able to express a true opinion. On 26 April 1854 a secret newspaper named *El Murciélago* (The Bat) appeared in Madrid, scurrilously attacking the Queen Mother, her husband and the prime minister, San Luis, on the grounds of corrupt practices. By June it was still in publication and turned its attention to Queen Isabel herself, giving details of her association with General Serrano. With these and other revelations of the scandals of the court clearly presented to the public an explosion could not be long delayed. On 28 June General O'Donnell persuaded a cavalry brigade exercising near Madrid to join him in a demand for a change of government, and an indecisive action was fought with loyalist troops at Vicálvaro on the outskirts of the capital (30 June). General O'Donnell renewed his demands and they were echoed by the Madrid mob. The organisation of the usual *juntas* in several of the large towns proved that the rising was more serious than a mere *pronunciamiento* by a disaffected general and at length the Prime Minister, San Luis, resigned (17 July).

To celebrate this event Madrid gave itself over to rioting. The Hymn of Riego was played at a bullfight, the houses of Queen Cristina, San Luis and other ministers were wrecked, the National Militia was revived by a hastily elected *Junta de la Seguridad, Armamento y Defensa de Madrid* and 284 barricades, 'stout pillars of freedom' were erected in the streets. A rival *junta* also arose in the unsalubrious district of Madrid named Lavapiés, under the leadership of a bullfighter, Pucheta. After executing an unpopular police officer, the *junta* took possession of one of the main gates of Madrid and did good business issuing safe-conducts at a stiff price to persons anxious to leave the city. Isabel's favourite was amongst those from whom this toll was exacted.

The only person able to put an end to these disorders was Espartero, now living in retirement at Logroño. The Queen, who was a prisoner of the revolutionaries, begged him to come, assuring him of her submission. After some hesitation he agreed and entered Madrid in triumph in an open landau, spreading out his arms as if to embrace the thousands of noisy patriots around him. General O'Donnell reached Madrid the following day and the two generals embraced dramatically in public in token of the fusion of the two parties they represented—Espartero the *progresistas* and O'Donnell the *moderados*. O'Donnell had in no way intended to bring Espartero to power when he initiated the revolt, but he was content to bide his time and allow the hero's popularity to wane. He had not long to wait, for Espartero had no constructive policy and replied to any question on his proposed actions with the phrase: 'Let the Will of the nation be fulfilled.' In any event his popularity with the extreme left slumped quickly. The mob was howling for the trial of Queen Cristina and breathed threats against anyone who connived at her escape from Spain. The Queen Mother, however, announced firmly that she was retiring to Portugal and insisted on taking formal leave of the ministers of the Crown. Espartero and his colleagues were forced to agree and Queen Cristina departed, complete with a guard of honour and all her jewels. The mob was pacified with difficulty and in retaliation Queen Cristina's pension was stopped once again; it made little difference to her since she had previously transferred the bulk of her fortune to Paris.

Having clashed with the extreme Radicals Espartero soon ran foul of Queen Isabel. The new regime had as usual reshaped the Constitution and among other provisions was proposing to renew sales of Church property, granting extensive credit facilities so that all but the poorest peasants could buy land. When this particular bill was presented by Espartero for signature, the Queen steadfastly refused to sign, stating that she would rather abdicate than betray her religion. Isabel for all her wanton behaviour was deeply devout and was surrounded by religious advisers of the most bigoted type. Of these the most notorious was Sor Patrocinio, the 'bleeding nun' on whom at times of stress the wounds of the stigmata were wont to appear. Espartero was, if nothing else, an obstinate man and he prevailed upon the Queen to sign, which she did under protest. She then wrote to the Pope claiming that she had been obliged to sign against the dictates of her conscience. The Pope severed diplomatic relations with the Spanish government which retorted by banishing Sor Patrocinio and other undesirable members of the Queen's entourage, in spite of a ludicrously theatrical threat by the effeminate King-Consort of armed resistance.

Queen Isabel, however, was soon to have her revenge. O'Donnell had been ingratiating himself with her, at the same time extending his influence in the cabinet, while mocking Espartero's rough appearance and peasant's manners behind his back. With the connivance of the Queen he manoeuvred Espartero into a position in which resignation was offered and accepted by Isabel, much to Espartero's surprise and indignation (13 July 1856). Meanwhile, O'Donnell had his own cabinet formed and waiting. Its first measure was to proclaim a state of siege throughout Spain in order to reduce dissension created by the reappearance of the National Militia. O'Donnell returned to the more Conservative Constitution of 1845, but hoped to secure the support of the more advanced radicals by passing an Additional Act authorising slightly more liberal modifications. Again the government tried to proceed with sales of Church property in order to conceal its own bankruptcy, but once more Isabel proved stubborn, and after she had slighted him openly at a Court ball on 10 October 1856 he resigned. He was replaced by General Narváez, who, though believing himself a Liberal, had no other policy than that of restoring the traditional power of Church and monarchy. His methods amounted to simple direct oppression, and as he was fundamentally an honest man he always commanded respect in the country. But he was frank and outspoken with the Queen who resented his plain speaking and was glad to find an excuse to dismiss him. Narváez departed with good grace after exactly one year in office.

The Queen was about to give birth to a child, and fearing that scandalous gossip might be rife throughout the country sought to appease popular opinion by forming a less repressive government. A son was born to her on 28 November 1857. The appearance of an heir to the throne caused much speculation about its paternity, which was generally attributed to a Catalan colonel. This was not Isabel's first son, one born in July 1850, though apparently a healthy child, had died within an hour of birth. Rumour had it that this had been the work of the Montpensier faction, who were intent on securing the succession for themselves. Such a suggestion seems to go beyond the bounds of credibility, but undoubtedly Isabel's unhappiness tinges with sympathy any subsequent censure of her conduct.

Civilian ministries proved ineffectual and by the summer of 1858 O'Donnell was back in office. His so-called Liberal Union achieved the distinction of retaining power for five years and for the first time the *Cortes* sat for the full period of its mandate. The secret of this success lay in the adroit manipulation of the election of the *Cortes* by Posada Herrera, known as *el gran sofista*. He was the first fully to realise that a complete majority in favour of the government usually led to endless bickering whereas a lively opposition kept government supporters united. Thus while securing an excellent working majority he allotted seats to the leaders of both the extreme Radical and Conservative parties. This double opposition when united gave unwonted solidarity to the government, but mostly fought amongst itself, leaving the ministry in peace.

A period of peace led to a more stable economic situation and Spanish trade expanded rapidly, helped by the improved communications afforded by the arrival of railway transport. (Queen Cristina is alleged to have profited greatly by dabbling in railway concessions.) Popularity was also obtained by the government in the renewal of activity abroad. In 1859–60 a moderately successful campaign against the Sultan of Morocco stirred the Spanish imagination as a renewal of the Crusade against the infidel. At the same time an attempted Carlist rising was suppressed with almost ludicrous ease and the Pretender, the Conde de Montemolín was captured. He was not made of the same obstinate stuff as his father and meekly signed a document abandoning his claim to the throne and humbly begging to be allowed to leave the country. The Queen could afford to be lenient and a general amnesty was proclaimed (1 May 1860). Her authority and that of her minister, O'Donnell, seemed complete.

Unfortunately, O'Donnell's next attempt to intervene abroad brought little profit and no credit. In October 1861 he joined Great Britain and France in an expedition against Mexico, where the republican leader Juárez had suspended payment on external debts. A Spanish squadron joined British and French naval units, and a Spanish force under the Catalan General Prim seized the town of San Juan de Ulloa. Juárez came to terms and in view of the grave displeasure of the United States at armed European intervention so near to home Great Britain and Spain withdrew. France persisted with a foolish plan to set up a puppet monarchy in Mexico and backed the claims of the Archduke Maximilian whom she soon abandoned to his fate at the hands of the republicans.

Such a discreditable affair harmed O'Donnell's reputation in Spain generally and weakened his influence with the Queen, who refused to accept his suggestion that Prim should be made scapegoat for the profitless expedition. He further clashed with the Court party when his ministry suggested formally recognising the King of Italy, for the unification of Italy had removed the temporal power of the Pope. The Queen's religious scruples, sharpened by the return of the Bleeding Nun and other bigots, could tolerate no offence to the Holy See and O'Donnell resigned (February 1863). Later the Pope rewarded Queen Isabel by bestowing on her the Order of the Golden Rose, and all Europe was stirred to laughter.

The governmental chaos of the reign continued, with ministries coming and going while the influence of the court party, the *camarilla*, remained permanent. Isabel had enjoyed popularity among the people of Spain for many years, but gradually it began to dawn on everyone's mind that there could be no stability of government so long as she remained on the throne. There was widespread disillusion everywhere and her gesture in allowing two-thirds of the Crown estates to be sold by the Treasury in return for a quarter of the proceeds found approval only in ministerial newspapers. Emilio Castelar, a professor at Madrid University in an article entitled *El Gesto*, maintained that the Crown estates belonged to the nation and that the Queen was to receive a share of the proceeds from a sale of property which did not belong to her. The court immediately demanded that Castelar should be dismissed from his professorial chair; the Rector refused to comply and was himself removed from his post. The students staged a demonstration of protest at which the large crowds were dispersed by cavalry charges. Several lives were lost and many people were wounded; the memory of the events of the *Noche de San Daniel* (April 1865) lasted long.

The Queen grievously offended General Prim, who, it is said, saw in a mirror Isabel putting her tongue out at him as he was leaving an audience. It is not easy to blame the Queen for disliking so harsh and touchy a man as Prim, but she made a bitter enemy who was not slow to conspire against her. His chance came when the *primeros sargentos* of the Regiment of Artillery in Madrid mutinied for the purely military grievance that in their regiment alone promotion from the ranks to a commission was debarred because, so they thought, of the haughty attitude of their officers. Some of these they shot, and then marched to attack the Ministry of the Interior with cannon (22 June 1866). This dangerous situation was averted by the prompt action of several generals, including Narváez who was badly wounded. All told 800 lives were lost. Sixty-six executions were carried out as reprisals and the public, adequately coached by Prim (who was in France) and others, were horrified at such severity. Even O'Donnell, who was Prime Minister at the time, declared privately that the blood would mount to the Queen's chamber and drown her. After this he resigned and was succeeded by Narváez.

The two generals on whom Isabel depended so much for support for her tottering throne died within six months of each other (1867–68). The Queen was obliged to turn to González Bravo to save the situation by energetic methods: he was certainly not wanting in courage and was determined to play the dictator in civilian clothes quite as well as any splendidly uniformed dictator. One of his first actions was to banish all the leaders of the Liberal Union, mainly generals, amongst whom was the erstwhile favourite Serrano. On their way to exile they passed through Cádiz, that cradle of revolutions, where they deliberated with a rebellious *junta* and also obtained the support of Admiral Topete, who commanded the Atlantic squadron, which was feeling aggrieved because the navy estimates had recently been drastically reduced.

Abdication of Queen Isabel

The credit for making a *pronunciamiento* was left to the navy. Topete's four frigates with Prim, Sagasta and other conspirators aboard bombarded in a mild fashion the shore batteries at Cádiz, and soon the city was taken with scarcely any opposition (18 September 1868). A manifesto entitled *España con Honor* was then drawn up, but its aims were necessarily vague because the views of the various conspirators were widely divergent. The only point on which they were agreed was that the scandals of the Queen's private life must cease: 'The person charged with the maintenance of the Constitution should not be its irreconcilable enemy. The considerations which decided the most important matters should be such as could be named before mothers, wives and daughters.'

Isabel was taking the waters at Zarauz on the Biscay coast and at first felt she could rely on the energetic González Bravo to deal with the situation. But *pronunciamientos* were being made in other parts of Spain and the government troops were defeated by the rebels at the bridge of Alcolea on the route from Cádiz to Madrid (29 September 1868). The capital too issued its *pronunciamientos* that very day and Isabel wisely chose to cross into France, remarking as she left: 'I thought I had struck deeper roots in this land.'

The nation had almost united in getting rid of Isabel, but once this had been achieved no one knew what to do next. The Spaniard is such an individualist that he can unite only in destruction; any constructive effort finds the nation torn by dissension. The Madrid mob was rejoicing over the 'final downfall of the spurious Bourbon race'; the Carlists were preparing for another effort and attracted many Conservative supporters, the Duc de Montpensier hurried back from Portugal where he had been exiled by González Bravo, but the eager offer of his services was rejected. A Republican party was in existence and included, not surprisingly, Emilio Castelar, but the majority of the generals and indeed of the nation favoured a monarchy, but where was a monarch to be found? 'Finding a democratic king in Europe', remarked Prim, 'is like looking for an atheist in Heaven.'

The search lasted for over two years. Espartero might have become king, for petitions flooded his humble home of retirement at Logroño begging him to come and save the nation, but whether from loyalty to the Bourbons or from the lethargy of old age he consistently refused. Prussia proposed Prince Leopold of Hohenzollern; France haughtily opposed this suggestion and was promptly invaded. By the autumn of 1870 there was still no king and the nation was in a chaos of wrangling. Some decision was necessary and eventually the crown was offered to the sons of King Victor Emmanuel of Italy. The second son, Amadeo, accepted it and the *Cortes* ratified the acceptance by the somewhat slender majority of 191 votes to 120, the largest minority group being the Republicans with 63 votes.

The experiment of inviting a foreigner to be King of Spain was unlikely to succeed, but the sole chance of success was eliminated by the assassination of General Prim, Amadeo's chief supporter. On 27 December 1870, three days before Amadeo landed at Cartagena, Prim's carriage was ambushed in the narrow *Calle del Turco* in Madrid as he was returning from the *Cortes* late on a snowy evening. The murderers were never discovered, but public opinion readily credited this brutal deed to the scheming Duc de Montpensier. Amadeo was left with nothing but his good intentions with which to combat the indifference and hostility all around him. The Madrid nobility deliberately snubbed him, while the Carlists in the north rallied enthusiastically to the banner of the hotheaded grandson of the original pretender. They were easily defeated by government forces, but the treaty signed at Amoravieta (24 May 1872) was so lenient that the Carlists interpreted it as weakness and bided their time for a further opportunity for revolt. The country indeed would have been inclined generally to accept Don Carlos, who by now had the support of the exiled Queen Isabel and had some legitimate claim to the throne. Unfortunately, Zorrilla, the Prime Minister, attempting to bolster Amadeo's position, had so drastically rigged the elections of September 1872 that only seven of his opponents were returned to the *Cortes*. Such a travesty of democracy showed the Carlists plainly that their cause could prevail only by force.

On the night of 18 July 1872 Amadeo and his wife narrowly escaped assassination in the streets of Madrid, and though his courage in the face of danger won some temporary popularity he realised that his position was untenable. In February 1873 he found an excuse for laying down his dangerous office; Zorrilla's extreme Liberal government dissolved the Regiment of Artillery after its haughty officers had refused to accept the appointment of General Hidalgo as Captain-General of the Basque provinces. This action by Zorrilla was directly against the advice of the King who after loyally fulfilling his constitutional obligation of signing the decree promptly vacated his throne and left Spain on February 12 observing that Spain's misfortunes were created by Spaniards.

Republican interlude

The large majority of Liberal extremists in the *Cortes* quickly proclaimed a Republic and for a while this sudden change of Constitution seemed to have been effected peacefully. But violence was not slow to appear, because the ignorant proletariat was an easy prey for political firebrands who advocated the abolition of all taxes as the first duty of a Republic. The whole of Andalusia was given over to outbreaks of mob violence, while at Cartagena mutineers manned the naval vessels and cruised up and down the coast, reinforcing their revolutionary speeches with cannon fire. Their erratic movements were discreetly followed by ships of the Royal Navy to ensure that no harm came to British persons or property in these escapades.

The Republicans in power at Madrid dreaded using generals to suppress this outburst of democratic enthusiasm because the higher ranks of the army were solidly monarchist. But military repression was a necessity and General Pavía was despatched to Andalusia with about 1,000 troops in two trains. With great ingenuity he seized Córdoba, Seville and Granada. There still remained the two most important centres of resistance, Málaga and Cartagena where the clamour for *Cantonalismo* or independent districts on the Swiss model, was loudest. Pavía was about to move against these towns when orders from Madrid stopped him; it was the Republicans who feared that a successful general might easily set up a military dictatorship throughout Spain in its weakened state. This halt only caused a renewal of violence and the President of the Republic, Salmerón, was replaced by Emilio Castelar, the fourth president in seven months. This doctrinaire *posibilista*, who had renounced bloodshed and militarism as political expedients, was now obliged to order the continuance of the campaign in Andalusia which was successfully accomplished, though Cartagena was recaptured only after a full-scale siege and a heavy bombardment (13 January 1874).

In the north the Carlists had once again taken the field and Castelar set about the task of reforming the army in order to fight this new threat. Castelar acted with energy and wisdom, and was ready to swallow his pride to create an efficient force, even restoring the aristocratic and mutinous artillery officers to their commissions so that this technical corps could take the field as a fighting force. To add support to his tottering government he sought to re-establish diplomatic relations with other countries and even negotiated a Concordat with the Vatican. Such measures seemed more consistent with a Conservative than with an avowed Liberal extremist, and they brought down the wrath of the Republicans on his head.

Just as Castelar was facing defeat in the *Cortes*, General Pavía, now

Captain-General of Castile and as muddled a thinker as he was an able commander, decided to intervene on the President's behalf. Late at night he surrounded the *Cortes* with troops and ordered the Deputies out. These noisily protested that they would die at their posts, but hastily slipped out by side doors after a few shots had been fired. Pavía's success was disappointing because the coalition he hoped for did not materialise; Castelar refused to join and so did the leader of the Alfonsist party, Cánovas del Castillo. Everyone was certain that the Republic could not last, but none felt that this was the right moment for a coup; a government was formed with Serrano as President of the Republic. Its main task was to fight the Carlists in the north, where many important towns had been seized and Bilbao itself was besieged. The government troops blundered badly, and at one stage a Carlist force reached Cuenca, no more than sixty-five miles from Madrid. But the Catalan Carlists were murderous, undisciplined ruffians, quite unable to exploit military success except for purposes of looting, and the Basque Carlists, though well organised in small groups, were never more than *guerrilleros*, and their command was torn by internal dissensions. The government forces, incompetent as they were, managed to relieve Bilbao and contain the rebels north of the Ebro.

Restoration of the Bourbons

The Alfonsists were waiting for a final victory over the Carlists, but this never came. In December Alfonso, Queen Isabel's son, then a cadet at Sandhurst, issued a carefully worded manifesto declaring: 'I shall always be a good Spaniard, a good Catholic like my ancestors and like the men of my own day, a good Liberal.' His civilian supporters favoured waiting a little longer, but the Army saw a chance for regaining political power by a restoration of the Bourbons, and on 24 December 1874 General Martínez Campos, the pacifier of rebellious Cartagena, proclaimed Alfonso XII at Murviedro (the Saguntum of the siege) and the more cautious civilians were forced by the sudden defection of the Captain-General of Castile, General Primo de Rivera, who having expressed surprise and horror at the action of Martínez Campos, whose loyalty he had guaranteed, promptly declared in favour of Alfonso.

The King reached Barcelona on 9 January 1875 and was rapturously welcomed both in Catalonia and Valencia. Madrid was more reserved, but the fact that government funds had risen in price by four per cent indicated that the world believed that the new regime would bring increased stability. A policy of reconciliation for all was immediately initiated, even the Carlists were given an offer of peace which they refused in the name of the precious *fueros* of the northern provinces. The war dragged on until the end of February 1876 when Primo de Rivera captured the Carlist stronghold of Estella and Martínez Campos drove Don Carlos across the frontier into France.

Meanwhile the political scene had been skilfully handled by Cánovas del Castillo, a scholar and thinker, who used unscrupulous means to achieve peaceful ends. He produced yet another Constitution, which allowed a degree of religious toleration and maintained a fiction of democratic elections, but unlike previous Constitutions it gave the government power to suspend constitutional guarantees without reference to the *Cortes*. Cánovas realised that stable government could only be achieved by the cooperation of the two main parties, and this he contrived by allowing the Conservatives and Liberals alternately to gain a victory in the elections, which were all rigged by the *Ministerio de Gobernación* (Ministry of the Interior). By this system the deputies were in reality the representatives of local cliques in the provinces, and gave rise to the power of local bosses to whom was given the Indian name of *cacique*. The dominance of local dictators has been a problem in Spain ever since.

Strangely enough this corrupt method of government gave Spain a period of internal peace for over twenty years, and with the absence of violent revolts the disastrous financial situation was gradually remedied.

Alfonso married in 1878 the second daughter of the Duc de Montpensier, Queen Mercedes, who had been born and brought up in Spain, and the marriage was one of affection and not of policy. Sad to say the Queen, not yet nineteen, died of fever in Madrid on 27 June, shortly after the end of the marriage festivities. Alfonso was heartbroken and never seemed to take an interest in life for the rest of his reign, though he did his duty as king nobly enough. He married again in obedience to the need for an heir, but the wedding to María Cristina of Austria (29 November 1879) was overshadowed by the gloom cast by disastrous floods in Murcia. The King himself was a victim of tuberculosis; his health gradually failed and his popularity waned too. His illness was kept secret from the nation and it came as a surprise when on 28 November 1885 he died at the age of twenty-eight. Spanish funds promptly dropped thirteen points and noblemen at the court who had known of the King's illness are said to have profited greatly by an early sale and subsequent repurchase. The curse of Cánovas's pacific system was that it perpetuated corruption in all forms.

Alfonso had no male heir, only two daughters, but at the time of his death the Queen was pregnant and the leaders of all parties were summoned to the Pardo Palace where they agreed to a *Tregua de Dios* (a Truce of God) pending the birth of the child. Should this child prove to be a third daughter, all hell would again be let loose in Spain, but in the meantime the nation behaved with the utmost decorum partly out of curiosity. There is nothing that appeals to the Spaniard more than some speculative event on which he can bet. After six months of suspense a son was born on 17 May 1886 and was proclaimed King Alfonso XIII, to the satisfaction of almost everybody except the Carlists.

That this dangerous period passed off reasonably quietly was due in large part of the tact and good sense of the Queen Mother, María Cristina, who as Regent won universal respect—a difficult accomplishment for a foreigner in Spain. She exercised her prerogative of mercy towards would-be rebels and thus made friends of many declared enemies of the monarchy.

Meanwhile the tacit understanding that Conservatives and Liberals should have alternate periods in power continued to work harmoniously, and there was little difference between the policies of the respective leaders, Cánovas and Sagasta. So perfect was the system of rigging elections that in 1890 Sagasta was able to introduce universal suffrage for men over twenty-four; Cánovas opposed this step, but confidently predicted that it would make no difference to the results of future elections. His confidence in the system was based on previous experience; in 1886, for example, some newspapers actually carried the results of the elections before polling took place. Sure enough when Cánovas was called on to form a government later in 1890 universal suffrage duly gave him a majority of 289 seats to 70 for the Liberals, with a consolation award of 30 to keep the Republicans quiet.

Such blatant trickery had a bad effect on public life in general and there was a scandal of the first magnitude when Cánovas had to admit that the neatly balanced budgets of the past fifteen years in fact concealed an average yearly deficit of £2,500,000. Spain was bankrupt and no politician could be found to accept the post of finance minister. The only solution was to force the whole cabinet to take responsibility for the budget. The electorate of Madrid was becoming too educated and too politically conscious to bear such chicanery much longer, and at the next elections early in 1893 the Madrid polls were so closely watched by the Republicans that they captured six out of the eight seats. This so alarmed the government that the impending municipal elections were postponed until new lists could be drawn up of voters whose support could be relied upon.

Not only in Madrid was there disaffection at the lack of effective government by so corrupt a regime. In the south the grinding poverty of the peasants on the *latifundios* (large estates belonging to absentee landlords) gave rise to sporadic outbursts of violence. The situation had been made worse by the fall in the exports of Spanish wine, which had greatly prospered when the French vineyards had suffered from mildew in the early 1880s. Full advantage of the situation had, however, not been taken; instead of marketing truly Spanish wines which could have established a permanent place in the world's cellars, the Spanish merchants were content to sell their products under counterfeit French names. When the French vineyards were replanted with American vines immune to the mildew disease, the spurious Spanish wines quickly became unsaleable.

Discontent was also widespread in Catalonia, where the separatist movement had been much strengthened during the lawless period of the Republic, and where poverty also provided ready hearers for Anarchist and Communist doctrines. In February 1892 the first bomb outrage occurred in Barcelona, which quickly gained an evil reputation for this kind of violence. In April of the same year a Catalan plot was discovered whereby the Congress of the *Cortes* was to be blown up, and the Government in alarm reacted strongly. Ruthless methods were employed to suppress the activities of agitators in Barcelona; suspects were arrested and held without trial and dark stories were told of torturing prisoners in the gaol at Montjuich. It was in revenge for the brutal treatment of Catalan agitators that an Italian anarchist assassinated Cánovas del Castillo when on holiday at the little seaside resort of Santa Agueda in the Basque Provinces on 8 August 1897.

War with the United States

At the time of his death a grave situation was threatening Spain, namely war with the United States over Cuba, Spain's last remaining colony in the New World apart from the Philippines, where trouble was also brewing. Cuba had been a hotbed of revolt for many years because the negro and half-caste population was treated as a dumping ground for Catalan exports and as cheap labour for sugar production. Treatment of the rebels by the Spanish garrisons of half-starved, fever-ridden troops had been exceptionally brutal. Frequent protests to Spain had been made by the United States Government, which was also fearful lest complete repression by the Spaniards would lead to the exclusion of American business interests in Cuba. Parties of United States filibusters were wont secretly to help the Cuban rebels, and when occasionally they were captured by Spanish forces they were roughly handled. Apologies for such incidents were made from time to time by Spain, and Sagasta had made the gesture of abolishing slavery in Cuba in 1886, but the general policy of successive Spanish governments had been uncompromising, with insistence on the unconditional surrender of the rebels before any reforms could be discussed. Cánovas, though by nature a man of peace, seemed aware of the inevitability of war with the United States and was even preparing for it when he was murdered.

Relations with the United States had been worsened by the rigorous campaign in Cuba carried out by General Weyler, who in 1896, using the most brutal methods, all but reduced the rebels to subservience. The final incident, which brought a declaration of war, was the blowing up of the U.S. warship, *Maine*, in Havana harbour (15 February 1898); 266 members of her crew perished in this disaster. The warship had been sent to Havana to watch over the lives and interests of United States citizens in Cuba. The cause of the explosion was declared by the American Consul to be an underwater mine; this the Spanish authorities strenuously denied and offered to hold a joint inquiry. This offer was refused and two national courts of inquiry found two totally different verdicts. The American commission insisted that the explosion came from outside, while the Spaniards were equally certain that the disaster was due to a flash reaching the *Maine's* powder magazine. The United States Congress declared war on 20 April 1898, calling on the Spanish to evacuate the island of Cuba.

Hostilities lasted only four months. The Spanish Pacific squadron guarding the Philippines was completely destroyed in Manila Bay (1 May 1898) by Admiral Dewey's ships, in which the total casualties were seven men wounded. A similar fate befell the Spanish squadron under Admiral Cervera, who had sailed to Cuba from the Cape Verde

The U.S. Warship Maine *after the hull had been raised in Havana harbour*

Islands on 27 April. Blockaded in Santiago harbour he was forced to sail out to give battle because American land forces were threatening the town. Running the gauntlet of the American fleets, all Cervera's ships were destroyed or captured, whereas American casualties amounted to only one man. Santiago surrendered a fortnight later and Spain, seeing that the situation was hopeless, sued for peace through the mediation of France. By the Treaty of Paris, ratified on 10 December 1898, Cuba and Puerto Rico became independent under American protection, while the United States acquired the Philippines for the sum of £4,800,000.

Though the war left Spain with a crippling debt, the loss of the last of her colonial empire was something of a relief, for the drain on money and men in seeking to pacify Cuba in the past fifty years had been excessive. The real blow was to Spanish pride, and the shock of such a humiliating defeat roused the educated element of the nation to clamour for a revival, if not of Spain's material prosperity, at least of her intellectual vigour. The *Generación de 98* was the name applied to a group of young intellectuals who sought to achieve this renaissance, and to their ability and their efforts is due the remarkable florescence of Spanish poetry and prose in the first half of the twentieth century.

In 1902 Alfonso XIII reached the age of sixteen, the age at which Spanish monarchs are by law considered fit to rule by themselves, and he assumed the reins of government from his mother. It was a difficult time in which to undertake such grave responsibilities. Violence still smouldered in the south, and Catalonia, having lost its protected markets in Cuba, was more than ever anxious to attain independence. The well-tried system of rotation of political parties was breaking down. Sagasta died in 1903 and Maura, a Conservative Prime Minister with greater vision or more confidence than his predecessors, did not deign to rig the elections in that year; his party at once lost forty seats. The King became alarmed and tended to turn more to the Army for political control. Cánovas and Sagasta had both sought to check the power of the Army to interfere in politics, but with no real success. The Army had too many high-ranking officers (in an expedition to North Africa in 1893 a force of 25,000 men had been commanded by twenty-nine generals) and these officers sought to find an outlet for their limited authority in dictating the political structure of the country.

They sought also to make the Army a privileged caste. For years they had been demanding that any civilian offending against the Army should be tried by court martial, but their demands had so far been resisted. When two Barcelona newspapers in 1906 published some cartoons offensive to the Army, some officers took the law into their own hands and broke into the newspaper offices, smashing the equipment. Far from punishing the officers concerned, the Government, a Liberal one under Moret, passed the *Ley de Jurisdicciones* giving the Army the right it desired to try civilian offenders in its own courts (20 March 1907).

Attempted assassination of Alfonso XIII on his wedding day, May 1906

Relations between Castile and Catalonia were further embittered by this move. Already in May 1906 a Catalan anarchist had attempted to kill the King and his English Queen, Victoria Eugenie, by hurling a bomb under their carriage on their wedding day. In July 1909 serious riots broke out in Barcelona as a protest against a futile and hopelessly mismanaged expedition in Morocco. A general strike was proclaimed in the city and the mob sacked and burned some twenty churches and thirty-four convents in a fury of anticlericalism. Order was restored only after many lives had been lost during this *Semana Trágica*, but the execution (13 October 1909) of the supposed ringleader, Francisco Ferrer, a railway clerk, caused such widespread protests throughout Europe that the King made a scapegoat of Maura, the Prime Minister, dismissing him from office.

The Great War

The outbreak of the Great War found Spain divided in its sympathies; the higher aristocracy on the whole favoured Germany because the defeat of the allies would lessen the influence of English liberal ideas and

Alfonso XIII

perhaps return Gibraltar to Spain. The Liberals naturally supported the allies, as did the Socialists, though somewhat grudgingly because they regarded the war as a clash of capitalist interests. Spain therefore declared herself neutral. Neutrality proved profitable since the sale of minerals and agricultural produce to the belligerents enriched the landowners, while the industrialists were able to capture some of the Latin-American markets from the belligerents, whose export trade had been either stopped or reduced by the war. The national debt accumulated after the Cuban disaster was liquidated and Spain's gold reserves rose from £23 million to £89 million.

Prosperity brought its difficulties. Prices in Spain rose quickly and wages failed to keep pace. The spread of an organised labour movement had been rapid and in March 1917 its leaders were strong enough to stage a nationwide general strike. The resulting disorders were suppressed by the Civil Guard and the Army, which oddly enough had formed a kind of officers' trade union of its own, *Juntas de Defensa*. The aims of these committees were not clearly defined, but in the main they demanded not only army reforms, but also more political power for the Army. They also had in mind the repression of the continuing demand for Catalan independence, which had grown more insistent when Europe had been split into so many segments after the Armistice of 1918. Attempts by various governments to impose order in Catalonia all failed. The Army was driven to a pitch of desperation by this failure and still more by a military disaster in North Africa in 1921, when a Spanish force opposing the Riffs was defeated, losing 15,000 men and large quantities of equipment. While the Army was enraged and hypersensitive at this defeat, the civilian population lost faith in both the regime and the Army, and there were further serious civil disturbances in 1923 when among others the Cardinal Archbishop of Zaragoza was assassinated.

Military dictatorship

The Army demanded stern measures to repress these outrages and in September 1923 the garrison of Barcelona revolted, its example being followed by others throughout the country. On 13 September a military government was formed under the leadership of the Captain-General of Barcelona, Miguel Primo de Rivera, nephew of the turncoat who had ushered in the Bourbon restoration of 1875. He was an aristocratic Andalusian soldier with no very clear ideas of policy beyond a desire to end violent disturbances and a profound distrust of politicians. These had protested to the King about the new dictatorship, reminding him of the oath he had sworn to observe the Constitution. The King dismissed them without an answer and thus threw in his lot with a regime which had no basis of legality, only force. It was the preoccupation of both King and Dictator to find some vestige of legality for their government that led to the downfall of both.

Primo de Rivera's first acts were not only successful, but beneficial. Civil agitation was suppressed by force and Catalan independence was curtly forbidden. The rigid censorship of the press and the curtailment of free speech, though deplorable in themselves, brought some order and discipline to a country where heated and fruitless argument is a national disease. The Dictator also gained considerable personal popularity by joining with the French against the Riffs, who were quickly defeated after Rivera had himself taken command of the Spanish–Moroccan army in October 1925. The whole area was quickly pacified, but Spain was forced to take second place to France in the affairs of the international city of Tangiers and withdrew in a huff from the League of Nations in September 1926.

With the nation controlled and the Army's prestige restored, Primo de Rivera was able to turn his attention to the vexed question of labour relations. Perhaps his basic intention was to try to strengthen the Socialists, who were mostly Castilians with a sense of discipline, against the Anarchists, who were mainly Catalan separatists. To further this end a series of *Comités Paritarios* were established, with five representatives of the employers and five of labour on each. Eventually these committees were to be expanded into a national organisation which would cover every trade and industry. These measures achieved a modest success, and for a few brief months Spain enjoyed a period of economic expansion which saw the building of new roads and railways and some much-needed modernisation.

The pattern of these social measures had been copied from Mussolini's Italy, with whom Spain signed a pact of friendship in 1926, but Spain was not Fascist in outlook nor could the aristocratic Primo de Rivera bring himself to ape the bombastic buffoonery of Mussolini. Taking his cue from King Alfonso he was still gravely worried about the lack of legality of his government, a scruple which never bothered his Italian counterpart. In fact his rule was no less illegal than the constitutional government with elections that bore no relation to the will of the people, but the outward form was lacking, and in 1926 Primo de Rivera strove to create some pretence of democracy by forming a new party called called the *Unión Patriótica*. In September 1927 he instituted an Assembly of nominees appointed by provincial governors, civil servants, commercial and agricultural bodies and labour organisations. This Assembly, which had no legislative powers, was to prepare a new Constitution to be approved by plebiscite, with subsequent elections in 1931.

This effort at legalisation hoodwinked nobody. The Army began to be sulky on the grounds that the Dictator was wooing civilians to make his regime appear democratic; intellectuals loathed the rigid censorship and suppression of many faculties in the universities, and the nobility disliked seeing their power and privileges being side-stepped. Several conspiracies were formed against Primo de Rivera, often with the connivance of the King, but the most extensive was that of *Noche de San Juan* in 1926, when Count Romanones led a motley collection of plotters, civilian and military. The plot was easily uncovered and was dealt with by Primo de Rivera in a clever way which made the conspirators appear ridiculous. They were each fined sums according to their means, Count Romanones 500,000 pesetas, the veteran General Weyler 100,000, Dr Marañón, a celebrated surgeon and historian, 100,000, Benlliure y Tuero, a journalist, 2,500, Amalio Quilez, an anarchist, 1,000. At least Primo de Rivera was not bloodthirsty, but this facetious form of punishment did not make his enemies love him any the more.

By 1929 the slump in world trade was bringing economic problems to add to the Dictator's other difficulties, and now the Army definitely deserted him. Primo de Rivera made one last appeal to the Captains-General and naval commanders in January 1930, after his finance minister, Calvo Sotelo, had resigned. His appeal was unanswered, and in February he too resigned and retired to Paris, where he died a month later. He had been perhaps one of the most benevolent dictators ever to have ruled, and one who least deserved so much unpopularity.

The King now found it impossible to recreate the Constitution which he had so precipitately abandoned in accepting the Dictatorship in 1923. He had even lost the support of the nobility, who, realising that a republic was an inevitability, wanted to create one where their interests would be of prime importance. After several abortive attempts to form governments the King withdrew to Paris on 14 April 1931 without formally renouncing the throne. This was two days after municipal elections had been held throughout Spain and, though the results were never published, all Captains-General had been informed that the principal cities were solidly republican.

The Republic established

The Republic was proclaimed amid great rejoicing, and the people were determined that no bloodshed should mar so joyful an event. The remaining members of the royal family (Alfonso had departed alone in a destroyer from Cartagena) were bowed out of Spain with a guard of young socialists. This passion for sobriety, good behaviour and social improvement was due mainly to the doctrines preached by the *Generación de 98*, whose ageing apostles, Ortego y Gasset, Unamuno and others now lent their support to the Republic. Unfortunately the

*José Antonio Primo
de Rivera*

new freedom for debate left Spain open to every form of oratory, and though elections for the *Cortes* were held in June, agreement on a Constitution was not reached until 9 December, by which time the forces of reaction in Spain, both oligarchical and anarchist, were in full flood. A series of jubilant strikes greeted the strong socialist element in the *Cortes*, while the abandonment of an established religion gave rise to wild demonstrations of anticlericalism, in which about a sixth of the convents and religious schools in Madrid were sacked and burned. Meanwhile the nobility and the Church were active in spreading propaganda which appealed to the mass of women who suddenly found themselves with a vote. The Church was also zealous in fostering the interests of the agricultural community by creating cooperative societies to finance improvements. In this way the oligarchy retained a firm hold on a large section of the nation.

The Government under Alcalá Zamora, in so far as it was able to act with any kind of unanimity, made efforts to introduce reforms. Attempts were made to extend both primary and secondary education in Spain by building new schools and *institutos*, but progress was desperately slow because many parents preferred to have their children earning a little money from odd jobs rather than sitting on the school bench acquiring unremunerative knowledge. Azaña, Minister of War, tackled the thorny problem of the Army, where he found that there were 800 generals and 21,000 officers, a ratio of one officer to six men. This top-heavy officer class was offered voluntary retirement on full pay, and 11,000 of them took advantage of this timidly generous offer. Unfortunately the officers who were thus tempted to return to civilian life on full pay were the unpretentious members of the middle class who had entered the Army to make a living, and who were mainly Liberal in political outlook. The wealthy aristocrats who had become officers for reasons of social prestige, and who were hostile to the Republic, remained in the Army. Azaña's reforms had therefore achieved no financial saving and had made the proportion of anti-Republican officers much greater than before. Out of 10,000 remaining officers it was estimated that only 3,000 were loyal to the government. It was hardly surprising therefore that as early as August 1932 General Sanjurjo felt able to make a *pronunciamiento* in Seville. His rebellion was easily defeated and he was condemned to death, though sentence was not carried out.

The forces of the right realised that the time for revolt was not ripe, but they continued to organise opinion in their favour throughout the country. A new Fascist organisation, the *Falange*, formed by José Antonio Primo de Rivera, son of the late Dictator, found much favour among the student population. In the elections of November 1933 the exertions of right wing propagandists bore fruit now that the women's vote was used for the first time. The swing to the right which involved the suspension of the law to give smallholdings to landless peasants caused serious outbreaks of violence in various parts of the country. Catalonia had been promised independence as a federal state and now saw its chances of gaining its freedom recede. The Catalans therefore acted quickly, and under the leadership of Companys proclaimed their independence, inaugurating their own *Le de Cultivos* for parcelling out land to peasants.

Profiting by the lead given by Catalonia, other northern states began to claim independence, as indeed they were entitled to do under the Republican Constitution of 1931. A real revolt burst out in Oviedo, where the Asturian miners, well armed with dynamite and expert in its use, fought a minor war which was ended only by calling in troops from Morocco. When the outbreak was finally crushed, 1,335 people lay dead and more than 3,000 wounded. Oviedo, the capital of the Asturias, was in ruins. Such slaughter had a sobering effect on Spaniards for a time, but the parties of the Right were unable to form satisfactory governments and political circles were split by disputes over revising the Constitution. The president, Alcalá Zamora, therefore exercised his right to dissolve the *Cortes* for the second time during his term of office and fresh elections were held in February 1936. The stage was set for a real battle between the Extreme Right and the loosely knit Popular Front which comprised republicans, socialists, trade unionists, anarchists and communists, and whose policies lacked coherence though its members were determined on action. The moderate parties of the centre had faded into insignificance. The total figures of the poll revealed a narrow division of opinion, 48·2 per cent for the Popular Front and 46·2 per cent for the Right, but the actual electoral contests gave a substantial majority to the Popular Front. All the elements of disintegration in Spain at once sprang into life. Companys again proclaimed himself President of the Independent Catalan *Generalitat*. Alcalá Zamora was removed from the presidency of the Republic, being replaced by the strong man of action, Azaña, who attempted to govern from the presidential office like an American president. His efforts at control were completely ineffectual and Spain gave itself up to an orgy of murder and arson. During the first four months of Popular Front government there were, so the *Cortes* were told, 269 murders, 249 cases of arson (mostly churches, but also newspaper offices and political clubs), 113 general strikes and 228 partial stoppages. In the south too peasants were anticipating agrarian reforms by seizing land from the great estates for their own use. In some instances this newly acquired property was quickly sold, and after an agreeable spree the peasants were as landless and poverty-stricken as before.

The Civil War

Violence was by no means confined to left wing sympathisers, for the *Falange* was active in using Fascist methods in attempting to spread its propaganda. The generals were known to be plotting a revolt and the Government attempted to break the conspiracy by sending General Franco, one of its leaders, as Captain-General of the Canary Islands. Far from making matters harder for the conspirators, this move actually aided their plans since they were able to organise their rising free from Government surveillance. Despite further Government attempts to break up the conspiracy, including the imprisonment of José Antonio

Primo de Rivera in Alicante, the date for rebellion was finally fixed for 18 July 1936. On that day General Franco flew to Tetuan in Morocco where he broadcast to the nation declaring 'Spain has saved herself. You can be proud to be Spaniards.' It was the classic military *pronunciamiento*.

The rebel plan was that the military garrisons in each of the large cities should rise and proclaim martial law. The various garrisons would then establish communications with one another so that within a few days the whole country would be in the grip of military government. The rebels counted on a brief campaign, though they had doubts about their chances of success in Madrid. Their plan therefore included a drive on the capital by General Mola from the north, while other attacks were to be mounted from the west, aided by the sympathy shown by Portugal to the insurgents. But they had not reckoned on the strength of the popular reaction to a rebellion which had the avowed intent of restoring repressive government in one form or another. In Madrid the workers were joined by the Civil Guard and units of the Air Force, and the military rising was suppressed after some bloody fighting. Forty-five miles to the south-west the garrison in Toledo was soon besieged in the ancient four square fortress, the *Alcázar*, where with typical Spanish obstinacy it held out under Colonel José Moscardo, despite terrible privations until relieved ninety days later. Visitors to Toledo are now told by the official guides how the Reds fired indiscriminately on women and children taking refuge in the *Alcázar*, but the Reds were no other than the ordinary citizens of Toledo fighting to retain a form of democratic government which they believed would eventually work in Spain despite its manifold initial failures.

The Toledo incident had a profound effect on the course of the war. The relief of the *Alcázar*, which the rebels felt bound to undertake, diverted troops from the assault on Madrid, and the Republicans were able to strengthen the defences of the capital which was not taken until the final surrender. But for Toledo Madrid might have fallen quickly despite the vigour and enthusiasm of its unarmed defenders, and the continuance of the war by the Republican Government would have been virtually impossible. As it was, the Republican Government had to move in November 1936 to Valencia, but by then its front was largely stabilised, comprising Catalonia, New Castile, La Mancha and Eastern Andalusia. Vizcaya and Guipúzcoa in the Basque provinces were also loyal to the Republic, but being cut off from their fellow Republicans they were overrun in June 1937 in a campaign in which

Guernica by Picasso,
on extended loan to the museum of Modern Art, New York, from the artist

Guernica, the historic centre of Basque government, was wantonly destroyed by German aircraft.

The rebels had been negotiating with Mussolini and Hitler for armed aid even before the rising had been made, and Italian troops under General Bergonzoli were quickly in the field in support of Franco's forces. The Germans were rather more cautious in lending assistance, but they found Spain a useful testing ground for various forms of aerial attack. The Republicans on the other hand were seriously hampered from the start by a grave shortage of arms and equipment. England and France were both pursuing a policy of non-intervention, and the only source of supply was Soviet Russia. To pay for supplies Spain's entire gold reserve, amounting to 51 metric tons, was transferred to Russia, but it is doubtful whether the Republicans ever received their money's worth in return. Stalin was willing to grant enough aid to maintain the Republicans on the defensive, but he seemed to have little desire to see them win the war. Russian assistance naturally led to a great increase of members of the Communist party, which had hitherto been insignificant in Spain, and some of the more distasteful adjuncts of Stalinism made their appearance in Republican Spain, such as political commissars with army units and the organisation of secret police *chekas*. Hence Franco was able to enlist much sympathy among Conservative opinion in all countries by dubbing his opponents with the opprobrious name of Reds; his own insurgents acquired the

Bomb damage in Guernica

more respectable title of Nationalists. Even many liberal thinkers in free democratic countries saw the struggle in Spain as a choice between the two evils of Fascism and Communism, and were inclined to feel that Franco's Fascism was the lesser evil.

In October 1937 the Republican Government moved from Valencia to Barcelona, where the Catalan Republic had its *Generalitat*. The presence of two governments in one city caused certain political tensions which did the Republican cause no good and presented a splendid target for aerial attack of which the Germans and Italians took full advantage. Franco's forces were also enabled to break through the centre and reach the Mediterranean at Castellón de la Plana (16 June 1938), splitting the Republic in two. By this time France had become alarmed at the success of her bellicose neighbours Germany and Italy in Spain, and tardily sought to bolster the Republican Government by allowing the transport of arms through (but not from) France. The Republicans were then able to mount almost their only large-scale offensive of the war, crossing the Ebro in force just below its junction with the Segre. They established a bridgehead of some twenty miles and killed or captured large numbers of the enemy, of whom many were Italians and Moors. This unexpected attack drew off Franco's forces from the assault on Valencia, but it only delayed the inevitable end of the war. By 15 November the Republicans could no longer hold their bridgehead west of the Ebro: the French had once again closed the frontier and they were unable to replace losses in men and munitions. In January 1939 an all out offensive, conducted mainly by Italian troops under Gambara, entered Barcelona. Vast hordes of refugees threaded their way to the French frontier and heartrending scenes took place, involving tragic loss of life and much human suffering.

The Republican Government escaped to France after the fall of Barcelona, but returned to Spain by way of Valencia to decide whether or how the war could be carried on. The Communists were determined to continue the fight and the Prime Minister, Dr Negrín, decided that the situation was not entirely hopeless. The Republic still had some 800,000 men under arms and its rule extended in a somewhat tenuous fashion over ten provinces containing 8 million inhabitants. The forces of disintegration, however, were strong in Madrid among the Republican military leaders: it was General Mola's prophecy of a 'fifth column within the city' come true. Not that the leaders were intentionally traitorous, but they infected others with their despair. General Miaja, Colonel Casado and Señor Besteiro formed a *Junta de Defensa*, claiming arrogantly that they were respected by General Franco and could obtain honourable terms of surrender. In fact the terms of surrender they set out were far more demanding than those which had been haughtily rejected by Franco when previously suggested by the Republican Government through British and French diplomatic channels.

The Communists were furious at the suggestion of surrender and on 5 March 1939 Communist troops* attacked Republican forces loyal to the *Junta de Defensa*. A week of fierce internecine fighting followed, during which the Communists, though they gave a good account of themselves, were defeated because they were simultaneously assaulted by forces of the *Junta* and of Franco, whose aircraft bombed their positions at Casa de Campo on the outskirts of Madrid. When the fighting ended, there were reprisals carried out by the *Junta*, which executed two Communist leaders and filled the prisons with the smaller fry.

Dr Negrín in despair had left for France and the *Junta* confidently went to parley at General Franco's headquarters at Burgos. They were surprised and shocked to find that the only terms of surrender possible were unconditional.

Meanwhile Republican soldiers were deserting to the Nationalists, who at this time received them with a kindness in marked contrast with

---

* The Republican army was organised into groups of Militia according to their party or trade union allegiance.

ABOVE *Shelter from the bombs in a Madrid subway*

BELOW *Spanish refugees crossing into France*

savage treatment later. By 29 March the Republican armies were in full process of disbandment, the roads choked with lorries and soldiers on foot homeward bound. Large numbers tried to leave Spain, congregating at Alicante, where 17,000 were rounded up by General Gambara's Italian division and placed in a concentration camp under inhuman conditions. On 1 April 1939 the Nationalists formally declared the war at an end, and the Republic, which had come into being amid such enthusiasm for sobriety, reason and education, ceased its existence after a welter of blood and destruction in which some 1,800,000 people perished.

This was by no means the finish of the bloodshed, for the Nationalists were vindictive to a degree. Bestial atrocities had been committed during the war by both sides and can only be attributed to the fundamentally cruel and savage nature of the Spanish character. Among the senseless executions on the Nationalist side had been the shooting at Granada in 1936 of the Andalusian poet and playwright, García Lorca. The Republicans for their part had shot in the prison at Alicante in 1936 the founder of the *Falange*, José Antonio Primo de Rivera, who was now exalted into a saint and whose death was savagely avenged. Before the end of 1939 it is estimated that about 100,000 persons were executed by Nationalist firing squads, and by 1940 some 2 million were in or had passed through prisons or had been shot by firing squads.*

The triumph of General Franco

Nevertheless, fears that Spain would become entirely Fascist or Nazi were not realised. In Italy and Germany it was the party that had imposed its will on the Army, whereas in Spain it was the Army itself that had rebelled and had used the *Falange* as an institution with similar aims. Franco had early shown that he would brook no dictation or insolence from the *Falange*, for during the civil war he had ordered the arrest and execution of its leader, Hedilla, for insubordination. Though he was saved from death by German intervention, the *Falange* has had to tread warily ever since. Its insignia of the sheaf of arrows is to be seen at the entrance to most towns, but its political influence has dwindled greatly.

The outbreak of the European war within six months of the ending of the Civil War was a source of difficulty and embarrassment to Franco. He desperately needed credit and supplies of all kinds to help rebuild

* A. V. Phillips, *Spain under Franco,* London 1940.

Hitler and Franco in Hendaye

the stricken country, and being under the greatest obligation to Germany he was always under the threat of seeing exhausted Spain drawn into the conflict. The danger was increased when in 1940 France fell and Franco's other creditor, Italy, entered the war to gather the pickings. Spain's neutrality then turned to non-belligerency, but with the Germans on the Pyrenean frontier casting longing eyes at Gibraltar, preserving Spain's independence and integrity was a delicate matter. It was now too that the *Falange* party in Spain became more belligerent, and its demands for foreign conquests had to be satisfied with the occupation of the international city of Tangiers, a situation which Great Britain tolerated as being preferable to German or Italian occupation.

Mussolini's incompetent efforts to conquer Greece focused German attention on the Mediterranean. Franco met Hitler at Hendaye, but Hitler found that there is no moving a Spaniard by persuasion or threats and *Führer* and *Caudillo*★ parted with only an official display of cordiality. In January 1941 Germany demanded the right to pass troops through Spain for the capture of Gibraltar, but Franco was no Godoy and the crisis was staved off. Hitler finally gave up hope of coming to terms with such an obstinate ally and on 22 June 1941 turned eastwards to invade Russia. This set Spain free from any immediate fear of invasion by her German friends, and Franco's foreign minister was able to

★ *Caudillo* means chieftain. Franco assumed the title in imitation of *Duce* and *Führer*.

thunder against Communism without deeply offending Great Britain, on whose tolerant interpretation of naval blockade Spain depended for essential supplies. Franco had signed the Anti-Comintern Pact in March 1939 and now felt justified in sending the Blue Division to Russia to assist Germany, who, he assumed, must soon win the war.

When the onslaught faded in the Russian winter, and Japan's precipitate action at Pearl Harbour brought the United States into the war, Spain's non-belligerency began once more to pale into neutrality. Certain concessions to democracy were made in the regime by the creation in March 1943 of a *Cortes* consisting of members appointed by the *Falange*, the trade unions and provincial delegates on a partially elective basis. Its function was, and is, to rubber stamp laws decreed by the *Caudillo*, but ostensibly it seemed that the full rigours of military dictatorship were being relaxed. The bellicose Serrano was replaced as Foreign Minister by General Jordana and late in 1943 the Blue Division was withdrawn from Russia.

As the allies groped their way to victory, the process of outward Liberalisation in Spain gained momentum. In 1945 a partial amnesty was granted to those in prison for political offences which did something by alleviate the bitterness engendered by the ruthless reprisals exacted by the Nationalists. The world in general was not deceived and Franco's regime was criticised at the Potsdam Conference in 1945, and was ostracised generally by a resolution proposed by Mexico and adopted at the San Francisco conference on 20 June. Finally in June 1946 the United Nations decided that member countries should withdraw diplomatic representation from Spain until internal political freedom should be restored in the country.

This move had the effect contrary to what was intended, because this foreign insult drew Spaniards together and Franco found himself ruling a Spain far more united than previously. In fact he was secure enough to be able to make new concessions to liberalism. A workers' charter was established with provision for social services giving some security of employment and various other benefits in return for loyal obedience from labour. A statute for the *Cortes* was also enacted for form's sake and provision was made for holding a national referendum. This was used to approve in March 1947 the law of succession which was Franco's most difficult problem. His proposal was adopted by the country (assuming the voting results were genuine) and Spain was declared 'in accordance with tradition a Kingdom', with Franco the regent in the absence of a king. His successor was to be of the blood royal and was to observe the five fundamental laws of the state, *Fuero de los Españoles*. As a sop to the still aggressive *Falange* it was announced that the royal successor was also to swear fidelity to the principles of the Falangist movement.

Alfonso XIII had died in Rome in 1941 and the claimant to the throne was now his third son, Don Juan, who at once refused to be bound by such pledges as Franco demanded. He was supported in this refusal by most of the nobility, who were further outraged when in 1948 Franco assumed for himself the right to distribute titles and grandeeships. Eventually, however, a compromise was reached, and in 1954 it was agreed that Don Juan's son, Don Carlos, then sixteen years old, should receive his education in Spain, though neither party gave any assurance as to the future.

Meanwhile, the continued truculence of Russia had brought the western powers to look more leniently on Spain, and since government in Russia was every bit as authoritarian as Franco's regime it was patently absurd to exclude Spain from the United Nations. She was therefore admitted in 1956, having already two years previously entered into an agreement with the United States for economic aid in return for bases in Spain. This was the chance for which the *Caudillo* had been waiting; hitherto his efforts at reconstruction and expansion had been gravely hindered by lack of foreign currency. Public works so far undertaken had seemingly been paid for by the additional printing of *pesetas* in defiance of all laws laid down by economists. The currency consisted almost entirely of shabby notes, down to the humble one *peseta* which though its value had decreased fourfold in ten years still held its own. The cheapness of life in Spain for the foreigner began to attract hordes of tourists, who were at first received with true Spanish reserve in the form of demands for visas and entry payments, but who were later welcomed and wooed when it was realised how much foreign currency they left behind. The value of the *peseta* was stabilised; new shiny *duros* (five *peseta* pieces) 25, 50 *peseta* coins began to appear; huge caterpillar tractors, bulldozers, rollers, cranes replaced toiling gangs of manual workers in constructional enterprises. When in 1961 the twenty-fifth anniversary of the Revolt was celebrated, Spain was outwardly a thriving nation, with more building in progress than in almost any other European nation and farm tractors rapidly ousting the patient plodding mules, donkeys and oxen.

To any foreigner who has seen Spain before the Civil War it is difficult to avoid admitting that Franco has done much for Spain.

Any authoritarian regime is detestable in the eyes of those accustomed
to centuries of democracy, but the Spanish nation, profoundly individualist and perhaps even anarchist by nature, appears at present
ungovernable by any other means.

It is undeniably true that behind the façade of increasing modernity
there is still cruel poverty in Spain, especially in the more barren
districts. Wages are low and work is often hard to obtain, but the hordes
of beggars who for centuries disfigured Spain are gone. No longer is it
likely that visitors should find cases of advanced starvation such as was
common in the 1930's. The standard of living may still be low, and the
eagerness with which Spaniards, especially Galicians, still emigrate to
find work testifies to this, but the general level has risen and a new
phenomenon can be seen: the emergence of a prosperous middle class
with their little *Seat* cars and general eagerness to enjoy life. The old
division of society between the very rich and the very poor appears to
be breaking down.

Not since the days of Philip II has there been such a long period of
comparative stability in Spain, and the country has benefited greatly.
Franco has avoided the mistakes of *Felipe el Prudente* (and indeed of
Hitler and Mussolini) by eschewing the temptation to make foreign
conquests. Indeed his recognition in 1956 of Spanish Morocco's
independence had put him in the forefront of modern colonial reform.
He has concentrated on the internal unity and reconstruction of Spain,
and despite gaps in achievement, injustices, jobbery, and tardy reprisals,
as in the case of Julián Grimau, executed in 1963 for crimes allegedly
committed during the Civil War, the lot of the ordinary Spaniard has
steadily improved. Whether on Franco's death, the forces of disintegration will again erupt in the traditional manner is impossible to forecast. It would be a rash prophet who would foretell the future of a
country so politically unpredictable as Spain.

Part 2
Literature

Enbiaredes por ellas adugan gelas aca

Fata en valençia dellas non uos partades

Dyxo auengaluo fer lo he de voluntad

Ella noch con ducho les dio grand

A la mañana pienssan de caualgar

Çiento le pidieron mas el co dozientos va

Passan las montañas q son fieras grandes

Passaron mata de toranz de tal guisa q ningu miedo no

Por el val de arbuxedo pienssan a de pruuar

E en medina todo el recabdo esta

Enbio dos cauallos mynaya albarfanez q sopiesse la uer

Esto non detarda en de coraçon lo han

El vno finco con ellos el otro torno a albarfanez

Virtos del campeador a nos vienen buscar

Afeuos aqui po vermuez muño gustioz q uos quiere sin

E martin antolinez el burgales natural

E el obpo don jeronimo coronado leal

E el alcayaz auengaluo con sus fuerças q traye

Por sabor de myo çid de grand ondal dar

Todos vienen en vno agora legaran

Essora dixo mynaya vaymos caualgar

Esso ffue apriessa fecho q nos quiere de tardar

Bien salieron den çiento q no parecen mal

En buenos cauallos a petriles a caxcaueles

E a cuberturas de gendales escudos alos cuellos

E en las manos lanças q pendones traen

Q sopiessen los otros de q seso era albarfanez

Chapter 6
The Middle Ages

Narrative verse

Castilian literature begins, it may be said, with the great epic *Poema de mío Cid* composed about 1140 by an unknown author. Clearly such a poem cannot spring into being without previous models and there must have been an extensive series of *Cantares de gesta* celebrating the deeds of heroes, but since they were all recited by *juglares* (troubadours) it is not surprising that no written version has survived. The *Poema de mío Cid* derives from a single manuscript copy written by one Pedro Abad in 1307, consisting of some 3,730 lines, three pages being missing. The poem is in three *Cantares*. The first deals with the exile of Don Rodrigo Ruiz de Bivar by King Alfonso VI of Castile as a result of the accusations of jealous courtiers. Don Rodrigo, with sixty faithful adherents who voluntarily share his exile, passes through Burgos, where the inhabitants weep for him but dare not help him for fear of the King. All they can do is to lament and exclaim: *Dios; ¡qué buen vasallo, si oviese buen señor!* (Oh God! What a noble vassal, if only he had a noble overlord!)

Don Rodrigo, however, is quite capable of looking after himself and raises a loan of 600 marks from two Jews on the security of two chests reputed to be filled with gold. In fact they contain merely sand, but the Jews, perhaps uncharacteristically, are hoodwinked into promising not to open them for a year. Now in funds after this piece of blatant trickery, Don Rodrigo moves on to the convent of Cardeña to bid farewell to his wife, Doña Jimena, and his two young daughters who had taken refuge there. Then he sallies forth with an army which is daily increasing in size to do battle with the Moors in the kingdom of

Toledo. His progress is a succession of splendid victories and a magnificent accumulation of booty which is described in great detail.

The second *Cantar* deals with the Cid's greatest triumph, the capture of Valencia and the fertile plain around it. With leave from the King (the Cid is always careful to legalise his actions) he brings his wife and two daughters and proudly shows them his conquests and his wealth. It is like a captain of industry showing his family over the works. Later he bids them stand on the ramparts and watch him do battle with the Moors to see *como se gana el pan* (how his daily bread is earned). Wealth and success bring the Cid reconciliation with the King who chooses husbands for his daughters. The suitors are the Infantes de Carrión, sons of the noblest in the land who are willing to marry beneath them for the sake of the dowries. The *Cantar* ends with the pomp and ceremony of the double wedding in Valencia.

The final *Cantar* tells of the cowardice and treachery of the Infantes de Carrión in the great battle against the Moorish host of King Búcar of Morocco whom the Cid defeats and kills:

> *Buen cavallo tiene Búcar e grandes saltos faz,*
> *mas Bavieca el mío Cid alcançándolo va.*
> *Alcançólo el Cid a Búcar a tres braças del mar,*
> *arriba alçó Colada★, un grant colpe dádol ha,*
> *las carbonelas del yelmo tollidas gelas ha,*
> *cortól el yelmo e, librado todo lo al,*
> *fata la çintura el espada llegado ha.*

> (Búcar has a good horse which takes great leaps, but Babieca, my lord the Cid's, is overtaking him. The Cid overtook Búcar three fathoms from the sea, he raised Colada aloft and struck him a great blow, the rubies in his helmet were all torn out; he cleft his helmet and splitting all the rest the sword reached down to his belt.)

The Cid's followers after the victory keep him in ignorance of the cowardice of his sons-in-law who beg permission to leave Valencia for a while. When they reach the oak forest of Corpes, they strip their wives naked, beat them with straps, dig their spurs into them and finally abandon them in the forest bleeding and unconscious:

> *Por los montes do ivan, ellos ívanse alabando:*
> *'De nuestros casamientos agora somos vengados.'*

> (Over the mountains as they go, they justify themselves: 'For our humble marriages are now avenged.')

Forthwith the Cid hastens to the King's court at Toledo, carefully

★ *Colada* was one of the Cid's swords; the other was *Tizona*.

dressed in magnificent armour and with his flowing beard safely encased in a net lest anyone should pull it. There he successfully demands the return of his two swords, stolen by the Infantes, and of his daughters' dowries. Having won his case the Cid feels emboldened to pull out his beard from the net and challenge the Infantes to single combat to vindicate his honour. Meanwhile, messengers arrive from the kings of Navarre and Aragon asking the hand of the Cid's daughters for their sons. This request is granted and the poem ends with the ignominious defeat of the Infantes de Carrión by the Cid's two nephews, who force their opponents to admit their guilt.

The narrative of the poem is reasonably accurate historically, though certain facts are glossed over, such as the Cid being in the pay of the Emir of Zaragoza when he fought the Christian Count of Barcelona. But the poem is not a crusading epic like the *Chanson de Roland*. The Spaniards knew the Arabs and had a profound respect for them; in fact this poem is thought to have been composed by a *Mozárabe*, that is a Christian born in a Muslim kingdom. The wars against the Arabs were forays for plunder as well as reconquest and the religious element was much less strong than later chroniclers claim. The *Poema de mío Cid* is more a social document, the story of a lesser nobleman who by his own exertions rises to wealth and power. The Cid was seeking *averes*, that is to say, property; he is certainly not aiming at religious conversion for he allows his Moorish subjects in conquered Valencia to worship as they please. He is a patriarch who looks after himself and his own; he is intensely loyal to his King, but is also sturdily independent when there is any hint of unjust or arbitrary use of the royal authority. He is in fact the ideal of Castilian manhood, brave, vigorous, fair-minded, devoted to his family. Of course, the portrait is idealised, but not unduly so, for no attempt is made to conceal his greed for plunder. But he is no demigod like Charlemagne in the *Chanson de Roland* for whom heaven works miracles. The Cid is the ordinary man of action, charging into battle on his warhorse Babieca, killing without malice until his arm is red with blood up to the elbow, then after victory congratulating his men and sharing the booty. Battle is big business; the weakest succumb and there is no room for sentiment.

So plain a tale demands a plain style and the verse in the *Poema de mío Cid* is almost wholly unadorned. Few adjectives are used and scarcely anywhere are there flights of poetic feeling to be found. Lyricism is shunned except when it occurs naturally in descriptions such as the Cid's arrival at the convent of Cardeña just as dawn is

hpstan.

historia hamaias
elgastton

ubius uuquodoboson septamorrac   rfilioseius lusulaq

Reproduction of a Códice, Cathedral of Seo de Urgel, Lérida

Woodcut of the Cid

breaking. There is also a moment of quiet lyricism in Doña Jimena's prayer before the Cid leaves her at Cardeña, but her husband's farewell is tersely stated in two lines:

> *A Dios vos acomiendo e al Padre spiritual;*
> *agora nos partimos; ¡Dios sabe el ajuntar!*

> (I commend you to God and the Holy Spirit.
> Now we must leave, God alone knows when we meet again!)

The versification consists of lines of about fourteen syllables with a marked caesura in the middle of the line. The lines are made up into stanzas of varying length with each line ending with the same assonance. It is perhaps a repetitive, monotonous system of versification, but it is highly effective in describing scenes of intense activity. As in all great stories of action, the reader or listener is unaware of the style of the author, who is content to let his tale tell itself and who ends an epic poem of 3,730 lines with the laconic statement:

> *Estas son las nuevas de mío Cid el Campeador;*
> *en este logar se acaba esta razón.*

(Such is the tale of my lord Cid the Champion;
at this point the poem ends.)

Lyric poetry

For lyric poetry in Spain in the early Middle Ages it is necessary to
turn to the Galician-Portuguese dialect, which produced so many
successful lyric poems that in the thirteenth century the dialect for such
poetry was used throughout the Peninsula. Even ALFONSO EL SABIO
(1221–84), almost the founder of Castilian as a written language,
composed lyrical poetry in Galician-Portuguese dialect. However, it
is certain that poets were using Castilian for lyrical verse, since there
are many allusions in the chronicles to *cantos* which are now lost.
The earliest lyric in Castilian to survive dates probably from the
beginning of the thirteenth century and is called *La razón de amor*. It is
a simple tale of a student who falls in love with a fair maid whom he
meets in a field so full of beautiful flowers:

> *que sol nombrar no las sabría,*
> *mas el olor que d'i ixía*
> *a omne muerto ressuçetaría.*

> (that he could not even name them, but the scent which
> came from them would revive a dead man.)

The couple make mutual declarations of love, but the time comes for
them to part and the maid consoles her swain by assuring him of her
eternal fidelity:

> *no vos cambiaxe por un emperador.*

> (I would not change you for an emperor.)

La razón de amor is a brief poem with no great felicity of language or
fertility of ideas, but it has the charm of freshness and simplicity.

Another style of poetry grew up in marked contrast to the popular
forms; this was the *mester de clerecía*, which might be translated as the
'learned art', being practised by monks and clergy who in the thirteenth
century alone formed the educated part of society. The style is defined
proudly, even haughtily in the *Libro de Alexandre*:

> *Mester trago fermoso, non es de joglaría;*
> *mester es sen peccado, ca es de clerecía;*
> *fablar curso rimado por la quaderna vía,*
> *a síllavas cuntadas, ca es grant maestría.*

(I present a style of great beauty, it has nothing to do with
minstrelsy; it is a faultless style, for it is a learned one; to speak
in rhymed quatrain with an even number of syllables shows
the highest skill.)

Regular the verse may be, but it mostly betrays the boundless monotony of life in a medieval monastery. The *Libro de Alexandre* contains
over 10,000 lines and tells of the legendary deeds of Alexander the Great,
but the unknown author parades his knowledge of classical mythology
in general, only raising a smile by occasional anachronisms such as when
the mother of Achilles hides her infant son in a nunnery. It does,
however, contain some traces of poetic inspiration and there are certain
descriptive passages of lyrical beauty. Similar in style is the *Libro de
Apolonio* dealing with the complex and improbable adventures of the
King of Tyre and his daughter Tarsiana. The poem is much shorter
(a mere 2,600 lines), the style is robust and free from the platitudes
characteristic of the *mester de clerecía*.

This school of poetry produced one writer of distinction, the first
Castilian poet to be known by name, GONZALO DE BERCEO (?1180–
?1247), a Benedictine monk in the monastery of San Millán de la
Cogolla. His output was considerable, but all his poems are on religious
subjects, lives of saints, miracles of the Virgin, and there is little
originality of ideas. Much of his verse is dull and pedestrian (he called
his poems *prosas*), but here and there real flashes of poetry can be seen,
as for example in the *Milagros de Nuestra Señora* when the poet finds
himself by chance in a beautiful meadow:

> *La verdura del prado, la olor de las flores,*
> *las sombras de los árbores de temprados sabores*
> *refrescáronme todo e perdí los sudores:*
> *podrie vevir el omne aquellos olores.*
>
> *Nunqua trobé en sieglo logar tan deleitoso,*
> *ni sombra tan temprada, ni olor tan sabroso.*
> *Descargué mi ropiella por yacer más vicioso,*
> *poséme a la sombra de un árbor fermoso.*

(The green of the meadow, the scent of the flowers, the shade
of the tree with its soft delights, refreshed me completely and
I shed the weariness of toil: man might live on those scents.
Never in the world did I find such delightful places. I took off
my habit to lie more at ease, and I sat in the shade of a beautiful
tree.)

Berceo's flat but expressive style has been imitated by several modern
poets including Antonio Machado. If he did nothing else, Berceo can

The Arcipreste de Hita

claim to have contributed most to the formation of Castilian as a
language for lyric poetry.

The Arcipreste de Hita

The greatest of all the poets of the middle ages was also a cleric, but
of a very different sort from the gentle, learned Berceo. The Arcipreste
de Hita, JUAN RUIZ by name, was born around 1280 probably in Alcalá
de Henares not far from Madrid. Little is known of his life except that
he was imprisoned at Toledo by order of the Archbishop and by 1350
he had disappeared from the scene altogether. It can only be conjectured

that some of the adventures told in his great collection of poems, the *Libro de buen amor*, are based on episodes in his own life. The narrator of the story is normally named Ruiz, though occasionally the name is given as Don Melón de la Huerta. His appearance is described in some detail and the description may be taken as a self-portrait of the archpriest: corpulent, with a large head, small eyes beneath thick eyebrows as black as coal, a long nose, big like his mouth, thick lips, a short powerful neck, unhurried gait, a good musician and a gay lover.

The poet in his prologue tries to pretend that he has composed his verses solely for the benefit of his fellow creatures by demonstrating the difference between divine love (*el buen amor*) and carnal love (*el loco amor*), but there his hypocrisy ends for he adds with disarming frankness that since to err is human, 'if any (though I do not advise him to do so) would wish to indulge in carnal love, here he will find some methods of doing so'. The poet himself was afire with love, but his first three attempts at seduction are fruitless and he takes counsel of Don Amor and later of Doña Venus who advises him to seek the aid of an old procuress. This cunning old go-between, Trotaconventos, fulfils the archpriest's desires by persuading a comely widow to yield to his advances. This is not achieved without difficulty:

> *Respondió la dueña, diz': 'Non me estaría bien*
> *casar ante del año, que a biuda non convien'*
> *fasta que pase el año de los lutos que tien'*
> *casarse; ca el luto con esta carga vien'.*

> *Si yo ante casase, sería enfamada,*
> *perdería la manda que a mí es mandada,*
> *del segundo marido no sería tan onrada,*
> *terníe que non podría sofrir gran temporada.*

> (The lady replied, saying: 'It would not be right for me to marry before the year is out, for it does not befit a widow to marry until her year of mourning is passed; for that is the duty that mourning involves. If I were to marry before, my reputation would suffer, I should lose the legacy that has been left to me, I should not be held in high esteem by the second husband, such a situation I could not bear for long.')

Despite these powerful reasons the widow, Doña Endrina, surrenders to the archpriest, but the joys of love do not last long, for the widow dies suddenly. The archpriest is left sick with grief and despair, but his natural buoyancy of spirit soon returns. After a bungled affair which involves a temporary quarrel with Trotaconventos he sets out on an excursion to Segovia and back across the high *sierra*. The observations on the journey with its difficulties and attendant dangers are full of interest, but his adventures with three ugly, rapacious, lustful *serranas* (highland cowherds) are somewhat mysterious. It would seem that the archpriest, who likes to display himself in a faintly ridiculous light, is satirising a form of courtly pastoral lyric called a *serranilla*, for his alarming experiences are written in a different metre from the usual *cuaderna vía*; instead they are composed in the form of *cantigas*, that is songs arranged in seven line stanzas with eight syllables to the line:

> De buen vino un quartero,
> manteca de vacas mucha,
> mucho queso assadero,
> leche, natas, una trucha;
> e dijo: '¡Hadeduro!
> Comamos deste pan duro:
> después faremos la lucha.'

> (A quart of good wine, a deal of cow's butter, plenty of smoked cheese, milk, cream and a trout. Then she said: 'Upsadaisy! Let's eat this dry bread and then we will get to work.'

In the archpriest's *serranillas* there are no Dresden shepherdesses, but instead cowgirls as tough and lewd as any from the Wild West.

Safely back in town just before Ash Wednesday the archpriest launches forth into a burlesque (very much in the style of Jean de Meung or Rabelais) of a battle between the forces of Don Carnal and Doña Quaresma (Lady Lent); the former's armies consist of hens, partridges, rabbits, goats, pheasants, while the latter's soldiers, all drawn up in appropriate squadrons, are sardines, cuttle-fish, eels, prawns. Doña Quaresma is victorious and Don Carnal is wounded, but after seven weeks of fasting he and Don Amor return in triumph, greeted by men and maidens, clergy and laity, monks and nuns. All this would appear to be a satire on the general laxity of morals at the time, for the church is openly ranged on the side of Don Carnal and Don Amor, the two emperors of the world, and the archpriest has no hesitation in placing himself among the eager followers of Don Amor; he would have been a detestable hypocrite had he not done so.

Once more in league with Trotaconventos the archpriest essays the most difficult of all conquests, the seduction of a nun, whose qualities the old procuress praises because nuns neither wish to marry nor let out the secret. But this nun proves to be virtuous and the archpriest has to be content with a platonic friendship, *limpio amor*, which is not to his liking, and his comments on nuns in general are somewhat waspish as a result. He is more successful with a Moorish girl for he

has a good knowledge of Arabic and a taste for Moorish music. Soon
after this happy liaison Trotaconventos dies and the archpriest is
griefstricken. He composes a heartrending lament for her:

> Cierto en paraíso estás tú asentada,
> con dos mártires debes estar acompañada.
>
> (I am sure that you are seated in heaven with two martyrs at
> your side.)

The place of the invaluable old hag is taken by a rascally servant,
Hurón, who, though he appears only for a brief moment, is a most
engaging person; he has fourteen capital faults, being among other
things a drunkard, thief, idler and slattern, but gay and witty. His one
errand of love on his master's behalf is a lamentable failure and as a
result the archpriest decides to forsake the pursuit of *loco amor*.

The *Libro de buen amor* is a vast satirical survey of medieval life
embracing all classes of society and employing every metrical form
known to the poetry of the age. From such a variegated hotch-potch
it is difficult to extract a coherent expression of opinion or a philosophy
of life. Perhaps the author's immense zest for life demanded a violent
counterblast to the dullness of medieval existence. Like Chaucer and
Rabelais he was a man of some standing, but he mixed freely with
the lower strata of society, writing songs to be performed by *juglares*,
who were often poverty-stricken entertainers. One such song is the
coarse *Trova cazurra* full of crude puns and telling how the poet is
betrayed by his go-between, Fernán García, who himself seduces the
baker's wife in his stead:

> Prometiól', por mi consejo,
> trigo que tenía añejo,
> e presentól' un conejo
> el traidor falso marfuz.
>
> (He promised her, on my advice, some good, ripe wheat
> I had and the smart, treacherous trickster gave her a rabbit
> himself.)

The archpriest is lewd and bawdy, but his zest, warmth and humanity
are a relief after the dull prolixity of the *mester de clerecía*. As an observer
of human life and character he is in the highest rank and the *Libro de
buen amor* is, like the *Canterbury Tales*, a historical document of the
greatest importance. What Chaucer did for English poetry the Archpriest of Hita did for Spanish verse, making it a supple mode of artistic
expression and bringing it into the main stream of European poetry.

The Cancioneros

The dominance of Castilian as the literary language of Spain is clearly demonstrated in the first great anthology of poetry, the *Cancionero de Baena* compiled about 1445 by Juan Alfonso de Baena *para alegrar e servir* King Juan II of Castile. There are indeed some poems in Galician dialect, but the vast majority of the 576 compositions are in Castilian. Every type of poetry is represented, poems of love, satires, burlesques and so on, almost all unfortunately uniformly dull and pedestrian. The poet who figures chiefly in the anthology is ALFONSO ÁLVAREZ DE VILLASANDINO (?1350–?1428) whose work is highly praised by the compiler. He was a professional poet who wrote verses by contract or commission, for instance he received a fee of 100 gold crowns from the town council of Seville to compose a poem each year at Christmas in praise of the city. It is not surprising that his themes tend to be conventional and uninspired. At times he is frankly obscene, for his commissions included not only hymns of praise or devotion, but also slanderous poems calumniating the reputation of some unfortunate lady, presumably out of revenge or spite. But even in obscenity he is dull and offers little incentive to any class of reader except possibly students of the medieval social scene.

Of the other poets represented in the *Cancionero de Baena* one of the most noteworthy is perhaps RUY PAEZ DE RIBERA, a well-to-do citizen of Seville who was reduced to indigence and whose laments on poverty have a heartrending personal note:

> Yo me vi solo en bravas montañas,
> anduve en la mar tormenta corriendo
> sin vela, sin remos, en ondas extrañas
> diversos peligros e miedo sofriendo,
> tormentos crueles e penas veyendo
> a vista de ojos sin comparación:
> con todo no iguala tal tribulación
> a la del pobre que muere viviendo . . .

> (I saw myself alone in rugged mountains, I went over the sea running before the storm, without sail, without oars in strange waters, suffering manifold dangers and fear, seeing at close quarters incomparably cruel pain and grief; such tribulation, however, in no way equals that of the poor man who suffers a living death.)

The twelve syllable metre in eight line stanzas, known as *arte mayor*, was now fashionable, taking the place, for long poems at least, of the clumsy *cuaderna vía*. For many years it was not a particularly successful metre, because Spaniards speak like machine-guns and they could not accustom themselves to gentler rhythms. Equally unsuccessful at first was the adaptation of Dante's *Divina Commedia* in eleven syllable lines composed by FRANCISCO IMPERIAL, the son of a jeweller from Genoa who had set up shop in Seville. His *Decir a las siete virtudes* is an allegorical poem based almost entirely on Dante, but although the work is mainly mere translation from the Italian, many of the lines are of remarkable beauty. These efforts were largely experimental and the older forms based on the needs of songs and dances remained popular. Best known of these, though not included in the *Cancionero de Baena*, is the *cosante* (round-song) to the tree about to bloom, composed by DIEGO FURTADO DE MENDOZA (d. ?1404):

> *A aquel árbol que mueve la foxa*
> *algo le antoxa.*
> *Aquel árbol del bel mirar*
> *face de maniere flores quiere dar:*
> *algo se le antoxa.*
>
> (That tree that is stirring its leaves has taken a liking to something. That tree of handsome appearance looks as if it wants to burst into flower; it has taken a liking to something.)

Also to be remembered among the medieval poets is MACÍAS EL ENAMORADO (d. ?1390), if not for his compositions, at least for his romantic love affair and death at the hands of a jealous husband. This tragic story has inspired many subsequent Spanish writers.

The *Cancionero de Baena* was the first of many anthologies which proliferated after the introduction of printing to Spain about 1474 and which culminated in the publication of the *Cancionero general* in 1511. This in its turn was followed by other anthologies, and there were also collections of poems by individual authors known as *Cancioneros particulares*, the first of which, by JUAN DEL ENCINA, had appeared in 1496. Poetry shows an increasing influence from Italy and a greater understanding also of classical Latin literature. One of the more successful poets of this humanist, renaissance trend was JUAN DE MENA (1411–56). His *Laberinto de fortuna* (1444) is an allegory which owes much to the *Divina Commedia*, but there are reminiscences of Virgil and Lucan in certain passages. His style is mostly over-erudite and the allegories are frequently obscure. He presents the heroes of antiquity in a somewhat frigid fashion, but he shows more eloquence and liveliness when preaching in favour of the holy crusade against the infidel in Spain. His inspiration is not wholly jingoistic, for besides bellicose passages in praise of former heroes of the Reconquest, he indulges in sharp censure of the nobility and clergy of his own time denouncing their greed and idleness. Nevertheless there is an air of artificiality about the whole poem for the writer is never at ease with the metre, which is *arte mayor* with lines of twelve syllables in eight line stanzas. Perhaps following the current fashion of Italy, Juan de Mena intended his poem to be sung, but the musical rhythm and cadences of Dante, Petrarch and Bocaccio are missing.

The Marqués de Santillana

Spanish poetry took another great step forward towards suppleness and variety at this period in the works of IÑIGO LÓPEZ DE MENDOZA (1398–1458), the first Marqués de Santillana. He came of a powerful noble family and took part in the struggle of the nobility against Juan II's favourite, Don Álvaro de Luna. He combined with his political aspirations a passion for poetry and without being a profound humanist scholar he had a real understanding of literature not only in Spain, but in Italy and France as well. It was he who wrote the first work of literary criticism in Spain in his *Proemio e carta*, prefacing a collection of his poems addressed to Don Pedro de Portugal (1449). He traces the development of poetry in the Peninsula, conceding that the Galician-Portuguese dialect has been the cradle of lyricism. He praises Italian poets, preferring them to French poets, whom he admires nonetheless for their metrical exactness. This was the view of a technician and a man of learning and it drove him to speak disparagingly of popular poetry in Spain. This patronising attitude today seems misplaced because, while most of his lengthy allegorical poems are entirely forgotten, many of his *villancicos, decires, canciones, serranillas,* all of popular inspiration, are still enjoyed.

The best of the longer poems are *El infierno de los enamorados,* imitated from Dante's *Inferno* and *El diálogo de Bias contra Fortuna*. The first is allegorical and the second is didactic, demonstrating the triumph of the philosopher, who, preferring poverty to riches, finds happiness listening to the dictates of his conscience. More passionate and more personal is the *Doctrinal de privados* written on the death of Don Álvaro de Luna on the scaffold. The condemned favourite meditates on the past and on the frailty of human greatness in this false and wicked world. He repents of his own misdeeds and gives advice to other favourites of kings, bidding them be upright, just and modest: *Lo que non fice, facet* (What I did not do, let it be done.) This is an unjust epitaph to Don Álvaro whose firm policies pacified Spain, but Santillana remained his implacable enemy.

Santillana has the credit of writing the first sonnets in Spanish, forty-two in number, reflecting the style and ideas of Petrarch's *Canzionere*, but in spite of Santillana's admiration for Italian forms his own inspiration is much more Spanish in origin, being based on the Galician lyrics which he had read in his youth. This native strain of inspiration is even more apparent in his best works, which are his *canciones, villancicos* and *serranillas;* this is where Santillana reveals his considerable poetic gifts especially for vivid and colourful description.

The *serranillas* have an obvious connection with those of Arcipreste de Hita. Santillana, in fact, owned a castle at Hita and it is not surprising that he places the encounters with cowgirls in the two *serranillas* on the same slopes of the Sierra de Guadarrama as those described by the Archpriest. The latter made his way on foot over the mountains whereas the Marqués de Santillana no doubt travelled in some state and tended to be welcomed respectfully by the peasants. Hence his *vaqueras* are beautiful girls instead of the lecherous monsters described by the Archpriest, whose buffoonish outlook on life led him to guy these fashionable pastoral poems. Santillana's *serranillas* reflect much more the idealised conception of love of the Galician poets and the theme frequently breaks off discreetly in the Galician manner as opposed to the squalid realism of the Archpriest:

> *En un verde prado*
> *de rosas e flores,*
> *guardando ganado*
> *con otros pastores,*
> *la vi tan graciosa*
> *que penas creyera*
> *que fuesse vaquera*
> *de la Finojosa.*

> (In a green meadow with roses and flowers, guarding her herd, I saw her so beautiful that scarcely would I believe that she was a cowgirl from la Finojosa.)

This is the strong, cantering rhythm of popular Spanish poetry, but perhaps Santillana's great achievement was that he managed to combine Galician and Italian rhythms and produce poetry with musical qualities in slower tempo. This is apparent in the beautiful *Villancico a unas tres fijas suyas* in which he sees three ladies in a garden sighing for love; they are his daughters and sadly he realises that their sighs are not for love of him:

> *Por mirar su fermosura*
> *destas tres gentiles damas,*
> *yo cobríme con las ramas,*
> *metíme so la verdura.*
> *La otra con grand tristura*
> *començó de sospirar*
> *e desir este cantar*
> *con muy honesta mesura:*
> *La niña que amores ha,*
> *sola, ¿cómo dormirá?*

(To see the beauty of these three charming ladies, I covered myself with the branches and hid under the green leaves. The second lady began to sigh and sing this song in a most decorous manner: The girl who is in love, how shall she sleep alone?)

Santillana indeed had not yet succeeded in fusing the Italian and Spanish styles, but he had made great progress in that direction and definitely foreshadows the final achievement attained in the next century by Garcilaso de la Vega.

Santillana's family was remarkable for their poetic gifts and it was his great-nephew, JORGE MANRIQUE (?1440–79) who composed the best known poem of the later Middle Ages, the *Coplas por la muerte de su padre*. This was in fact his only achievement as a poet, rather as Thomas Gray is remembered only for his *Elegy in a Country Churchyard*. Manrique's other poems are conventional and superficial, but it is fair to remember the early age at which he died of wounds received in battle fighting for Queen Isabel I against her rival la Beltraneja. Then again medieval poets did not strive after originality, but sought to produce harmonious verse in certain well known and well defined forms. As writers of condoling letters know, it is hard to be original about the sorrow that bereavement brings; Manrique's *Coplas* are stereotyped in ideas, reproducing the well worn themes of the transitory nature of life and the vanity of the pomp of this world. Like Villon in his *Ballade des dames du temps jadis* he calls on the great, the powerful, the magnificent of times past:

> *¿Qué se fizo el rey Don Juan?*
> *Los infantes de Aragón,*
> *¿qué se fizieron?*
> *¿Qué fue de tanto galán?*

¿Que fue de tanta invención
  como truxieron?
Las justas y los torneos,
paramentos, bordaduras,
  y cimeras,
¿fueron sino devaneos?
¿qué fueron sino verduras
  de las eras?

  ¿Qué se fizieron las damas,
  sus tocados, sus vestidos,
    sus olores?
¿Qué se fizieron las llamas
  de los fuegos encendidos
    de amadores?
  ¿Qué se fizo aquel trobar,
  las músicas acordadas
    que tañían?
  ¿Qué se fizo aquel dançar,
  aquellas ropas chapadas
    que traían?

(What has become of King John? The princes of Aragon,
what has become of them? What has become of so many
gallants? What has become of all the innovations they
brought? The jousts, the tourneys, ornaments, embroidery
and crests, were they but vanity? Were they but grass on
the winnowing floor? What has become of the ladies
with their head-dresses, their gowns and their perfumes?
What has become of the flames of the fires that lovers
kindled? What has become of minstrelsy and the harmonious music they played? What has become of all the
dancing, those exquisite dresses they wore?)

If Jorge Manrique has nothing new to say about death, he has succeeded
perfectly in echoing the time-honoured sentiments in grave and solemn
language that never seems to date, just as Gray in his *Elegy* has chosen a
stately style that never becomes old-fashioned in order to epitomise
thoughts on life and death evoked by a country churchyard. Manrique
is the last medieval poet and he has summed up all the aspirations and
stoic resignation of the Middle Ages.

Development of Castilian prose

Apart from legal or ecclesiastical documents there are no records of
the use of Castilian literary prose before the middle of the thirteenth
century when Fernando III *el Santo* (1217–52) interested himself in

literature and caused translations of legal, didactic or historical works
to be made from Latin, Arabic and Hebrew. Of these the most important were the revision of the Gothic code of laws, the *Fuero Juzgo* (1241),
a version of oriental fables such as *El libro de Kalila et Digma* (1251) and
the *Anales toledanos* which ambitiously sets out to record events from
the time of Christ up to the reign of Fernando III. Both as history and
literature the *Anales* is no more than a museum curio because the facts
are improbable and the style is arid and frequently incoherent. However,
Fernando had imparted his interest in literature to his son, Alfonso X
el Sabio in whose reign (1252–84) Spanish made huge strides forward
as a literary language.

Alfonso gathered round him scholars of all types and creeds,
Christians, Moors and Jews alike. His ambition was to collect all the
scientific knowledge of the day and to publish it in coherent form in a
series of works in Spanish and under his personal supervision more than
twenty works appeared on history, astronomy, law, natural sciences.
Alfonso was eager that these works should be written in correct and
elegant language and the preface to the *Libro de la esfera* states that the
King himself amended any sentences which he did not consider to be
in *castellano derecho*. Since such works were compiled by several writers
it is impossible to expect unity of style, but in the main the language is
apt and at times colourful and gracefully fluent even when dealing with
such dry material as the revision of laws in the *Siete Partidas*. The *Tablas
Alfonsinas* and the *Libros de saber de astronomía* show a notable advance
in astronomical knowledge and calculations, correcting many previous
errors. Even recreation is not neglected and the *Libro de ajedrez* is one
of the earliest handbooks on the technique of playing chess.

The early chronicles

Alfonso's greatest achievement was the compilation of the *Primera
crónica general* which was begun about 1270 when, so the prologue
states, the King ordered his scholars to *ayuntar cuantos libros pudimos
aver de istorias en que alguna cosa contassen de los fechos d'Espanna* (gather
together all the books we could find on the subjects of history in which
something might be told of the deeds of Spain). It is one of the earliest
chronicles to give a reasonably full bibliography detailing the works
consulted by the compilers. Such works included Latin poems (both
medieval and classical, for the chronicle goes back to the earliest times),
Arabic poems and tales, and Castilian *cantares de gesta*. Though the

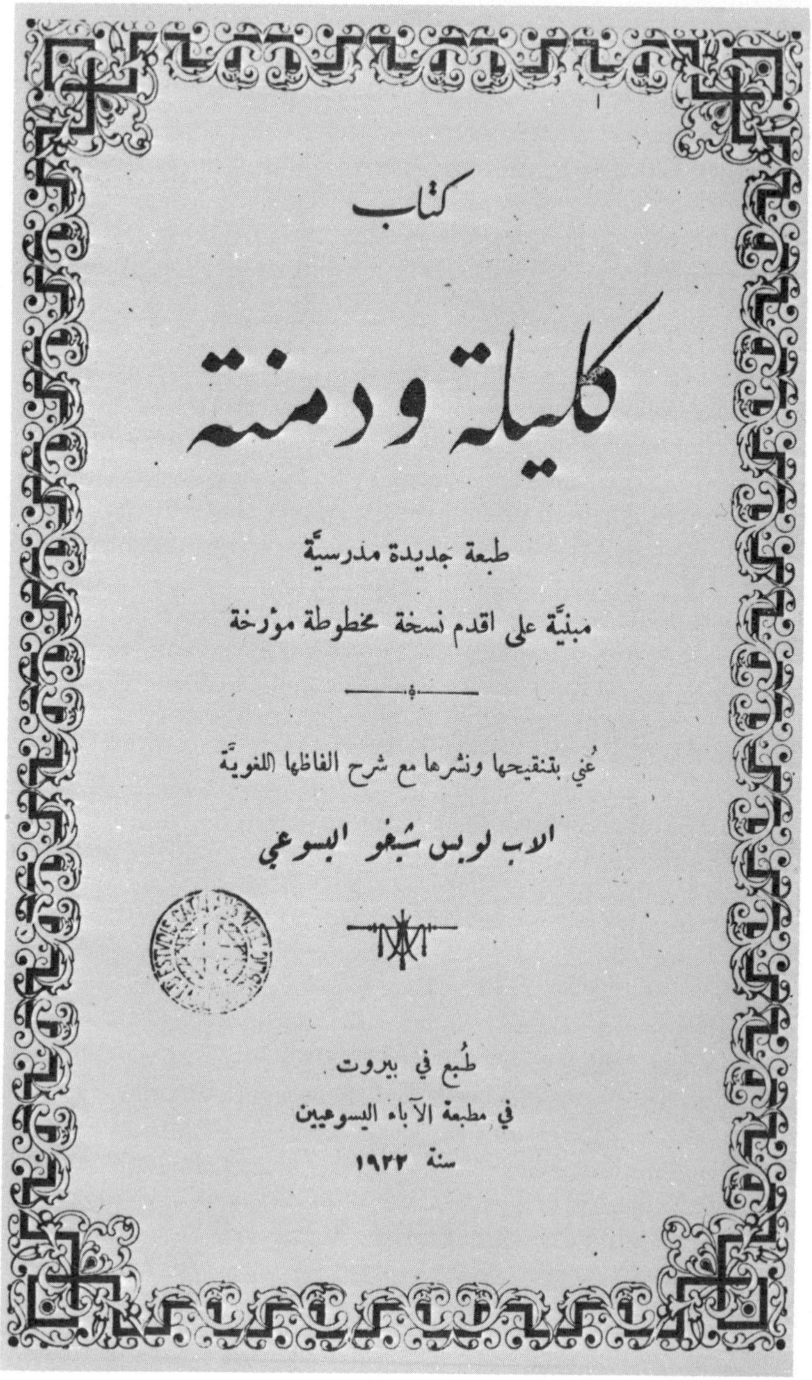

كتاب

كليلة ودمنة

طبعة جديدة مدرسيّة

مبنيّة على اقدم نسخة مخطوطة مؤرخة

عُني بتنقيحها ونشرها مع شرح الفاظها اللغويّة

الاب لويس شيخو اليسوعي

طُبع في بيروت

في مطبعة الآباء اليسوعيين

سنة ١٩٢٢

Title page of El Libro de Kalila et Digma

compilers often seem naively credulous, they have made conscientious efforts to examine facts and incidents with a critical eye; frequently they qualify the more fanciful episodes of the *cantares de gesta* with the warning that '*no podían seer*'. The *Crónica* has a coherent and concerted plan in spite of its varied sources, and it shows a real concern for literary style, even though in places the writer is merely translating from the original source.

The *Primera crónica general* is undoubtedly superior to the chronicles of the three subsequent reigns compiled by order of Alfonso XI in the first half of the fourteenth century, for these are bald, incoherent narratives which do little but reiterate praise for the kings. Of greater historical accuracy and clarity are the chronicles dealing with the period 1350–96 written by PERO LÓPEZ DE AYALA (1332–1407), chancellor to four kings and a shrewd observer of contemporary events. Most of his narrative is strictly impartial, but he occasionally builds up a situation with dramatic intensity and allows himself the pleasure of a comment. His description of Pedro *el Cruel* is undoubtedly fair, but equally not flattering:

'*Era muy temprado e bien acostumbrado en el comer e beber; dormía poco, e amó muchas mujeres. Fue muy trabajador en guerra; fue cobdicioso de allegar tesoros e joyas . . . E mató muchos en su regno, por lo cual le vino todo el daño que avedes oído.*'

(He was very temperate and well-mannered in eating and drinking; he slept little, and loved many women. In war he toiled hard; he was greedy to acquire riches and jewels—And he slew many in his reign and thereby brought upon himself all the misfortune of which you have heard.)

This personal view of history was carried a step further in the next century by FERNÁN PÉREZ DE GUZMÁN (?1376–?1460) whose historical biographies transformed the bald narrative of the chronicles into a psychological study. In his *Mar de historias* he recounts the lives of a wide variety of historical personages from Alexander the Great to Pythagoras and St Francis, but his most interesting work lies in his comments on contemporary history in what has been classed as the third part of the *Mar de Historias;* this is a study of the physical and moral qualities of famous men under the title of *Las generaciones, semblanzas y obras*. Guzmán defines the qualities required of an historian as twofold: 'First that the historian should be wise and learned and have a good way of expressing himself so as to compose his history in a handsome and dignified style . . . Second that he should have been present at the most important and notable deeds of war and peace.' It is this personal knowledge that makes his portraits so real and fascinating, though he maintains a constantly strict impartiality in his judgments and his style is notable for being concise rather than florid. This conciseness adds piquancy to the analysis of character by hinting much in a few words; thus his exalted predecessor, Chancellor Pero López de Ayala, is summed up in the stark sentence: 'he was very fond of women, more so than befitted so learned a gentleman.'

Medieval prose fiction

Fictional prose works in Spanish may be said to have originated from the imitation of oriental fables which were didactic in purpose, presenting exemplary tales in which the characters were usually animals. The earliest and best known of these is the *Libro de Kalila et Digma* translated from the Arabic in 1251. The third story gives the book its title and deals with the intrigues of two lynxes, Kalila and Digma, in the court of the lion. Out of envy for the bull, who is the lion's confidant, they persuade the King that the bull is a traitor and he is condemned to death. Soon, however, the charge is proved to be false and Digma, the originator of the plot, is sentenced by the lion to a lingering death: *con fambre e con set, et murió mala muerte en la cárcel* (With hunger and thirst and he died a painful death in prison). The fables are insignificant in themselves, but they had a profound influence on prose literature in the century following.

The first prose work in Spanish that can be described as a novel is the *Historia del Caballero Cifar* written probably by a priest or monk between 1299 and 1303. It bears traces of oriental influence since the scene is set in India, but much of the material seems to have been drawn from Spanish sources. There is a strong resemblance in certain details to the story of the Cid, since the knight, Cifar, is dismissed by the King because of the jealous intrigues of courtiers. The good knight wins the hearts of all people with whom he comes in contact by reason of his valour, piety and uprightness, for which virtues he receives the title of the *Caballero de Dios*. Eventually he triumphs and having royal blood in his veins succeeds to the kingdom of Menton on the death of the King who had treated him so badly. His road has been a hard one because a curse has been laid upon him whereby any animal he owns dies within ten days of coming into his possession. Moreover, his two sons disappear, one stolen by a lioness, the other getting lost in a strange city. To cap it all, his wife, Grima, is captured by pirates and undergoes incredible adventures in the manner of a Byzantine novel, but finally the whole family is miraculously reunited through divine intervention.

The second part of this lengthy work contains fifty-three chapters of sound parental advice given by Cifar to his sons on the duties and responsibilities of the perfect knight, all illustrated by moral tales and anecdotes. Thus adequately briefed the second son, Roboan, sets forth in the third part of the novel to seek adventures in the true style of the knight errant. Needless to say his outstanding qualities and personal charm enable him to become the favourite of an Emperor, who, having no heir, leaves his throne to the handsome, virtuous, valiant Roboan.

As may easily be imagined, this novel does not make for light reading, for it exudes the overwhelming dullness of medieval moralising, but it is an interesting reflection of the ideals and aspirations of the age and contains one character of great vividness and typically Spanish in origin: this Ribaldo, Cifar's squire, who is the prototype of Sancho Panza and all the able, practical, sensible servants of Spanish literature. He is cheerful and witty in a caustic fashion (*socarrón* in Spanish) and has a fund of popular wisdom and common sense, speaking like Sancho Panza (and indeed like rustics of any nation) mostly in proverbs. Contrasted with his master, the rather dreary, moralising Cifar (whose character, however, is much less clearly defined), Ribaldo seems to bring a breath of earthy sense to this high-faluting medieval romance.

The ideals of knighthood are reiterated in the works of the INFANTE DON JUAN MANUEL (1282–1348), nephew of Alfonso *el Sabio*. He was an aggressive and turbulent nobleman who rebelled against his King, for whom he had formerly acted as regent. However, he was later reconciled when he saw that the King and his adherents were obviously gaining the upper hand. Such were the qualifications that enabled him to retire to his estates from time to time to compose such moral treatises as the *Libro del caballero y del escudero*, a dialogue between a knight and his squire on the whole order of knighthood. To this are added discourses on heaven, hell, the elements, planets, birds and other subjects. The squire is, as Queen Victoria once complained, 'treated as a public meeting', for he has the chance to speak only on four or five occasions in the whole book. Don Manuel improved to some extent on the dialogue form in another didactic work, *El libro de los estados* (1330) which is composed of 'questions and answers between a king and a prince, his son, and a knight who brought up the prince and a philosopher'. It is a study of the various estates of society in the fourteenth century, the first part dealing with the laity (in one hundred chapters) while the clergy are summed up in half the space in the second part. Again the form of the book is not true dialogue, for the characters are allowed to utter without interruption the lengthiest of speeches, which evoke admiration for the stamina of the medieval listener.

Though still patently didactic, Don Manuel's masterpiece, *El Conde de Lucanor* (1335) shows a considerable advance in literary technique. The book consists of fifty-one chapters called *exemplos*, each telling a story whose moral implication is summed up in a concluding rhymed couplet. It is the Conde de Lucanor who is capping the moral tale told by his counsellor Patronio, as for instance in the story of an Empress (*Exemplo XXVII*) who shortly after her marriage becomes captious and difficult to please. The Emperor wishes to eat, but she has decided to fast; if he is ready for bed, she wants to stay up. Patronio's conclusion is that '*cumple mucho que al primero día que el omne casare de a entender a su muger que él es el sennor e le faga entender la vida que an de pasar en uno*' (it is most important that on the first day of marriage a man should make his wife understand that he is master and make her realise the kind of life they are to lead together). The Count is impressed by such sage advice and causes the couplet to be written at the end of the tale:

> En el comienço deve el omne mostrar
> a su muger como tyene de pasar.
>
> (At the beginning the man must show his wife how she is to behave.)

Such an unvarying method in fifty-one chapters may make for monotony, but in fact Don Manuel's tales, allegories and fables are varied and interesting, being gathered from widely differing sources— Spanish history, Greek, Latin and oriental mythology. The dialogue is natural and convincing, the style is flowing, well-constructed, elegant, and the author's personality is clearly evident. Don Manuel reveals himself as artistic in temperament, distrustful, aloof and possessed of an ironical turn of phrase. It is a personality that is scarcely attractive, but his workmanship has the delicate refinement of the conscious artist who was confident enough to deposit the original copies of his works in the monastery of Peñafiel (high on a barren hill near Valladolid) so that posterity should be able to read them unsullied by later additions and alterations.

Popular poetry

While prose remained formal and stiff and uncompromisingly didactic, poetry in Spain had veered to a more popular style by the beginning of the sixteenth century. Instead of the ponderous poems in *cuaderna vía* and *arte mayor*, the *villancico* (carol) with its brief lines and repeated refrain became fashionable as songs in court circles and at noblemen's houses. Popular in origin and probably descended from Moorish narrative songs, the *villancico* was reduced in length to suit the needs of chamber music and was especially suited to accompaniment by a *vihuela*, a primitive form of guitar. The result of reducing the length of the *villancicos* is that much is left to the listener's imagination since the whole story is not told. The song is highly suggestive and impressionistic, often using symbols such as a heron or a poplar tree to suggest a graceful girl in love:

> *Al revuelo de una garza*
> *se abatió el neblí del cielo,*
> *y por cogella de vuelo*
> *quedó preso en una zarza.*

(As the heron flew by, the falcon swooped from the sky and in trying to seize her by the wing became caught in a bramble.)

> *De los álamos vengo, madre*
> *de ver como los menea el aire,*
> *De los álamos de Sevilla,*
> *de ver a mi linda amiga.*

(I come from the poplars, mother, from seeing how the breeze stirs them, from the poplars of Seville, from seeing my pretty friend.)

This impressionistic imagery was something new in the poetry of Spain and to some extent it resembles some of the symbolical poetry of the Old Testament: 'Or ever the silver cord be loosed, or the golden bowl be broken, or the pitcher be broken at the fountain or the wheel broken at the cistern.' The new imagery spread quickly throughout western European literature and though it was lost in the enthusiasm of the Renaissance with its emphasis on Italian forms, the *villancico* has inspired modern poets, in particular Lorca who has based much of his style on creating word pictures by vivid similes.

The romances

Another form of popular poetry emerges in the early fifteenth century and has remained ever since the basic form of Spanish verse. This was the *romance* or ballad. Its origin and date of introduction are uncertain. One theory is that the *romances* were snatches of the epic *cantares de gesta* which had appealed greatly to the populace and which were repeated in a somewhat altered form after the *juglar* had gone, rather as an amusing after-dinner story is repeated with additions, omissions or alterations depending on the memory and veracity of the hearer. The case for spontaneous creation remains plausible because many of the *romances* deal with the same subjects as the epics—the Cid, the seven Infantes de Lara who were slaughtered in a blood feud, the supposed betrayal of Spain to the Moors by Conde Julián. Moreover, the *romances* use the same system of assonance as the *cantares de gesta* and basically the same metre (sixteen syllables with a pause after the eighth). The objection to this theory is that the evidence of the type of language used and of references in the text proves that very few *romances* date from before the beginning of the fifteenth century. This is not altogether conclusive because they may well have been circulating verbally much earlier, but a scribe would write them down in the most up-to-date version. Certainly they were becoming popular in Santillana's time because in his *Proemio* (1449) he contemptuously alludes to those who *'sin ningún orden, regla ni cuento, facen estos romances e cantares, de que las gentes de baxa e servil se alegra'* (without any method, rule or syllable count make these ballads and songs which are enjoyed by people of low and servile degree).

Like many a haughty literary critic after him, the Marqués de Santillana was proved utterly wrong in his judgment, for the *romances* prospered and were enthusiastically adopted by cultivated court poets who cut them down in length to suit their musical needs and who later arranged the metre in lines of eight syllables (the form, however, remains unaltered). This arrangement adopted in the sixteenth century became the most usual metre in drama and in Spanish poetry generally. The *romances* were collected and printed (from about 1550 onwards) in volumes called *Romanceros* and have been a source of inspiration to literary men not only in Spain, but in France, England, Germany and America as well. There is no doubt that the romances form some of the greatest literary productions of the world.

They can be divided roughly into three groups: epic subjects of a legendary or historical nature, subjects dealing with the struggle against the Moors (*romances fronterizos*), and fictional subjects. The *romances* dealing with epic themes have a remarkable energy combined with terseness and stark diction which strongly hints at their popular origin. Thus King Rodrigo is described after his defeat by Don Julián:

Iba tan tinto de sangre   que una brasa parecía:
las armas lleva abolladas   que eran de gran pedrería;
la espada lleva hecha sierra   de los golpes de tenía;
el almete de abollado   en la cabeza le hundía;
la cara lleva hinchada   del trabajo que sufría.

(He was so stained with blood that he seemed like a glowing coal; his jewel-encrusted armour was dented; his sword was notched from the blows it had received; his helmet was so dented that it sank down on his head; his face was swollen from the grief which he was suffering.)

It is remarkable what a depth of feeling and at times of passion too is contained in these matter of fact statements where nouns stand by themselves rarely needing support from attendant adjectives.

The *romances fronterizos* are possibly of even greater interest, for they are contemporary accounts of the fighting on the frontiers of the Moorish kingdom of Granada; one in fact is known to have been composed by order of Enrique IV to commemorate a foray made into Moorish territory. The war sounds like some long drawn out series of sporting contests with its single combats, capture or loss of frontier towns, ambushes and skirmishes. The ballads are by no means fierce crusading literature for they reveal sympathy for the bitter feelings of an enemy in defeat, such as the chivalrous Spanish gentleman must have felt for the Moor. One such is the lament of the Moorish King on the capture of the town of Alhama:

Paseábase el rey moro   por la ciudad de Granada
desde la puerta de Elvira   hasta la de Vivarrambla.
¡Ay de mi Alhama!
Cartas le fueran venidas   que Alhama era ganada
las cartas echó en el fuego   y al mensajero matara.
¡Ay de mi Alhama!

(The Moorish king was riding through the city of Granada from the gateway of Elvira to the gate of Vivarrambla. Alas for my Alhama! Letters were brought to him that Alhama was won; he threw the letters in the fire and killed the messenger. Alas for my Alhama!)

The later courtly *romances* are generally of less interest for much of the sturdy vigour has gone. In some, however, it is replaced by a genuine lyrical feeling which the earlier ballads completely lacked. Some also, being shortened in form, have the same capacity for suggestive imagery as the courtly *villancicos*. One ballad which is outstanding in this respect is the *Romance del Conde de Arnaldos:*

> ¡Quién hubiese tal ventura   sobre las aguas del mar
> como hubo el Conde Arnaldos   la mañana de San Juan!

> (Who could have had such fortune on the waters of the sea as had the Count Arnaldos on the morn of St John's Day!)

How far the brilliant evocation of this ballad is due to art or chance is uncertain because it has been shown that the poem is a rehash of earlier versions with omissions and also the interpolation of three lines from a completely different ballad. The result, however, with this ballad is remarkably impressive.

La Celestina

Another masterpiece which seems to have sprung to life fortuitously at this period is the novel in dialogue form now known as *La Celestina* (1499). There is only one copy of the first printed edition and its titlepage is missing, but it is presumed to have borne the title of *La comedia de Calisto y Melibea* which is the name given to the second edition printed at Seville in 1501. This edition contains a prologue which states that the first *auto* (act) was written by an *antiguo autor*, but some prefatory verses contain an acrostic of the name Fernando de Rojas, the writer responsible for the remaining fifteen acts. FERNANDO DE ROJAS is a shadowy figure, born about 1465, still alive in 1538. He was a converted Jew who practised as a lawyer mostly in Talavera where he became mayor. The 1502 edition has an additional five *autos* and the work is now called a *tragicomedia*. All editions after 1519 print these additional acts which detract from the merit of the novel and which may not be the work of the original author. The significant fact is that the title after 1519 is firmly fixed as *La Celestina*, the name of the character on whom the main interest is focused.

That the novel is the work of more than one author is obvious, for the story begins as a simple, pathetic tale of thwarted love that ends in tragedy and subsequently turns into a survey of almost all strata of medieval Spanish society. Calisto, a noble youth of many virtues but little experience, falls in love with Melibea, equally high born and vivacious, passionate and candid by nature. To win her affection (under

Ragicomedia de Calisto y
Melibea. En la qual se cõtie
nen demas de su agradable y dul
ce estilo muchas sentēcias philoso
fales y auisos muy necessarios pa
ra mácebos: mostrádo les los en
gaños q estã encerrados en siruiē
tes z alcahuetas. ⁊ Cõel tratado
de Centurio y el auto de Traso.

Calisto y Melibea

medieval rules) is no easy affair and the naive Calisto unwisely heeds
the advice of his servant Sempronio to employ a go-between, an old
procuress, *vieja barbuda que se dice Celestina, hechicera, astuta, sagaz en*

cuantas maldades hay (a bearded old hag named Celestina, a cunning witch experienced in every form of wickedness). The novel now begins to turn from the sentimental love story to a penetrating analysis of the underworld of bawds, pimps and procuresses whose services are so well-known and so much in demand that even the nobility and clergy greet Celestina affectionately and respectfully.

Celestina then presses Calisto's suit on Melibea in an interview in which she makes masterly use of innuendoes and insinuations. Melibea's first reaction is one of indignation, but Celestina is accustomed to such rebuffs and in a subsequent conversation patiently persuades Melibea to grant her suitor an interview. Calisto, speaking in high-flown language such as would have done credit to Don Quijote, immediately captivates Melibea who promises him free entry to her house the following night.

Celestina gains so rich a reward from Calisto for her good offices that she is loath to share it, as promised, with his two servants, Pármeno and Sempronio who, infuriated by her treachery, fatally wound her. They are arrested by the watch and are put to death, but two women, friends and protegées of Celestina, resolve to avenge themselves on Calisto who, they feel, is responsible for her murder. While Calisto is visiting Melibea by night, he hears cries from two pages whom he had left on guard in the street outside. Despite Melibea's urgent entreaties that he should be careful, Calisto hastens to their assistance, but while descending a rope ladder which he has placed on the garden wall he slips and falls to his death. Melibea, unconsolable, finally flings herself from one of the towers of the house and dies beside her lover.

The theme of the novel is the tragic impulse of love. It is love that is responsible for the entire catastrophe, but it is not the charming, gentle love of Romeo and Juliet; it is fierce, compelling and crude, and it is Celestina who lives only to ensure that the passionate frenzy of love is gratified whenever possible. Her character is drawn with astonishing vividness, like a personage in a Goya painting. Wicked, unscrupulous, shameless, she revels in fornication; too old to indulge in it herself, she derives an unholy joy in procuring it for others. She will flatter, scheme and insinuate until she attains her object, yet for all her wickedness, drunkenness and deceit, she has qualities of warm friendliness and real enjoyment of life that evoke affection in all who meet her. *La Celestina* has its moments of tedium, but its tragic intensity and powerful portrayal of the manners of a crude age make it a novel of outstanding merit, and its success both in Spain and abroad was phenomenal. It achieved sixty-six editions in Spain before the end of the sixteenth century, and was translated into Italian, German, French and English, being the first Spanish work to appear in an English translation. No Spanish novel apart from *Don Quijote* attained such widespread popularity, or indeed deserved it. *La Celestina* is a stark tale of passion and its tragic consequences, but it is tempered with gaiety and humour and an incomparable observation of human nature.

Early attempts at drama

Although *La Celestina* is divided into acts and is written entirely in dialogue form, it could clearly never have been staged. At this period theatrical performances had scarcely developed at all. In Spain as in other European countries the origins of the theatre are to be found in the church services in which on festival days scenes from the Bible were enacted in a simple form. These *autos* or *misterios*★ did not exclude comic elements and such incidents as Balaam and his ass provided scope for knockabout farce. Uproarious laughter in church shocked some pious priests and there was a tendency to move these less reverent performances to the courtyard outside. In this lay the beginnings of the secular theatre. When these *autos* were first introduced into church services is not known, but a fragment of one of them dating fom the end of the twelfth century (*El auto de los Reyes Magos*) is extant. Apart from this, none is known to exist before the middle of the fourteenth century and it may be assumed that such performances were hastily contrived affairs similar to church *tableaux* of the present day.

The custom was, however, firmly established and it was greatly extended by JUAN DEL ENCINA (?1468–?1529) who had been brought up as a chorister in Salamanca Cathedral where he was well versed in the ceremonies held at festival times. After studying at Salamanca University he entered the service of the Duque de Alba in 1492 as a court musician and poet. His training in the humanities at the university on the brink of the Renaissance gave him a preference for Latin forms and his first compositions were two eclogues in which two shepherds discuss the birth of Christ and celebrate his coming by singing a *villancico* and setting off to Bethlehem to worship the infant Jesus. These two *Églogas* were recited on Christmas Eve and Christmas Day 1492 before the Duke and Duchess and their court. They contain no dramatic action and are merely short and simple dialogues. However, a little later it is evident that Encina's *Églogas* were followed by

★ *Misterio* in this sense means church service (from Latin *ministerium*).

Tower of the new Cathedral, Salamanca

representaciones, one of the Passion and the other on the Resurrection. More characters are introduced into these *representaciones*, not only the disciples but also (in the first one) two hermits and a pious woman named Verónica. Such performances were the forerunners of the religious plays (*autos sacramentales*) which gained such prominence in the two following centuries in the expert hands of dramatists of the Golden Age.

Encina was a better musician than he was a poet and his musical settings of the *villancicos* which end his *Églogas* are charming. His verse is insipid and there is an air of bogus simplicity which too often characterises poems on pastoral themes. Encina's value lay in the trend which he created and which his numerous imitators extended and developed. GIL VICENTE (?1470–?1539), a Portuguese by birth, began with a monologue, spoken this time by a cowherd, in the style of Encina in 1502, but later turned his attention to comedies in which real characters are portrayed, whereas Encina had dealt merely with situations. His comedies have little or no plot, but they are fresh and spontaneous and give a vivid picture of Portugal at the end of the middle ages, when her ties with Spain were so close that many Portuguese writers like Vicente composed a considerable part of their works in Castilian. The *Comedia del viudo* (1514) is a fair sample of his farces, depicting an inconsolable widower who has two beautiful daughters. A young gentleman is attracted by their beauty and enters the widower's house disguised as a servant. His dilemma is that he finds himself in love with both the beauties and pays equal court to the pair of them. Not unnaturally the ladies demand that a choice be made and the gentleman in an agony of indecision consults a member of the audience (Prince John, who attended the performance). He is advised to marry the elder and a happy ending is achieved by the arrival of a friend of the gentleman coming in search of him. Very conveniently he marries the younger daughter and a dangerous situation is tidied up. In this trifling and ridiculous episode Vicente manages to infuse strong comic elements and delicate satire. His lyrical qualities enable him to make the love scenes between the young gentleman and his two sweethearts not only convincing, but beautiful.

Vicente wrote two long tragicomedies on themes from the novels of chivalry, *Don Duardos* (?1525) and *Amadís de Gaula* (1533), but though again the verse is delightful, the improbability of the theme of knightly romance leaves Vicente ill at ease. Not that he is lacking in the qualities of fantasy and imagination, for in his *autos* (sacred plays) he depicts a wide variety of characters, Judaic, Pagan and Christian, but they are all real people based on the peasants and nobles whom he had observed in life, whereas Amadís de Gaula could never be anything but preposterous. The *Auto de Sibila Cassandra* (?1513) was written to be performed at Christmas time: it reveals Vicente's rich vein of invention and his ability to slip from comedy and satire to love scenes and religious rhapsodies with astonishing ease. Cassandra is a village maiden who refuses to marry because she regards herself as a woman chosen to bear a son to God. Her suitor Solomon, her three uncles Abraham, Moses and Isaiah, and her three aunts, all try in vain to persuade her to change her mind. She remains adamant, pointing out in parentheses the miserable situation in which married peasant women find themselves in Portugal. Isaiah reproaches Cassandra for her presumption and declares in a most poetical passage that all the beauties of nature herald the loveliness of the maid who will bear a son to God. The aunts are sybils and fall to prophesying that the moment of deliverance has come to a world oppressed. A curtain is drawn back, revealing a cradle surrounded by four angels singing a lullaby. The peasants with the biblical and mythological names unite in worshipping the child and the play ends with a *villancico*.

The delicate poetic conception of this work contrasts strongly with a Castilian work of the same period by LUCAS FERNÁNDEZ (?1474–1542), professor of music at Salamanca. His *Auto de la Pasión* is beautiful and moving, but is filled with the obsession with the physical torments of the Crucifixion which still besets the Spanish mind in modern processions and ceremonies. Spaniards dwell incessantly on the suffering of Christ and the tragedy of his death rather than on the glory of his resurrection. Resignation to death and destruction is characteristic of the Spanish mentality.

The development of the technique of drama was carried a stage further by BARTOLOMÉ DE TORRES NAHARRO (d. ?1531) who was the first to postulate rules for dramatic composition. These are to be found in the *Proemio* to a collection of lyric poems and plays entitled *Propaladia* (that is, the first fruits of his muse). He defines comedy as 'nothing else but an ingenious sequence of outstanding events (which end happily) narrated by the characters'. The number of these characters should not be 'so few as to render the performance dull nor so many as to cause confusion', that is to say, between six and twelve. Two sorts of comedy are sufficient, he declares, the *comedia a noticia* (comedy of manners) and the *comedia a fantasía* (comedy with a plot like a novel). Finally he divides comedy into five *jornadas* (that is, action taking place within the space of a day) and this division remained standard in Spanish drama for close on a century.

It would be too much to ask that Torres Naharro should abide by his own rules, but there is no doubt that his best comedy *Himenea* (1517) shows an immense technical advance on any previous dramatic work in Spain. Directly inspired by *La Celestina* it describes how Himeneo falls in love with Febea and eventually wins her hand despite her brother's opposition. Their servants are engaged in a parallel love affair and the lofty language of Himeneo in pressing his suit on Febea is admirably parodied when the servants are courting. The contrast between high and low, and their resemblance too, were subjects that were to occupy the attention of Spanish and European playwrights for centuries to come until the French Revolution made Figaro a dated figure. Though Torres Naharro was only a second-rate poet, he was a keen observer of people and his satire shows that he had a strongly developed sense of moral philosophy. He left the Spanish stage well prepared for the masterpieces of the Golden Age which directly followed.

Joannes Morenus, pinx.   London. R.Bentley. 1846.   Joseph Brown, sc.

Chapter 7
The Golden Age

Italian forms in Spanish poetry

The unification of Castile and Aragon in 1479 had, through the Aragonese possessions in Italy, brought Spain much closer to Italian influence. After the accession of Carlos V in 1516 Spain formed a close association with Flemish culture, and the full tide of Renaissance enthusiasm for learning flooded into the Peninsula. In literature the first impulses came from Italy, when in 1526 the Venetian Ambassador in the court of Spain, Andrea Navagero, a scholar and humanist, persuaded a Catalan poet, JUAN BOSCÁN (?1490–1542) to attempt Spanish poems in Italian forms. The discussion occurred in the gardens of the Alhambra at Granada, and Boscán was so deeply impressed that on his return to Barcelona he immediately set about adapting the Italian eleven syllable line with its flowing musical rhythm to the sharp, harsher rhythm of Castilian. This, as has been seen, was nothing new in Spain, since the Marqués de Santillana had experimented successfully with sonnets a century before, but his works in manuscript only were little known. Boscán was an excellent prose writer and had a ready ear for rhythm, which enabled him to master the eleven syllable line, but his style is flat and lacking in colour. The metre is correct, but apart from the versification Boscán might as well have been writing in prose:

> Soy como aquél que vive en el desierto,
> del mundo y de sus cosas olvidado,
> y a descuido veis donde le ha llegado
> un gran amigo, al cual tuvo por muerto.

> (I am like a man who lives in the wilderness, forgotten by the world and its business, and by chance you see the arrival of a great friend whom he took to be dead.)

Boscán's achievement lay not in the poetry he produced, but in the fact that he realised the need for the rejuvenation of the Spanish poetry of his day, which was frivolous and lifeless. Moreover he had a collaborator of genius who seized his idea and perfected the Italianate forms in Spanish verse.

GARCILASO DE LA VEGA (?1501–36) was of noble birth, being a descendant of the Marqués de Santillana. He was a man of splendid ability, skilled in anything he attempted whether it was jousting, music, or composing Latin verses, and such was his modesty that his attainments excited the minimum of jealousy at court. He married in 1525 a noble lady, but since in his poems he never mentions his wife, it may be assumed that this was a marriage of convenience. He was in fact disappointed in his love for a Portuguese lady in waiting, Isabel Freire, and his melancholy found relief in writing poetry and also in acts of rash bravery in war. Losing the favour of Carlos V, Garcilaso was exiled first to an island in the Danube and later to Naples where he formed friendships with the leading literary men and humanists. It was there that he learnt of the premature death in 1533 of Doña Isabel Freire, who had unromantically married a Portuguese nobleman, Don Antonio de Fonseca el Gordo (the fat). Her death inspired Garcilaso's greatest poem, the first Égloga. Three years later Garcilaso who for all his culture never lost his taste for battle was killed imprudently leading, without helmet or cuirass, a charge on a tower near Fréjus held by French peasants. His Spanish poems (the Italian ones are lost) were given to his friend Boscán, but he died in 1542 and it was his widow who published in the following year the collected poems of her husband and Garcilaso, thereby initiating a literary revolution of the first magnitude.

Garcilaso's output (or what remains of it) was slight, consisting of three eclogues, two elegies, an epistle, five odes, thirty-eight sonnets and some minor poems. The Primera Égloga (it was in fact written in 1534, a year later than the second) is deservedly his best known work, for in it the level of inspiration never falters. Dedicated to his friend and protector, Don Pedro de Toledo, the Viceroy of Naples, it tells of the gentle laments of two shepherds, Salicio who sees his Galatea prefer another man and of Nemeroso who mourns the death in childbirth of his Elisa. The pastoral convention sits lightly on Garcilaso, who makes his shepherds cultured people, unlike Encina who clumsily attempts to imitate peasant dialogue. Clearly Garcilaso is recalling his own experiences and the personal feelings expressed are admirably sincere and restrained.

¿Quién me dijera, Elisa, vida mía,
cuando en aqueste valle al fresco viento
andábamos cogiendo tiernas flores,
que había de ver con largo apartamiento
venir el triste y solitario día
que diese amargo fin a mis amores?
El cielo en mis dolores
cargó la mano tanto,
que a sempiterno llanto
y a triste soledad me ha condenado;
y lo que siento más es verme atado
a la pesada vida y enojosa,
solo, desemparado,
ciego, sin lumbre en cárcel tenebrosa.

(Who could have told me, Elisa, my dearest, when in that valley in the cool breeze we were picking those fresh flowers, that I was to see that sad and lonely day with its long separation that would put an end to my love? Heaven has loaded me with grief with such a heavy hand that it has condemned me to everlasting tears and sad solitude; and what grieves me most is seeing myself bound to this plodding, wearisome life, alone, unaided, blind, without light in a dark prison.)

The versification consists of stanzas of fourteen lines of which 1–6 and 10–12 and 14 are of eleven syllables; the remainder contain seven syllables. This is the classic metre of the italian *canzone* and was well suited to such a musical language as Italian. It might well have been awkward and clumsy in Spanish, but Garcilaso makes every stanza flow with a soft, continuous rhythm and chooses his simple words with such a sure touch that the whole poem is a stream of soft melancholy music. It is indeed like the gentle murmuring of rivers which Garcilaso described with such delicacy. His feeling for nature is exquisite and is full of charm and grace like that of Fray Luis de León and other Spaniards, who, though living in a harsh and barren land, appreciate nature in its softest mood:

Cerca del Tajo soledad amena
de verdes sauces hay una espesura,
toda de yedra revestida y llena,
que por el tronco va hasta el altura,
y así la teje arriba y encadena,
que el sol no halla paso a la verdura;
el agua baña el prado, con sonido
alegrando la yerba y el oído.   (*Égloga tercera*)

(Near the Tagus in pleasant seclusion stands a thicket of green willows, all filled and clothed with ivy, which climbs up the trunk to the top and so weaves up around it and chains it that the sun finds no way to the green grass; the water bathes the meadow, charming the grass and the ear with its murmuring.)

Here in the *Égloga Tercera* is the first example in Spanish of the *octava rima* (eight line stanza) and Garcilaso manages this metre with equal ease and grace. He experimented in many other measures, using *tercetos* (three line stanzas) in the two *Elegías* and for the first time *verso suelto* (blank verse) in the *Epístola* addressed to Boscán from Avignon, the birthplace of Petrarch's Laura. In the well known *Canción Quinta*, usually entitled *La Flor de Gnido*, Garcilaso uses *liras* imitated from Tasso, verses of five lines of which 1, 3, 4 contain seven syllables and 2, 5 contain eleven. This poem was written to help a friend in Naples whose love was not being returned by a certain beauty, Doña Violante Sanseverino, in the Gnido district of the city. Garcilaso describes the sufferings of her lover and reminds her of the nymph whom the Gods turned into cold, hard marble because of her lack of love.

> *Hágate temerosa*
> *el caso de Anajárete, y cobarde,*
> *que de ser desdeñosa*
> *se arrepintió muy tarde;*
> *y así, su alma con su mármol arde.*

(Be fearful and afraid of the tale of Anaxarete who repented too late of being scornful, and so her soul burns within her marble body.)

It would seem that Garcilaso de la Vega was little else but an imitator and it is true that he follows closely the models of Ariosto, Petrarch, Tasso, not to mention Horace, Virgil and other classical poets, but in Renaissance days imitation was considered, as in seventeenth century France, closely allied to genius. Though Garcilaso adopts the forms of Italian poetry and the classic simplicity and restraint of the great Latin poets, his style, feeling and sensitivity are all his own. His whole personality is projected into his work, except perhaps his taste for war, which was no doubt an outlet for his melancholy and complementary to his poetry. His poems, despite the pastoral convention of the age, have suffered not a whit by the passage of time and are as fresh and charming today as when they captivated literary circles in Spain and Italy in the sixteenth century, running through more than twenty editions in thirty years.

Though the younger generation particularly accepted the Italianate forms with great enthusiasm, the traditional Spanish metres continued in use; by the end of the century the Italian style had been completely assimilated and existed side by side with the older measures. DON DIEGO HURTADO DE MENDOZA (1503–75), a man of great learning and a leading politician, cultivated both styles alike, though he was far more successful with the traditional metres. Even CRISTÓBAL DE CASTILLEJO (?1490–1550), who satirised most fiercely the Italian forms as being unsuitable for the Spanish language, occasionally uses sonnets and *octava rima*, perhaps to prove that his criticism was not mere sour grapes.

Mystic poetry

The new forms had quickly become an integral part of the armament of Spanish poets and were used with splendid effect in a type of verse in which Spaniards excelled: mystic poetry. The foremost mystic poet of the sixteenth century was FRAY LUIS DE LEÓN (?1528–91). The son of a magistrate of Belmonte in La Mancha, he was sent to the university of Salamanca at the age of fourteen. Two years later he took his vows as an Augustinian monk and devoted himself to his studies, achieving such distinction as a scholar of Latin, Greek, Hebrew and Theology that in spite of fierce competition he was elected to a professorship. Silent, melancholy and intolerant of fools, he nevertheless gained a reputation as a lecturer with a clear, pungent style of speech. Academic rivalries brought grievous trouble to him and in 1572 he was arrested by the Inquisition on the secret denunciation of two colleagues. For nearly five years he was kept in prison facing charges of having attacked the Vulgate by indicating mistranslations, and of having himself translated the *Song of Songs* into Spanish. This indeed he had imprudently done, contravening both canon and civil law, but it was established that he had made the translation to oblige a nun who knew no Latin and that the poem was never intended for publication. Fray Luis was eventually released by the Inquisition and was welcomed back to the university with acclaim. People flocked to the first lecture he gave at the end of January 1577 expecting to hear some caustic reference to his imprisonment, but he contented himself with opening his remarks as if in the middle of a course, *Dicebamus hesterna die* (we were saying yesterday), thereby maintaining his reputation as *el hombre más callado que sea conocido* (the most silent man ever known).

Beset with all the bickering and intrigue of the academic world, Luis de León was able to give expression in poetry to his longing for peace and retirement. In this he echoes Horace, his favourite Latin poet, and indeed such yearning for tranquillity is frequently uttered by urban Spaniards, though they rarely forsake city life. But Fray Luis always seems to be searching the heavens to find the place where his soul will find mystical union with God. He is deeply sensitive to the beauty of nature, but he sees natural beauty as a preview of the everlasting felicity that the soul can attain with God.

> *Despiértenme las aves*
> *con su cantar sabroso no aprendido,*
> *no los cuidados graves*
> *de que es siempre seguido*
> *quien al ajeno está antenido.*

(Let the birds awaken me with their delightful, untutored singing, not the heavy cares which always beset a man subjected to another's will.)

Vida retirada 1557

Quiet country life is not sufficient for him; he scorns the things of this world and yearns for the glory of the heavens. Contemplating the night sky adorned with countless stars, he sees the world sleeping unaware and his heart grieves that he has not yet achieved liberation from his earthly prison.

> *Morada de grandeza,*
> *templo de claridad y hermosura,*
> *mi alma que a tu alteza*
> *nació, ¿qué desventura*
> *la tiene en esta cárcel baja, oscura?*

(Abode of grandeur, temple of light and beauty, my soul which was born equally high, what misfortune keeps it in this low, dark prison?)

Noche serena, c. 1571

Like Garcilaso, Fray Luis attains perfect simplicity in his poetry, but there is perhaps an even greater intensity of feeling. His theme is more positive—man searching for his God rather than regret for unrequited love. Moreover Luis de León's power of description is outstanding; with the utmost concision he can vividly suggest scenes from nature, as for example the storm in the ode to Felipe Ruiz (*c.* 1587). He uses the *lira* extensively, perhaps because the form was invented by Tasso when endeavouring to convey the meaning and rhythm of Horace's Odes. It is a form which suits Luis de León to perfection, for it seems to exemplify with its short and long lines the surging of his soul's aspirations.

His poetic output was small; he was writing for himself to find relief from the feuds of university life and his poems were never intended for publication, though at the instance of a friend he did once classify them. In fact they were known only to a circle of friends and were not published until 1637. Luis de León was more concerned with his prose works, in which he took the utmost pains to attain in Spanish the purity and dignity of style of the greatest Latin authors. In prison he had begun the compilation of a book in the form of dialogues on the names given to Christ—arm of God, prince of peace, good shepherd and so on. This was printed together with a treatise in prose on the duties of a wife—*La perfecta casada*. Surprisingly he shows himself well acquainted with the psychology of women and offers sensible and unbigoted advice, castigating severely those wives who neglect their household duties to *calentar el suelo de la iglesia tarde y mañana* (to warm the church floor morning and evening).

Another mystic poet who wrote with even greater feeling but more obscurity was SAN JUAN DE LA CRUZ (1542–91). His life was devoted to the severest asceticism and most passionate mysticism, believing himself to have been saved by the Virgin when at the age of five he fell into a well while playing with his friends. Entering the Carmelite order he took a degree at the university of Salamanca and then began practising the severe reformed regime initiated by Santa Teresa, starving himself and passing the night in prayer and meditation. Such zeal for reform found little favour with his fellows, who kidnapped him on a December night in 1577 and cast him into prison at Toledo, where he was ill-treated, starved and whipped. Eventually he was inspired once more by a vision of the Virgin to make his escape by knotting his blankets together and climbing down from a window.

It was in prison that he began to write poetry and almost all his poems (which are very few in number) were composed there. The best known is the *Cántico espiritual entre el alma y Cristo, su esposo* written in *lira* form. The theme of the poem is the road taken by the soul from the beginning of the service of God until the perfect state of spiritual union. The soul bearing the allegorical name of *La Esposa* journeys over hill and vale seeking her loved one: she asks the woods, meadows, birds and animals whether they have seen him pass. The creatures answer:

> *Mil gracias derramando*
> *pasó por estos sotos con presura*
> *y yéndolos mirando*
> *con sola su figura*
> *vestidos los dejó de hermosura.*

(Shedding countless graces he passed through these woods hastily and merely by gazing at them as he passed he left them clothed in beauty.)

La Esposa hurries on in despair searching for her beloved until at last she finds him beside a crystal spring in a flowery meadow and blissfully she devotes herself to the joy of contemplative love.

Such a religious allegory may appear a trifle indigestible, but the spirit of the poem is of burning intensity and the words pour forth in rich cadences with an astonishingly varied vocabulary. Poetry of this type can only be written in a frenzy of inspiration. Unfortunately San Juan de la Cruz composed forty chapters of commentaries for the poem's forty verses and, though his glosses are well written and closely reasoned, modern readers may often dispense with them.

SANTA TERESA DE JESUS (1515–82) also composed a few mystic poems and many more attributed to her including the famous anonymous sonnet *A Cristo crucificado:*

> *No me mueve, mi Dios, para quererte*
> *el cielo que me tienes prometido.*
>
> (I am not moved to love thee, O my God, by the heaven thou hast promised me.)

This, in its passionate sincerity, is one of the most deeply moving poems in all Spanish literature, but at present it cannot be ascribed definitely to any one author.* Santa Teresa's chief works are in prose and were written either for the guidance of nuns in the convents which she had reformed or else at the instance of her confessors to give vent to her thoughts and feelings of mystical religious ecstasy. The *Libro de las misericordias de Dios* (1566) is a kind of spiritual autobiography and is a highly personal record of the experiences of a most remarkable woman whose mind could dwell on thoughts of highest heaven or descend to the most practical details of everyday life; she was in fact an ideal combination of Mary and Martha. She used to sit down and write after receiving communion, and she wrote with feverish haste, scarcely pausing for thought and making no corrections. Her prose is the normal conversational language of educated people of the day and, despite the grammatical errors and digressions, her writing charms with its freshness and spontaneity as well as the beauty of her mystical thoughts and the clarity and intelligence of her practical ideas. She can describe the soul as a *pobre mariposilla, atada con tantas cadenas, que no te dejen volar lo que querrías* (poor little butterfly, tied with so many chains that they do not let you fly where you would like). She can also exclaim about the extreme thinness of San Pedro de Alcántara (who had been practising

* The latest theory is that the poem is the work of a Mexican priest, Miguel de Guevara.

rigorous asceticism for more than forty years) *que no parecía sino hecho de raíces de árboles* (that he seemed to be made only of tree roots). Perhaps Santa Teresa's writings scarcely come into the category of literature, but her *Libro de las fundaciones* and her four hundred and more letters throw light on the mind of an administrator of genius, while the *Camino de perfección* and *Las Moradas* are a most clear and original exposition of the aspirations of the human soul. Fray Luis de León said that in many parts of her writings it was not the human mind at work, but the Holy Spirit speaking through her, guiding her pen and her hand.

Development of the novel

Spanish literature formed the cradle of the novel in Europe, and such was the proliferation of novels in the sixteenth century in Spain that the word hotbed might well be substituted for cradle. There was a craze throughout the century for novels of chivalry touched off by *Amadís de Gaula* (1508) compiled by Garcí Rodríguez de Montalbo. Based on the Arthurian romances it is at least readable, which most of the later novels of chivalry are not, at any rate for the modern reader, although they were avidly devoured in sixteenth-century Spain. In 1558 a Portuguese Jorge de Montemayor (?1520–61) produced a pastoral novel, *La Diana*, imitated from the *Arcadia* (1481) by the Italian writer Jacobo Sannazaro. Again the reading of such a lengthy, discursive novel with its absence of action, its mixture of prose and indifferent verse and its utter artificiality would nowadays be heavy going; it was, however, much appreciated in its day and the pastoral episodes in Shakespeare, not to mention the plot of the *Two Gentlemen of Verona*, are echoes of it.

The really original contribution that Spain made to the novel was the establishment of a completely new type—the picaresque novel. *Pícaro* in Spanish means a rogue and the picaresque novel deals with the adventures of someone who has to live by his wits. This type of social predator was on the increase by the middle of the sixteenth century, for the early prosperity and the influx of bullion from America had greatly fostered the idea of gaining a livelihood without working. The first picaresque novel was brief and anonymous: *La vida de Lazarillo de Tormes*, published in 1554, but compiled possibly as early as 1539. The book achieved immediate popularity and three separate editions appeared in a year in Alcalá de Henares, Burgos and Antwerp; numerous subsequent editions followed with translations into French, Dutch

English, German, Italian and even Latin. The reason for its success is that it paints a picture of life as it was in plain, even vulgar language; there is no pretension or artificiality, but humour (often of the cruellest type), satire, excellent characterisation and a portrait of the triumph of human pertinacity and ingenuity over the extremes of adversity.

The story is told in the first person by young Lázaro whose father has been transported for stealing and his mother whipped for the same offence. She commends Lázaro to a blind beggar of Salamanca whom he is to serve as a guide. Lázaro's apprenticeship begins at once, when his master tells him to place his ear to a stone bull on the bridge at Salamanca and hear the strange sounds within. Lázaro obeys and the beggar promptly bangs the boy's head against the stone exclaiming: *Necio, aprende que el mozo del ciego un punto ha de saber más que el diablo.* (Fool, you must learn that a blind man's boy must be a jump ahead of the devil himself.) Lázaro thereupon reflects: *Verdad dice éste, que me cumple avivar el ojo y avisar, pues solo soy, y pensar como me sepa valer.* (He is right, I must keep my eyes open and be on the alert, because I am alone in the world and I have to make my own way.)

The blind beggar was cunning to a degree and extorted much money from kindly passers-by, but his treatment of Lázaro was mean and cruel; he starved and beat him, compensating him only by sage advice on how to extract a living from a hard world. Lázaro at length decided to leave so pitiless a master and departed after playing a savage trick on the blind beggar who was left half dead with his head split open. Lázaro's next master was a priest who was infinitely more miserly than the beggar. *Escapé del trueno y di en el relámpago* (I escaped from the thunder and struck the lightning), is Lázaro's comment. So little was he given to eat that he could scarcely stand on his feet and would have died had he not been able to steal bread with elaborate cunning from the chest in which it was kept locked. When the priest discovered the thefts, he put Lázaro out into the streets saying that he did not want in his household *tan diligente servidor* (such a hard-working servant).

Lázaro, almost dead from hunger, begs some crusts from charitable people, who, as soon as he is partially recovered, turn him loose, telling him to find a master. He is engaged by a well-dressed gentleman who dashes Lázaro's hopes by spending the whole day without eating, except that he borrows for his own use one of the crusts that Lázaro had hidden in his shirt. The gentleman lives in a dark house bare of furniture as of food, but he takes infinite care of his clothes, delights in his magnificent sword, which he would not sell at any price, walks abroad with all the airs and graces of a grandee, attends mass and with heroic determination hides from the world the fact that he is a starving pauper. This is the earliest portrait in Spanish literature of the impoverished *hidalgo* who figures so largely later on. Lázaro takes a liking to his stoic master, but for practical reasons leaves him for a succession of others with whom he fares little better, until he enters the service of a, chaplain who is liberal enough not only to feed him but also to pay him so that in four years he is able to save enough to buy a decent suit of clothes. Finally Lázaro finds himself serving the town crier of Toledo and married to the maid (and mistress) of the Archpriest of San Salvador. Lázaro closes the account of his life rejoicing that thanks to the favour shown to his wife by the Archpriest he himself is able to live *en la cumbre de toda buena fortuna* (at the peak of good fortune).

The charm of this brief novel lies in the directness of the narration and the wittiness of the style. There is no moralising, no comment on good and evil, no lesson drawn—just a succession of incidents drawn from life and vividly described. The reader is left to decide for himself how much the scenes are intended to be satirical, and it is a relief to be credited with intelligence and free to make a choice. Finally there is an unshakable gaiety and optimism in Lázaro, who faces adversity resolutely and realistically, never lamenting but always with a wry comment to make on every disaster and every human failing, as for instance when the charitable folk of Toledo turned him out only half cured from his prolonged starvation he observed that *ya la caridad se subió al cielo* (now charity has gone up to heaven).

It is strange that a book so immediately popular was not quickly followed by imitations or sequels. Perhaps *Lazarillo de Tormes* was ahead of its time and that the grandiose expansion of Philip II's empire masked the poverty of life at home, or perhaps such a book, with its implied criticism of the Spanish economy, was dangerous to write. At all events no similar work appeared in Philip II's reign. In 1599 MATEO ALEMÁN (1547–?1614) published his *Guzmán de Alfarache*. The public devoured it, and twenty-nine editions were printed in less than five years, after which a second part was produced. Mateo Alemán was well qualified to write the autobiography of a *pícaro* since he had led a wandering life of great hardship, supporting himself with minor governmental posts, supervising sales, auctions and contracts and finding himself frequently imprisoned for debt. His novel begins in a fashion similar to *Lazarillo de Tormes*, with the youthful Guzmán leaving his home to make his way in the world; unlike Lázaro he has had quite a soft upbringing because his mother was the kept woman of a rich old man, and Guzmán goes forth into the world with confidence in God and in the goodness of the human race. A series of rude shocks awaits him, like Candide, and from the very outset he suffers cruelly from the baseness of men. He has not the uprightness of Candide and he is corrupted by the company he keeps.

> Perdíme con las malas compañías ... Cuando comencé a servir, procuraba trabajar y dar gusto; después los malos amigos me perdieron dulcemente. La ociosidad ayudó gran parte, y aun fue las causa de todos mis daños. (I was ruined by evil company—When I began in service, I tried to work and give satisfaction; later evil companions gradually corrupted me. Idleness contributed considerably and was indeed the cause of my entire downfall.)

Guzmán's adventures take him over most of Spain and a good part of Italy. At times he is in the service of exalted persons such as a cardinal and the French Ambassador in Rome, but he can never settle and a series of unhappy adventures with women always reduces him to his real profession, which is thieving. When his second wife (on whose immoral earnings he has largely been living) deserts Guzmán, he resorts again to robbery, but he is arrested and sent to the galleys where the savage treatment (vividly described) drives him to the repentance of despair. He denounces a plot to revolt by his fellow slaves and is rewarded by the promise of freedom.

Here the second part ends with the author heralding a third instalment, which fortunately was never written, for the book is already too long and far too diffuse. Unlike Lázaro, Guzmán is of a moralising turn of mind and all the incidents are subjected to lengthy commentaries; the novel ceases to be a satire and becomes a cautionary tale. These moral digressions are well written and form an interesting study of national psychology, but they reduce the interest of the novel by slowing up the action.

The scenes, incidents and characters are rich in variety and vividly portrayed, but the author is filled with the bitterest pessimism; everybody and everything are corrupt—officials are incompetent, the law is inept and biased, tradesmen are thieves, innkeepers are robbers, women are faithless. Guzmán, who has a conscience, a feeling of responsibility, a sense of national pride, can find consolation in nothing. His final conversion to God is forced by harsh circumstances and his freedom is won only by the betrayal of his comrades. Lázaro despite the hardships he suffers never loses faith in himself and remains cheerful to the end, describing his gradual rise in the world in the witty, racy language of the gutter. *Guzmán de Alfarache* is written in literary language, dignified and elegant, but natural and easy, as good prose as Cervantes himself composed.

Miguel Cervantes

MIGUEL CERVANTES (1547–1616) suffered as many hardships in life as Mateo Alemán, if not more, but he maintained his optimism and faith in human nature. The son of an obscure surgeon in Alcalá de Henares, Cervantes went early in his life to Rome, probably in the service of Cardinal Acquaviva. In Italy he entered the army and saw service at the battle of Lepanto (1571) where he was wounded, losing the use of his left hand. On his way home to Spain in 1575 with letters of recommendation from Don John of Austria, he was captured by Berber pirates and spent five years as a prisoner at Algiers, where he made vigorous but unavailing efforts to escape. He was at length ransomed in 1580 and returned to Spain, where wounded ex-soldiers were treated with ungrateful indifference. To earn a living he turned to literature, for which he had early shown talent.

First he tried his hand at writing plays and according to his own account produced twenty or thirty between 1582 and 1587. Of these only two survive, *El trato de Argel* and *La Numancia*. The first provides interesting autobiographical details since it deals with the life of captives at Algiers, but apart from the realism of the subject matter it is not a convincing play because its development is clumsy and its characterisation is weak. *La Numancia* is an epic of Roman Spain which might well suit some modern Hollywood producer, but to portray Scipio's siege of Numancia with all the attendant horrors of the heroic defence strained the primitive stage technique of Cervantes's day beyond its limits.

Achieving only modest success in the theatre Cervantes turned to the fashionable literature of the time and published in 1585 his pastoral novel *La Galatea*. Written in noble prose, it has its moments of passion and excitement, but much of it is taken up with the colourless courting of artificial shepherds. Cervantes long cherished an affection for this work, for he talks about a second part of it in *Don Quijote* (Part 1, Chapter 6), but though some critics praised *La Galatea*, only three editions appeared during the author's lifetime. The book is interlarded with poems, some of which, like the *Canto de Calíope*, are unduly long. Cervantes all his life longed to succeed as a poet and his output (leaving aside his plays in verse) is extensive, but unfortunately his poetry is mostly heavy, clumsy and often prosaic in the choice of words, and it seems that he never mastered the difficulties of rhyme.

Disappointed with the rewards that literature afforded and constantly in debt, Cervantes between 1587 and 1597 took various posts in public administration in Andalusia, meeting all types of people and storing up rich material which was to appear later in *Don Quijote*. At one time he was engaged in collecting stores for the navy and the army, but his manipulation of public funds, though not dishonest, was so inept that three times (1592, 1597 and 1602) he was imprisoned for irregularities in the accounts. Possibly an unscrupulous man would have made a fortune by speculation in such posts and Cervantes could claim, as does Sancho when leaving the Duke's service (Part II, Chapter 53), *que saliendo yo desnudo, como salgo, no es menester otra señal para dar a entender que he gobernado como un ángel* (that leaving, as I do, broke, I need no other witness to testify that I governed like an angel).

In 1603 Cervantes was living at Valladolid, possibly having followed the court there in the hope of preferment. He was living in the utmost poverty with two sisters, a niece and his illegitimate daughter Isabel (his marriage in 1583 to a girl eighteen years his junior had been a failure and the couple had quickly separated). The women earned a little money by sewing while Cervantes was working away on his novel about a madman, the idea for which is said to have occurred to him while in prison in 1597. At length the long first part of *Don Quijote* was published in 1605 and immediately achieved extraordinary success. By 1607 *Don Quijote* was well known as far afield as Germany and Peru, and Cervantes's playful prophecy in the dedication of the second part that the Emperor of China wanted to use the novel as a textbook for learning Spanish was not far from fulfilment.

Success may have brought fame, but certainly did not bring riches, and Cervantes, who had moved to Madrid, in 1606, continued to live in poverty until the end of his life. For reasons unknown he was unable to complete the promised second part of *Don Quijote* for some years and in the meantime published in 1613 his *Novelas Ejemplares*, a series of short stories, some of which must have been written considerably earlier. Apart from *Don Quijote* itself these short stories form the most readable part of Cervantes's works. They are called Exemplary Tales, so the author declares, because each contains a moral lesson. It may be that Cervantes was anxious lest some of the stories which deal with low life and its brutality, would be taken amiss. He need not have worried;

although the twelve tales deal with a varied cross-section of Spanish life, including gypsies, thieves, soldiers and shepherds (far removed from those of the pastoral convention), Cervantes's outlook on life is serene and optimistic, so that low life sheds much of its sinister aspect. Indeed there is a tendency towards sentimental idealisation, as in *La Gitanilla* where the heroine Preciosa is a jewel amid a band of gypsies who have as little vice in them as the Pirates of Penzance. Similar to *The Pirates of Penzance* it turns out that she is the long lost child of noble parents and is enabled conveniently to marry the young gentleman who has fallen in love with her. A similar conventional ending is to be found in *La Ilustre Fregona* where the dazzingly beautiful scrubbing maid inspires love in a well born student who is doing some slumming; fortunately she turns out to have blue blood in her veins and the danger of a mixture of classes by marriage is averted. It would, of course, be foolish to condemn these tales because of the different outlook on social matters in modern times; equally silly is to damn them on the grounds of unreality. Realism is not an essential ingredient of the short story and these two tales have grace and charm and give colourful descriptions of gypsy life and the thronging bustle of a busy inn.

The story of *Rinconete y Cortadillo* is a surprising satire on organised crime. It describes humorously how two ragged young ruffians are unable to practise their particular line of swindling in Seville until they have become members of the *hermandad* or trade union of ruffians organised by Monipodio. At a somewhat rowdy *merienda* (supper party) the rogues discuss the various jobs they are about to undertake, a few knifings, a little blackmail and so on. Their work is mainly accomplished at night and by day they are highly respectable citizens and regular churchgoers. Perhaps the picture is too genial, but there is a wealth of colourful and picturesque detail which makes the story delightful to read. On similar picturesque lines is the *Coloquio de dos perros* in which one dog, Berganza, of a jovial and talkative nature, tells another dog, Cipión, wise and solemn, his long story of adventures with various masters—shepherds, a merchant, a constable, soldiers, a witch, gypsies, strolling players and finally a hospital. It forms a valuable social document of the times as well as being of literary interest for the vividness of the series of scenes it presents.

Possibly the best known of the *Novelas Ejemplares* is the *Licenciado Vidriera*, the story of a young graduate of the University of Salamanca who loses his reason as a result of an aphrodisiac administered by a lady in love with him. His particular form of madness is to believe that he

Strolling Players from a seventeenth century illustration of Don Quijote

is made of glass and he begs all others not to come near him for fear he shall get broken. Though his reason is turned, his intelligence remains unimpaired and he gains a widespread reputation for his apt, witty and satirical comments on poets, pimps, priests, doctors, apothecaries, judges and so on. At length he is cured of his lunacy by a monk and finds that although everyone consulted him while he was mad, no one is interested in his opinion now that he is sane. Disappointed he joins the army in Flanders where he dies honourably on the battlefield. Apart from the personal recollections of Cervantes's service in the Spanish armies (the story opens in Italy) there is the interesting study of insanity and the bitter reflection on the failure of the intelligent graduate when sane. There is no telling when this particular story was written; if it was composed before the success of *Don Quijote*, it might be an echo of Cervantes's own sense of failure in life. At all events the situation of Don Quijote and the *Licenciado Vidriera* can stand close comparison.

Don Quijote's Encounter with the Windmills vol I part

Don Quijote tilting at windmills

Both are studies in insanity and both are failures since neither would have been heard of but for his delusions.

It is quite possible that Cervantes at first intended *Don Quijote* to form one of the *Novelas Ejemplares*, for the tale might well have ended with the return of the knight across the donkey's back after the drubbing he received at the inn. It would then have formed a brief satire on the doleful effects of misguided idealism, but clearly Cervantes realised the infinite possibilities of the theme provided the madman could set forth again accompanied by someone the world considers sane. Hence the second sortie of Don Quijote mounted on his faithful but broken-winded nag Rocinante, in company with Sancho Panza on his ass, as practical and earthy as his master is idealistic and vague. Then begins an interminable series of adventures, many of which have become so famous that they are almost proverbial, tilting at windmills which Don Quijote insists are hostile giants, the visit to the inn which the knight assumed to be a castle, the freeing of the galley slaves, the strange events on the Sierra Morena, the dream in which Don Quijote fights with the wine-skins. Finally the knight, who is always talking of enchantments, is persuaded that a spell has been cast upon him and is taken back to his village caged in the back of a bullock cart. Once at home Don Quijote, to the despair of his friends (the canon, the vicar and the barber) merely shows himself disposed to sally forth again in search of knightly adventures. Here the first part ends without any promise of a sequel, but the extraordinary reception given to the novel encouraged Cervantes to embark on a second part. Whether he began writing at once is not known, but as late as 1614 (nine years after the publication of the first part) only half the work had been done. Shortly afterwards a spurious second part was published under the name of Alonso Fernández de Avellaneda, presumably a pseudonym, for nothing is known of any such author, although the book is of some literary merit. This piece of literary piracy so angered Cervantes that he quickly finished the genuine sequel, which was printed in 1615.

The action is resumed a little over a month after Don Quijote's humiliating return in the bullock cart and the persevering knight sets forth for the third time with his faithful squire, Sancho Panza, who by now is well versed in the conventions of knight errantry and who is becoming, if possible, more deluded than his master. The first task that Don Quijote sets himself is to seek his patroness, the imaginary peerless lady, Dulcinea del Toboso. When they reach the miserable village of El Toboso, not unnaturally they can find no one who can direct them to the lady's abode. Meeting three village girls Sancho Panza makes out that they are Dulcinea accompanied by two maids of honour. Don Quijote is incredulous seeing the ugliness and slatternliness of the rustic maidens, but Sancho cunningly persuades his master that he must be bewitched, declaring the females to be in reality beautiful and high-born ladies. The knight's protestations of undying love and devotion fail to impress the country girls who continue on their way making angry and vulgar comments on the behaviour of the Knight of the Doleful Countenance.

Many other adventures follow until Don Quijote is kindly received in the palace of a real Duke and Duchess, who humour his insane notions. There at last the knight is able to fulfil his promise of giving Sancho Panza an island to govern, for his squire is put in charge of a small township (*villa*) on the Duke's estates. Sancho finds that the burden of responsibility is heavier than he had imagined and is not sorry to be relieved of his duties in order to accompany his master to a jousting festival in Barcelona, where Don Quijote as a medieval knight cuts a strange figure in a modern, bustling, commercial city. He is defeated in battle by the knight of the White Moon, none other than his neighbour Sansón Carrasco, who with the laudable intention of ending Don Quijote's knight errantry bids him return home as a condition of defeat. The victor's commands are dutifully obeyed and on reaching home Don Quijote falls mortally ill, recovering his reason shortly before he dies.

The danger with *Don Quijote* is that commentators are apt to read into the novel far deeper philosophical meanings than Cervantes ever intended to convey. Part of the charm of the book is that the reader is free to speculate, to make his own interpretation of the rich variety of incidents and characters displayed and of the meaning of the endless series of discussions between the knight and his squire. It would be foolish to insist that Cervantes had any motive other than that of entertaining his public, first with a short burlesque of a lunatic who imagines himself to be a knight errant, and subsequently taking advantage of the ease with which the theme could be extended. It is tempting also to assume that Cervantes was portraying himself in his hero, whose physical description coincides with the author's—*aguileña y algo corva la nariz, los bigotes grandes y caídos* (an aquiline and somewhat hooked nose and large drooping moustaches). Moreover, the hero's character matures and develops, especially in the second part, where Don Quijote is no longer a pantomime figure constantly receiving ill-deserved drubbings, but an eccentric idealist, capable of shrewd judgment and sensible advice, but always seeking to achieve what is beyond his physical powers.

Eager Cervantine scholars have counted no less than 669 characters in Don Quijote, but throughout both parts of the novel the focus is always on the two central figures to such an extent that occasionally Cervantes indulges in pastoral episodes to ease the tension. But these are digressions which displeased his readers and from which he later desisted. The remarkable feature is the way in which the two characters, from constant companionship, almost exchange natures; late in the second part it is Sancho who seems besotted with romantic dreams and Don Quijote who counsels caution. Perhaps the two characters are one and the same person with the conflicting elements of personality projected in double image. The popularity of the novel in Spain must surely be due to the fact that knight and squire exactly sum up the greatness and shortcomings of the national character—those yearnings for magnificent achievement, the courage and patience in adversity, the inability to depart one iota from ideas or opinions once declared. Like Don Quijote, who when vanquished still maintains that

Dulcinea del Toboso es la más hermosa mujer del mundo, y yo el más desdichado caballero de la tierra, y no es bien que mi flaqueza defraude esta verdad. (Dulcinea del Toboso is the most beautiful woman in the world, and I the most unfortunate knight on earth, and it is not right that my weakness should distort the truth.)

Yet Spaniards for all their idealism and tenacity of purpose accept all sorts of makeshift devices to render the business of living possible. Anyone who visits Spain cannot fail to be struck by the grandiose designs and indeed achievements side by side with squalid expedients— such as a glorious architectural triumph festooned with drooping, badly insulated electric wires.

But Don Quijote is not only a national book; it is a universal one. It is in fact almost the only Spanish literary work known outside Spain to anyone other than students. This is perhaps because everyone to a greater or less degree has the dual personality portrayed by the knight and his squire. We all long for great deeds and have to be content for the most part with humdrum mediocrity. A group of persons assembled anywhere will reveal this fact at once. Cervantes chose to portray, no doubt quite unwittingly, timeless and universal characters who would undergo an astonishing series of adventures covering every aspect of life and these adventures are told in language equally rich and varied. Don Quijote uses stately and archaic turns of phrase while Sancho employs common speech with that colourful tinge so often found among countryfolk, together with an unending string of proverbs. When Cervantes is narrating events, his style is careful, but apt, expressive and natural. He has moreover the gift of clarity; he writes so that all shall understand him, explaining thieves' slang, gypsy dialect, technical terms and provincial words, yet never being tedious. He writes in fact as if he were aware that he was writing for posterity.

The last work that Cervantes prepared for publication (it appeared posthumously in 1617) was *Persiles y Sigismunda* a long, discursive tale of the loves of the son of the King of Iceland and the daughter of the King of Frisland. The episodes in the mists and ice of northern lands are tediously fantastic; only when the couple move south to the Peninsula and then on to Rome does the story come alive, with Cervantes describing scenes and persons from observation and not from imagination. Two years previously (1615) his reputation as the author of *Don Quijote* had enabled him to publish a collection of *Ocho comedias y ocho entremeses, nunca representados*. The eight comedies scarcely deserve notice, but the short farces or interludes are remarkable for their wit and able characterisation and on them alone Cervantes merits fame as a dramatist.

The drama of the Golden Age

In his youth Cervantes had witnessed the actors of the troupe of the great LOPE DE RUEDA (d. 1565), the founder of the Spanish theatre. He and his company presented plays in towns and villages, using as a theatre the market place, a blind alley or a *patio*; all their props and costumes were contained in a sack and two blankets hung on a string served as a dressing room and as a concealment for the musicians who modestly chanted ballads anonymously at various points of the performance. The stage consisted usually of benches placed in a square with planks laid across. With such primitive scenic arrangements the plays performed were of necessity simple in construction and were normally mere dialogues in the pastoral convention. Such colloquies tended to be dull, and to enliven them brief farces were performed as interludes and the custom has remained in force ever since in Spanish theatres. As with Cervantes, Lope de Rueda's best compositions were not his plays, which are clumsy and in poor taste, but his *pasos* (sketches or tableaux), which are lively comic incidents drawn from real life with witty, satirical dialogue (*socarronería*).

The efforts of Lope de Rueda, chiefly in Madrid and Seville, gave rise to a veritable passion for theatricals throughout Spain; the villages were entertained by strolling players—a *bululú* (single actor), a *ñaque* (pair of actors), a *gangarilla* (four actors) or a *cambaleo* (five actors and an actress). Even to this day such itinerant players are not unknown, and high up in the *sierra* at some dingy inn it is possible to meet a dilapidated omnibus transporting a seedy troupe which gallantly bawls *Madam Butterfly* to audiences of grave, attentive yokels. The large towns in the sixteenth century soon had proper theatres (by 1584 there were three in Madrid) and the technique of staging and presenting plays advanced rapidly. The theatre appealed to all classes and unlike France in the next century it was the populace not the gentry on whom dramatists depended and whom they set out to please. As a result Spanish drama (which is the real glory of the Golden Age) is essentially romantic in inspiration, packed with incident, with strong sentiment and love interest and composed for the most part in traditional *romances* instead of Italianate verse forms.

The man who satisfied the gluttonous appetite of the Spanish public for plays was LOPE DE VEGA (1562–1635), who was credited by his biographer (Montalbán) with having written 1,800 plays and 400 *autos* (sacred dramas). So popular was Lope de Vega in his day that authors willingly ascribed their plays to him, prefering anonymity and box office appeal to literary glory. Nevertheless, some five hundred plays of all types have survived and can be attributed with reasonable certainty to the facile pen of Lope de Vega, *el monstruo de la naturaleza*, as Cervantes calls him. The son of a modest artisan who had moved from Santander to Madrid, Lope de Vega early showed his prodigious capacity for writing verse and was credited with having composed a play by the age of twelve. He received an excellent education in the Jesuit College at Madrid and later at the university of Alcalá de Henares. Passionately religious, he was preparing for the priesthood when he fell in love with the wife of an actor, Elena Osorio, but he later broke with her because he suspected that she was having dealings with a gentleman at court. For publishing libellous satires on her parents Lope de Vega was prosecuted and exiled from Madrid (1588). In the same year he eloped with a girl named Isabel de Urbina, whom he deserted after marriage in order to join the Armada. During this disastrous expedition he found the time to write a poem of some 11,000 lines, *La hermosura de Angélica*, a continuation of Ariosto's *Orlando Furioso*. Safely back in Spain in December 1588 he set up home for a time in Valencia writing plays for the Madrid theatres. Later he entered the service of the Duque de Alba and shortly after his return to Madrid (now a widower) he fell in love with an actress, Micaela de Luján, who bore him five illegitimate children.

In 1598 he married Juana de Guarda, the daughter of a rich butcher, whose humble origin at times left Lope a target for snobbish literary wits. Nevertheless he settled down into respectable married life until his wife died in 1613, whereupon he took holy orders, for despite all his adventures his devotion to religion was still intense. Unfortunately his weakness for women overcame his aspirations to the priesthood and in 1616 he fell violently in love with a woman named Marta de Nevares. Any happiness that this affair engendered was of short duration for Doña Marta went blind and then mad, although she continued living until 1632. Two years later Lope's only son, much beloved, was drowned on a voyage to America and not long afterwards the aged

RIGHT   *Lope de Vega*

playwright succumbed to a chill caught while tending his small but highly prized garden in Madrid.

Lope de Vega was a man of violent contrasts and considerable moral instability, but of his creative genius there can be no doubt. The astonishing fact is that nearly all his plays still read today are of a uniformly high standard in spite of the fact that they were composed in the shortest time possible, some in as little as twenty-four hours. To achieve this a system was needed and Lope de Vega reveals his formula for play-writing half seriously, half comically in a poem addressed to the Spanish Academy in 1609, *Arte nuevo de hacer comedias en este tiempo*. He reduced plays from five to three acts; the first act is the exposition in which the situation is described, in the second act complications are introduced and these are maintained until well over half way through the final act, for if it were possible to guess the dénouement earlier the audience would not stay till the end. Spanish audiences according to Lope were hard to please and he declared that the 'fury of the seated Spaniard is not soothed unless he is shown in a period of two hours everything from Genesis to the Last Judgment'. He discovered an admirable method of extending and complicating the action as well as introducing comic relief; this was the presentation of the *gracioso* and sometimes the *graciosa* too, characters of inferior status who guyed the actions of the main personages by their parallel love affairs. This device was not new, for Torres Naharro had made use of it (p. 241), but Lope de Vega exploited it with such skill that for centuries it became the standard practice in Spanish, French and Italian drama.

Lope de Vega at times affected to scorn rules for writing plays:

> *y, cuando he de escribir una comedia*
> *encierro los preceptos con seis llaves*
> (*Arte nuevo*)

(and when I have to write a play, I lock up the rules with half a dozen keys)

At other times he is apt to blame his audience and the tyranny they exercised for his not being able to write plays in the classic mould of Plautus and Terence; he had to content himself with stuffing his poems with classical allusions expressed in Italianate forms. In drama he studied carefully the tastes of his audiences and gave them what they liked—a mixture of tears and laughter, rapid action, romantic and patriotic sentiment, the triumph of the weak against the strong and finally the happy ending. Only two of his plays really end tragically and one of them, *La Estrella de Sevilla*, is possibly not his work. Lope is a realist, but in common with most Spaniards his realism is based on optimism and the sordid side of life is generally excluded. His range of subjects and his facility for invention are astounding, but basically all his plays are composed on the same solid framework. In old age he was regularly writing two plays a week, and to achieve this required genius, but Lope's genius is firmly harnessed to a reliable method.

Lope de Vega was a skilful and fertile poet, but he applied a rule of thumb to the verse which he chose for his plays:

> *Acomode los versos con prudencia*
> *a los sujetos de que va tratando:*
> *las décimas son buenas para quejas,*
> *el soneto está bien en los que aguardan,*
> *las relaciones piden los romances;*
> *aunque en octavas lucen por extremo,*
> *son los tercetos para cosas graves,*
> *y para las de amor las redondillas.*
>
> (*Arte nuevo*)

> (Suit the verse with care to the subjects which are being treated: ten line stanzas are good for laments, the sonnet is fine for moments of expectancy, narratives demand ballad form; although eight line stanzas are particularly brilliant, triplets are best for solemn matters and for the affairs of love, roundelays.)

The *romance* is the normal verse form employed and though it is highly suitable for relating rapid action, it lacks the grandeur of the longer line such as English blank verse, and sometimes Lope's plays have a startling terseness which actors have to conceal by their skill, as occasionally happens in Shakespeare. Often Lope's style tends to be ambiguous (as with Shakespeare's clowns), but this was done deliberately because the equivocal way of speaking was popular with the groundlings, who liked to show how clever they were in understanding conundrums. It might be thought that simple people would demand simple speech, but this is by no means so in any country; when the Cockney removal man talks of 'shifting the Joanna' (rather than piano) he is unwittingly displaying the same liking for mystification in speech as the audiences of Shakespeare and Lope de Vega. But Lope like Shakespeare realised also the plain man's appreciation of real poetry and his plays are full of passages of great lyrical beauty.

His production is too huge and too uniform in standard to make it easy to single out plays for special study, but some have come to fix themselves firmly in the minds of critics and public alike. Two of them are similar in subject, *Fuente Ovejuna* and *El mejor alcalde, el rey*, in that they both portray the sturdy independence of ordinary Spaniards and also extol the sense of justice and democratic feeling of Spanish monarchs. Such a theme is calculated to appeal to an audience of Spaniards, in whom hatred of tyranny and loyalty to the King are fixed tenets. In *Fuente Ovejuna* the ordinary people of an obscure township in Extremadura struggle against the tyranny of the local overlord and finally kill him. The officers of the law cannot discover the murderer since the killing was a concerted effort of the whole town, and the King, realising the provocation, pardons the inhabitants. In *El mejor alcalde, el rey* the theme is more intimate, for the local overlord after giving his consent to the marriage of two of his vassals forcibly kidnaps the bride. Sancho (the husband) journeys to León to beg the aid of King Alfonso VII (1126–57) who gives him a letter to the overlord, Don Tello, sternly ordering him to restore Elvira to her husband, but Don Tello snaps his fingers at the King's authority and threatens Sancho. The King himself subsequently arrives disguised as a magistrate and expostulates with Don Tello, who roughly brushes him aside. King Alfonso then reveals his true identity and pronounces sentence with grim terseness:

> *Da, Tello, a Elvira la mano,*
> *para que pagues la ofensa,*
> *con ser su esposo; y después*
> *que te corten la cabeza,*
> *podrá casarse con Sancho,*
> *con la mitad de tu hacienda.*

> (Tello, give Elvira your hand so that you shall redeem the outrage by being her husband; and after your head is cut off, she will be able to marry Sancho with half your estate.)

Such a plot told in outline appears banal and sentimental with the kind of serve-him-right ending which children appreciate, but Lope's skill infuses dramatic tension as well as poetical tenderness in the love scenes and humour too with the gross *figura del donaire* (comic character), Pelayo. Lope de Vega is wonderfully adept at portraying ordinary people, peasants in particular, convincingly and sympathetically, not caricaturing them as clodhoppers as Shakespeare tends to do.

Loyalty to the Monarch is also strongly depicted in *La Estrella de Sevilla*, one of the really great plays of the Golden Age. Here the King conceives a criminal passion for the beautiful Estrella, betrothed to Sancho Ortiz. He gains access to her bedroom, but is surprised by her brother Busto Tavera who reproaches him, but spares his life out of loyalty. The King to gain his revenge orders Sancho Ortiz to challenge and kill in a duel a person, guilty of treason, whose name is written in a folded piece of paper. Sancho, discovering the person to be Busto Tavera, wrestles with his feelings of love and duty, but decides he must sacrifice all to obey the royal command. While Estrella is decking herself in gala clothes to meet her lover, her brother's body is brought to her. Sancho Ortiz is cast into prison, but he is resolved to die rather than incriminate the King, who, however, repents of his misdeeds and releases Sancho. All seems set for a happy ending, but the lovers part for ever, Sancho to find death upon the field of battle and Estrella to enter a convent, unable to bring herself to marry her brother's slayer.

The original edition of the play (which is not quite complete) appears to be a revision of an earlier one and various points of style as well as the uncharacteristic tragic ending have caused critics to doubt its authenticity as Lope de Vega's work. There is, however, no disagreement on the adroit management of the plot and the tenderness of the love scenes, especially those where Estrella, bent on revenge, visits Sancho in prison and is won over by his loyal nature and true devotion. Corneille may well have had this sort of episode in mind when writing *El Cid*. Lope de Vega (an experienced lover) was an expert at portraying women in love and his female characters usually stand out more vividly than the men. He would also have been quick to exploit the dramatic value of a conflict between love and duty, and the lovers' parting at the end coincides with the growing concern of the Spaniard for his honour which became an obsession as Spain decayed in the seventeenth century. A Spaniard would feel dishonoured not by committing an offence, but by having an offence committed against himself and condoning it. How then could Estrella marry Sancho and preserve her honour? The same theme of love and duty and personal sacrifice in loyalty to the King came more and more to occupy the attention of dramatists who followed Lope, and gradually replaced the pure *comedias de capa y espada*, dealing with the loves of the *galán* and the *dama* with consequential challenges and duels.

Lope de Vega's plays are larger than life and slightly resemble good scripts for romantic films. His reputation has suffered because all his plays are of similar quality and because, ingenious though they are, they have a certain superficiality. The characters are alive, but Lope appears to hire a set of characters to suit the situation. In Shakespeare it is the characters that create the situation and form a more interesting

Scene from one of Lope de Vega's plays

study for the reader. Nevertheless, Lope de Vega was indeed a 'wonder of nature'; he created the modern Spanish theatre by his systematic inventiveness and power as a poet, and when viewing his defects account must be taken of the speed with which he wrote and also of the fact that he intentionally left much to the skill of the actor. A Lope play well acted is quite a different play from the mummified corpse of the annotated edition.

The popularity of the theatre produced a large number of dramatists of the first rank who carried on the tradition that Lope de Vega set. The most cogent defence of the *drama nuevo* as opposed to the classical drama based on the so-called rules of Aristotle came from a monk Gabriel Téllez better known under the literary pseudonym of TIRSO DE MOLINA, who flays the convention of the unity of action (1621). How can character be developed if for example two people have to meet, go through their courtship and marry all in the space of twenty-four hours? Such criticism was true enough for the type of play that Tirso de Molina wrote with its plot filled with action often of an improbable or even supernatural sort—girls disguised as men, mistaken identities, statues coming to life. But if his plays are romantic in style, his characters are remarkably interesting and save his plays from lapsing into melodrama, as so often happened with dramatists in the nineteenth century.

Tirso de Molina (1571–1648) was a prolific writer, composing over four hundred plays according to his own statement (eighty-six survive) and his work is similarly bedevilled by the need for haste. The best of his comedies is perhaps *Marta la Piadosa*, in which the leading female character is outstandingly realistic, if unattractive. Marta is in love with a young gallant, but her father is planning to marry her to an elderly captain. To avoid so odious a match she pretends to be seized with fervent devotion for religion and makes her father believe that she has taken a vow of maidenhood. To perform her works of devotion and charity she has free run of the house and is thus able regularly to meet her lover, who later appears at the house disguised as a poor, starving student. Marta piously insists on taking him in and nursing him back to health. When he is sufficiently recovered, in gratitude he sets about teaching her Latin, the better to understand her books of devotion. Many complications follow, but finally the lovers are united in matrimony.

The interest of the play lies in the problem posed of whether all is fair in love, whether unreasonable parental demands can be countered by underhand methods on the part of the children. Marta is only deceitful in order to win her rightful lover and the audience sympathises with her, but such wiles inevitably incur the danger of self-corruption and we feel that Marta is on the brink of moral degradation. As a psychological study the play is of exceptional interest as well as being a powerful satire on the folly of arranged matches.

Tirso de Molina was a vigorous satirist and attacked fearlessly the abuses of his day—the ignorance of doctors, hypocrisy in religious matters, the selfishness and excessive wealth of churchmen, the vanity of great ladies, the debauchery of noblemen. Indeed as an unwitting forerunner of socialism (he never attacked institutions or principles) Tirso de Molina always presents the common people as infinitely more worthy than the nobility. *La desvergüenza en España se ha hecho caballería*, (In Spain shamelessness has become genteel), he states in *El Burlador de Sevilla*, the play which established the legend of Don Juan Tenorio. Hurriedly and roughly written, it consists of a loosely connected series of scenes and the spectator, confused, may wish that Tirso de Molina was not so scornful of the unities of time, place and action, but despite this episodic treatment Don Juan is the most extraordinary and arresting character in almost the whole of literature, matched only by Faust, Don Quijote and Hamlet.

The opening scene is in Naples where the young nobleman, Don Juan Tenorio, seduces the Duquesa Isabela by means of a trick and then escapes from a balcony when the alarm is raised. He is next found shipwrecked on the coast of Catalonia, where his servant carries him unconscious to the cottage of a beautiful fisher-girl, Tisbea, who nurses him back to health and is seduced for her pains by a false promise of marriage. Back in Seville, Don Juan hears from a friend and fellow libertine, the Marqués de la Mota, of the beauty of Doña Ana de Ulloa, with whom the Marqués is deeply in love. Such information is a challenge to Don Juan who finds his way at night again by base trickery into Doña Ana's house where he is surprised by her father, the Comendador de Ulloa. Don Juan is forced to draw his sword to defend himself and easily kills Doña Ana's father, escaping unrecognised from the house.

Exiled from Seville by the King because of the scandalous affair in Naples, Don Juan disports himself in the neighbouring village of Dos Hermanas where he attends a rustic wedding. With his fatal fascination for women he seduces the bride almost under the very eyes of the groom. Defying the King's command Don Juan returns secretly to Seville to meet his servant Catalinón in a church at night. There by chance they discover the Comendador's tomb with the inscription:

> *Aquí aguarda del Señor*
> *el más leal caballero,*
> *la venganza de un traidor.*

> (Here the most loyal knight of the Lord awaits vengeance on a traitor.)

Don Juan, unabashed, pulls the stone beard on the Comendador's statue, jokingly inviting him to supper. The appointment is kept and in a moment of tense drama the statue makes his entrance into Don Juan's dining-room with all the servants quaking in terror; only the master is arrogant, mocking and unafraid. At the end of the meal the statue invites Don Juan to supper in return the following night in the church and the invitation is promptly accepted. It is a point of honour with Don Juan to accept a challenge and punctually he arrives with his servant for the supper which consists of the hideous meats of the dead. Finally, the statue bids Don Juan to give him his hand, asking whether he is afraid. Don Juan contemptuously gives his hand and then for once he feels fear, for all the fires of hell flow through the statue's hand and burn up Don Juan while the statue pronounces his epitaph:

> Esta es justicia de Dios.
> Quien tal hizo, que tal pague.
>
> (This is God's justice. As ye sow, so shall ye reap.)

So weird a play may easily border on laughable melodrama, but *El Burlador de Sevilla* is sustained by the force and energy of the character of Don Juan. Apart from his obsession with the seduction of women he is not an unsympathetic person (in the shipwreck he risks his life to save his servant Catalinón) and certainly all his victims are in love with him and would readily forgive him, but he himself is incapable of love. He regards the seduction of a pretty woman both as a joke and as a challenge; the more difficult and dangerous the conquest, the more insistent is the urge to accomplish it. Don Juan has no principles except valour, no redeeming features except energy. This is what makes everyone, particularly Spaniards, admire him so much. He is the type of man who is propelled by an inner force stronger than himself that drives him to destruction as if preordained by destiny. This superlative creation by Tirso de Molina so frequently copied in literature with varying success, has broadcast a false impression of the Spanish male as a militant philanderer and Spain a land of easy conquests, whereas in reality courtship in Spain is hard labour.

If the plays of Lope de Vega and Tirso de Molina were for the most part robustly romantic, a less exuberant type of comedy as provided by JUAN RUIZ DE ALARCÓN (?1581–1639). Born in Mexico City he came to Spain in 1600 and took a degree in law at Salamanca University. After a brief return to Mexico he finally settled in Spain in 1613. His career as a playwright was brief because he abandoned all literary work about 1626 when he took up a government post in the *Consejo de las Indias*. In one of his plays he describes his own appearance; he was extremely short with a hump back and front, bow legs and a red beard. The cruel wits of the literary world dubbed him as a dwarf, ape, crookback, nature's frippery and so on. Alarcón bore these onslaughts with dignity and good sense although he must have been deeply wounded by them. In *Los pechos privilegiados* a character expresses his thoughts:

> al que le plugo de dar
> mal cuerpo, dio sufrimiento
> para llevar cuerdamente
> los apodos de los necios.
>
> (To him whom God was pleased to give a misshapen body, he gave tolerance enough to bear with equanimity the nick-names bestowed by fools.)

Later when the first part of his *comedias* was published in 1628 he strikes uncharacteristically at the public in the Preface, calling it, 'a wild beast' and declaring that 'if his plays are ill-received he will be comforted in the knowledge that they must be good'. Alarcón was no doubt relieved to abandon the world of the theatre and to withdraw to the less hectic life of the civil service where he was greatly respected.

Perhaps Alarcón stirred up so much jealousy among his contemporaries because he was different from them in so many ways. He wrote slowly and carefully (his output was a mere twenty-three plays) whereas the others composed in frenzied haste; his plays, while lacking the lustre and brilliance of those of Lope de Vega or Tirso de Molina, have an aristocratic polish reminiscent of French classical literature. His contemporaries fed the public on what it liked, thrilling drama; Alarcón offered the public what was good for it, thoughtful comedies with a moral purpose.

It is true that his earlier plays were in the romantic mould and he acquitted himself well. *El tejedor de Segovia* is one of the best constructed of this type of drama with swift, interesting (though improbable) action and fiery passions of hatred, love and vengeance. The scene is set in the early middle ages in the reign of Alfonso VI of Castile (1069–1109). Don Fernando is accused falsely of conspiring against the King and has to flee for his life. Posing as a weaver's son in Segovia, he becomes involved in a quarrel, kills his opponent and is himself imprisoned. He makes a daring escape and becomes a bandit chief, being the prototype of the chivalrous highwayman. He is betrayed and arrested, but burns his bonds asunder, knifes his captor and escapes once again. After many adventures he kills in a duel the two enemies who had falsely incriminated him and finally he is restored to the King's favour.

All this is strong meat and seemingly ready for scenario treatment. Well managed as the drama is, Alarcón was patently out of his element and only came into his own in a far more sophisticated type of play, of which the best example is *La verdad sospechosa*. The central figure in this comedy is Don García, a young man about town with all the attributes of wealth, intelligence and handsome appearance, but with one deadly fault: the truth is not in him and he spends his time romancing futilely and unnecessarily, even to his confidential servant. To the lady to whom he is paying court he pretends to be a man of fabulous wealth lately returned from the Indies. He boasts to a friend that he has treated the lady, Doña Jacinta, to a lavish entertainment on the river. He lies hastily and shamelessly to his father when the question of marriage is suggested. The upshot of all this frenzied prevarication is that Don García loses his beloved (she was the person whom his father intended for him as a wife), quarrels with his friend, is humiliated in front of everybody and finally finds himself obliged to marry a woman he does not love.

This insistence on the punishment that vice brings is the cardinal feature of Alarcón's moral lessons; he does not set out to kill vice by bitter satire so much as by pointing out the disaster it entails. Nevertheless, *La verdad sospechosa* is filled with sparkling comedy. Don García is a master of the art of lying, so quick, so convincing, so full of corroborative detail, so adroit and imperturbable at escaping when caught out. Lying for him is his recreation as well as his second nature. When he claims that he can speak ten languages, his servant ruefully reflects that *todas para mentir no te bastan* (all ten are not enough for your falsehoods). The whole action of the play springs from Don García's fantastic inventions and all the manifold incidents are woven together with consummate skill. Corneille copied it in *Le Menteur* (1643) and Molière declared that 'if I had not read *Le Menteur*, I think I should never have written any comedies'. Such was the profound effect that Alarcón, untypical of his age in Spain, produced on the literature of France.

Of equal importance in the shaping of the French theatre was a drama by another Spanish playwright, GUILLÉN DE CASTRO (1569–1631). His *Las mocedades del Cid* was borrowed once again by Corneille for *Le Cid* (1636), which marks the beginning of French classical tragedy. The subject is frankly romantic, dealing with how Don Rodrigo in honour bound to avenge an insult to his aged father finds himself compelled to challenge and kill the Conde Lozano, father of his beloved Doña Jimena. Rodrigo, after the deed is done, presents himself to Jimena begging her to kill him in revenge. She, knowing that honour alone impelled Rodrigo to slay her father, can neither kill him nor forgive him. Rodrigo goes to war against the Moors and the King tests Jimena by pretending that Rodrigo has been slain. Jimena is grief-stricken, but recovers herself on hearing that in fact he has been victorious and she resumes her demands for his execution. The same process is repeated when Rodrigo fights the champion of Aragon in single combat and finally Jimena, yielding to her love and the entreaties of the court, gives her hand to the *Cid Campeador*.

The treatment of the story is on the epic scale; everything is larger than life, as for example the episode of the leper from whom all recoil in horror except naturally our hero, who covers him with his cloak and makes him sit beside him at table. All the incidents and the sonority of the verse have but one object, namely to extol the greatness of character of the national hero. Corneille conceived his drama in the same heroic mould, but he strove to compress the epic into the narrow confines of the three unities which had recently been promulgated anew in France. The result with Corneille is something of a foaming, brimming pot of ale, but ale of a noble brew. Guillén de Castro's version is unrestricted and freely romantic, but lacking in the fierce interior action that Corneille puts into the minds of Don Rodrigue and Chimène.

By the time that Lope de Vega died in 1635 all the many playwrights whom his genius had inspired were either dead or no longer writing for the stage, and the last dramatist of the Golden Age in Spain, PEDRO CALDERÓN DE LA BARCA (1600–81), was fundamentally different, reflecting the greatness of Spain in decadence. He was the son of a minor official in the Treasury in Madrid where he received his education in the Jesuit College before going on to Salamanca University. There he studied theology with a view to taking a chaplaincy of which his family had the gift, but he abandoned this idea and after the premature death of both his parents he competed as a dramatist in the literary festival at Madrid in 1622. For two years he may have been with the Spanish armies in Italy, but from 1625 onwards for twelve years he was in the service of the Duque de Frías, busy writing for the stage and leading the life of a gay, philandering and quarrelsome courtier. By 1636 he was at the height of his fame; his musical play, *El mayor encanto, amor*, dealing with the adventures of Ulysses on Circe's island, was chosen for the opening of the recently constructed palace of Buen Retiro. The performance took place on a floating stage on the lake with the court watching from gondolas; the stage effects were lavish and dramatic and included the destruction of Circe's palace accompanied by fireworks and the discharge of ordnance. The success of this performance earned Calderón the honour of a knighthood of the Order of Santiago.

Spain was at this time heading for disaster and in 1640 the blow fell. Catalonia and Portugal rebelled and in a vain effort at austerity in a time of national crisis all public and private theatricals were forbidden. Calderón volunteered for the heavy cavalry and spent some eighteen months fighting in Catalonia. Disillusioned he returned to Madrid to enter the household of the Duque de Alba. After various personal bereavements, including the death of his mistress, he abandoned court life in 1650 to become a priest. Living almost in retirement at Toledo or Madrid, Calderón gave up writing for the stage except for two *autos sacramentales* for religious festivals in the capital and some plays on mythological themes for performance at court. Just as Spain herself descended into the gloom of decay, Calderón withdrew into sombre gravity after the brilliance and violence of his youth.

Calderón's dramatic production is extremely varied, ranging from sketches, musical comedies, historical plays, *comedias de capa y espada* to philosophical plays, tragedies based on the theme of jealousy and religious dramas. His musical comedies deserve mention since their type is perpetuated in the Spanish theatre under the name of *Zarzuela* and enjoys wide popularity today. The word *zarzuela* is derived from the name of a hunting lodge near the Pardo Palace outside Madrid where Calderón's musical comedies were frequently staged. Among his historical plays is one dealing with the divorce and execution of Catherine of Aragon, *La cisma de Inglaterra*, where the characters of Henry VIII and Anne Boleyn, though strongly outlined, perhaps offend English historical conceptions. Another, *El sitio de Breda*, provided the scene which Velázquez has immortalised in *Las lanzas*, in which Justin of Nassau hands over the keys of Breda to the Marqués de Espinola who receives them with Spanish courtesy (and pride):

> *Justino, yo las recibo,*
> *y conozco que valiente*
> *sois, que el valor del vencido*
> *hace famoso al que vence.*

> (Justin, I receive them and I acknowledge that you are a brave man and that the bravery of the vanquished enhances the reputation of the victor.)

A third historical play is a tragedy, *Amar después de la Muerte*, based on an episode during the revolt of the Moriscos of Granada (1569). Tuzani, a Morisco, seeks out and stabs to death a Christian soldier who has killed Tuzani's betrothed while attempting to rape her. Two points of interest emerge from this play; first is the presentation of the Moriscos as noble heroes at a time when they had recently been finally expelled from Spain—and Calderón was by no means alone in doing this. The second point is the drama of revenge (here quite justifiable), a theme which becomes an obsession with Calderón.

Calderón's real strength lay in his ability to manage his plots; in consequence he excelled in the *comedias de capa y espada* in which an intrigue with two pairs of lovers is ingeniously woven in a mass of complications and finally resolved in the last scene. This form of play he imitated from Lope de Vega, but in many ways he outdid his master in concocting situations and fitting in complex ramifications. What he lacks is Lope de Vega's spontaneity and naturalness; he is also inferior to Tirso de Molina in creating live characters, but his fine wit, his vigour and brilliant stagecraft make his *comedias de capa y espada* amusing and enthralling, even though by their very nature they are entirely artificial.

Among the best is *Casa con dos puertas mala es de guardar* (1629) in which a highly intelligent heroine manages to trick her suspicious brother and meets her own lover in the house of her brother's sweet-heart—the house with the two doors. The complicated plot moves with remarkable precision, the verse flows easily and smoothly and the whole play is an interesting study of the manners of the day. Calderón's own favourite comedy was acted in the same year, *La dama duende*; in it we are shown a discontented shrewish widow, who resorts to such diabolical and mysterious methods of gaining the attention of a guest of her brother that the whole household is paralysed with terror, thinking that there is a ghost in the house; the guest himself roundly declares that he has seen it. In the end the ghostly enchantress is successful.

Calderón, in reflecting so vividly the customs of his age, tends to make the servants or *graciosos* the only comic characters. The upper classes assume more and more the gravity and touchiness that charac-terised Spain in decline. It was an age of decorum and pomp and since humour is often associated with lack of dignity, it was rigorously eschewed (Philip IV never smiled in public) for fear of loss of self-respect or honour. Even in the *comedias de capa y espada* honour provides the gravest obstacle to an easy life and the theme of honour so absorbed Calderón that it induced him to compose plays in which jealousy leads to a bloody ending. Of these the most terrifying is *El médico de su honra* (1635) in which Don Gutierre suspects his wife of an affair with the King's brother, the Infante Don Enrique. In fact she was in love with the Prince before her marriage, but she has been entirely faithful to her husband. The tragedy lies not only in the wife's innocence, but also in the fact that Don Gutierre is in love with her, but his jealousy grows more frantic as he ruminates on his suspicions. The Prince he cannot touch, but honour demands that he should kill his wife. This he does in a horrible and premeditated manner, bringing a *sangrador* (blood letter) to the bed where his wife is drugged and bound, bidding him open a vein. The King comes to the house and finds Don Gutierre, his hands stained with his wife's blood, but exultant that his deed has saved his honour. To kill one's wife in the heat of a jealous argument might be understandable and the slayer has a measure of protection under the law, but murder so carefully planned that no one shall suspect anything but an accident makes Don Gutierre not a tragic figure but a butcher. Nevertheless his action receives the King's approval, as does a similar slaughter in Calderón's next play, produced also in 1635, *A secreto agravio, secreta venganza* (Secret vengeance for a secret insult). The reason perhaps for approving such conduct lies in the fact that it was not considered dishonourable to have an affair with another gentleman's wife; shame lay in being a passive cuckold. Such a philosophy of life can indicate decadence, and Spain, though not yet prostrate, was on the road to ruin. *El héroe calderoniano*, relentless where honour was concerned, no doubt influenced Corneille, but since France was on the rising tide of vigorous achievement his popularity was short-lived and by 1660 Corneille's heroes no longer reflected the dominant mood.

For the most part honour is confined to gentlemen of standing; common folk, like David in Sheridan's *The Rivals*, were no doubt content to do without it. However, such was the obsession of Spaniards with their individuality that in one of Calderón's greatest plays we find a farmer avenging his daughter's disgrace at the hands of an arrogant army captain. *El Alcalde de Zalamea* (1642) is believed to reflect Calderón's experience in the Catalan campaign, but it was based on an incident during the conquest of Portugal (1578) and had already been used for a play by Lope de Vega. Don Álvaro, captain of a company of soldiers bound for Portugal, is billeted on a farmer, Pedro Crespo, whose beautiful daughter he attempts to seduce. Pedro Crespo forestalls him and is about to punish him for his lecherous impudence when the Commander, Don Lope de Figueroa, appears and upbraids him for daring to lay hands on a captain of his Majesty's army. Pedro turns on the Commander, answering with justifiable wrath. Such bold and frank words impress Don Lope who takes a liking to Pedro, and gives him sound fatherly advice on hearing of his predicament. When the soldiers march away, Don Álvaro abducts Pedro's daughter whom he ravishes and abandons on the hillside. Pedro, who has just been nominated *alcalde* of Zalamea, arrests Don Álvaro, obliges him to marry his daughter and then hangs him. The King, Philip II, then appears, grave and dignified, and hearing that a village mayor has dared to arrest one of his captains demands that the prisoner should be delivered to him at once. Pedro's only answer is to produce the body. In the face of the

King's reproaches, Pedro states his case energetically, but with the utmost respect to his monarch, declaring that so far as his honour is concerned he himself is the sole judge. Philip is impressed by the courage and dignity of Pedro, whom he names as permanent mayor in recognition of the justice of his action against Don Álvaro.

Summarised in this way the play may seem yet another version of the David and Goliath story with the usual exaltation of the monarch at the end. This would be doing less than justice to the rich pattern of the drama with its mixture of tragedy, pathos, brutality, burlesque and gaiety, giving a cross-section of Spanish life. Comic relief is provided by the jolly but chicken-hearted soldier, Rebolledo, whose ebbing courage is reinforced by the firmness of his friend, Chispa the *vivandière*. The characters stand out more vividly than is usual with Calderón; Pedro Crespo is a solid yeoman, loyal, honourable, obstinate, yet with a tinge of quiet humour often found in countryfolk. Endowed with the gift of the gab he argues in forthright manner with Don Lope, the old Commander, gouty, irascible, touchy (like the traditional English colonel), but beneath the fiery exterior generous, sympathetic, kindly. Don Álvaro is the conceited, selfish, licentious officer who cannot believe that members of the lower orders can have feelings. As a comment on the times the play seems almost revolutionary in tone, but it merely reflects the extraordinary paradox that Spaniards would brook tyranny from no one except the King and the Church, from whom they received more than their share.

Calderón's best known philosophical play is *La vida es sueño* (1635), which is based on oriental tales, though he probably knew them in Spanish forms, for Lope de Vega had already utilized the theme. Segismundo, son of King Basilio of Poland, had been imprisoned in solitary confinement since his childhood because an astrologer had predicted that he would be a monster of cruelty and impiety. The King's conscience bids him test the possible truth of this prediction and consequently he has Segismundo (now at the age of reason) brought drugged to the palace where on waking he finds himself treated as King with all due pomp and adulation. Embittered by his long imprisonment, Segismundo behaves with startling violence, throwing a servant over a balcony, trying to kill his former guardian, almost knocking over a beautiful lady, and insulting his father, who hastily has his son drugged once again and carried back to his prison. When Segismundo awakens, his guardian, Clotaldo, persuades him that his experiences were but a dream. Basilio announces that he intends to disinherit Segismundo and make Astolfo, Duke of Moscow, his heir. His subjects, however, rebel at this proposal and Basilio is forced to submit to Segismundo, who in victory behaves with generosity and moderation. He has realised in prison that the greatness of this world is fleeting, that all life is a dream, that faith and hope can be fixed alone on eternal life.

La vida es sueño is uncharacteristic of Calderón in that the plot is confusing, and a somewhat clumsy byplot with Rosaura disguised as a man detracts from the main focus of the play, which is the personality of Segismundo. As in *Hamlet*, much time is given to soliloquies on the mystery of life and these are the most effective passages. Segismundo is not perhaps a person but a symbol of mankind, chained and bound in his body while his soul longs to roam free. Suddenly liberated he gives way to his instincts of violence, passion, impulse. But pomp and power are mere illusions and in the solitude of renewed confinement he learns that the secret of life is the mastery of self. In his victory he exclaims:

> *Pues que ya vencer aguarda*
> *Mi valor grandes victorias, hoy ha de ser la más alta*
> *Vencer a mí.*
>
> (Since now to conquer my valour expects great victories, today must be the greatest of them all, to conquer myself.)

Critics have claimed that Segismundo's conversion is too rapid to be convincing, but surely they miss the point. This is not a realist play, but an allegory in which the deepest problems of the soul of men are discussed; much is to be pondered on, much that can be only half understood, much that could be interpreted in several ways. Moreover, it is possible to see in Segismundo Calderón's own image—the violent youth turning to grave old age. His literary methods reflect the same tendency. His tastes are baroque and the baroque style favours melo-dramatic contrasts and the blending of unlikely objects. Yet with all the love of the extraordinary, shipwrecks, volcanoes, earthquakes, thunder and lightning, goes a passion for order, method and symmetry. The grandeur of Calderón's poetry is always rightly admired, but when analysed all his imagery is founded on a method which is basically simple. This does not mean that anyone could have written Calderón's poetry, which has a splendour that only genius can infuse.

Góngora and the new poetry

Since 1613 there had been war among the poets, who argued fiercely about the merits and absurdities of a high-flown style known as *culteranismo* perfected by LUIS DE GÓNGORA (1561–1627). Born in Córdoba of a well-to-do family of gentry, he studied at Salamanca University and then returned home to lead the life of a young gentleman with a reputation as a poet, wit and lavish spender. In 1585 he took deacon's orders so that he could fill the post of prebendary (lately vacated by his uncle) in the Cathedral at Córdoba. His duties were not onerous, but he fulfilled them in a casual fashion, preferring to frequent bullfights rather than the choir stalls. Wisely the Chapter transferred him to organising processions on festival days and later sent him on missions to distant parts of Spain where his social connections and brilliant wit would make him readily acceptable. These long, slow journeys over the parched countryside sharpened his awareness to natural beauty and gave him the time he needed for contemplation, because in Córdoba his life was gay and flighty, more occupied with amorous dalliance and gambling parties than befitted a prebendary of the cathedral. He tried life at court, then at Valladolid and spent some time also at Salamanca and Toledo, meeting the leading intellectuals of the day. Suddenly in 1611 there came a complete change in his way of life, inspired possibly by his journeying through rural Spain or by his friends' exhortations to compose really serious poetry. He retired to a country place two miles from Córdoba and there wrote the *Fábula de Polifemo y Galatea* and the first part of the *Soledades*. It was the circulation of these two poems in manuscript in 1613 that caused such a furore in literary circles. Góngora himself seems to have been surprised and shocked at the violence of the reaction, for he never finished the second part of the *Soledades*. He also felt the need, possibly for financial reasons, to move in 1617 to Madrid, where he took up a royal chaplaincy after taking orders as a priest. He found the court atmosphere unconducive to the writing of poetry and further debts forced him to publish his poems. He had previously not taken his poetry very seriously and only once before had any of his poems been printed, the collection entitled *Flor de varios romances nuevos* (1589). He died before he could complete the editing of this further collection of poems which when it appeared a year after his death was banned by the Inquisition.

Góngora as a poet is like Picasso as a painter, capable of producing traditional work as well as compositions in his own particular style. Most of his earlier poems are in popular metres, *canciones*, *romances*, *letrillas*, but they have a marked tendency to strive for original imagery and also an exact sense of balance in the lines and verses. From the begin-

Góngora

Calderón

ning he was clearly an intellectual poet rather than a popular one, though in many ways he combines both elements.

> *La más bella niña*
> *de nuestro lugar,*
> *hoy viuda y sola*
> *y ayer por casar,*
> *viendo que sus ojos*
> *a la guerra van,*
> *a su madre dice*
> *que escucha su mal.*
> Dejadme llorar
> orillas del mar.

(The loveliest girl in our village, today a lonely widow, yesterday a bride, seeing that the light of her eyes has gone to the war, says to her mother who is listening to her lament: *Let me weep by the seashore.*)

The image in lines 5 and 6 is highly suggestive and foreshadows the *conceptos* or 'conceits' of Góngora's later style. The careful balancing of the lines is evident and, though perhaps this is a characteristic of Spanish ballads, it is much more pronounced in Góngora than in other poets, and bears some resemblance to the formal antithesis found in eighteenth-century English poetry.

The search for imagery is intensified in Góngora's earlier sonnets and the images frequently approach the *culterano* style, though their meaning is clearer and their appeal more immediate:

> *La dulce boca que a gustar convida*
> *un humor entre perlas destilado.*

(Her sweet mouth inviting a kiss, moisture distilled among pearls.)

Of course to translate *humor* as 'moisture' is both prosaic and confusing since it means any of the liquids which form the living body and the reader can interpret the word as he pleases. It is perhaps one of the charms of Góngora's poetry that it is usually not fully appreciated at once. It provokes thought, and real enjoyment comes only through repeated study of the lines.

This is even more applicable to the two works which caused such a literary storm in 1613. They are undoubtedly obscure, they are full of mythological allusions (mainly from Ovid and Virgil), they have a specialised poetic vocabulary, and the structure of the sentence is almost as free as in Latin. The ordinary reader would be well advised to acquire a copy of Professor Wilson's translation (Cambridge 1965) before embarking on a study of the *Soledades*. Góngora's detractors have labelled all the various devices he employs as affectation and it is difficult entirely to rebut the charge, but all Renaissance poets were faced with the same difficulty of a vocabulary rapidly enriched by the new learning and discoveries. Similar problems confront the modern poet who is surrounded by all the jargon of the scientific, industrial, medical and technical worlds. Góngora was seeking not only a purified form of poetic diction, but was also experimenting with the sound of words to give 'colour'. He is a symbolist in his poetry like Mallarmé and Baudelaire in nineteenth-century France, but it must be admitted that like them Góngora infuses a tinge of decadence into his style. For all its many qualities, it is not the good, honest, straightforward stuff of the traditional Spanish *romances*. It is Garcilaso and his school exaggerated to twisting point.

The *Fábula de Polifemo y Galatea* is a long poem of sixty-three stanzas of *octavas* and is based on Ovid's story of the water nymph Galatea who fell in love with a faun, Acis. His rival, the one-eyed giant Polifemo, in a fit of jealousy crushed him with a rock. Góngora creates an atmosphere of the shimmering heat of a burning Mediterranean summer with Acis asleep in the noonday sun; Galatea finds him and is smitten at once with love for him:

> *Llamárale, aunque muda, mas no sabe*
> *el nombre articular que más querría . . .*
>
> (She would call to him, though she is dumb, but she cannot utter the name that she would love most . . .)

In this drowsy summer haze the passion of jealousy arises, fierce and uncontrollable. Polifemo loves Galatea deeply, and she is

> *blanca más que las plumas de aquel ave*
> *que dulce muere y en las aguas mora.*
>
> (whiter than the feathers of that bird that gently dies and dwells in the waters.)

The meaning is at times vague and nebulous, but the style fits the subject and the impression which the poet intends to convey; the musical effects are at once evident and beautiful as can be seen from the exquisite cadence of the line *que dulce muere y en las aguas mora.*

Polifemo y Galatea was a mild innovation compared with the *Soledades*, which were the real cause of the literary battle. The poem is far more irregular in construction, being written in *silvas*, that is eleven-syllable lines interspersed with seven-syllable lines at varying intervals. There are some two thousand lines in the two parts, but the poem, originally intended to have four episodes, was left unfinished. There is almost no plot, merely a series of pastoral scenes. A young man is shipwrecked on an unknown coast where he is befriended by goatherds; later he meets peasants on their way to a wedding and shares in the festivities, which end with athletic contests. In Part II the youth sets out with fishermen in their boat down an estuary and they land on an island where they meet an old fisherman with six beautiful daughters, themselves adept at sea fishing. The next day the fishermen set out again in their boats from which they watch some gentlemen who have emerged from a castle for a hawking expedition. At this point the poem abruptly ends.

The theme of the poem is a mere reiteration of the idealised picture of rustic life that courtiers conjure up for themselves. There was nothing new in that, but for Góngora perhaps this life symbolised the unattainable ideal of pure poetry. There is a constant impression of striving and seeking in the poem, of vagueness, confusion, uncertainty, fleeting feelings and sensations, though also there are passages of keen and exact observation which occur rather like sudden moments of clarity in the midst of swirling mists. The poem is filled almost to choking point with metaphors and similes often apt and beautiful, but in general too numerous and occasionally too extravagant. To describe a fishing net as: *siempre murada, pero siempre abierta* (always walled, but always open) is fine, but to allude to a ship steering by compass as: *En esta, pues, fiándose atractiva del norte amante dura, alado roble* (Thus winged oak trusting to the attraction of this steadfast lover of the north) seems clumsy and strained. Moreover the unusual word order, as in this sentence, tends to become tedious; Góngora's defenders claim that this strange syntax produces subtle effects, but the ordinary reader may well agree with the critics who maintain that it is artificial and affected. The *Soledades* is plainly caviare to the general.

The protests which the *Soledades* evoked led Góngora to return in the main to more conventional poetry, but the younger generation of poets seized on his style with the utmost eagerness and some of his imitators carried the conceits to the point of absurdity. PEDRO ESPINOSA (1578–1650), one of the most talented poets of Góngora's school, after a disappointment in love at the age of twenty-eight retired to live as a hermit in a cave in the mountains for twelve years. His highly decorated poetry could only be tolerated in an age which enjoyed Baroque ornamentation. Góngora indeed did not create the *culto* style; it was a general trend which made its appearance in many countries in different forms—euphuism in England, *préciosité* in France for example, but Góngora was the only Spanish poet to infuse a deeper meaning and lyrical musical qualities into a style that by nature was highly artificial. It is right then that *gongorismo* should be the usual term applied to this style.

Quevedo—'conceptismo' and satire

There were many fierce contemporary opponents of *gongorismo*, including Lope de Vega, who personally disliked Góngora, Calderón, who being younger saw more of the imitators' work than Góngora's, and Quevedo, whose pale verses stood little comparison with those of Góngora. Curiously enough Quevedo's rich and varied prose style initiated another literary fashion called *conceptismo* which later declined into bombast. FRANCISCO DE QUEVEDO (1580–1645) was born in Madrid of a noble family, his father being secretary to the Queen and his mother a lady-in-waiting. His father died when he was very young and his childhood was spent unhappily in the care of governesses. At the Jesuit school and at the university of Alcalá de Henares Quevedo showed himself a prodigy of learning, but it is doubtful whether he found much happiness there. He was of a quarrelsome nature and in 1611 had to flee to Sicily after gravely wounding an opponent in a duel. Returning to Spain a few months later he settled down on an estate belonging to his mother, Torre de Juan Abad in La Mancha, but in 1613 he embarked once more for Sicily at the invitation of the Viceroy, the Duque de Osuna. Quevedo held important posts in Sicily and later in Naples to which the Duke was transferred, and he had an excellent opportunity of seeing how the business of politics and diplomacy was conducted. It was not an edifying experience, for the Duke was plotting to overthrow the independent government in Venice and seize power. Quevedo was sent there as his agent in disguise and narrowly escaped with his life when the plot failed. Back in Spain he was exiled to his estate and the Duque de Osuna was imprisoned. Quevedo escaped punishment by grovelling to Philip IV's favourite Olivares and was released from house arrest.

For ten years he devoted himself to massive literary production, much of which was satire, since Quevedo had set himself up as the

Jeremiah of Spain. His faults were many, but at least he had the courage or obstinacy to voice his criticisms, and despite previous dangerous experiences eventually came to attack Olivares's despotic rule. In 1639 while on a visit to Madrid he was arrested and carried off to imprisonment in a monastery in León. The reason for his arrest is said to have been that a set of satirical verses appeared under the King's plate at table and were at once attributed to Quevedo, whose sharp tongue and sarcastic pen had made many enemies at court. Despite all appeals he was confined in an underground cell that ran with water and not till 1643, after Olivares's downfall, was Quevedo released, broken in health. For two more years he gallantly laboured at setting his papers in order and helping to prepare a complete edition of his works before he died worn out, but pugnacious to the end.

Quevedo's contribution to poetry is extensive and varied, ranging from satirical *romances*, licentious *letrillas* to lofty *silvas* on the grandeur of ancient Rome and religious poems. He was a facile versifier, but his poetry is unimpressive because it seems but a reflection of all the great poets of the day including Góngora whom he detested. The sensitivity necessary for a poet was withheld from Quevedo and his verse lacks any lyrical qualities. He is best suited to satirical subjects where his sharp wit and mastery of words have full rein, as in the *letrilla, Poderoso caballero es Don Dinero:*

> *Madre, yo al oro me humillo;*
> *él es mi amante y mi amado,*
> *pues de puro enamorado*
> *anda contino amarillo;*
> *que pues, doblón o sencillo,*
> *hace todo cuanto quiero*
> *poderoso caballero*
> *es Don Dinero.*

> (Mother, I prostrate myself before gold; he is my lover and my beloved, because in pure love he goes forever yellow, and sovereign or half-sovereign, does everything I wish; *a powerful gentleman is Don Dinero.*)

A note of firmness and a feeling of the responsibility of the social and political critic is to be found in the austere, vehement *Epístola satírica y censoria* (1639) addressed to Olivares.

> *No he de callar, por más que con el dedo,*
> *ya tocando la boca o ya la frente,*
> *silencio avises o amenaces miedo.*
> *¿No ha de haber un espíritu valiente?*
> *¿siempre se ha de sentir lo que se dice?*
> *¿nunca se ha de decir lo que se siente?*

Villegas

(I will not be silent, however much, your finger touching your lips or your brow, you warn me to hold my tongue or threaten me with terror. Must there not be one bold spirit? Does one always have to feel what one says? Must one never say what one feels?)

Bold words indeed, but not poetry.

In prose, too, Quevedo is remembered as a social satirist. His long political dissertations like *La política de Dios* (1626–55), dedicated to Olivares, and *Vida de Marco Bruto*, are now forgotten, clear and well reasoned though they are. His best known work is a picaresque novel

Vida del Buscón, begun probably in 1603, but not published till 1626. The story follows the familiar pattern of a boy, Pablos, whose father is a barber-cum-thief, subsequently hanged and whose mother is a scamstress and spare-time witch. He enters the service of a young gentleman, Don Diego Coronel, at a school in Segovia kept by a cleric, Maestro Cabra, whose avarice and capacity for ill-using his pupils make Mr Squeers seem a pamperer of the young. Finally Don Diego's father hears of the state of affairs and takes his son away, sending him to Alcalá de Henares with Pablos still attending him. There they suffer the initiation ceremonies reserved for freshmen before joining in undergraduate pranks and follies. Pablos receives news that his father has been hanged for robbery; the circumstances are given in great detail by his uncle who should know what has happened since he is the public hangman in Segovia. Pablos journeys to Segovia to claim his small inheritance and then makes for Madrid where he joins a company (*cofradía*) of crooks as a cardsharper (*buscón*), ending up in prison. He escapes by means of bribery and after various adventures finds his way to Seville where his ill luck still pursues him. He determines to make a fresh start in the Indies, but with little hope of success. Pessimistically he points the moral of the tale: '*Fueme peor, pues nunca mejora su estado quien muda solamente de lugar, y no de vida y costumbres.*' (It was worse for me, because he never betters his lot who merely changes his abode, but not his way of life or his morals.)

The novel shows little originality in conception since it follows closely the style of previous picaresque novels, though it has a far wider range of characters and incidents than *Lazarillo de Tormes*. It is powerfully and wittily written, but it lapses too readily into gross caricature and can be compared with Dickens in this respect. The chapters on the horrors of boarding school and university education are clearly based on personal recollections, but the portrait of the schoolmaster is too weird and horrific to be credible.

> *Las barbas, descoloridas de miedo de la boca vecina, que de pura hambre, parecía que amenazaba a comérselas, los dientes, le faltaban no sé cuántos, y, pienso que por holgazanes y vagamundos se los habían desterrado; el gaznate largo como de avestruz, con una nuez tan salida, que parecía se iba a buscar de comer, forzada de la necesidad; los brazos, secos, las manos, como un manojo de sarmientos cada una. Mirado de medio abajo, parecía tenedor o compás. Si se descomponía, le sonaban los huesos como tablillas de San Lázaro.*

(His beard, pale for fear of the nearby mouth, which, out of sheer hunger, seemed to be threatening to gobble it up; his teeth, goodness knows how many were missing and I think that they had been banished as idlers and wastrels; his neck, long as an ostrich's, with an Adam's apple so protruding that it looked as if it were from necessity searching for food. His arms, withered; his hands each like a bunch of sticks. Viewed from halfway down he looked like a fork or compass. If he tried to hurry, his bones rattled like lepers' clappers.)

It is all larger than life and as such is less convincing than the sober, factual narrative of *Lazarillo de Tormes*. Perhaps all social protest has to be exaggerated in order to draw the public's attention to the vices of the age.

If the *Buscón* is largely caricature, Quevedo's other well-known work, *Los sueños* (published 1627), provides essays in the macabre and grotesque. The first edition contained five episodes, but three more were added later. The title indicates the nightmarish atmosphere of each episode, in which social satire is expressed in weird and often horrifying scenes. In the first episode, the *sueño de las calaveras*, the last trump sounds and dead begin to rise from their graves, gentlemen, players, doctors, lawyers, judges, soldiers, misers, gossips, all try to justify themselves before the throne of Jupiter, but their faults, sins and vices are obvious and all are damned. The third episode, *Las zahurdas de Plutón* (Pluto's pigsties) gives a picture of hell and the torments which various classes of persons suffer there—clowns and comics are shut up in a cave and have only each other as an audience for their quips and puns, pastrycooks are closely watched (for how many stomachs would bark if all the dogs they had caused to be eaten were to come to life again?), poets have to hear their rivals' works praised. Quevedo is particularly vehement against women (he had married, but the union lasted only a few months). Almost all the *sueños* attack the female character, but none more violently than *El mundo por de dentro* which is a diatribe against hypocrisy and double dealing.

'¿Viste esa visión, que acostándose fea se hizo esta mañana hermosa ella misma y hace extremos grandes? Pues sábete que las mujeres lo primero que se visten, en despertando, es una cara, una garganta y unas manos, y luego las sayas. Todo cuanto ves en ellas es tienda, y no natural.'

(Did you see that vision who went to bed ugly, but this morning made herself beautiful and puts on such airs and graces? Well you should know that women when they first dress after waking have one face, one throat, one pair of hands and then on go the decorations. Everything you see on them is artificial and not natural.)

The most frightening *sueño* of all is *La visita de los chistes* where the scene opens in Quevedo's bedroom during one of his dreams (he had recently suffered an illness in 1621) and there appears a procession of physicians, apothecaries, surgeons, with their hideous implements, chanting 'cut, tear, saw, open, flay, prick, slice, burn'. Death then appears and leads him to her kingdom where seated on her throne surrounded by sundry causes of death—hunger, fear, cold, love, laughter —she allows the dead to hold converse with Quevedo who answers their questions on events in the world.

These macabre scenes may have been inspired by Dante and the paintings of Bosch; certainly they influenced Goya in his treatment of the *Caprichos* and *Disparates;* but largely they are the product of Quevedo's own brooding temperament. He was the supreme pessimist, the man with the largest chip on his shoulder. Brilliant scholar though he was, his mind closed in later life; he made no friends, only enemies, he did not know the meaning of love, everything in the world was wrong. Moreover, he had no remedy for the state of affairs of which he disapproved so profoundly; he diagnosed the diseases of the age, but had no suggestions about the causes and the remedies. He approved of the Inquisition, the war in the Netherlands, he hated the Jews, Moriscos, foreigners of all types, trade and commerce. In fact he supported all the causes of disastrous decay in Spain and then criticised the results of such a policy. He hoped for salvation and the restoration of Spain's glory by urging Spaniards to raise their moral standards, but he never stopped to enquire why standards had fallen. Negative criticism induces a brooding sense of personal injustice and hence the strange, paranoiac tendencies observable in the *sueños* with their fantastic images and violent conceits. Powerful he certainly is, but his writings are decadent and reflect the chaos of Spain in the shadows.

The strangling of intellectual progress at this period was evident in the treatment of another philosopher and eminent stylist, BALTASAR GRACIÁN (1601–58). Aragonese by birth, he joined the Jesuits at the age of eighteen. His books were published under an assumed name, but his literary activities came to the notice of the Provincial of Aragon and after the appearance in 1653 of the second part of his great work, *El criticón*, he was formally forbidden to publish more books. Refusing to obey, he published the third part, having tried to leave the order. He was sent to a lonely monastery in the mountains and kept in a cell on a diet of bread and water. Such treatment effectively rid the order of a troublesome member.

El criticón is an allegorical work with a slender thread of plot. Critilo, a wise man of middle age and of a philosophical turn of mind, is ship-wrecked on the island of Santa Elena where he meets the island's sole inhabitant, Andrenio, whom he teaches to speak Spanish and thus hears his strange story. Waking as a child in a cave Andrenio had found himself among wild animals which fed him and raised him as one of their young until one day the light of reason dawned on him. Then he began to contemplate and ponder upon the great work of creation— the sun, the moon, the stars, the mountains. Andrenio is *par excellence* the child of nature in the manner of Rousseau. Critilo and Andrenio together contrive a rough boat and escape from the island, landing in Spain. Together they journey through a great part of Europe studying the customs and motives that govern human behaviour. Andrenio is amazed at the follies and wickedness of civilised society even though Critilo does his best to explain them and comment on them.

El criticón is a highly original book, full of shrewd observations of human behaviour and with well reasoned and logical arguments. Though the picture of life presented by Gracián is grim, it is not weird, macabre and without hope like Quevedo's hysterical scenes. As in Voltaire's *Candide* there is a glimmer of positive philosophy. Once in this world man must strive towards perfecting himself and seek to acquire immortality through his deeds and works. Such counsel of hope and exhortation to use one's talents found no favour in an age in Spain in which the sole remedy for any problem was one of destruction; with too liberal use of weed-killer flowers and grass tend to suffer too. Gracián succumbed and would never have been known again, but for the enthusiasm of Schopenhauer who in 1832 wrote: 'My favourite author is the philosophical Gracián. I have read all his works. *El criticón* is for me one of the best books in the world.'

Chapter 8
Decadence

The century and a half from the death of Calderón (1681) until the death of Fernando VII (1833) was a barren period for Spanish literature. Yet the eighteenth century saw the establishment of many cultural institutions: the *Biblioteca Nacional* (1711), the *Real Academia* (1714), the *Academia de Historia* (1738). The fact is that the Bourbon kings were enlightened and eager for the advancement of culture in Spain, while the Spaniards resolutely resisted and clung to traditionalism. In a way this reactionary attitude was right because the culture offered them was wholly French in origin and in a form which in no way suited the Spanish genius. Nevertheless, Spain failed to take advantage of the intellectual offerings provided by the Bourbon kings; in the early sixteenth century Spanish poetry had taken a new life from the inspiration of Italian verse forms, and the glittering literature of seventeenth century France might equally have inspired a revival, but there was no intellectual aristocracy in Spain such as was created in France by the influence of the salons, and literature modelled on that of France was received in Spain with the darkest suspicion by all except a handful of intellectuals. When literature springs from intellectual rather than popular origins it tends to be didactic in nature rather than artistic, and the urge to spread propaganda is as strongly marked in eighteenth-century Spanish writers as it was among the *philosophes* in France.

The greatest propagandist of the eighteenth century, the so-called Voltaire of Spain, was a mild Benedictine monk, FRAY BENITO JERÓNIMO FEIJÓO (1676–1764). A native of Casdemiro in the province of Orense in Galicia, he taught theology in the university of Oviedo and later, after 1739, retired to a secluded monastery from which he treated the world to an astonishing series of letters and essays dealing with every conceivable subject from medicine and public hygiene to religious

LEFT *Goya, Incómoda elegancia, the Prado*

reform and literary criticism. How a monk came to be so well informed is a mystery, but Feijóo seemed to have read everything, remembered everything and judged everything with such sound common sense that his opinions are eminently valid today. Though he accepted the discipline of the Catholic religion he was bold enough to admire Francis Bacon and other English philosophers and to speak out frankly against the Inquisition. 'I grant,' he says, 'that to close the door to all new doctrine may be a precautionary remedy against noxious error. But it is a very violent remedy besides being an unnecessary one; it is condemning the soul to harsh slavery; it is tying human reason with the shortest of chains; it is confining to a narrow prison innocent minds solely to avoid the remote contingency that some follies may be committed in the future.'

His two great collections of essays and letters reveal in their titles the fact that they are directed against abuses, ignorance and superstitions. The first was the *Teatro crítico universal* or 'Divers essays on all kinds of subjects for the disproving of common errors'. This was in eight volumes and was published between 1726 and 1739; it was followed by five more volumes of *Cartas eruditas y curiosas* 'refuting or casting doubt on divers opinions commonly believed'. The range of Feijóo's interests makes his work almost an encyclopaedia, and the boldness of his opinions drew much hostility to him, though he was championed by King Fernando VI, who forbade any attacks to be made against him. Feijóo had warm sympathy for all the human race as is shewn in his letter addressed to a Jewish theologian of Bayonne when he says: *Todos los hombres debemos contemplarnos como hermanos* (we must look upon all men as brothers). But sympathetic and tolerant as were his ideas Feijóo was an intellectual, who believed in the reform of society but despised the masses and the ignorant multitude. Like Voltaire he preached universal brotherhood but fell short of practising it. Like Voltaire he had the gift of explaining erudite matters clearly and simply, but Voltaire could never be dull with his glitteringly witty style whereas Feijóo, though devoid of pomposity, is often insipid and colourless in expression and his influence on the general public in Spain was negligible.

Luzán and neoclassicism

Equally unpalatable to popular opinion was the apologist of neo-classical literature in Spain, IGNACIO LUZÁN (1702–54) whose *Poética*

(1737) proposed to *subordinar la poesía española a las reglas que sigue en las naciones cultas* (subordinate Spanish poetry to the rules observed in cultured nations). Such a proposal seemed a direct insult to Spain, but Luzán had spent many years in Italy, where he had steeped himself in classical learning and had acquired a love of classical simplicity and orderliness. He closely follows the judgments of Aristotle on literature as he knew it and draws inspiration from Boileau's *Art poétique*. Luzán is beset by the didactic purpose of literature though he does admit that poetry may aim solely at pleasing the reader; even so he feels like Horace that it is preferable for poetry to educate the mind as well as to delight the ear. Hence springs his lack of enthusiasm for Góngora, whose *conceptismo* was deliberately aimed at supplying aesthetic appeal rather than moral fare. Nevertheless Luzán is a man of keen critical judgment and excellent taste and he recognises the merits of Spanish Golden Age dramatists; his praise for Lope de Vega is grudging indeed, for he fails to recognise his work as an innovator and blames him for aggravating the defects of Spanish drama. Calderón he blames too for not observing the classical rules, but he admits that he knew the supreme art of interesting the audience or reader and of carrying them from scene to scene not only without tedium, but with an eager desire to see what finally happens; a most essential attribute which cannot be credited to many poets of other nations, who scrupulously observed the rules.

Despite this sensible recognition of the sovereign need to interest the audience Luzán is wholly in favour of the so-called Aristotelian rules for drama and stressed the need for the unities of action, place and time in their strictest application, so that not only should there be but one plot and one scene, but also the time of the action should be limited to the period required for performing the play (some three hours in all).

Such rigid rules were hard to accept and Spanish playwrights continued cheerfully in the style of Calderón. The impetus, however, was gone and no works of any lasting merit were produced. Towards 1750 attempts were made to produce plays on the French classical model and the leader of this new school was NICOLAS FERNÁNDEZ DE MORATÍN (1737–80). His *Lucrecia* (1763) was a ponderous Roman tragedy, extremely declamatory in style and with the action artificially compressed for the sake of the unity of time. His *Hormesinda* (1770) is a more eloquent tragedy on a Spanish theme, though it met with little success. Munuza, the Moorish governor in Spain, holds captive the

Christian princess, Hormesinda, and attempts to seduce her. She resists him and out of revenge Munuza sends false letters to her brother Don Pelayo accusing Hormesinda of faithlessness. Don Pelayo (a ranting fool in the play) swears to kill his sister, but later finds that she is guiltless. He marches his troops against the Moors who are defeated and Munuza is slain. The play represents a compromise between the traditional and neo-classical styles and relies for appeal on nationalistic claptrap, as does N. F. Moratín's *Guzmán el Bueno* (1777), which deals with the most famous act of devotion in Spanish history. Guzmán el Bueno defending Tarifa against the Moors discovered that the enemy were holding his son as a hostage. He flung down his dagger from the walls, bidding the Moors kill his son with it, and firmly refused to surrender Tarifa in exchange for his son's life.

Superior as literature and far more successful with the public was *La Raquel* by GARCÍA DE LA HUERTA (1734–87). This was to some extent a compromise between Spanish traditional drama and the classical rules for tragedy. There is no mixture of tragedy and comedy and the action takes place within the space of twenty-four hours, but the subject is one dear to the Spanish theatre, namely loyalty to the King. It is the story of Raquel, the beautiful Jewess who became the favourite of Alfonso VIII (died 1214). The Castilians in Toledo rebel against such a liaison, but Raquel manages to retain the King's favour and attempts to revenge herself on the Castilian nobles by provoking them to a fresh revolt. Whilst Alfonso is away hunting, the rebels decide to kill Raquel, though one, García, attempts to save her not out of regard for her but from loyalty to his King. However Raquel's confidant, Rubén, deserts her and is persuaded by the Castilians to kill her. As Raquel dies, Alfonso returns and in fury slays Rubén with his own hand. On García's advice, Alfonso pardons the Castilian nobles, admitting that he is much to blame for the catastrophe. Cynics would attribute the play's success to the narrow appeal to racial purity, but there is in addition some excellent characterisation and fine poetry, though indeed it remains a hybrid drama in the style of Voltaire with Iberian undertones.

Reaction against French drama

There was a strong popular reaction to the French dramatic style and it was mercilessly satirised by RAMÓN DE LA CRUZ (1731–94), perhaps for the very reason that his attempts to imitate the style had been singularly

José Camarón Borouat, Dos Petimetras Biblioteca Nacional, Madrid

ineffectual. The opportunity for satire was all the more readily grasped because of the liking of Spanish audiences for comic interludes between the second and third acts of tragedies. These dated from Lope de Rueda in the sixteenth century, and Ramón de la Cruz revived them vigorously under the name of *Sainetes*, which provided with their witty comment on contemporary Spanish life a gay antidote to high-flown tragedy. In *Manolo* Ramón de la Cruz claimed he would write a tragedy not with three unities, but with three thousand. The satire is perhaps heavy and clumsy, but the Madrid public enjoyed a twenty-minute interlude in which the dregs of the capital spoke in high-flown language and died in droves in ludicrous circumstances of tragedy.

So great was the success of this popular reaction that in 1770 the Conde de Aranda as first minister attempted to forbid in Madrid all plays not in the French style, but this arbitrary effort to impose French culture was a signal failure and Ramón de la Cruz continued to enjoy great popularity, even though his style is frequently crude in the extreme.

The real interest of Ramón de la Cruz's work is the detailed picture the *sainetes* give of middle and lower class life in Madrid in the second half of the eighteenth century. Thanks to the enlightened policy of the Bourbon kings this was a period of comparative prosperity for Spain and life in Madrid was gay. The aristocracy acquired French tastes in clothes, furniture, food and amusements, but Ramón de la Cruz is not concerned with the nobility, whom he had no opportunity to observe. The middle classes aped the aristocracy and a new type of dandy appeared in Madrid, known as the *petimetre* (from French *petit maître*). His wife was given the name of *petimetra* and she was even more pleasure-loving than her husband for he of necessity usually had to spend his day working. She was left in a state of utter boredom and sought the consolation of a *cortejo*, a gallant who danced attendance on well-to-do married women, often with the full knowledge of the husband who found this a convenient method of having his wife looked after. The husband himself was not above dallying with a *corteja*. *Petimetres* wore French fashions and their wives spent endless time and trouble on decking themselves out in hooped dresses and huge high headdresses.

Ramón de la Cruz was staunchly conservative and thought the slavish copying of everything French, with dainty food and fragile furniture, was a betrayal of the old manly Spanish way of life with its plain, solid fare and massive furniture, and its undoubted discomfort. His sympathies were entirely with the lower classes. But prosperity had thrown up a new, low-class beau named the *majo*. He wore traditional Spanish dress, but far more fanciful than the normal sober garb of unrelieved black. He would swagger around Madrid accompanied by his *maja* dressed in black lace with a high mantilla, and woe betide anyone who objected to his swashbuckling manner, for the *majo* was violent and ready to use a knife at the slightest provocation. The *maja* was equally vindictive, though she submitted meekly enough to rough treatment from her own *majo;* if, however, another rival *majo* appeared on the scene the most vicious fighting immediately occurred. So colourful were the *majos* and *majas* on the Madrid scene with their

Goya, Majas y Majos

picnics, *paseos* and dances that the nobility began to copy them, and
by the end of the century it was quite frequent for Goya to paint
countesses or duchesses or even the Queen in *maja* costume.

Ramón de la Cruz may indeed be called the Goya of the Spanish
theatre because his *sainetes* give such a vivid impression of life in Madrid
with the various classes of Spaniards and the flocks of French men and
women who had poured into Spain during the eighteenth century.

English influence in Spain at this time was slight, though English cloth
was highly prized and the Sir Roger de Coverley was a popular dance.
Only one Englishman, named Jones, appears in the *sainetes*. In an inn
he beckons the waiter, points to his mouth and holds up a gold coin.
When the waiter asks him to leave, Jones sits still and stares the waiter
into silence. He finally leaves of his own accord, making a polite bow,
never having uttered a single word.

Moratín and social drama

Though the *sainetes* form a fascinating social document they can
scarcely be classed as dramas, being more sketches with hardly any
plot. The best full-length dramatic works came from the pen of
LEANDRO FERNÁNDEZ DE MORATÍN (1760–1828), son of the author of
La Hormesinda. They are few in number because the author, a protegé
of Godoy, allowed himself to be identified with the French in the War
of Independence and spent the last years of his life in exile in France.
His was a complex character and his shyness made him flee from
society; only occasionally in company with his closest friends did his
power of observation, his wit and his gift for mimicry really become
apparent. Mostly he withdrew into himself, hiding away in his house
at Pastrana or finding consolation in foreign travel, made possible by
the generous patronage of Godoy. Moratín visited England and was
so deeply impressed by Shakespeare that he made a translation of
Hamlet (1794), though his allegiance to neo-classicism led him to
criticise the lack of attention to the rules on Shakespeare's part. There
was something of a romantic in Moratín's nature; in his *Cartas* and
Autobiografía he shows himself remarkably sensitive to natural beauty
and his description of Vaucluse foreshadows Chateaubriand or Lamar-
tine.

> *La tremenda soledad del bosque y el rumor incesante de las aguas, que asorda el valle y*
> *retumba en la concavidad del monte, todo inspira una melancolía deliciosa que se siente y no*
> *se puede explicar.*
>
> (The terrifying solitude of the wood and the ceaseless noise of the water, which
> deafens the valley and echoes in the hollow of the hillside, everything inspires a
> delicious melancholy which is felt but cannot be explained.)

Even in his comedies, which are plainly inspired by Molière, there
is a sentimentality reminiscent of Marivaux and a tenderness which
anticipates de Musset.

As with Molière, the themes are based on social problems, but there is a liberal character too in Moratín's attitude to life, particularly in the relations between the old and the young, and in this his work differs from the conservative satire of Ramón de la Cruz. This is especially noticeable in his last and best known play, *El sí de las niñas* (1806), in which a girl is to be married to an elderly man for the sake of his wealth. The play conforms strictly to the unities, the action developing in a space of ten hours all in an inn at Alcalá de Henares. The scene is described in minute detail and in no way resembles the *banale antichambre* of which Victor Hugo complained, but rather heralds the arrival of realism with *la mugre del cuarto, las sillas desvencijadas, las estampas del hijo pródigo, el ruido de campanillas y cascabeles* (the filth in the room, the rickety chairs, the prints of the Prodigal Son, the ringing of handbells and jingling of harness bells). Don Diego, an elderly bachelor of comfortable means, is fetching Doña Francisca aged sixteen from her convent to take her to Madrid, where he intends to marry her. He is by no means unaware of the disparity in age and is eager not to force the girl into an odious marriage against her will. He attempts to question Doña Francisca about her feelings, but this is unavailing because her widowed mother, the scheming Doña Irene, constantly interrupts, declaring how eagerly her daughter is awaiting the marriage. Doña Francisca has a secret lover, Don Carlos, a young cavalry officer, who arrives at the inn after receiving a despairing letter giving news of the intended marriage. The lovers meet and vow eternal devotion, and Don Carlos hopes to enlist the aid of a rich uncle of his in Madrid. Unfortunately this uncle is none other than Don Diego, who on meeting his nephew at the inn immediately orders him back to his regiment in Zaragoza. Don Carlos attempts one last meeting with Doña Francisca, throwing a note up to her window. Don Diego finds the note, overhears the lovers' conversation and confronts Don Carlos, telling him to renounce for ever any intention of marrying Doña Francisca. He also tells Doña Irene what has happened and she becomes so angry that, but for Don Carlos's intervention, she would have laid hands on her daughter. The situation is then resolved by Don Diego, who, having discovered where Doña Francisca's true affections lie, gives his leave for the lovers to marry and protests vigorously against the usual methods of bringing up girls whereby *las juzgan honestas luego que las ven instruidas en el arte de callar y mentir ... Todo se les permite menos la sinceridad* (they are judged virtuous as soon as they are seen to be instructed in the art of keeping silent and lying ... Anything is permitted for them except sincerity).

The theme was no new one. Molière constantly pleaded for more liberal treatment of the young, especially as regards marriage, but hitherto the aged bridegroom had usually been painted as a ridiculous figure whose plans are frustrated more often than not by trickery, but here Don Diego is a man of goodwill and of finer feelings. Indeed the whole play is imbued with an atmosphere of gentle melancholy, due perhaps to the fact that the situation may have been based on an actual incident in Moratín's life. Though the comedy is in prose, there is a delicacy of style reminiscent of poetry (several of Moratín's early plays had been in verse) and one is left with a bewildering impression that Moratín, though a typical product of the eighteenth century, had romantic leanings as well, such as were conspicuously absent from most of the other writers of his age.

Eighteenth-century academic verse

Poetry in Spain in the eighteenth century was notably undistinguished. Nearly all the men of letters composed poetry, but it was cold, hollow verse which is now mainly forgotten. When literature concentrates on the propagation of ideas, poetry normally withers; a thinker is not necessarily a poet, for poetry demands intense feeling and an instinct for sound and rhythm. Two eighteenth century poets are still read for their fables, which were likewise a typical product of propagandist literature. The first was TOMÁS DE IRIARTE (1750–91) whose collection of Fábulas literarias (1782) is lively, witty and apt. The seventy-six fables all propound some literary precept in a style half humorous, half serious; El mono y el titiritero (The monkey and the puppeteer) demonstrates the need for clarity in literature, El caminante y la mula de alquiler (The traveller and the hired mule) satirises the high-faluting style, while La campana y el esquilón (The big bell and the handbell), one of Iriarte's best known fables, gently makes fun of those who by saying little and adopting a grave demeanour pass themselves off as great men:

> Muy verosímil es, pues que la gravedad
> suple en muchos así por la capacidad.
> Dígnanse rara vez de despegar sus labios,
> y piensan que con esto imitan a los sabios.

> (Very true to life it is for solemnity in many people thus makes up for ability. They rarely deign to open their lips and believe that in this way they are imitating the wise.)

Iriarte was a true neoclassicist and stressed the need for observing rules in literature, for without them only rarely does a literary work succeed, like a donkey playing the flute (*El burro flautista*):

> *Sin reglas del arte,*
> *borriquitos hay*
> *que una vez aciertan*
> *por casualidad.*

> (Without rules for the art there are donkeys who once by chance succeed.)

Less original than Iriarte, but more readable perhaps, was FÉLIX DE SAMANIEGO (1745–1801) whose *Fábulas morales* (1781–84) are almost all imitated directly from Aesop, Phaedrus or La Fontaine. Nevertheless they are more natural and spontaneous in style than those of Iriarte, though less witty and inventive. The author neatly points out the moral lesson at the end of each fable, unlike La Fontaine who may well insert it at the beginning if he so chooses or leave it to the reader's imagination:

> *Dijo la Zorra al Busto*
> *después de olerlo*
> *—Tu cabeza es hermosa,*
> *pero sin seso.—*

> Como éste hay muchos,
> que aunque parecen hombres
> sólo son bustos.
>
> > (*La zorra y el busto*)

> (Said the Vixen to the Bust, after smelling it: 'Your head is beautiful, but brainless.' *There are many like that, for although they appear men, they are only busts.*)

The greatest lyric poet of the eighteenth century was without doubt JUAN MELÉNDEZ VALDÉS (1754–1817), who had a true instinct for flowing, harmonious language. He was greatly influenced by the poems of Fray Luis de León as well as seeking inspiration among Greek and Latin poets such as Anacreon and Horace. His early work is entirely lyrical in inspiration, with a real feeling for nature and a gentle melancholy of expression. There may indeed be a hint of artificiality typical of some eighteenth-century art but beneath the elegant perfection of form, as most certainly in Mozart, there is a deep understanding of the mind and a charming serenity. One of Valdés's most delightful *letrillas amorosas* is *La flor del Zurguén*, the name he gives to a beautiful girl after the valley of Zurguén near Salamanca:

> *Parad, airecillos,*
> *y el ala encoged;*
> *que en plácido sueño*
> *reposa mi bien;*
> *parad, y de rosas*
> *tejedme un dosel,*
> *do del sol se guarde*
> *la flor del Zurguén.*

(Stay, gentle breezes, and fold your wings, for my beloved is resting sweetly asleep; stay, and with roses weave me a bower where from the sun will be shaded the flower of Zurguén.)

As well as love poems Valdés composed odes reminiscent of those of Luis de León and eclogues showing the influence of Garcilaso de la Vega, of which the best is *Égloga primera*, in praise of country life. He was also master of the ballad style and among his best *romances* mention may be made of *Los segadores* (The Reapers), *Doña Elvira*, a colourful historical poem, and above all *Rosana en los fuegos:*

> *Del sol llevaba la lumbre,*
> *y la alegría del alba*
> *en sus celestiales ojos*
> *la hermosísima Rosana,*
> *una noche que a los fuegos*
> *salió la fiesta de Pascua,*
> *para abrasar todo el valle*
> *en mil amorosas ansias.*

(She bore the fire of the sun and the gladness of dawn in her heavenly eyes, the lovely Rosana, one night when amid the festive fires of Easter she sallied forth to set the whole valley ablaze with the yearnings of love.)

It was perhaps a pity that this pastoral poet should have been persuaded by his friend GASPAR MELCHIOR DE JOVELLANOS (1744–1811) to turn his attentions to philosophical poetry, for which he was by no means so well suited. Though his instinct for poetry is still plainly to be seen, the odes, epistles and elegies mostly have a cold and hollow ring. How can a poet be sincere addressing an epistle to such a man as Godoy, even though he had recently acquired the title of 'the Prince of Peace' and even though he was a generous patron of the arts? Admirable sentiments abound in Valdés's later poems, such as *La presencia de Dios*, but they tend to sound trite and conventional and very different from the deeply felt emotions of the poems of the earlier period.

Another poet typical of the late eighteenth century was MANUEL JOSÉ QUINTANA (1772–1857), who was a statesman as well as a bold liberal thinker. His main themes in poetry are progress, liberty and *la patria*, but though his poems are elegant and correct and though there can be no question of their sincerity, their vehemence leaves the reader as little moved as when listening to impassioned oratory at a political election meeting. *A la invención de la imprenta* (1800) is scarcely a suitable theme for poetry, indisputable though the benefits of the printing press have been. Similarly an ode *A la expedición española para propagar la vacuna en América* (1806) is pedestrian in tone because vaccination, admirable though its results are, does not inspire true poetic feeling; odes to penicillin or antipolio serum are rightly eschewed by modern poets because their praises are best told by the diminishing incidence of disease. But the modern age expects progress from its scientists and it would be wrong to smile too patronisingly at the genuine enthusiasm of eighteenth-century thinkers and men of letters for the spread of scientific knowledge in a country still wallowing in the darkness of medieval superstition.

Quintana was apt to find the patriotic muse difficult to manage also. After praising *Juan de Padilla* (1797) for leading the popular front against the despotism of Carlos V and castigating Philip II in *El panteón del Escorial* (1805), he finds himself nobly apostrophising the French and Spanish fleets at Trafalgar, fighting as they were for Napoleon's tyranny, which dominated Europe including the cowardly Spanish government. Fortunately he has a good word to say for Nelson, since only three years later the English were to become Spain's glorious allies:

> También Nelson allí . . . Terrible sombra,
> no esperes, no, cuando mi voz te nombre,
> que vil insulte a tu postrer suspiro:
> inglés te aborecí, y héroe te admiro.
>
> (Nelson too was there . . . Dread shade, fear not that when my voice names thee it shall vilely insult thy last breath: as an Englishman I detested thee and as a hero I admire thee.)

When Napoleon invaded Spain Quintana was insistent in his call to fight for the independence of the nation. His ode *A España* (1808) urges all Spaniards to remember Spain's past glories as the *reina del mundo* (largely made possible by Carlos V and Philip II of course) and to rise in arms, *¡Antes la muerte que jamás ningún tirano!* (Rather death than ever any tyrant!) To modern ears far from the misery and horrors of

the *Guerra de la Independencia* Quintana's calls to arms seem bombastic
rhetoric, just as Churchill's speeches of 1940 may sound stirring only
to those who lived through those dark days. But Quintana, as a prophet
of victory in his poems, gave hope and courage to Spaniards in their
unequal fight against the Napoleonic armies. His muse is nothing if
not majestic.

Philosophic and didactic prose

The remaining prose literature of the eighteenth century was chiefly
philosophical and didactic in purpose. JOVELLANOS (1744–1811) was
perhaps the most illustrious intellect of the century, a statesman,
reformer and writer. His style attains clarity and elegance, but his
works lack fire and inspiration. Nevertheless, the ideas expressed
retain their interest; severely classical though he was in outlook, he
recognises that imitation of the ancient writers is a sterile occupation:

> *'porque los antiguos crearon y nosotros imitamos; porque los antiguos estudiaron en la
> naturaleza y nosotros en ellos . . . Dad más a la observación y la meditación que a una
> infructuosa lectura y sacudiendo de una vez las cadenas de la imitación, separaos del
> rebaño de los metodistas y copiadores, y atreveos a subir a la contemplación de la naturaleza.*

(Because the ancients created and we imitate; because the ancients studied nature
and we them. . . . Pay more heed to observation and contemplation than to fruitless
reading and shaking off once and for all the chains of imitation, separate yourselves
from the herd of followers and imitators and dare to rise to the contemplation of
nature.)

This sounds like some faint foreshadowing of the plea by the romantics
for natural inspiration in literature.

Colonel JOSÉ CADALSO (1741–82) was even more pronounced in
his romantic and sentimental tendencies, implausible as they may sound
in a distinguished regimental officer. His *Noches lúgubres* (c. 1771),
imitated from Edward Young's *Night Thoughts*, form a prose elegy of
a poetic, heartrending and even febrile nature. Cadalso was in despair
at the sudden death of his lover and conceived the fantastic idea of
digging up her body and taking it away. He was prevented from so
doing by his friends, but this mournful work commemorates the
Colonel's anguish and foreshadows the passionate fantasies of Chateaubriand.

Cadalso was also a man of his century and his *Cartas Marruecas*
(published posthumously in 1793) are modelled on Montesquieu's

Lettres Persanes; they reveal shrewd observation, impartial judgment and subtle satire. The letters represent the correspondence of two Moors, one of whom is travelling in Spain and who describes in detail and with a sharp wit the manners and customs of the Spaniards. Cadalso was a writer of ability, but he lacks the sure touch of the professional man of letters. He conveys the impression of feeling his way towards his objectives without having formed his style sufficiently firmly to be able to forget about it.

Although French prose literature was extensively imitated in Spain during the eighteenth century, the native Spanish style following the example of Cervantes, Quevedo and the picaresque novel was never entirely abandoned. The autobiography of DIEGO DE TORRES Y VILLA-ROEL (1693–1770) reads like a picaresque novel with the tense satirical phraseology of Quevedo. Though Villaroel was up to date in his passionate interest in science and other questions of the day, his rumbustious, rowdy career was out of keeping with that of most men of learning in the eighteenth century. He was the son of a bookseller at Salamanca where he studied at the university. After falling foul of his father he ran away and earned his living in a variety of ways, as a village bullfighter, seller of patent medicines, beggar and dancing master. Later he revived interest in mathematics in Spain by publishing a series of almanacks based on astrological calculations, and correctly forecast the death of Luis I, son of Philip V. Another accurate prophecy was of the French Revolution, but this event did not occur during the author's lifetime. So great was the public interest in mathematics that Salamanca University reinstituted the Chair of Mathematics and appointed Villaroel to lecture.

With such a varied career it is not surprising that Villaroel has much to say of interest in his *Vida*, published between 1743 and 1758 in several parts. His style is eminently readable and his autobiography is a valuable social document giving curious details of life in Spain at all levels. Villaroel had the reputation of a cure-all and besides having taught himself to be a doctor in thirty days, he was consulted on the problem of strange noises in the house of the Condesa de los Arcos, whose servants were living in a state of terror. In spite of Villaroel's jaunty demeanour a sense of horror is conveyed when he finds himself alone and unarmed in an attic where the lights suddenly go out and huge pictures crash down from the walls. In general he exhibits the eighteenth-century dislike for heroics and describes himself in terms of deprecatory geniality.

A mi parecer soy medianamente loco, algo libre y un poco burlón, un mucho holgazán, un si es no es presumido y un perdulario incorregible; porque siempre he conservado un aborrecimiento espantoso a los intereses, honras, aplausos, pretensiones, puestos, ceremonias y zalamerías del mundo.

(In my opinion, I am half mad, something of a freethinker and a bit of a jester, extremely lazy, a trifle conceited, an incorrigible wastrel; because I have always had a terrible hatred of interests, honours, applause, pretensions, jobs, ceremonies and flattery in this world.)

In spite of his claims to an egalitarian outlook (he boasted that he treated his servants as equals) he displayed all the snobbery of a social climber and his debonair manner failed him when confronted by the Inquisition. Nevertheless he was an optimist; he believed in the future and in the advance of science. If for nothing else Villaroel impresses by his zest for life in an arid age.

The eighteenth century was a period when writers revelled in quantitative production. The *España sagrada* by the Augustinian father, ENRIQUE FLÓREZ (1702–73) was a monumental encyclopaedia of the Church in Spain, covering not only ecclesiastical affairs but also geography, archaeology, numismatics, palaeography and much else besides. In Flórez's lifetime twenty-nine folio volumes appeared, and the labours of subsequent Augustinian friars brought the total to more than fifty. The *Historia crítica de España* by JUAN FRANCISCO MASDEU (1744–1817) reached twenty volumes, but never progressed beyond the eleventh century, while the history of Spanish literature by the brothers MOHEDANO was twenty-five years in writing and filled ten volumes, but dealt with literature only to the time of Seneca. This prodigious prolixity was largely the result of the abundance of monasteries in which too many educated men had far too little to do in life.

Such a situation is well satirised by the Jesuit father, JOSÉ FRANCISCO DE ISLA (1703–81) in his novel *Fray Gerundio de Campazas* (1758). Although it displays eighteenth-century French influence especially in its tedious insistence on the didactic element, there is a strong resemblance to the picaresque novel in the descriptions of Fray Gerundio's youth and upbringing, and there is a touch of Cervantes's satire in the way in which the florid, bombastic style of preaching is guyed. Gerundio at an early age captures the heavily latinised style of a popular preacher, and even when his infant lips cannot properly pronounce the sonorous words his parents mark him down as a suitable candidate for the pulpit. The picture of life in a remote village in León is admirably drawn, revealing the endless boredom of such an existence. Life in the monastery, with the clash of personal feelings, is equally well depicted, but here again the keynote is the unbearable tedium which drives men to compose voluminous works on absurd trivialities and to preach sermons filled with misplaced classical quotations and allusions to pagan mythology. The curious fact (though eminently true to life) was that these flights of highflown nonsense were received with enthusiasm by congregations of ignorant and illiterate peasants. Indeed Padre Isla himself left six volumes of sermons couched in the very style he satirised so skilfully. *Fray Gerundio* is still a readable novel; in fact it is the only Spanish novel of this period that is ever read today, apart from Padre Isla's adaptation of Lesage's *Gil Blas*, which was itself modelled on the Spanish picaresque novel.

The eighteenth century was an undistinguished period for Spanish literature, but the writers of the age left their mark on the nation. Their ideas of liberalism spread widely, and in the following century it was the nation that struggled for freedom against a bigoted and repressive monarchy, whereas the early Bourbon Kings had struggled in vain to edge their obdurate and hidebound subjects into some semblance of modernity.

Chapter 9
Romanticism and realism

Romantic drama

It is always said that romanticism came late to Spain for the very good reason that all writers of note had been exiled under Fernando VII's oppressive rule, but in actual fact its triumph on the Spanish stage with the performance of Martínez de la Rosa's *La conjuración de Venecia* in 1834 came only four years after the famous battle for romanticism in France when Hugo's *Hernani* was first acted. It is true that Spanish romantic writers found their inspiration at first from abroad, being especially influenced by Scott and Byron, Chateaubriand and Manzoni, but when they came flocking back to Spain after Fernando's death in 1833, they found the ground well prepared, for romanticism was in reality a return to traditional forms of Spanish literature, the ballads, the laments, the strong feeling for colour, the violent action in plays which were essentially popular in atmosphere and not solely intellectual like French classical tragedies. Neo-classical literature in Spain was not a natural growth and romanticism, when it returned, bloomed at once like any native flora. Interest in traditional Spanish literature had been revived through the work of foreign scholars, mostly German. The brothers Schlegel had made studies of the old *romances* and of the theatre of Calderón; Herder had popularised the *Romancero del Cid* in Germany while Nicolás Böhl de Faber (whose daughter became the first realist novelist in Spain) had published his *Floresta de rimas antiguas castellanas* between 1821 and 1825.

All was ready then when MARTÍNEZ DE LA ROSA (1787–1862) presented his drama to an expectant and wildly enthusiastic audience. *La conjuración de Venecia* contains all the ingredients of romanticism, a tale of

LEFT *Ballet of The Three-Cornered Hat*

the Middle Ages with lovers' meetings in a tomb-house and a melodramatic denouement of mistaken identity. The theme is the conspiracy
in 1310 against the Doge of Venice in which the leader, a handsome and
mysterious young stranger named Rugiero, falls in love with Laura, a
member of the Morosini family who head the rival faction. The lovers
meet secretly amid the tombs in the Morosini family vault and pledge
undying fidelity to each other. The conspiracy is uncovered, Rugiero
is arrested and condemned to death by Morosini. As Rugiero dies it is
revealed that he is in fact the long lost son of Morosini who has unwittingly ordered the execution of his own child. Laura goes mad with
grief.

A bald summary of the plot gives the impression that the play is
nonsensical and indeed the elaborate stage directions raise involuntary
smiles on occasions especially in the trial scene. There are three doors,
each headed with a single dramatic word; the door of the prison is
marked *SOLEDAD*, the torture chamber is labelled *VERDAD* while
the door to the execution shed bears the word *ETERNIDAD*. It would
be unfair, however, to dismiss *La conjuración de Venecia* with a con-
temptuous smile, because it is both moving and convincing. Martínez
de la Rosa is restrained and is not infected by the grosser exaggerations
of romanticism; he manages the ramifications of the plot neatly and his
characters, though conventional, are not mere puppets. Nevertheless,
it must be admitted that as a play it can hardly justify the romantic
claim that it was true to life; in fact the only concession to reality is the
substitution of prose for verse and the style, in the main, is fluent and
simple and avoids over-rhetorical phraseology.

Martínez de la Rosa represents in fact only a transition to romanticism
which burst in its full bloom in the theatre during the following year
with the performance of *Don Álvaro o la fuerza del sino*. Its author Don
ÁNGEL DE SAAVEDRA (later Duque de Rivas) (1791–1865) had served with
distinction at an early age·in the Spanish armies opposing Napoleon.
Exiled for his liberal opinions during the reign of Fernando VII he
visited Italy, France and Malta where he was introduced to English
literature by the governor, Sir John Frere. Converted to the new ideals
of romanticism he published on his return to Spain *El moro expósito*
(1834), an epic poem on the theme of the Infantes de Lara. In the preface
to the poem the well-known critic, Galiano, wrote a manifesto of the
new doctrines similar to Hugo's *Préface de Cromwell*, claiming freedom
to write without fixed rules, to mingle tragedy with comedy, verse
with prose, taking truth and beauty as the sole criteria of literature.

Don Álvaro is the embodiment of these doctrines, though it is doubtful whether truth plays much of a role. The theme resembles the Don Juan legend and its basis of the power of destiny seems at variance with catholic doctrine. Don Álvaro is a spirited young stranger lately returned from America, who falls passionately in love with Doña Leonor, daughter of the Marqués de Calatrava. Consent to the marriage is refused and the lovers attempt to elope, but they are surprised and Don Álvaro unwittingly causes the death of the Marqués, who curses his daughter as he dies. Don Álvaro, wounded in the struggle with the servants of the Marqués, believes Doña Leonor to be dead, and he is next found with the army in Italy where he hopes to find death on the battlefield. Fate places him face to face with one of the Marqués's sons whom he is forced to fight and whom he kills. Don Álvaro is driven by remorse to seek solitude in a monastery in the mountains near Córdoba where for four years he does penance. He is discovered by another son of the Marqués and although Don Álvaro struggles to keep his fiery nature in check, at length he is driven by the taunts of his adversary to fight. Together they go to a lonely place near a cave where there lives a mysterious hermit who attempts vainly to intervene between the duellers. The Marqués's son falls mortally wounded, but suddenly recognising in the hermit his sister Doña Leonor, he stabs her crying: *¡Toma, causa de tantos desastres, recibe el premio de tu deshonra!* (Take that, thou cause of so many disasters, receive the reward of thy dishonour!) In the confusion of the crowd that has gathered Don Álvaro is seen to cast himself in despair from the top of a lofty precipice.

Once again a plain outline of the plot makes the play seem preposterous melodrama, but again it is unfair to criticise too hastily. There is immense vigour in the play; the action is astonishingly rapid, but is managed with great skill. There are few plays which contain greater variety than *Don Álvaro* with its gay and vivid crowd scenes (written in prose), the tender love story and the passionate episodes in which the Marqués's curse is worked out. Melodrama it may well be, but fire and poetic inspiration are never lacking and make *Don Álvaro* a moving play to read or watch. If it is now forgotten by all except students of Spanish literature, it is undeserved oblivion, but at any rate the theme has been preserved in Verdi's adaptation for his opera *La forza del destino*.

Romantic plays are highly suitable for conversion to Italian operas and another Spanish drama now well known as *Il Trovatore* is *El*

trovador by ANTONIO GARCÍA GUTIÉRREZ (1812–84), who was a poor
soldier in the national militia when this play achieved phenomenal
success in 1836. The theme is medieval and the scene is set in Aragon in
the fifteenth century, but the plot and characters are entirely fictitious.
Manrique, the troubadour, and Doña Leonor are in love, but the
powerful Conde de Luna is also pressing his suit with the lady. In a
duel with his rival the count is grievously wounded. Doña Leonor
receives false news that Manrique is dead and she retires to a convent.
Manrique is able to find where she is and woos her in true troubadour
style. The lovers elope, but Manrique is captured by the count's soldiers
and is condemned to death for rebellion. Leonor visits him in his cell,
takes poison and dies in his arms. As Manrique is beheaded, an old
gypsy woman who is thought to be his mother informs the count that
he has in fact executed his long lost brother.

This last unnecessary development of mistaken identity is an inescapable feature of romantic drama and is irritating to modern readers.
The tragedy has occurred and there is no need to attempt to emphasise
it by such an improbable device. Nevertheless, *El trovador* is well worth
reading because not only is the verse fluent and melodious, but the
characters are drawn with a care that is surprising for a melodramatic
theme in which puppets would suffice.

A more sober romantic play is *Los amantes de Teruel* (1837) by JUAN
EUGENIO HARTZENBUSCH (1806–80), a son of a German father and a
Spanish mother. He began life apprenticed to his father who was a
cabinetmaker, but his taste for learning led him to make a prolonged
study of the dramatists of the Golden Age and he ended as director of
the Biblioteca Nacional. Dramatically *Los amantes de Teruel* is the best
constructed of Spanish romantic plays, but it has never achieved the
widespread popularity of *Don Juan Tenorio* (1844) by JOSÉ ZORRILLA
(1817–93). This has now become a tradition in Spanish life and is acted
every year throughout Spain on All Saints Day (1 November). It is
perhaps fortunate to have achieved annual revival for it is a loosely
constructed imitation of Tirso de Molina's *El burlador de Sevilla* in no
less than seven acts. But if it has blemishes due to carelessness, the play
sparkles with life and its verse flows gracefully. It has in addition a
lofty moralising and religious tone which may be regarded as a defect,
but which probably induced ecclesiastical authorities to approve it as
suitable for performance on an important church festival day.

Don Juan Tenorio

Poetry of the romantic movement

Nearly all the romantic playwrights were poets as well, though some
like Martínez de la Rosa composed poems of frigid conventionality.
The Duque de Rivas, however, was a prolific poet and perhaps his
greatest contribution lay in his revivals of ballads as a literary form.
His *Romances históricos* were published in 1841 and all but three of the
poems deal with varied themes from Spanish history. Rivas aspired to
resuscitate the vigour and energy of the old eight syllable ballad metre,
but he was not uniformly successful. His style is somewhat laboured and
often exudes the same bogus air of antiquity as Walter Scott's poems,
but many of his descriptions are vivid and powerful, such as that of the
Arab palaces in the *Alcázar de Sevilla*. Often too he achieves a real
simplicity and effective sobriety in his use of words, as in *El fratricidio*
which begins:

> *Era una noche de marzo*
> *de un marzo invernal y crudo,*
> *en que con negras tinieblas*
> *se viste el orbe de luto.*
>
> (It was a night in March, a raw, wintry March when in
> blackest darkness, the earth is clothed in mourning.)

Zorrilla as a poet was more gifted and imaginative than Rivas, and
his whole life was one long piece of romantic make-believe. His

autobiographical work *Recuerdos del tiempo viejo* tells the story of his escape from his stern father; he leapt from a coach in the dead of night and rode away on a mare grazing by the roadside. Subsequent flights from matrimonial entanglements sent him wandering over Europe and Mexico, but he returned to Spain in 1866 where until his death he enjoyed immense popularity, especially with the older generation. Like Tennyson and Hugo he continued writing romantic poems long after the taste for such themes had passed. Like Tennyson he is often desperately pedestrian, but he has also some of Hugo's mastery of words. Zorrilla was the most spontaneous of poets, for melodious verses streamed from his pen; he described himself as *el pájaro que canta*, but there is possibly something of the repetitiveness of birdsong in his poems, and the melodiousness is sometimes wasted because of vacuousness and verbosity.

Zorrilla shook the dust off the old legends and furbished them up in a readable form. His *Leyenda del Cid* (1882) gives modern readers an insight into the most famous episodes of the life of the national hero. It is, if anything, less true to historical fact than the old *Poema de mío Cid* and is far less sober and realistic. *Granada* (1852) is another long poem (unfinished) which attempts to recreate the atmosphere of the reconquest and to describe life in the Arab kingdom; there are indeed moments of brilliance, but the picture of Granada under the Moors is somewhat conventional, with the feastings and delights of the luxurious life of the harem, just as the Christian camp, with the ardent faith and generous valour of the soldiers, equally fails to convince. His *Cantos del trovador* (1840-1) are perhaps more successful and many provide stirring narratives coupled with passages of lyrical beauty. One of the best poems in the collection is *A buen juez, mejor testigo* based on an old Toledo tradition. A young gallant promises to marry his sweetheart and pledges his troth at the foot of the image of the *Cristo de la Vega*. He goes off to the wars and on his return denies ever having made such a promise. The girl appeals to her only witness, the sacred image, and the Christ in confirmation of her evidence lowers his hand. It is indeed a recurring theme in Spanish poetry and song. Zorrilla contrives to make his narrative simple and moving:

> Asida a un brazo desnudo
> Una mano atarazada
> Vino a posar en los autos
> La seca y hendida palma,

Y allá en los aires ¡'Sí juro!'.
Clamó una voz más que humana.
Alzó la turba medrosa
La vista a la imagen santa . . .
Los labios tenía abiertos,
Y una mano desclavada.

(At the end of a bare arm a torn hand laid a dry, pierced palm on the legal depositions and in the air a more than human voice cried: 'I swear it be true!' The multitude in fear raised their eyes to the sacred image. . . His lips were opened and one hand was unnailed.)

The greatest of the Spanish romantic poets was JOSÉ DE ESPRONCEDA (1808–42) and his poems can still be read with great enjoyment, for he is less concerned with recreating Spanish legends than with expressing his own passionate personal feelings. His life was the embodiment of the romantic ideal; handsome and manly with a pale complexion and flowing dark hair he looked at once like a Byronic hero; hating all forms of tyranny, he fought in the barricades in the streets of Paris in July 1830 and later enlisted in a crusade to liberate Poland. On his return to Spain he took part in revolutionary activities in the streets of Madrid in 1835 and 1836. He showed his magnanimous nature during a serious cholera outbreak in Madrid when he went from house to house doing what he could to relieve suffering. Like most romantic heroes Espronceda had a tragic love affair; the lady was named Teresa and he met her when in exile. She was prosaic enough to desert him in order to marry a Paris merchant, but she died in 1839 of consumption in the flower of youth, though it was rumoured that her death was hastened by drink. It was this tragic love affair that inspired possibly the most beautiful of his poems, *Canto a Teresa*, which he declared was *un desahogo de mi corazón* (an unburdening of my heart).

Espronceda was a supreme egoist and as the apostle of revolt he longed for complete freedom for himself, though he did not extend this freedom to others. In the *Canción del pirata* he glories in the life of a pirate captain who can defy all authority:

Que es mi barco mi tesoro,
que es mi Dios la libertad,
mi ley la fuerza y el viento,
mi única patria la mar.

(For my ship is my treasure, my God is freedom, my law strength and the wind, my only home the sea.)

Like Keats, his sole requirement is perfect beauty:

Y lo cogido
yo divido
por igual.
Solo quiero
por riqueza
la belleza
sin rival.

(And the booty I divide equally. All I want as riches is peerless beauty.)

No doubt this poem is inspired by Byron's *Corsair*, for Espronceda had been deeply influenced by Byron when in exile in London in 1829. The poem is notable for its musical qualities, for the words echo the thunder of guns, the howling of the wind or the soothing lapping of the waves in a calm sea. The abrupt changes of metre reflect the poet's changing moods and the masterly flow of words in the short lines can be matched only by Hugo in *Les Djinns*.

Another poem displaying the same ability to manage short lines which seem to have an indignant staccato sarcasm is *El Mendigo*. The beggar revels in his freedom and delights in embittering with his presence the pleasures of the rich:

Y a la hermosa
Que respira
Cien perfumes,
Gala, amor,
La persigo
Hasta que mira,
Y me gozo
Cuando aspira
Mi punzante
Mal olor.

(And the beauty who exudes countless perfumes, finery and love, I pursue her until she looks at me, and I am glad when she breathes in my pungent stench.)

This is the beggar at his most spiteful. At other times he reverts to a longer metre to indicate the Spanish beggar's long drawn out whine:

Mío es el mundo: como el aire libre,
Otros trabajan porque coma yo;
Todos se ablandan, si doliente pido
Una limosna por amor de Dios.

(The world is mine: free as the air, others work so that I may eat; all hearts soften if dolefully I beg alms for the love of God.)

The beggar makes no concession to society; it is the duty of everyone to support him.

Espronceda's aggressive protest against organised society rises to its shrillest pitch in the *Canto del Cosaco*. He expresses his contempt for stagnant European society and would welcome virile, violent Cossack invaders from the east who would slaughter and plunder. His panacea for Spain's ills seems to foreshadow the anarchist movement of the early twentieth century:

> *¡Hurra, cosacos del desierto! ¡Hurra!*
> *La Europa os brinda espléndido botín:*
> *Sangrienta charca sus campiñas sean,*
> *de los grajos su ejército festín.*
> *¡Hurra! ¡a caballo, hijos de la niebla!*
> *Suelta la rienda, a combatir volad.*

> (Hurrah! cossacks from the wilds! Hurrah! Europe offers you magnificent plunder: Let her countryside be a bloody pool and her army a feast for the crows. Hurrah! To horse, sons of the mists, at full rein fly to the battle.)

Espronceda also attempted long narrative poems in the conventional romantic style. The first, *El Pelayo*, was an early effort and was never completed. It tells the story of the Arab invasion of 711 and of the first Christian victory at Covadonga in 718. There are the conventional scenes of the Moorish king's harem inescapable in any romantic description of the Arabs in Spain, but there is vivid realism in the description of the hunger and desolation in Seville after the Christians had been driven out. Espronceda's best narrative poem is *El estudiante de Salamanca*, based on a popular legend of the Don Juan type. Don Félix de Montemar, the student of Salamanca, is a character after Espronceda's own heart who refuses to conform to society. He leads a dissolute life and seduces an innocent girl, Doña Elvira, whose brothers he kills in a quarrel; for this Don Félix is condemned to death and dies on the scaffold hand in hand with a spectre.

Though *El estudiante de Salamanca* is artistically convincing and the fantastic episodes of the legend are well contrived, Espronceda is more at home with contemporary themes and perhaps his most characteristic poem is the lengthy *El diablo mundo* which sets out to be a compendium of Madrid society in the nineteenth century. A disillusioned old sceptic, Adam, is miraculously made young again and through his eyes the reader is introduced to all the vices and miseries of society. There are seven *cantos* in the poem, which is too long and chaotic to be read all together; there are useless digressions followed by passages rigidly condensed, there are episodes of pure fantasy and sketches of crude realism; sentiment, pessimism, sarcasm, humour are all intermingled with such irregularity that the reader is bewildered and is forced to select the passages that appeal to him. The *Canto a Teresa*, the second of the seven forming *El diablo mundo*, is a masterpiece. Espronceda is in a mood of resigned despair and the long eleven syllable lines express his grief with quiet dignity:

> *Un recuerdo de amor que nunca muere*
> *Y está en mi corazón; un lastimero*
> *Tierno quejido que en el alma hiere,*
> *Eco suave de su amor primero;*
> *¡Ay! de tu luz, en tanto yo viviere,*
> *Quedará un rayo en mí, blanco lucero,*
> *Que iluminaste con tu luz querida*
> *La dorada mañana de mi vida.*

> (A memory of love which never dies, but stays in my heart; a piteous, tender cry of grief which wounds the soul, gentle echo of its first love: oh! as long as I live, there will remain in me a ray of your light, bright star which bathed with its beloved light the gilded morning of my life.)

Espronceda was not alone among romantic writers to experiment with realistic descriptions of contemporary life and Spanish romanticism seems to contain the elements which destroyed it. It represented a revival of traditional Spanish themes and in seeking these and accompanying local colour within Spain itself the attention of romantic writers was struck by the actual state of affairs in the country. It was a time of bitter despair and disillusionment, which suited the mood of the romantics; the wild hopes occasioned by the liberal revival on the death of Fernando VII faded quickly amid the chaos of the Carlist war and the general corruption with María Cristina as regent. Espronceda bitterly describes the state of Spain as all 'misery and greed, money and prose'. It was precisely the prose writers who developed this tendency to analyse contemporary Spanish manners until it became a definite literary trend known as *costumbrismo*.

Costumbrismo

The greatest exponent of *costumbrismo* was MARIANO JOSÉ DE LARRA (1809–37). His short tragic life was that of a thorough-going romantic;

failing with a novel and a drama in verse both on a medieval theme, he turned to journalism, writing short articles on life in Madrid, and with these he quickly gained fame. Married at twenty he suddenly left his wife and two children and plunged into adulterous love affairs. At length rejected by his mistress he shot himself dramatically in her house. His death is foreshadowed in an article *Fígaro en el cementerio* written shortly before his suicide and reflecting his mood of black despair by picturing the whole of Madrid as a graveyard. His despair was heightened by the fact that all Madrid laughed at his mordant articles and regarded him as a humorist.

> *Supone el lector en quien acaba un párrafo mordaz de provocar la risa, que el escritor es un ser consagrado por la naturaleza a la alegría, y que su corazón es un foco inextinguible de esa misma jovialidad que a manos llenas prodiga a sus lectores. Desgraciadamente, y es lo que éstos no saben siempre, no es así.*

> (The reader supposes when a mordant paragraph has just evoked laughter that the writer is a being consecrated by nature to gaiety, and that his heart is an inextinguishable focus of that same joviality which he so lavishly bestows on his readers. Unfortunately, and this is what they are not always aware of, it is not the case.)

Larra wanted to believe in romanticism as a sincere artistic reaction against neoclassical artificiality, but he could not tolerate the equally artificial exaggeration to which romanticism was particularly prone. He wanted to believe in freedom and progress, but he was driven to cynicism by the blind refusal of the ordinary Spaniard to accept changes of any kind, even those which would patently bring improvements. In the article *El castellano viejo* he satirises the foolish pride, obstinacy, boastfulness and self-deception of the average Spaniard who seems to glory in incompetence and discomfort because that is the Spanish way. *Vuelva Vd. mañana* castigates the idleness of shopkeepers, officials, ministers and Spaniards in general who prefer to procrastinate even if thereby they lose valuable custom. *¿Entre qué gentes estamos?* returns to the same theme only with greater bitterness; a hustling Frenchman, M. Sans-Délai, is eager to invest money in various enterprises in Spain, but everywhere he is greeted by officials who are either openly insolent or lazily obstructive. M. Sans-Délai's applications are hopelessly becalmed in official channels and the once optimistic investor returns to France in despair taking his money with him.

The satire in Larra's *Artículos de costumbres*, which he wrote under various pseudonyms such as *Fígaro* or *El pobrecito hablador*, is entirely destructive in its criticism, as is usual with satire written by the young. He has nothing constructive to offer, but unlike many youthful satirists, he is restrained and never outrages good taste, bold though he is in his attacks. He carefully avoids personal and spiteful allusion; he satirises types, not individuals. *Solo hacemos pinturas de costumbres, no retratos.* (We are only doing paintings of manners, not portraits.) This restraint gives his satire extra force.

Larra is surprisingly modern in tone and can be read today with the same keen interest as in Madrid of the 1830s. He has seized the permanent features of the Spanish character rather than ephemeral manifestations. Moreover, he writes in a simple even racy style which exudes a bitter joviality: *Reírnos de las ridiculeces, ésta es nuestra divisa; ser leídos, éste es nuestro objeto, decir la verdad, éste es nuestro medio.* (To laugh at follies, this is our motto; to be read, this is our aim; to speak the truth, this is our method.) In fact Larra's prose represents a welcome return to the direct irony of Cervantes or Quevedo replacing the Johnsonian pomp of the eighteenth century and the highflown bombast of romanticism.

Most writers of the period tried their hand at the romantic historical novel in the style of Walter Scott, including MARTÍNEZ DE LA ROSA and ESPRONCEDA whose *Sancho Saldaña* (1834) was an imitation of *Ivanhoe*. Some of these novels are of considerable merit like *El Señor de Bembibre* (1844) by ENRIQUE GIL Y CARRASCO (1815–46). Its plot resembles that of the *Bride of Lammermuir* and the novel is patently sincere and moderate in tone, but there is too much insistence on the pathetic note and its somewhat languid style induces monotony. Spain had her Dumas in MANUEL FERNÁNDEZ Y GONZÁLEZ (1821–88) whose fertile imagination and gift for narrative enabled him to produce more than 200 novels, all now entirely forgotten. Though romantic novels remained popular long after the movement had lost its initial impetus, *costumbrismo* quickly gained favour and literary influence. ESTÉBANEZ CALDERÓN (1799–1867) was brilliantly successful with his *Escenas andaluzas* (1847), which, though somewhat affected in style, give vivid pictures of the life of the poorer classes in Andalusia, the most picturesque and un-European part of Spain, then scarcely known. MESONERO ROMANOS (1803–82) rivalled and continued Larra's work in his articles describing life in Madrid. His first *artículos de costumbres* were collected in 1820–21 under the title of *Mis ratos perdidos;* other collections followed, *Panorama matritense* (1835–38), *Escenas matritenses* (1842), *Tipos y caracteres* (1862). Though not so pungent as Larra, Mesonero Romanos is a brilliant observer; his satire is light and genial and the style is clear and natural.

Costumbrismo shaped the course of the novel in the second half of the nineteenth century by turning it towards a realistic survey of contemporary life in the author's native district. This *regionalismo* is a feature common to almost all the realist novels of the latter part of the century; even Juan Valera who had travelled as a diplomat to places as far apart as Washington and St Petersburg wrote novels set in his native Andalusia. Only Pérez Galdós could be called an international novelist.

The first realist novel was by a woman CECILIA BÖHL DE FABER (1796–1877) who wrote under the name of FERNÁN CABALLERO. She had at first continued the work of her father, the German consul in Cádiz, collecting Andalusian popular poetry and songs. In this way she came to interest herself in the doings of the lower classes and in 1849 her novel *La Gaviota* caused something of a literary sensation by describing in much of the novel ordinary peasant life rather than the adventures of medieval knights and ladies. La Gaviota (the Seagull) is the name given to a boorish country girl with whom a young artistic and ideal-istic German doctor falls in love. They marry and at the invitation of the Duque de Almansa go to live in Seville where La Gaviota who has a fine natural voice is taught operatic singing. She achieves a triumphant success as an opera singer in Madrid where she forms an adulterous liaison with a bullfighter. Her husband in despair leaves her and even-tually dies of yellow fever in Cuba. Meanwhile La Gaviota sees her lover killed in the bullring and is deserted by all her patrons and friends. Having lost both her health and her voice she returns to her native village where she becomes the wife of the local barber who ill treats her.

The novel still displays many romantic tendencies such as the unlikely operatic triumph of La Gaviota and the excessive sentimen-tality of the lachrymose German doctor, Stein, but the characters are plausible and the peasant scenes are especially well observed. It suffers also from a ponderous moralising tendency which Fernán Caballero must have acquired from her German father rather than from her mother who was half Spanish, half Irish. She aspired to the re-establishment of Spanish customs and traditions and was opposed to any influence from without which might loosen the strict moral-ity of patriarchal or more precisely matriarchal country life. This tendency to moralise is apparent in the realist novels of nearly all the writers who followed this new trend inaugurated by Fernán Caballero.

The realist novel

A short novel *El sombrero de tres picos* (1874) by PEDRO ANTONIO DE ALARCÓN (1833–91) is a masterpiece, though some critics have dismissed it somewhat contemptuously as sentimental. Alarcón was born in Guadix, a small cathedral town in Andalusia honeycombed with inhabited caves, and the novel is clearly set in the author's home town although no name is given. The date of the action also is not precisely stated, but may be taken as 1805, though Alarcón was thinking no doubt of his own times when satirising the social injustice and local tyranny inherent in Spanish government. A well-to-do miller, Tío Lucas, ugly and hunchbacked, is married to the lovely Señá Frasquita, whose beauty attracts the attention of all the local gentry including the bishop. They gather at the mill where they are entertained and flattered by the miller and his wife who in return receive various favours and privileges. Unfortunately the local Corregidor, the representative of the King, casts lustful eyes on Señá Frasquita and attempts to seduce her, drawing away her husband to a nearby village by a trick. The Corregidor falls into the mill race and has to make his passionate advances while dripping wet. These advances are indignantly rejected by Señá Frasquita who takes fright when the Corregidor collapses in a shivering fit. She hastily leaves the mill to seek her husband leaving the Corregidor to the care of his *alguacil* who has been waiting in a lane nearby. He undresses his swooning master and puts him in the conjugal bed. Then at his master's bidding he leaves the mill to pursue Señá Frasquita, who, they think, has gone to the town to complain to the Corregidor's wife. Meanwhile, Tío Lucas who has escaped from the village where he was detained returns to the mill unbeknown to anyone, notices the Corregidor's clothes in the kitchen, applies his eye to the keyhole of the bedroom door and sees framed in it the Corregidor's head on the pillow. His worst fears are confirmed. After rejecting his instinctive desire to kill his supposed rival, he puts on the Corregidor's clothes and sets off towards the town, mimicking the Corregidor's walk and voice and declaring: *También la Corregidora es guapa*. (The Corregidor's wife is not bad looking either.) Not long after, Señá Frasquita who has drawn blank at the village returns with the *alcalde* and meets the Corregidor emerging from the mill dressed in the only clothes available, those of Tío Lucas. After a scuffle due to mistaken identity the party sets out for the town with Señá Frasquita weeping, and the Corregidor uttering ferocious threats against all and sundry. At the Corregidor's residence they are at first refused admission, being told that the master has already returned and is in bed with his wife like any God-fearing gentleman should be at that time of night. Eventually the Corregidor gains admission and is received by everyone including the Corregidora as Tío Lucas who in fact shortly appears as the Corregidor. The joke is finally ended and the two men exchange clothes while the whole affair is satisfactorily explained to Señá Frasquita. The miller and his wife are reconciled, but the Corregidora categorically refuses to explain to her husband what passed between her and Tío Lucas. She banishes him henceforth forever from her bedroom. The old reprobate merely smiles and mutters to himself: 'I did not expect to get off so lightly. Garduña (his *alguacil*) will fix me up somewhere else!'

The novel which was first intended as a short story for a Cuban magazine is based on the old ballad (*El molinero de Arcos*) and it has been said that in no way can it be classed as a realist novel since it is merely a tale of a village maiden and a wicked squire whose evil designs are frustrated. It is true that the disguises and mistaken identities strain credulity, but the book has a broad basis of realism because the characters are wholly lifelike. Tío Lucas is upright enough, but he is grasping and well aware of the value of his pretty wife in obtaining favours from the gentry. She in her turn, though horrified at the attempted seduction, is quite capable of flirting with the Corregidor to obtain her nephew's nomination as clerk to the town council. The Corregidor, lecherous though he may be, is more weak than wicked, managed by his scheming *alguacil* and in constant fear of his cold, dominating wife. These characters are no mere puppets, for each is carefully and realistically drawn, even those who play minor roles like the village mayor. The style too is natural, easy and gently ironical; perhaps there are moments when Alarcón is too consciously facetious, as for instance when he compares Señá Frasquita courted by the Corregidor to Pamplona bombarded. The theme of the novel is a recurrent one in Spanish literature, the triumph of the little against the big, the humble against the great; as in Lope de Vega's *Fuente Ovejuna* it is the common people who display sound sense and sturdy independence of spirit. If as in *El sombrero de tres picos* the story ends happily, it is none the less realistic; Spanish realism always displays a healthy, optimistic view of life very different from the sombre picture presented by Balzac and the de Goncourt brothers in France. There is perhaps a tendency with Spanish writers to idealise surroundings; the description of the mill and the marvellous contrivances which Tío Lucas and his wife have arranged is too *ameno* (neat and agreeable) to be credible for it sounds as if it were written by a house agent. This trend is noticeable in many Spanish realist novelists and may well be an inescapable development from *regionalismo* for any author is liable to view his native heath in a glowing light. *El sombrero de tres picos* is of immediate appeal to readers in all countries and has achieved phenomenal success; besides being translated into twelve languages it has been adapted as a musical comedy and a ballet.

Of less popular appeal, but perhaps of greater literary interest, are the novels of JUAN VALERA (1824–1905). He too came from Andalusia, being a native of Cabra, a small town near Córdoba. A man of wide culture and learning he made the diplomatic service his career and was stationed in many foreign capitals, Rio de Janeiro, Naples, Lisbon and later Washington, Paris, Vienna and St Petersburg. Though forced to earn his living as a diplomat, he was by nature drawn to literature and between periods of service abroad published numerous poems, coldly classical in tone, and critical essays of the highest value. These literary efforts brought meagre financial rewards and at the age of fifty, when on a visit to his home town, he conceived the idea of writing a novel in the hope that it would earn him a larger sum of money. The result was *Pepita Jiménez* (1874).

Valera states that he had been reading a number of books on religion and mysticism and that these provided the main theme for his novel. The story is of Don Luis who on the eve of ordination pays a visit to his father, a rich landowner or *cacique* in Andalusia, and meets a beautiful young widow whom his father is courting. The first part of the story is told in the form of letters from Don Luis to his uncle, the Dean, who for the last ten years has been preparing him for ordination. The letters reveal all the confidence and half-digested learning of a young student aspiring to be a hero of the Church. He speaks at first loftily of the young widow and answers his uncle's anxious enquiries by saying that he is interested in her merely as a 'beautiful creature of God'. To be polite to her and to his father he learns to play *tute* (a card game) at her *tertulias* and at her suggestion he learns to ride because, he says, it might be useful to him later as a missionary in some savage land. Gradually his self-assurance fades and he realises with horror that he is in love with Pepita. With a mighty effort and with characteristic youthful lack of consideration for the other party, he decides to give up seeing her.

Pepita, however, is not to be defeated so easily. She makes it quite clear how shabbily he is treating her, and her outspoken, interfering old nannie, Antoñona, induces Don Luis to come and bid farewell to

Pepita. The lovers have a discussion on love, both human and divine, which would do credit to two doctors of theology. Don Luis remains firm and Pepita rushes from the room to her boudoir to which Don Luis in remorse follows her and where his stern resolve is utterly broken. Realising that his ecclesiastical ambitions are at an end Don Luis is galvanised into unwonted action now that his long agony of mind is over. He deliberately picks a quarrel in the casino with a young count who has been making disparaging remarks about Pepita; in the ensuing duel both antagonists, hopelessly inept, are wounded, Don Luis less seriously than the Count. Don Luis now faces the task of informing his father that he is about to marry the lady whom his father is courting. It turns out, of course, that his father (and indeed the whole village) has been fully aware of the situation and has been secretly encouraging the match. All therefore ends happily.

Any attempt to classify Valera's work into some neat literary pigeonhole is bound to fail. He is an eclectic who writes to please himself. The setting of *Pepita Jiménez* is as idyllic as a scene from a romantic ballet where all the peasants are neat and clean and the alfresco picnic seems to have been supplied by high-class caterers. There is practically no external action in the novel apart from a few incidents verging on the improbable; for instance Don Luis learns to ride in an incredibly short time and of course tames the tiger horse right under Pepita's window. On the other hand interior action is continuous and often violent. *Pepita Jiménez* is a magnificent psychological study developed with great subtlety. The main interest is the birth and growth of the passion of love and the behaviour of the lovers under varying circumstances, but there are endless subsidiary sources of interest and indeed amusement. There is a splendid description of Don Luis's wounded feelings when on a picnic expedition he watches his father, his cousin and Pepita herself galloping around on mettlesome Andalusian horses while he has to follow with the parish priest and his mountainous aunt Casilda on mules specially selected for their docility.

The style of the novel is serenely classical with elegant but natural turns of phrase. Perhaps the characters, including Pepita, speak too much like university dons (only Antoñona uses an incomprehensible Andalusian dialect) and it is undoubtedly true that Valera indulges too much in long theological disquisitions to suit his own pleasure, but the impression which the novel conveys is calm, reflective, observant and smiling, and fresh charms are to be found in it with each subsequent reading.

Pepita Jiménez was an immediate success and Valera was encouraged to write other novels, none of which have had quite so much appeal for the reading public. One of them, *Doña Luz* (1879) is on a similar theme to *Pepita Jiménez*, describing how a middle-aged priest, Padre Enrique, falls in love with a beautiful *marquesa*, Doña Luz, to whom he has been giving spiritual advice. He conceals his passion heroically and she, unaware of the love she has inspired, marries. Only after Padre Enrique's death does she discover by reading some of his papers how bitter has been his struggle to remain faithful to his priestly vows. Most of Valera's other novels deal in one way or another with the problems raised by the union of an elderly husband and a young wife (he himself married at the age of fifty-two). The best known is *Juanita la Larga* (1895) set once again in Andalusia in idyllic surroundings and describing the courtship of an old man of substantial fortune with the beautiful daughter of an impoverished widow. Valera's last novel *Genio y Figura* (1897) is the story of a Spanish courtesan who marries an elderly rich Brazilian. There is an international flavour about the book, for the scene is laid in Rio de Janeiro and later in Paris. Valeria is not so happy, well though he knew these cities, as when drawing his serene, idealised picture of his native Andalusia.

The masters of the novel

Less charming but infinitely more powerful are the novels of JOSÉ MARÍA PEREDA (1833–1906), an uncompromising traditionalist from Polanco near Santander. A man of good family, he went to Madrid in 1852 to study, but spent most of his time in theatres and at literary gatherings. In 1854 he returned to his home and thereafter rarely left it. He is the most emphatic apostle of *regionalismo;* his books are filled with long descriptions of the mountains of his native district, and brilliant though they are such passages sometimes grow tedious. He is a passionate believer in patriarchal rural life, with the squire caring for the welfare of his tenantry and ruling them with firm discipline. His earliest work *Escenas Montañesas* (1864) are sketches in the *costumbrista* style: several similar collections followed and then in 1878 he launched into his first novel on his favourite theme. *Don González de la Gonzalera* is a fierce caricature of a common uneducated man who returns rich from South America and tries unsuccessfully to be a country gentleman.

Galdós, who was a friend of Pereda and who was as gently tolerant as Pereda was sternly rigid, had already published two novels in defence of tolerance (*Doña Perfecta* and *Gloria*) and Pereda countered with *De tal palo, tal astilla* (1879), which is a manifesto in favour of strict catholicism. For a man of such uncompromising views Pereda was remarkably sensitive to his critics who, while praising his descriptions of country life, maintained that he lacked breadth and was unable to depict life in the great capitals. Pereda's answer to this was *Pedro Sánchez* (1883) which is a novel almost picaresque in character; the hero first appears in his native village but then goes to Madrid as a revolutionary writer. Surprisingly he finally ends up as the governor of a province. All types of society are depicted in the course of the hero's wanderings and the satire is unexpectedly gentle in tone.

But Pereda was not happy describing life elsewhere than in the province of Santander and his masterpiece is a novel, *Sotileza* (1884), depicting the fisherfolk of his native province. The central figure of the story is an orphan girl called Silda who is taken in and cared for by some fisherfolk. Because of the gentleness and purity of her nature she is given the name of Sotileza, a dialect form of *sutileza*, meaning the finest thread of a fishing line (the novel is somewhat overloaded with *santanderino* jargon). Several of the villagers are in love with her, but for some mysterious reason she prefers to marry an ugly, bestial creature named Muergo. He is drowned in a catastrophic storm and Silda eventually marries into an honourable fishing family. The plot is slight and the main interest is in the study of the life of the fishing community with its poverty, hardships and dangers. Pereda has a horror of false idealism and does not shrink from depicting the brutal and bestial aspects of a primitive community, but he also shows the virtues of the fisherfolk, who are a virile, generous race. Their endless struggle with the sea teaches them courage and patience and gives them a sense of responsibility in caring for each other.

Sotileza attracted much attention and brought forth a crop of imitations such as *José* by Palacio Valdés and *La Pesca*, a long narrative poem by Gaspar Núñez de Arce. Strangely enough Pereda himself turned away from Santander and made another attempt to portray life in Madrid with *La Montálvez* (1888). It is the scandalous chronicle of a lady who regards marriage as merely a means of gaining wealth and social position. Having a husband by no means prevents her from having affairs with a series of lovers. Her ideal is to be admired by all men of good taste and to be envied by all elegant women. The picture of a vicious society lady is exaggerated and suffers from the prejudices of a country gentleman who has had limited opportunities of observing life in the capital.

Once again literary critics began to murmur in their oracular fashion that Pereda's powers as a novelist were declining and as if in answer he produced one of his greatest works, *Peñas Arriba* (1895), on the recurring Wordsworthian theme of the superiority of country life. Again the plot is slight and the main interest is centred on the description of patriarchal life in the Cantabrian mountains. Don Celso lives in his lonely *casa solariega* and, although a man of superior education, he shares the troubles and problems of the villagers. Having no heir, Don Celso sends for a nephew from Madrid hoping that he will eventually settle as the village patriarch. Don Marcelo arrives with vast quantities of luggage, having suffered a nightmare journey on horseback from the railhead, and does nothing but pine for Madrid and Paris. Gradually, however, he is charmed by the peaceful beauty of rural life and after Don Celso's death assumes the role of squire amid the simple, happy peasant community. At first sight the novel appears prejudiced and exaggeratedly idealistic, but Pereda has remarkable powers of description and his characters are real and convincing. His language is at times archaic in flavour like his political ideas, but it is rich and vigorous and occasionally resembles that of Cervantes in the mastery of picturesque phrases.

Pereda represents traditional Spain at its best. His friend, PÉREZ GALDÓS (1843–1920) shows a more liberal outlook and has broader vision. Like Larra he is not deceived by the charm of life *a la antigua española* and takes a freer and more cosmopolitan view. Perhaps it is for this reason that he was unappreciated by many Spanish critics, and their narrow censure caused the rest of Europe also to neglect Galdós, whose work deserves to be placed among internationally known novelists like Dickens and Balzac and Tolstoi. He was born in Las Palmas in the Canary Islands and his family had connections with England through the fruit trade. He went to an English school in Las Palmas and later spent some time in England. He acquired an admiration for English literature, particularly the works of Dickens, and for the English in general. His flattering descriptions of the chivalrous behaviour of the British navy after the battle of Trafalgar are positively embarrassing in their enthusiasm.

At the age of nineteen he was sent to Madrid to study law, as was usual with youths of promising ability, but he knew his real vocation was literature. A visit to Paris confirmed his taste for Balzac's novels and his own first novel *La fontana de oro* appeared in 1870 with moderate success as a picture of Spain during the tyranny of Fernando VII's reign. Three years later he embarked on an ambitious series of novels which he named *Episodios nacionales* and which dealt with historical events during the momentous period 1805 to 1814. They are short novels in which the same hero, Gabriel, recounts his experiences of national events; by some miraculous means he appears to witness all incidents of any importance, being a cabin boy at Trafalgar and a battalion commander at the battle of Los Arapiles (1812). The success of this first series encouraged Galdós to write a second covering the years 1814–34, told in the same autobiographical manner, but with another omnipresent hero, Monsalud. In 1879 Galdós abandoned historical novels to devote himself to studies of contemporary life. In 1897, however, when he felt himself too closely identified with the characters he observed in life and represented in his novels, he returned to the more objective study of history. The result was three further series of *Episodios nacionales* bringing the survey of Spanish history up to the beginning of the reign of Alfonso XIII (1885). The last novel was *Cánovas* written in 1912 in which year Galdós' eyesight failed and he became completely blind. He wrote no more novels after a lifetime of composition, but in the last eight years of his life he still found the energy to dictate four plays.

The total *Episodios* amount to forty-six volumes; each is a complete novel in itself and can be read separately. The best known in England is the first, *Trafalgar*, but it is not of outstanding merit. There are indeed vivid descriptions of the battle and especially of the storm that followed, but the characters are of a somewhat conventional kind, the old retired naval captain, Don Alonso, determined to get back to the fleet which is preparing to sail to meet Nelson, and his abettor, Marcial, a retired boatswain with forty years' service in the navy. The battle has a slightly over heroic and intensely honourable flavour like an account of the Eton and Harrow match in a Victorian sporting journal. Perhaps the most lifelike character is the old captain's domineering wife, Doña Francisca; she is quite determined that he shall not make a fool of himself by returning to the fleet for the battle. To escape her vigilance the old man has to give her the slip while visiting the fortifications at Cádiz. Nelson's cannons hold no terrors for him, but he cannot face his wife without trembling.

Galdós had remarkable ability in portraying female characters and his first *novela de costumbres* is a powerful study of a bigoted possessive mother and her neurotic daughter. *Doña Perfecta* (1876) is a plea for religious tolerance and also a less narrow outlook on the treatment of

children. Doña Perfecta is a widow who is the principal lady in the
small cathedral town of Orbajosa. Being under an obligation to her
brother, she agrees to a suggestion that his son, Don Pepe Rey, should
come to stay in Orbajosa in the hopes that he will form an attachment
to Doña Perfecta's daughter, Rosario, and thus unite the two branches
of the family. Pepe is a young engineer of great intelligence besides
being manly and kindhearted. On arrival he bears with great politeness
his aunt's maddeningly fussy attentions and such repeated phrases as
'How you have grown!' (he is thirty-four), but he has a fatal habit of
speaking his mind somewhat frankly. He declares that the shoddy
decorations inside the cathedral are hideous, especially the ridiculously
ornate clothes of the Virgin and Child; the local priest, Don Inocencio,
points out with mild triumph that this holy image is cared for lovingly
by none other than Doña Perfecta and Rosario. The priest has considerable ascendancy over Doña Perfecta and he never fails to goad
Pepe Rey by taunting him in the most honeyed tones about how
clever and progressive young men are nowadays, but how he prefers
the traditional Spanish way of life. No doubt the priest sees in Pepe Rey
a rival, for he himself entertains hopes that his priggish young nephew
will marry Rosario. Doña Perfecta, seeing that Pepe and Rosario have
at once taken a liking to each other, betrays all the jealous feelings of a
mother who cannot bear a young man to steal her daughter's affections
from her. She begins to persecute him in mean underhand ways,
ensuring that his father's letters do not reach him, stirring up the
townsfolk to bring footling lawsuits against him and quarrelling with
Pepe about his alleged lack of reverence in the cathedral. Finally she
shuts Rosario in her room and will not allow Pepe to see her, pretending
that she is suffering from a congenital melancholia. The lovers meet
secretly and finally plan to elope. The plan is discovered after Doña
Perfecta has mercilessly cross-examined a maid who has acted as a note
carrier. On the night that Pepe is in the garden preparing to carry off
Rosario, Doña Perfecta, claiming that the house is being broken into,
orders a retainer to shoot Pepe Rey in the darkness. After his death,
which is conveniently labelled suicide, Rosario who has always been of
a highly nervous temperament, becomes mad.

It may seem that the novel is overdramatic and a mere caricature,
like so many of Dickens's works, but Doña Perfecta is a convincing piece
of observation and the final catastrophe is the result of a momentary
decision in the heat of fury by a jealous mother who has convinced
herself that she is acting for the best in preventing the marriage. The

picture of the cathedral town with its faded charm, the complete inability of this small community to criticise itself and its hostility towards a young stranger who is disarmingly frank, are as clear and penetrating as Trollope's Barchester, where passions run as high as in Orbajosa and intrigue is quite as intense, though temperaments are less violent. As in Trollope's novels, there is no lack of humour in *Doña Perfecta*. There is the gay young officer, Pinzón who billets himself on Doña Perfecta and allows Pepe to impersonate him in order to have secret meetings with Rosario. The boisterous spirits of the Troya girls cast a light amid the encircling gloom when they throw stones into a neighbouring courtyard and inadvertently hit Don Inocencio. With them too a sentimental note is sounded; they are orphans in the most straitened circumstances, but nevertheless display remarkable exuberance and unconcern about their bad reputation in Orbajosa for receiving visits from gentlemen—even though their virtue is in fact impeccable.

Sentiment is never far away in Galdós, who had a fund of sympathy for fellow creatures in circumstances less fortunate than his own. *Marianela* (1878) is frankly sentimental and is only redeemed from slushiness by Galdós's vigorous style and uncanny powers of observation. Marianela is an ill-favoured girl who acts as a kind of housekeeper to a rich young man, Pablo, who has been blind from birth. She has great gifts of tenderness and affection and Pablo falls in love with her, believing her to be as beautiful as she is kind. When a doctor pronounces it possible to cure Pablo's blindness, Marianela runs away so that the secret of her ugliness shall not be revealed. Pablo, recovered from his blindness, now falls in love with a cousin of his, Florentina, who eventually discovers Marianela lying gravely ill in a house in the neighbourhood. She is brought back to Pablo's house where she dies in his presence, still adoring him, and with Pablo struggling to conceal his disillusionment.

Marianela is touching and pathetic, but it does not bear the stamp of reality apparent in Galdós's next series of twenty-one novels dealing with life in Madrid. These contain his most mature work. The first, *La desheredada* (1881) is a study of a middle-class girl with ideas and aspirations above her station. Isidora Rufete has been led to believe that she is the daughter of a *marquesa* and she arrives in Madrid to press her claim at law. She has a dread of anything common or vulgar and is attracted by the glamour of new clothes. Despite her high principles, her pride and the proffered help of friends and relations, she is unable to resist the temptations of luxury and sinks into virtual prostitution. Her gradual fall has all the essence of tragedy for she is in no sense wicked and accepts with dignity the consequences of her weakness. As an analysis of the female mind strongly tempted, yet filled with revulsion for anything sordid, *La desheredada* is a masterpiece.

Two short novels, *Tormento* and *La de Bringas*, appeared in 1884 and deal with a family of civil servants. Don Francisco is a man of meticulous methods and order and in *La de Bringas* he is to be found making a picture of a mausoleum for a bereaved lady out of the hair belonging to her daughter recently dead. His wife, Doña Rosalía, meanwhile is lured by the desire for luxury and fine clothes into disreputable liaisons. *La de Bringas* is admirable comedy, giving a faithfully accurate picture of the jobbery and intrigue at court in the last year of the reign of Isabel II.

Galdós's longest and perhaps greatest novel is *Fortunata y Jacinta* (1886–87) which, though having the simplest of plots, embraces the whole network of Madrid society. The characters, incidents and background are so realistic that the book gives the illusion of life itself and the vast length of the novel passes unnoticed by the reader. The central theme is of a selfish, spoilt young man of a wealthy family who marries a charming girl, Jacinta, of the same social class as himself. He also keeps a working-class mistress, Fortunata, who bears him a son whereas his wife is childless. The interplay of feeling in these circumstances is skilfully managed and in the background are all the various friends and relatives, one lot well-to-do and refined, the other poor, but far from unassertive. Low life seemed to interest Galdós more than previously and he spent much time investigating the squalid conditions of the Madrid slums. This interest may have been inspired by Dickens or it may have sprung from the French school of naturalist writers led by Zola. Galdós is fascinated too by the study of mentally abnormal characters, as for example Maxi Rubén who persuades Fortunata to marry him and who preaches a new religion that death is the only way to freedom.

The preoccupation with poverty appears again in *La misericordia* (1897) which describes the life of an old servant, Benigna, who is forced to beg at a church door to keep her mistress from penury. In return she receives nothing but cold ingratitude. Meanwhile, in *Ángel Guerra* (1891), another very long novel, Galdós in presenting a convincing description of a sudden, impetuous conversion from agnosticism to catholicism, indulges in such a parade of abnormal types, criminal and neurotic, that most readers are likely to be repelled. Indeed Galdós

finally made himself mentally sick, for by instinct he reflects the fundamental optimism of the Spanish realists, and with relief he returned to
the *Episodios nacionales*.

Galdós knew all classes of Spanish society except the aristocracy,
which is the least typical because it is the most cosmopolitan. His real
mastery lies in depicting ordinary life and especially the lives of families
or social groups. This is a far more difficult task than that of novelists
who write of high adventure in which excitement is inherent. With
Galdós the humdrum existence of middle and lower class society takes
on a throbbing interest, as in Dickens or Balzac. Galdós avoids the
melodrama of Dickens and his characters are drawn lifesize; he has
none of the heaviness and bad taste of Balzac at his worst. It is true that
Galdós can be tedious and longwinded at times, but his style is rescued
by the never failing fund of solemn irony that characterises the greatest
Spanish writers such as Cervantes, Lope de Vega or Tirso de Molina.

Bazán and naturalism

The credit for introducing French naturalism to Spain is usually given
to DOÑA EMILIA, CONDESA PARDO BAZÁN (1851–1921) because in the
prologue to her second novel, *Un viaje de novios* (1881), she praises the
French naturalist school for its detailed observation of life. She had
travelled extensively before settling down in Madrid where she gained
the reputation of being one of the wittiest and most intelligent women
of the century as well as one of the ugliest. She was certainly a most
distinguished literary critic with mature judgment and discerning
insight. Her two main works of literary criticism are *Los poetas épico-
cristianos* and *La literatura francesa moderna*, but she wrote in addition
numerous articles of great interest on contemporary writers such as
Alarcón and Campoamor. In these she makes valiant efforts not to
appear prejudiced and on the whole she succeeds; only on the subject
of Pereda does she show herself violently antipathetic.

From a person with such a mixture of interests native and foreign a
variety of methods and styles is only to be expected and Pardo Bazán
can be romantic, realist, naturalist in rapid succession, as can be seen in
her many and varied collections of short stories in which sentiment
and cold reality are readily mixed. At her best she is typical of Spanish
realism in that she describes her native Galicia frankly and brutally,
but without prejudice. Her best novel is *Los pazos de Ulloa* (1886)
which depicts life in and around a Galician manor house (*pazos* is

dialect for *palacios*). In this solitary country mansion lives a young *marqués* of despotic tendencies; his mistress is the beautiful Sabel, daughter of his *mayordomo* who attempts to exploit this liaison. The *mayordomo* recognises an enemy in the newly appointed chaplain and tries all methods of discrediting him, including making Sabel flirt with him. The *marqués* marries a cousin whom he treats with great brutality and who is immediately the object of the hatred of the *mayordomo* and Sabel. Her one spiritual support is the young chaplain, and the *mayordomo* finds the opportunity to spread further scandal about him, eventually forcing him to leave. Before he goes, however, he sees the body of the sinister *mayordomo* who has been murdered in an act of local revenge. The *marquesa* is left to suffer the martyrdom of an unhappy marriage.

The grim and gloomy house which is falling into decay because of the impoverishment of Galician agriculture exudes the same weird atmosphere as *Wuthering Heights*. But it is not only events in the house which are powerfully described, but also life in the locality. Outstanding is the account of a rigged election in the neighbourhood, engineered by two rival *caciques*. Galician writers are noted for their Celtic strain of melancholy sentiment, but in Pardo Bazán there is no such trace; she is remarkably direct and vigorous and at times is boldly frank, but Spanish restraint prevents her from being obscene. Her picture of Galicia is very different from Pereda's eulogies of country life. With Pardo Bazán rural life in Galicia is wretched, violent, corrupt, and therefore probably she tells only half the truth.

The sentimental novel

The brighter side of the picture is presented by ARMANDO PALACIO VALDÉS (1853–1938) who saw his native Asturias as the earthly paradise, and recalled that when he was sent away to study in Madrid he felt like *Adán expulsado*. Being well-to-do he could afford to return to the Asturias and settle down to a life of modest literary activity. He wrote in a smiling, benevolent fashion, usually about rich middle-class people whose problems are trifling and whose lives can be described with gentle frivolity. Following the fashion for realistic studies of life among the common people, he occasionally launched into *novelas de costumbres* as in *La aldea perdida* (1903) or *José* (1885), but even here the idyllic note predominates and Valdés delighted in stressing the good to be found in simple folk.

Valdés had great talent and his characterisation and powers of description often outweigh his basically amateurish style and methods. *José*, which is a small scale imitation of *Sotileza* is only half convincing as a study of an Asturian fishing community. The hero, José, is somewhat too gentle and kindhearted, while the heroine, Elisa, appears insipid; it seems as if they scarcely deserve to break down the opposition to their marriage. Conventional too is the portrait of the impoverished but proud nobleman, Don Fernando, who finally sells the crumbling ruins of his ancestral house to enable José to buy another boat and to get married. Much better is the description of the respective mothers-in-law who come to blows in the end, scratching, biting and tearing out each other's earrings. José's mother is a railing widow worn out by a lifetime of hard work, whereas his prospective mother-in-law is a grasping fish-dealer and ship's chandler who uses José's affection for her step-daughter, Elisa, as a means to buy fish from him at reduced prices. At the same time she opposes the marriage in order to retain for herself the money Elisa is due to inherit from her mother's will. To this end she persuades the village idiot to sabotage the new boat for which José has long saved up. This episode is especially well managed and the suggestions and innuendoes employed to put the idea into the idiot's head are subtle and cunning. Eventually the lovers with Don Fernando's help manage to defy this termagant and prospects for their marriage seem to be improving when the village fishing fleet is caught in a storm, which is vigorously described and from which José at length returns unscathed. There is something of the unreality of a film scene about the storm, which in fact has no bearing on the main plot; but a novel on the life of fisherfolk must include a storm and the reader is certain that Valdés will be too tenderhearted to allow his hero to perish amid the waves. The final chapters of the novel are therefore of moderate interest only.

More appealing, though equally unrealistic, is *La Hermana San Sulpicio* (1889). A young Galician poet on a visit to Seville falls in love with Gloria, a young lady about to confirm her vows as a nun. The poet has to overcome the unwillingness first of Gloria and then of her mother before marriage is possible. This gently amused observation of the psychology of a reluctant lover has a flavour of *marivaudage* about it, but the plot is in fact an excuse to describe Seville and the colourful life of the city with its gypsy dancing, *tertulias* and general effervescence so very different from the gravity of the northern Spaniard through whose eyes the story is told. It is undoubtedly a brilliant description of the gayest city of Andalusia, but again it has the unreality of a stage set. Delightfully and charmingly though Valdés wrote, there is no depth of truth in his novels. Like Valera he wrote to please himself and his taste was for everything that is agreeable in life, but he lacked Valera's keen psychological insight into human behaviour and his stories lapse at times into triviality.

Insipid verses

The same charge can be levelled at much of the poetry of the post-romantic period. Like Valdés, RAMON DE CAMPOAMOR (1817–1901) came from the prosperous middle class. When he was governor of Alicante, he married an Irish lady and settled down to a life of happiness without financial worries and without great ambitions. His verse seems un-inspired and tepid, gently ironic and mildly disillusioned. His long poems such as *El drama universal* (1860) are chaotic and incoherent, but his short poems, *Dóloras* (1846) and *Humoradas* (1886–88), form inter-esting epigrammatic comments on the social life of his times. Like Wordsworth he took his craft as a poet very seriously, publishing a *Poética*, in which after examining traditional poetic values he outlined theories of his own. He claimed to have invented both the name and form of *Dóloras* as being a short poem combining lightness with depth of feeling and conciseness with philosophy. The name might be new, but the form was not, for it was based on that of popular songs or *coplas* and the subject matter is often a conventional generalisation. But many of the hundreds of *Dóloras* composed by Campoamor are appealing and none is more popular than the charming *¡Quién supiera escribir!* in which a girl is dictating a love letter to a kindly old priest who is acting as her amanuensis:

> *Escribidme una carta, señor Cura.*
> *Ya sé para quién es*
> *¿Sabéis quién es, porque una noche obscura*
> *Nos visteis juntos?—Pues*
> *Perdonad; mas . . . No extraño ese tropiezo*
> * La noche . . . la ocasión . . .*
> *Dadme pluma y papel. Gracias. Empiezo*
> * Mi querido Ramón:*
> *¿Querido? . . . Pero, en fin, ya lo habéis puesto . . .*
> * Si no queréis . . . —¡Sí, Sí!*
> *¡Qué triste estoy! ¿No es eso?— Por supuesto.*
> * ¡qué triste estoy sin tí!*

(Write me a letter Señor Cura—I already know whom it is
for—you know whom it is for, because one dark night you
saw us together? Well—Forgive me, but—I am not surprised
at this peccadillo. The night . . . the opportunity, . . . Give me
pen and paper. Thank you, I will begin . . . *My dear Ramón.*
Dear? Why, you have already put it . . . if you do not love
him . . . I do, I do! *How sad I am!* That is right?—Of course—
How sad I am without you!)

The *Humoradas* are even briefer than the *Dóloras* as the poet strives
after conciseness, but often the thoughts expressed are as trite as those
on Christmas cards.

Todo en amor es triste;
mas, triste y todo, es lo mejor que existe.

(Everything in love is sad; but, sad and all, it is the best that
exists.)

It is unfair to judge Campoamor by the most pedestrian of his products,
but there is little doubt that his inspiration is very uneven. He wished to
free poetry from pompous phrases and to make his style natural and
direct. He wished also to be considered as a poet of ideas. Like Victor
Hugo he felt himself a philosopher, his motto being: *Pensar alto, sentir
hondo y hablar claro* (To think loftily, feel deeply and speak clearly).
Unfortunately he lacked Hugo's magic mastery of words and his
thoughts and expression are sometimes equally commonplace.

More sonorous, but seemingly less sincere is GASPAR NÚÑEZ DE ARCE
(1834–1903), a politician and a poet who sought to enlighten the
collective conscience of the Spanish people by his verse. He is the poet
of *la actualidad política*. An excellent versifier with a fine command of
language and metre, his poems appear flat because clearly he does not
believe in what he is saying. He shrieks for freedom and demands that
the bonds of tyranny be broken, but at the same time deplores revolutionary excesses (*Gritos del combate*). He calls for the reform of the
church of Rome (*La visión de fray Martín*) and regrets the decline of
catholicism in Spain. His effort at an epic poem, *Última lamentación de
Lord Byron*, is a windy hymn of praise for romanticism; the fashion for
realism is reflected in *La pesca* with the familiar theme of the fisherman
drowned despite his gallant efforts while his relatives wait in an agony
of anxiety. It is wrong to be cynical about such themes, but a poet must
feel sincerely about what he describes and Núñez de Arce fails to convey
this impression.

Bécquer's 'Rimas'

Quite different is GUSTAVO ADOLPHO BÉCQUER (1836–70) whose *Rimas* are filled with deep personal feeling. Orphaned at the age of ten he was brought up by his godmother. At eighteen he set out from Seville for Madrid with little more than the fare in his pocket, hoping to earn his living by his pen. This he found a wretchedly difficult task and he was always poverty-stricken. He fell in love with a girl who did not return his love and he made an unhappy marriage with another woman. His health was poor and at the age of thirty-four he died of consumption aggravated by malnutrition and unhappiness.

As a literary hack his production of prose works was considerable. A large collection of essays and literary criticisms was published under the title of *Desde mi celda*. A series of stories rather on the lines of the *Tales of Hoffmann*, entitled *Leyendas*, are clearly the work of a poet for they are luxuriant in style and rich in fantasy. By a strange contrast his poetical work, the *Rimas*, is completely plain and unadorned but with an unusual depth of feeling. They consist of seventy-six short poems, all of which link up to form a spiritual survey of Bécquer's life. The idea for this collection of poems on a single theme may have been inspired by Heine's *Lyrisches Intermezzo*, but the matter and form are entirely original, for Bécquer is the most subjective and personal of poets. He is unconcerned with the outside world, but is content to find his poetical inspiration in searching his own heart, which is consumed with unrelieved melancholy.

The *Rimas* begin with the poet feeling the sovereign attraction of his art (I–VIII). Then he is vaguely aware of the passion of love which takes definite shape when he sets eyes on a woman of fascinating beauty (IX–XV). Together their souls achieve perfect harmony (XVI–XXIX), but suddenly the idyll is broken by some disaster, presumably treachery on the part of the lady (XXX). The poet is consumed with sorrow and for the first time he is seized with the thought of death; he remembers with sadness the happy days now past and yearns to forget his sorrows in *la lejanía y el vértigo* (XXXVII–LII). Sadly and gently he proclaims his undying passion (LIII), but later he loses faith in love and his scepticism increases (LIV–LIX). He is pained by the loss of all the joys that sweetened his life (LX). His heart is beset with the constant thought of death (LXI). In the world all is tears and sorrow which serve to increase the longing for the infinite (LXII–LXXVI).

Such a brief analysis must necessarily make the *Rimas* appear sickly nonsense and they are indeed an acquired taste; they need to be read as a whole and to be read several times over to be appreciated. One hasty glance cannot give the full savour of the poet's agony of mind or of the musical qualities of the words. Their simplicity is deceptive because on each new reading fresh effects of startling vividness become apparent. All this requires time and for those who desire a brief acquaintance with Bécquer the *Rimas* mentioned singly in the summary above will be enough.

Another poet of deep feelings and inspissated gloom is ROSALÍA DE CASTRO (1837–85). She was a native of Santiago de Compostela, but her mother, though a woman of good family from the nearby town of Padrón, was unmarried and the stigma of illegitimate birth remained deep throughout Rosalía de Castro's life. She was formally adopted by her mother and was brought up in the ancestral mansion where she learned many Galician folk tales and songs. In 1856 she went to Madrid, which she loathed, and there she married a young Galician writer named Murguía, a dwarf who ill-treated her. Living in constant poverty she bore him five children and her misery was increased by her longing to return to her native Galicia. She was suffering from cancer and could find relief only by spending long periods in her home in Padrón where she used to sit watching from her window funeral processions winding up to the nearby cemetery. It was in Padrón that she died, worn out by suffering.

Nearly all Rosalía de Castro's poems are in the Galician dialect which has some affinity with Portuguese, but is not at all difficult to read for those who know Castilian. She was not perhaps so much at ease when in her last collection of poems she used Castilian, which is harder and rougher in texture than Galician. Nevertheless, in this collection entitled *En las orillas del Sar* she displays marked ability for producing lines which flow with a gentle musical rhythm. Her main themes are homesickness and a longing for life after death, but she introduces subject matter little seen in Spanish poetry, namely pity for the poor and needy. Galicia is a province which cannot support its population and its inhabitants have long been forced to emigrate to Castile, South America and in recent years to domestic service in England. The absence of menfolk in most cases causes great hardship for the families left behind and there is always a note of hysteria in their grief at separation. The Galician has always been something of a beast of burden in Spain, hardworking, patient, badly treated and unshakeably obstinate. Rosalía de Castro writes about the sorrows of the poor in Galicia with a hatred for their Castilian oppressors and for the callous indifference of well-to-do *Gallegos*. She has something of the same understanding of the poor and sympathy for them that Burns displays and like Burns she is more expressive in dialect verse.

Realistic drama

While the romantic theatre had been in full but brief activity, there existed side by side a more realistic form of drama in the style of Moratín. The chief exponent of this type of play was BRETÓN DE LOS HERREROS (1796–1873) whose literary output was enormous, including one hundred and three original plays and seventy-four translations and adaptations. It may well be imagined that such quantity necessarily involved sacrifice of quality. He was an able versifier with a sense of the dramatic and a gift for comedy, but his preposterous characterisation makes it hard to read his plays with any enjoyment.

Nearer to the truth of life, but with less geniality is MANUEL TAMAYO Y BAUS (1829–98). He came of a family of actors and was early imbued with the craft of the stage. After beginning with romantic plays in verse filled with action, Tamayo y Baus attempted a more realistic type of drama in prose with the psychological interest paramount. His first effort in this direction was *Locura de amor* (1855), a historical play about *Juana la Loca* in which the romantic element is still strong. *La bola de nieve* (1856) is a play about modern times analysing the effects of jealousy and suspicion on two lovers. Tamayo was becoming more and more preoccupied with simplicity of action and scenic effects and aimed at concise expression. He is obsessed like many contemporary novelists with the necessity for literature to teach a moral lesson. *Lo positivo* (1862) deals with the problem of marriage for wealth and position or marriage for love. A girl has to choose whether to obey her father's wishes for a wealthy match or to obey the dictates of her heart. She herself has some regard for the advantages that money brings, but eventually idealism wins and the audience sighs with relief.

Lo positivo is not a stimulating play because the author, try as he will, is never at home with a psychological subject. He was at heart a romantic with a longing for dramatic action and his best play, *Un drama nuevo* (1867), satisfies this craving to the full. The scene is set in Elizabethan England; Yorick, the clown in Shakespeare's troupe, has made a second marriage to a girl named Alice whom he adores. He is also very proud of his son by his previous marriage, Edmund. 'Alas, poor Yorick!' says Shakespeare because it is known in the troupe that Alice and Edmund are lovers. Yorick begs Shakespeare to allow him for once to play a tragic role in place of Walton, who immediately becomes furiously jealous. By one of those coincidences so beloved of romantic dramatists, the situation of the play within the play is identical with the circumstances in which Yorick is placed. The Count Octavius finds his ward Manfred in love with his wife Beatrice; Yorick as the Count is being warmly applauded by the audience for his splendid acting when Walton as Landolph brings him a letter to warn him of Beatrice's infidelity. In fact he hands a genuine letter from Edmund to Alice discussing plans for flight. The Count has to kill Manfred (played of course by Edmund) and his part becomes a real tragic role for in his despair and rage at his son's treachery he stabs Edmund to death.

The plot is improbable in the extreme and too obviously contrived, but for all that the play is moving because the characters are well drawn. Yorick is a person of faithful devotion, but his possessive nature is enough to drive his wife into another's arms. Alice and Edmund are young and gay and their love for one another springs naturally without sinister intent. But Edmund is weak-willed and cannot face a situation which has become impossible. The catastrophe originates from the defects in the characters of the protagonists, but the plot is so preposterous that the play fails utterly as a psychological study.

In fact the Spanish theatre was destined never to lose its romantic nature during the nineteenth century because after Tamayo y Baus had failed to establish realism on the stage there was a return to full romanticism engineered by the remarkable JOSÉ ECHEGARAY (1832–1916). He was a mathematician and an economist, and once occupied the thankless office of finance minister. At the same time his powerful personality and compelling writing made him the monarch of the theatre. He maintained that '*lo sublime del arte está en el llanto, en el dolor y en la muerte*' (the sublime substance of art lies in tears, grief and death) and he never had any compunction in killing off his characters, innocent and guilty alike, or alternatively driving them mad. In *El conflicto entre dos deberes*, of the five characters in the play only two remain sane in the end. In *Mar sin orillas* Leonardo de Aguilar kills his wife whom he idolises, saying:

LEONARDO	*¡Morir debes por culpable!*
LEONOR	*¡Pero si no lo soy!*
LEONARDO	*Pues por honrada*
	que de Aguilar la esposa no consiente
	la duda de la sombra de una mancha.

LEONARDO   You must die for you are guilty!
LEONOR   But suppose that I am not!
LEONARDO   Then you must die as an
honest woman because the wife of an Aguilar never
allows the slightest doubt of a stain on her honour.

There is no escape from Echegaray's butchery.

After 1885 Echegaray under the influence of Strindberg and Ibsen tried to edge away from romanticism and to make profound psychological studies of his characters. But in reality almost all he achieved was to substitute prose for verse, for he always lurched unconsciously into melodrama and still death or the asylum gaped for all the main characters. *El hijo de Don Juan* depicts a man who inherited a deformity from his father and is thereby deprived of happiness and love; he dies a madman. However much one may smile in a lofty way at these oratorical melodramas which are quite out of fashion, the fact remains that Echegaray's plays roused critics and audiences to wild displays of enthusiasm not only in Spain but over half Europe as well. Perhaps taste will one day veer back towards these displays of passion, death and lunacy.

Galdós composed some twenty-two plays of which the first was *Realidad* (1892). This raised a storm of controversy because it attempted to break the vogue for sentimental claptrap. Galdós was never successful in establishing a more realistic trend in the theatre and perhaps he too was unconsciously influenced by the prevailing fashion, as his best play *El abuelo* certainly contains its fair share of sentiment. An elderly nobleman has two granddaughters of whom he knows one to be illegitimate, though he does not know which. He tries to guess the answer by observing their characters closely. In the end it turns out that the better of the two is the bastard and the old man realises that nobility of character does not depend on nobility of lineage.

It is strange that the nineteenth century in Spain should have produced so much excellent literature at a time when Spain was in the throes of continual political strife. The fact is that the rush of liberal ideas gave a new impetus to intellectuals and even during the last years of Isabel II's inglorious reign Madrid was an active cultural centre with a mass of literary clubs. Spain was also blessed with a critic of gigantic stature in MARCELINO MENÉNDEZ Y PELAYO (1856–1912), whose touch was of the surest when dealing with the literature of any nation at any period. His work greatly helped to recreate the image of Spanish literature of the Golden Age and his sound judgment constantly guided contemporary writers into channels of good sense and good taste. His *Historia de las ideas estéticas en España* (1883–91) is perhaps too wide in scope for, despite its title, it reviews aesthetic ideas throughout Europe, but it enabled Spanish writers to examine themselves by comparison with the culture of other nations. His numerous works are filled with the spirit of enthusiasm for the recreation of Spanish aesthetic achievements and his style, which is solid without pomp, made criticism an interesting form of literature on its own.

Chapter 10
The generation of '98 and after

Intellectual crusade

The full tragedy of the final disruption of the Spanish Empire in 1898 was felt most keenly by a group of young intellectuals who embarked on a crusade to restore the spiritual greatness of Spain. With such an end in view it was natural that literature should take on a markedly didactic tone and there was a rapid increase in the production of philosophical works, chiefly in the form of essays. There was also a revulsion from the style which had dominated nineteenth-century literature; efforts were made to break away from realism and to produce perfection of form. This was noticeable particularly in poetry, but in the novel too Don Ramón del Valle-Inclán shows a similar stylishness. It is a mistake, however, to try to classify exactly the aims of the generation of '98, for many divergent styles are apparent. It was an age of experiment, but if there was one common factor, it was a desire to banish the prosaic from literature and to return to originality and vigour of expression.

The inspiration of most of the writers of this generation came from the remarkable *Institución Libre de enseñanza* founded by FRANCISCO GINER DE LOS RÍOS after the government in 1879 had begun to interfere with education, dismissing several professors whose views were held to be dangerously liberal. The aim of the *Institución* was to train men to have a sense of vocation in life and its influence was strong and widespread. Young writers set out with enthusiasm to make Spain aware of her heritage. The first attempt in this direction appeared in 1897 shortly before the final catastrophe occurred; this was the *Ideariuni español* by ÁNGEL GANIVET (1865–98). He was a young man of strong feelings and deep convictions, but his unhappiness became unbearable after a

LEFT   *Ramón del Valle-Inclán*

disastrous love affair and he committed suicide at Riga where he was stationed in the consular service. Strangely enough his *Idearium español* urges a stoic philosophy and it shows no great belief in the ability of Spaniards to govern themselves except in an authoritarian manner. The book, aided no doubt by Ganivet's tragic death, exercised considerable influence over the young writers of the day because they saw in it a plea for Spain to regain her dignity. Every nation, Ganivet claimed, has its own typical figure; Greece has Ulysses, Spain Don Quijote, England Robinson Crusoe, Germany Dr Faustus. Of all these Don Quijote has the most spiritual idealism and this is what Spain should cultivate. Materialism must be abandoned and intellectualism developed; only thus can Spain restore her spiritual power.

The philosophy of Unamuno

While Ganivet's *Idearium español* was urging Spain to seek intellectual regeneration, the greatest philosopher of the age MIGUEL DE UNAMUNO (1864–1936) proclaimed: *Es una ciencia divina la ciencia de la ignorancia; es más que ciencia, es sabiduría* (It is divine knowledge the knowledge of ignorance; it is more than knowledge, it is wisdom). There may well be an arguable case for such a statement, but Unamuno was a man of contrasts and all his life was spent trying to educate people. He was from 1891 until his death in 1936 professor of Greek at Salamanca University, apart from a period of exile under the Primo de Rivera dictatorship. His formal teaching as a professor was stimulating and exciting, though he was never truly a man of learning; he was a warrior, a man with a message, fiercely battling to educate his fellow Spaniards, to Europeanise them, as he put it; like Bernard Shaw, Unamuno uses characters in his works as pulpits to expound his ideas. Like Shaw too, he had the ability to express abstruse thoughts with singular clarity so that readers could grasp the meaning of Schopenhauer or Nietzsche without knowing that they were being introduced to philosophy. Finally, like Shaw, Unamuno propounds a welter of ideas so that it is difficult to decide which side he is taking. The commonest theme that runs through all his works is the problem of life and death. The only certainty in man's life is death; reason tells him that death is but an ending, a negation of life, and yet man never ceases to hope and yearn for immortality.

This is the subject of Unamuno's greatest philosophical work *Del sentimiento trágico de la vida* (1913). Man, he states, could not endure life on earth without the hope of immortality; he believes in God solely because of the promise given by religion of life after death. Yet man's reason tells him that there is no evidence whatever for believing in survival after death. Is man then to give way to despair? Unamuno rejects such a supine attitude. Man must battle for immortality, he must deserve to be immortal by his deeds on earth. It may be that his hopes will be disappointed, but at any rate he will have striven. There is egoism in Unamuno's outlook; he himself passionately longed for immortality, no doubt because he was conscious that he had much to give the world. But there is nobility in his view; he urges men to be positive in their egoism, to do their task well in order to deserve immortality, and if every man's egoism were channelled along positive lines no doubt the world would be a better and a happier place. As a philosopher Unamuno is unsystematic and to the pure reasoner his conclusions may be unsatisfactory, but for the ordinary reader *Del sentimiento trágico de la vida*, with its clear arrangement of argument and its forceful style, is a deeply moving book. There is an underlying feeling of passion that conveys the sense that Unamuno really believes in his message. There is no cynicism, only deep sincerity.

Unamuno applies the same views to interpreting Don Quijote in his *Vida de Don Quijote y Sancho* (1914) where he sees the knight's hallucinations as his yearning to achieve fame and so win immortality. Dulcinea is a symbol of love, but she represents the desire for survival. Sancho Panza may seem at first to be earthy and matter of fact and to take life as he finds it, but soon he is infected with Don Quijote's passionate longings, for he yearns to be ruler of the island which for him represents life immortal. It is a startlingly original interpretation of Don Quijote and sets the reader thinking about the springs that activate men's behaviour, even though Cervantes, writing his novel possibly in prison, never dreamed of such underlying motives.

Unamuno is not an orthodox catholic; he has little regard for God, in whom he wants to believe, but cannot. He is, however, deeply stirred by the thought of Christ striving and suffering to give mankind immortality and this admiration for Christ as man rather than as God is brought out strongly in Unamuno's long poem *El Cristo de Velázquez* (1920). It is a series of meditations on Velázquez's painting of Christ crucified and it is the man in Christ that Unamuno emphasises:

> *Es el hombre*
> *éste es el Dios a cuyo cuerpo prenden*
> *Nuestros ojos, las manos del espíritu.*

(It is the man who is the God on whose body our eyes are fastened, our eyes that are the hands of the mind.)

Perhaps this insistence on representing Christ as a man rather than as God is typical not only of Unamuno alone but of all Spaniards, for in Spain all paintings or statues of Christ suffering are realistic in the extreme. The poem is written in blank verse (*verso suelto*) with eleven syllables to the line, and the style is solemn, grave and passionately sincere. Unamuno had not the gift for the musical expression of many contemporary poets, but he excels them all in the vigour of the ideas he conveys.

Although Unamuno's novels are likewise fascinating in their originality of thought, it is true that they are mere pulpits from which Unamuno preaches. The first, *Paz en la guerra* (1897), is perhaps less typical of Unamuno's completely personal view of the novel. It is a story of the Carlist War of 1874–76 and contains recollections of the author's childhood; the focus is not on Unamuno but on Bilbao, his native town, which was particularly involved in the war. Subsequent novels by Unamuno have less action, less concern with external surroundings; the characters argue, reason, discuss, all preoccupied with the analysis of ideas and feelings. In *Amor y pedagogía* (1902) a father tries to educate his son to be a genius, but the result leads to disaster and suicide. All through the novel the characters mouth the author's ideas:

¿De dónde ha nacido el arte? De la sed de inmortalidad. Me llaman materialista. Sí, materialista, porque quiero una inmortalidad de bulto, de sustancia.

(Whence was art born? From the thirst for immortality. They call me a materialist. Yes, materialist because I desire a solid, substantial immortality.)

In *Niebla* (1914) the personal note is even more strongly reinforced by the introduction of the author as a character in the book. The hero, Augusto Pérez, is introduced to Unamuno whom he consults about his plan for suicide. The author forbids suicide, but nevertheless condemns him to die. Augusto Pérez bursts out:

¿No quiere usted dejarme ser yo, salir de la niebla, vivir, vivir, vivir, oírme, tocarme, sentirme, dolerme, serme; conque no lo quiere? ¿conque he de morir ente de ficción? Pues bien, mi señor creador Don Miguel, también usted se morirá, también usted, y se volverá a la nada de que salió.

(You won't let me be myself, to emerge from the mist, to live, live, to see myself, to hear myself, to touch myself, to feel myself, to suffer, to be myself; so you won't do it? So I must die a creature of fiction? Well then, my lord creator Don Miguel, you will die, you too, and you will return to the void from which you came.)

This interview between character and author is not only highly original (it anticipates Pirandello), but it is also convincing and moving. *Abel Sánchez* (1917) is better known than *Niebla* and is more conventional but again it harps on the theme of life and death which obsessed Unamuno. The story represents a modern version of Cain and Abel; Abel Sánchez and Joaquín are supposedly the best of friends, but in reality they are the bitterest of enemies. In *San Manuel Bueno, mártir* (1933) Unamuno paints a picture of a saint, a Franciscan monk, but his heterodoxy is typical of the perplexity and moral agony of the Generation of '98.

Self examination

Unamuno was a Basque and perhaps he was not entirely at ease writing in Castilian; many other Spanish men of letters have written more stylishly than he, many have been less contradictory than he and more stable, but few have borne the agony of a mind beset by doubt more heroically than he or have expressed themselves with such energy. He might be compared with the real Spanish fighting bull in the ring; he knows he is condemned to die, but while there is life, there is vigour. By his deeds he will deserve immortality.

Another writer who cultivated the personal novel was JOSÉ MARTÍNEZ RUIZ (1876–1967) who became so identified with the chief character of one of his novels that he assumed the name of Azorín as his literary pseudonym. Antonio Azorín first appears in *La voluntad* (1902); he is a lonely young man apparently without aim in life, incapable of any sustained effort who flits like a butterfly from one idea to another. The novel has no plot because, as Azorín points out, life has none; the book is a collection of thoughts, comments, observations and memories. Two similarly constructed novels with the same central figure followed, *Antonio Azorín* (1903) and *Las confesiones de un pequeño filósofo* (1904). These are impressionistic in form, being recollections of places and incidents in the life of Azorín accompanied usually by lighthearted musings. All the incidents are insignificant in themselves and their presentation is coldly impersonal and unemotional, but they are vivid and evocative like impressionist paintings.

Better still are the novels *Don Juan* (1922) and *Doña Inés, historia de amor* (1925); they likewise show Azorín as an exquisite painter of trivial realities and states of mind, but he is not a creator of life and was thus bound to fail as a novelist. His real ability was as an essayist especially gifted at describing scenes of country life as in *Los pueblos* (1905) and *Castilla* (1912) where he evokes the impressions by focusing on tiny details such as the whistle of a train. He applied this impressionistic method to literary criticism as well. His *Lecturas españolas* (1912) consist of essays not only on scenes in the country and towns, but historical and literary sketches. In literature he lights up details quoting a few lines of a poem or prose work and concentrating upon them. Such criticisms tends to be biased and Azorín at times drifts into wild assertions; for example, he claims that the drama of the Golden Age in Spain is of no interest whatever. Azorín is nothing if not inconsistent in his judgments, but through his artistic sensitivity his literary criticism, especially *Al margen de los clásicos* (1915), gave the general public a new insight into Spanish literature. He uses short sentences, scorning conjunctions, so that his style has all the rapidity and clarity of a lightning sketch as well as the deeper feeling and colour of a master of impressionism.

Later in time than the Generation of '98, but carrying on the work of national self-appraisal was JOSÉ ORTEGA Y GASSET (1883–1955). He received his education mostly in Germany and as a result never really understood Spain or appreciated the qualities of the Spaniard and his literature. His approach is largely negative, whereas the true members of the generation of '98 were passionately positive in their desire to recreate Spain's intellectual glory. His *España invertebrada* (1921) is a highly suggestive piece of work, but the theories he puts forward are open to question. He regrets that the Visigoths arrived in Spain already latinised because their culture was merely a decadent form of what the Romans had to offer and Spain, unlike the more northerly European countries, never knew the impact of feudalism. He rightly sees most Spanish cultural activity as popular in origin and he deplores the fact that there are no select minorities in Spain. He attributes the florescence of literature and art in the sixteenth and seventeenth centuries to a momentary cohesion on the part of Castile alone, but the very centralisation of government in Madrid killed all possibility of intellectual expansion. Much of this is true beyond question, but he underrates Spanish culture, which combines in an almost unique fashion popular and intellectual elements. He also shows himself heavily prejudiced in favour of Germanic as opposed to Hispanic culture, a prejudice which led him to despise Spanish literature apart from Don Quijote.

More positive from the philosophical point of view is *El tema de nuestro tiempo* (1923), in which he attempts to apply Einstein's theory

Miguel de Unamuno, by Solana

of relativity to the conquest of truth. Each life, he says, represents a different outlook on the universe and each individual is indispensable in the search for truth. In 1925 Ortega y Gasset published *La deshumanización del arte*, which had a remarkable influence on the young writers of the time. It is in fact another expression of tendencies noticeable among many of the Generation of '98, namely the search for perfection of form. As society becomes increasingly egalitarian and drab, art of all kinds seeks to become totally abstract and to depend solely on its technical qualities. It disassociates itself from humanity. This is a plausible explanation of many modern artistic and literary styles, but Ortega y Gasset in his eagerness to be modern is prejudiced against former artistic productions. Though it is refreshing to find a critic praising contemporary works, there is a feeling that Ortega seizes too much on ephemeral manifestations. He was after all a journalist, though his admirable style puts him in a class high above most members of his profession. It was his stock in trade to reflect the latest ideas of the moment and he could turn all his literary talent to the discussion of trivial as well as transcendental matters, witness his *Conversación en el golf*. Nevertheless, his influence on modern culture has been extensive, not only through his books, but also by his efforts to spread cultural ideas from other countries, notably Germany. As a craftsman in the art of essay writing he is outstanding. It was perhaps this care for his craft that made him conscious of the gulf between the intellectuals struggling for progress and the amorphous mass of the middle-class who were either reactionary or uninterested. In his *Rebelión de las masas* (1930) he sees the increasing importance of technicians, salesmen, executives and the like as the real threat to European culture.

The novel in the early twentieth century

The first novelist of the generation of '98 was VICENTE BLASCO IBÁÑEZ (1867–1928), but he was not for the most part typical of the movement. Born in Valencia, he was a man of enormous vitality and great strength, and early found himself a champion of the cause of the poor and oppressed. He saw himself as a kind of Prometheus, a Titan fighting for the humble. He was a fervent republican and suffered imprisonment and exile for his radical views, which he proclaimed with passionate oratory. In 1909 he emigrated to the Argentine with grandiose plans for founding colonies where men should live in freedom and harmony; such was his energy that he actually founded two such colonies, one in the cold wastes of the Tierra del Fuego and the other in the sticky jungle of Paraguay. Economic conditions forced him to abandon these projects and in 1914 he returned to Europe and flung himself ardently into pro-ally propaganda, especially with his novel *The Four Horsemen of the Apocalypse*, which was filmed with great success in America. Blasco Ibáñez was enabled with the proceeds to build an expensive villa at Menton from where he continued to heap vituperation on the head of King Alfonso, fighting his cause unremittingly until his death.

His greatest period as a novelist was when he was engaged in a fierce battle to spread his liberal ideas in Valencia between 1894 and 1902. He operated a printing press which published a federalist newspaper and several of his novels were scribbled down in the early dawn after seeing the daily edition through the press. They were novels about Valencia and Blasco Ibáñez really knew the people and the scenes he was describing; as a result the novels of this period have a freshness and a spontaneity which he never recaptured later in his career.

In *Arroz y tartana* (1894) he describes the shopkeeping class in Valencia among whom he had grown up, but movement and action were what he really loved and his next novel *Flor de mayo* (1895) was greatly superior, dealing with smuggling trips and jealousy and hatred among the fisherfolk of the Valencian coast. He had himself made a smuggling trip to Algiers in a staggering, leaking boat and his picture of the life of the Valencian community is as clear and glittering as the Mediterranean itself. The greatest novel of all was *La barraca* (1898), the rough draft of which had been scribbled in violet ink in the attic of a wineshop while Ibáñez was hiding from the police in 1895. It is a story of *la huerta*, the great market garden around Valencia. A family from outside the district comes to work an allotment which has been left uncultivated as a reprisal against the meanness of the landlord. The other smallholders gang up against the newcomer both because he is a stranger and because he has broken their boycott of the avaricious landlord. They ruin his crops and finally burn his *barraca*, driving him from the neighbourhood. There is almost no book in Spanish literature which, when once taken up, is so hard to put down so vivid is the description and so well conceived the plot and characters. There is no superfluous detail and the reader is made to feel that he has been born and bred in *la huerta*. The opening description of dawn over the *vega* is superb while the judgment of the *Tribunal de las aguas* outside Valencia cathedral is tersely realistic and convincing.

Almost equally masterful is *Cañas y barro* (1902), a novel about the ricegrowers beside the freshwater lake, La Albufera, near Valencia. Two young people Tonet and Neleta are fatally attracted by one another and lapse into adultery. All the primitive, earthy quality of peasant life is portrayed frankly but with a sympathy that could spring only from someone intimately acquainted with the virtues and vices and miseries of the agricultural classes.

If Blasco Ibáñez had confined himself to writing about the district he knew so well, he might be remembered as one of Spain's greatest novelists, but he turned his attention to other fields and his later novels were mostly sentimental and melodramatic; though two of them at least became bestsellers abroad in translations, they damaged his reputation at home. Already in 1901 he had attempted an historical novel, *Sónnica la cortesana*, on the theme of a rich Athenian courtesan who perishes in the siege of Saguntum when Hannibal's armies storm the city. Though Ibáñez took great pains over historical research, the novel has the heavy-fisted feel of a Hollywood epic, thus foreshadowing his later screen triumph.

After some equally ponderous novels on social themes of which the best known is *La catedral* (1903) Blasco Ibáñez turned to the national sport of bullfighting with *Sangre y arena* (1908) in which he traces the career of a popular *torero* who has a love affair with a great lady, but who ultimately perishes in the ring, largely unmourned. The novel was highly successful and contains brilliant descriptions of bullfights and of Holy Week in Seville, but by now Ibáñez seemed capable of describing only exteriors or scenes of high excitement; his characters have little resemblance to real life and the story drags because of over-emphasis. The light touch is lacking; he is too strong and powerful and humourless.

It seems that Blasco Ibáñez conceived the idea of writing a series of novels about South America, for *Los Argonautas* (1914) describes the voyage of Spanish emigrants across the Atlantic in a liner, but the Great War broke out and he turned his energies to denouncing German militarism with his most famous novel, *Los cuatro jinetes del Apocalipsis* (1916). It is a long ragged novel beginning in the Argentine (it was clearly started as a novel in the Argentine series before the outbreak of war) and then switching to a description of the early days of the fighting in France and ending with the battle of the Marne. Again Blasco Ibáñez excels in depicting external events and the scene when the Uhlans first approach a French town, which a scratch force of French

Una barraca near Valencia

stragglers defends for a few brief moments despite the entreaties of the mayor, is almost photographic in its clarity. Likewise the description of the French counterattacking across the Marne and blasting the Germans out of the château is brilliantly managed because it brings war down to a level of personal experience. Characterisation is, however, weak. The hero, Desnoyers, owner of the château, is a vague uncommunicative person with excellent intentions, but lacking colour while the German officers who billet themselves in the château are villainous to a man. The General appears at first a cultured person, but his morals are clearly suspect when he is found playing the piano wearing a lady's Japanese *kimono* and he turns out to be as callous and cruel as the rest. Even a humble middle-class staff captain who talks of nothing but his fat *Frau* and square-headed sons, proceeds in a drunken fit to rape the lodge-keeper's daughter. All this may be good propaganda, but it is mediocre literature.

Encouraged by the worldwide popularity of *Los cuatro jinetes del Apocalipsis* both as a novel and as a film, Blasco Ibáñez produced another war book, *Mare nostrum* (1918) with the same strongly melodramatic

A matador in difficulties

ingredients. The captain of a Spanish merchant vessel, Ferragut, falls in love in Naples with a beautiful adventuress who turns out to be a German spy. She induces him to provision a U boat operating in the Mediterranean. The submarine sinks a certain French ship in which Ferragut's son perishes. Ferragut, bent on revenge, places his ship at the disposal of the Allies and eventually dies in their service. The atmosphere of the novel is dark with secret plotting and machinations, but Blasco Ibáñez's old skill in describing the Mediterranean has in no wise deserted him. The novel has its moments of thrilling intensity, but one longs for a return to the terse rapid action and natural development of events and people which characterised his early novels of Valencia.

It would have been surprising if the writers of the generation of '98 had not been influenced by the *fin de siècle* styles and attitudes fashionable in the rest of Europe. In the novel this influence took the form of a highly finished elegance of expression combined usually with erotic subject matter. The leading exponent of this type of novel, somewhat resembling the work of Oscar Wilde, was DON RAMÓN DEL VALLE-INCLAN (1869–1936). He was a *poseur* who wove such fantastic tales about himself that little definite is known about his private life or his antecedents. Born in Galicia, he studied law in the University of Santiago de Compostela, but then went to Mexico because, he said, it was the only country in the world that has an X in it. Even this mild statement is of doubtful truth coming from a Spaniard since Méjico is the normal spelling. On his return to Pontevedra in Galicia he wrote a series of six short stories which he published in 1894 under the title of *Femeninas*. The stories are highly erotic in character, chronicling the lives of amorously wicked women in stylised prose. A year later he came to Madrid and began to frequent the literary circle that gathered at the Café Regina. He was a striking figure, tall and thin with piercing eyes and a beard that reached almost to his waist. On his shoulder perched a black cloak which drew attention to the fact that his left arm was missing. How he came to lose it is a matter for conjecture because his version of the accident was different every time. The disability gave him an additional touch of romanticism for it inevitably reminded his hearers of Cervantes and Valle-Inclán (the name was not his real one, but had been chosen for its sonority) thrived on an attentive audience for his weird and preposterous tales.

Meanwhile, his literary success had been meagre until in 1902 he published the first of his *Sonatas* of the four seasons. With characteristic perverseness Valle-Inclán could not write these in order and the first was the *Sonata de otoño* in which the hero, the Marqués de Bradomín, finds himself at that stage in life when his powers are beginning to decline. He meets one of his former lovers, Concha, who is dying. Gallantly he pretends to love her still and together they enjoy moments of ecstasy with Concha's health temporarily restored. Soon, however, she suffers a relapse and dies in the Marqués's arms. This touching episode does not prevent him from seducing that very night Concha's cousin, albeit because of a misunderstanding. Next morning the Marqués weeps not out of sorrow for Concha nor from remorse for his actions, but because he feels that his youth has slipped from him.

The following year saw the appearance of the second story in the series, *Sonata de estío* which is set in the highly coloured, voluptuous and violent atmosphere of Mexico. Here the Marqués describes his love affair with a fascinating half-caste, la Niña Chole. The Marqués is doubtless the projection of Valle-Inclán as he saw himself and such is his conceit that in all the love affairs he plays an almost passive role; it is the women who are fatally attracted by him. The *Sonata de primavera* (1904) describes the Marqués's first and only sincere love which ends in ignominious flight because the Marqués is in fear of his life, being justly blamed for the misfortunes he has brought upon his lover, María Rosario. This is a different side to his nature, for in his maturer years he scorns danger like a true Don Juan and stands to confront his foes unashamed and undismayed. The final *Sonata de invierno* (1905) sees the aged Marqués somewhat crushed in spirit, unloved now by women, except for his daughter, devoting himself with proud resignation to a lost cause, that of Don Carlos (who styled himself Carlos VII) still claiming the throne by his appeal to sentimental rather than practical values.

The *Sonatas* are sickly productions in many ways, false in every note, with a style whose carefully studied cadences weary the ear after a time. But there is a luxuriance in the language rather like the tropical house at Kew Gardens and beneath the florid expression there is a violence and sharpness especially in the dialogue passages. The *Sonatas* indeed have a fascination as unusual and original works of art, but their appeal is limited and they must be sipped in the smallest doses.

Valle-Inclán's other works are less well known, but they include three novels on the second war waged in 1874 by the Carlists whose caused he espoused precisely because it was unsuccessful. He also wrote a number of farces which he called *esperpentos;* some of these are in verse and Valle-Inclán proved himself an excellent poet. His last novels were

Tirano Banderes (1926), a satire on a Mexican dictator, *La corte de los milagros* (1927) and *Viva mi dueño* (1927) which both deal with the last shameful years of the reign of Isabel II. Gone is the pretentious elegance of the *Sonatas* and the latent violence of Valle-Inclán comes to the surface. The satire is virulent and tragic and the humour, if humour it can be called, is more like that of the *guignol* theatre where laughter is evoked by bare brutality. Valle-Inclán is a writer capable of abrupt changes; indeed he is incapable almost of coherent development. His achievement is uneven, but in places he is extraordinarily compelling, not because he has no exact parallel in literature (he has been compared with Cervantes, Quevedo, Oscar Wilde), but because no comparison is complete. Valle-Inclán is a mystery on his own, but his influence on younger writers was extensive. He was copied as a model of *modernismo* with its craving for elegance and the *deshumanización del arte*, that is to say, divorcing literature from real life.

PÍO BAROJA (1879–1956) provides a complete contrast to Valle-Inclán's carefully cultivated style, for he seemed to care little for elegance of expression, being intent on portraying sharp and fleeting pictures of life as he saw it. His novels tend to be filled with rapid action and have all the startling speed and intensity of a film trailer. But such is his power of observation and ability to describe events he can probably be classed as the greatest Spanish novelist so far in the twentieth century. Like Unamuno a native of the Basque provinces, he became a doctor for a time in the small town of Cestona, not far from San Sebastián. Saddened by the sight of so much poverty and suffering, he moved to Madrid, where he managed his brother's bakery with such conspicuous lack of success that it was obliged to close after eight years. Success, however, came to him as a novelist and though excessive shyness made him something of a hermit, he found pleasure in travelling abroad, a fact which gives his work a broader and more cosmopolitan outlook than that of many contemporaries.

He himself has grouped his novels mainly into trilogies, though in many instances the connection is tenuous in the extreme. The first three novels deal with the Basque provinces. *La casa de Aizgorri* (1900) is in dialogue form, a development in which the generation of '98 specialised in some degree. It is a factual, unemotional description of a family tainted with alcoholism. Similar in theme, but depicting the degeneration of a whole village is *El mayorazgo de Labraz* (1903) while the third novel of the trilogy, *Zalacaín el aventurero* (1909) deals with the second Carlist war, chronicling the adventures of a young Basque

Pío Baroja, by Sorolla

whose obstinate, independent outlook eventually leads him to his death.

The next series of novels was of a more intimate nature and forms to some extent psychological studies with a satirical basis. The second and third novels deal with a character that is tough, bitter, but sincere (like Baroja) named Silvestre Paradox. The last novel is perhaps Baroja's most famous work, *Paradox Rey* (1906), in which the adventurous hero after trying his hand at journalism, at being an inventor, tutor and tramp, goes off to Africa to found a Jewish colony. He and his companions are captured by a tribe of savages who elect Paradox king. His acts of government provide opportunities for a comprehensive satire on twentieth century civilisation. Baroja reveals himself in *Paradox Rey* (also written in dialogue form) as beset with scepticism, rebellion and general disillusion.

His next set of novels published in 1904 were given the title of *La lucha por la vida*. They depict the life of the Madrid underworld with its rogues and pimps and gamblers and in no sense do these novels have any connected plot or action, but they form a kind of portrait gallery, intensely realistic and true to life. Especially vivid is the description of Madrid urchins and ragamuffins in *La Busca*. More conventional as novels is the following trilogy *El pasado* (1905); the first, *La feria de los discretos*, is set in Córdoba while the second and third are concerned with revolutionaries both Spanish exiles and Frenchmen during the 1870s.

Of greater interest to English readers is the trilogy entitled *La raza* (1908). The first novel, *La dama errante*, is based on the attempt to assassinate Alfonso XIII and his English bride on their wedding day in 1906. The central figure is a woman implicated in the plot who flees to London where she undergoes adventures which are told in the second novel, *La ciudad de la niebla*. This is a study of Edwardian London life as Baroja saw it with sharp contrast between the wealth of capitalism and the degrading poverty and grinding struggle for life in the East End. Baroja hated poverty, suffering, cruelty and injustice and the third book of this trilogy, *El árbol de la ciencia* is a savage attack on accepted institutions in Spain. He is indeed an anarchist, though he renounces militant anarchism, but he hates all laws and his bitterest hatred is reserved for catholic morality, for he regards the Christian religion as a mere illusion to keep people in their place. His general view of life is one of disgust at the vileness of men.

Though his novels are so brimming with vitality that they are never depressing, it is perhaps a relief to find Baroja turning from contemporary life to a series of historical novels which he called *Memorias de un hombre de acción*. These appeared between 1913 and 1916 and deal with the period of the *Guerra de la Independencia* and the restoration of the Bourbon monarchy. The central figure, Don Eugenio de Aviraneta, is a real historical person, conspirator, *guerrillero* and revolutionary, but in the various adventures he undergoes in the novels fact and fiction are freely mixed. Inevitably they recall Galdós's *Episodios nacionales*, but they are in fact very different. Like all Baroja's novels they give a series of impressionist pictures and the story is connected only very loosely.

Baroja continued to pour out a stream of novels which tended to decline in value and interest as he grew older. As a novelist of such experience he is curiously lacking in technique; he despised care for his craft and style and in consequence his novels frequently lack unity and logical development. The impressions he produces are often confused and fragmentary; in *El mundo es ansí* (1910), for example, the reader is whirled from Spain through France, Belgium, Holland, Germany, Poland and on to Russia and the feeling that remains is that of a traveller in an express train with the blinds half drawn. But his great merit is his vigour and intensity and his power of observation. He is curious about all aspects of life and inquires into everything he meets; he writes with a passionate sincerity that never fails to convince. He may indeed at times be abrupt and even trivial, but he gives the impression of feeling deeply about everything he describes.

In contrast RAMÓN PÉREZ AYALA (1880–1962) stands out as one of the most cultured and intellectual novelists of the century, with a depth of thought and ideas as well as a welcome sense of humour so gravely lacking in the writers of the generation of '98. Born in the Asturias, he retained, like Palacio Valdés, a deep love for his native district and in many of his novels Oviedo appears only thinly disguised by fictitious names. Yet he is a widely travelled man (for a period he was Spanish Ambassador to the Court of St James) and understood Spain's problems in relation to the rest of the world. He is a distinguished poet and critic as well as a novelist whose style is the richest and most personal of any writer of this century,

His early novels were satirical and realistic in their presentation of life. *Tinieblas en las cumbres* (1907) is almost a picaresque novel with a touch of tragedy in it and subtly ironical in style; the preface especially is highly entertaining for its disrespectful sarcasm while later the description of an eclipse shows the latent poetry in Ayala's style. *A.M.D.G.* (1910) is even more fiercely satirical in its portrayal, biased and exaggerated in places, of a Jesuit community in which are contrasted *el padre* Sequeros, a mystic tortured by doubts, and *el padre* Mur, vulgar and sadistic. The pessimistic, almost melodramatic tone of the novel is relieved somewhat by the sympathetic portrait of yet another Jesuit father, Atianza, who is plainspoken and sincere. *Troteras y danzaderas* (1913) is a description, satirical, pessimistic and even tragic, of bohemian literary and artistic circles in Madrid, and offers a rich field for identifying real personalities, lightly veiled.

The publication in 1921 of *Belarmino y Apolonio* showed that Ayala had changed his approach to the novel and his study of life becomes more personal. The two main characters, both shoemakers, are scarcely real persons; they represent Ayala's ideas in bodily form. Though they are by no means puppets, they are a special form of humanity created by Ayala, perhaps following the general trend for the *deshumanización del arte*. Along with these more complex creations goes a style rich in vocabulary, striving after effect, sometimes obscure, but offering passages of great beauty. The same method is continued in *Luna de miel, luna de hiel* and *Los trabajos de Urbano y Simona* (1923) which form a pair of novels with the same characters. Here Ayala seems to have slowed life down and draws a leisurely picture rather in the style of the story of *Daphnis and Chloe* with deep insight into human problems and the creation of characters of great vividness and great complexity.

The two masterpieces of his later style are without doubt *Tigre Juan* and its sequel *El curandero de su honra* (1926). Tigre Juan is a manly, rough, vital person sharply contrasted with Vespasiano Cebón, a smooth, effeminate philanderer. Herminia has to choose between the two; she is first attracted by the crude virility of Tigre Juan, but then in a moment of folly allows herself to be lured by the scented charms of Vespasiano. Finally she realises how repugnant this emasculated creature is and marries the human powerhouse, Tigre Juan, in spite of his face, which is 'square, obtuse, mongolian with protruding cheek bones and eyes like a wildcat'. The deeper significance of the theme is summed up by Tigre Juan when in the moment of triumph he says to his shrinking rival: 'You are a part of me which is missing just as I ought to be a part of you.' Nature rarely achieves the perfect balance in human character.

In *El curandero de su honra* Tigre Juan, unlike the hero of Calderón's drama, intends to save his honour not by killing his wife whose conduct has been guilty, but by killing himself. In the end he comes to realise what has happened and why it has happened and he forgives Herminia with manly generosity. This behaviour at first appears uncharacteristic of a man of such dynamic personality as Tigre Juan, but he is in fact a man of deep feeling for whom faith in his wife is a basic necessity of life. The novel with its terse, yet poetical style is extremely moving and the scene in the train when Tigre Juan answers forcefully and nobly the cheap jibes of his friends is magnificent. For dramatic intensity of the action and lyrical quality of the style there are few modern writers who can rival Ayala.

'Modernismo'

The poets of the generation of '98 were almost wholly under the influence of the Parnassian and Symbolist poets of France who had reacted first against the personal style of the Romantics and then against the materialism of the Naturalist School. The Parnassians had sought to be entirely objective in their poems and insisted on careful composition and technical excellence; the Symbolists sought to convey ideas by means of word pictures and laid stress on the musical quality of the style. Finally, the decadent school of writers at the end of the century relied for their effect on morbid subjects and sensations. The result of this mixture of trends on Spanish poetry was the creation of a style called *modernismo* which, if it differed in outlook from the ideals of the thinkers and essayists of the generation of '98, at any rate desired to endow Spanish poetry with fresh vigour and new rhythms.

The man largely responsible for the spread of new forms was a Nicaraguan, RUBÉN DARÍO (1867–1916). His poems had already won fame in America when in 1892 he arrived in Spain to represent Nicaragua at the quatercentenary celebrations of the discovery of America by Columbus. From Spain he went to Paris where he immersed himself in French poetry and the *fin de siècle* atmosphere of the cafés on the left bank where the literary swells gathered. In 1896 he produced a book of poems named *Prosas profanas* which created a sensation in Spain and had all the young intellectuals worshipping at the shrine of Rubén Darío. He for his part gave his worshippers plenty to wonder at, for he was nothing if not flamboyant. He travelled with his mistresses, drank to excess, thereby suffering from delirium tremens, and in the meantime gave himself the airs of a great lord, declaring that 'poets of our generation should wear gloves and patent-leather shoes, because modern art is aristocratic'. He was an exotic figure like Oscar Wilde, producing aphorisms of doubtful originality and ideally suited for a society lion.

The very title, *Prosas profanas*, gives a hint of affectation for it was a borrowing from the medieval Spanish poet Berceo, who called his sacred poems on the lives of saints *Prosas*. Nearly all Rubén Darío's poems exude the nineteenth-century predilection for medieval legends on the lines of Wagner and the pre-Raphaelites, or imagery of Greek mythology popularised by Leconte de Lisle's poems. But Leconte de Lisle was a genuine Greek scholar whereas Rubén Darío relied on French poetry to tell him about Pan and the Satyrs: *Amo más que la Grecia de los griegos, la Grecia de los franceses.* He was in fact a cosmopolitan exotic drawing his inspiration from many nations and periods of history, eighteenth-century France, Florence in the Middle Ages, the Germany of Lohengrin, the Spain of Mérimée and Bizet with its gypsies and bullfighters. Any age interested him provided it was colourful and unmaterialistic—at any rate to the imagination.

Rubén Darío is a master of colour and music in words. His style is smooth and flowing with delicate cadences and soft qualities of rhythm. Moreover the rhythms were all new to Spanish poetry for he was able to transpose French metres into Spanish with astonishing skill. Most noteworthy is his adaptation of the French alexandrine which in Spanish poetry had been little used because its length and sonority were ill suited to the staccato bark natural to Castilian diction. Rubén Darío uses the alexandrine (fourteen syllables to the line, not twelve as in French verse) to great effect, producing a soft, dignified, mournful melody. The best example is to be found in the *Sonatina:*

> *¡Oh, quién fuera hipsipila que dejó la crisálida!*
> *(La princesa está triste. La princesa está pálida)*
> *¡Oh visión adorada de oro, rosa y marfil!*
> *¡Quién volara a la tierra donde un príncipe existe*
> *(La princesa está pálida. La princesa está triste.)*
> *más brillante que el alba, más hermoso que abril!*

The cadences here are especially interesting with their alternations of stress, *esdrújulo* in the first two lines, *agudo* in the third and sixth, and *grave* in the fourth and fifth. With such magic in words it is disappointing to find the subject matter so banal—the Princess in the golden prison of her palace sad and dejected, but at the end enlivened by the Fairy Godmother's promise of the arrival of:

> *el feliz caballero que te adora sin verte*
> *y que llega de lejos, vencedor de la Muerte,*
> *a encenderte los labios con su beso de amor.*

In other metres Rubén Darío is equally masterful in his choice of words and management of rhythm. In the *Sinfonía en gris mayor* he uses with great skill an *agudo* ending to the second and fourth lines of each stanza conveying the impression of greyness; often the words chosen are foreign in origin and are strikingly original—*un cielo de zinc, su*

frasco de gin, sus biceps de atleta, su blusa de dril. All this is a clear imitation
of Théophile Gautier's *Symphonie en blanc majeur*, in which an impression is evoked of a woman in white and beautiful as snow, but equally
cold and untouchable. Rubén Darío's picture of the old sea dog is far
more commonplace and less satisfactory and scarcely fits in with the
atmosphere of greyness; indeed his skin has been toasted by the fiery
Brazilian sun while his nose has been reddened by imbibing from his
flask of gin amid the raging typhoons of the China Sea.

It is when Rubén Darío is entirely engrossed in manipulating words
that he is most successful. His *Eco y yo* is a *tour de force* in the intricate
combination of words that give the effect of echoing in the woods or
beside a lake and yet convey a coherent series of ideas:

> —*Eco, divina y desnuda*
> *como el diamante del agua,*
> *mi musa estos versos fragua*
> *y necesita tu ayuda,*
> *pues sola peligros teme.*
>   —*¡Hewe!*
> —*Tuve en momentos distantes,*
>   *antes,*
> *que amar los dulces cabellos*
>   *bellos,*
> *de la ilusión que primera*
>   *era,*
> *en mi alcázar andaluz*
>   *luz,*
> *en mi palacio de moro,*
>   *oro,*
> *en mi mansión dolorosa,*
>   *rosa,*
> *Se apagó como una estrella*
>   *ella,*

> (Echo, my muse divine and bare like a diamond drop of
> water is forging these lines and needs your help, because
> alone it fears the dangers.—Behold I am here!—Formerly
> in far-off moments I must needs love the soft and beautiful
> hair of the illusion that first was light in my Andalusian
> fortress, gold in my Moorish palace, a rose in my gloomy
> mansion. Like a star it faded.)

The translation murders the original in which, though the imagery
may be lush and conventional, the management of the impressionism,
metre and rhythm is brilliant. It was small wonder that these poems
with their surprising innovations seemed fascinating after the stilted

drabness of Campoamor and Núñez de Arce. All the young literary men of the day fell under the spell, including Unamuno, Juan Ramón Jiménez, the Machado brothers and particularly Valle-Inclán. It was like another Garcilaso de la Vega bringing foreign metres to inject life into Spanish poetry. Rubén Darío's influence, however, was short-lived; his subsequent collections of poems, *Cantos de vida y esperanza* (1905) and *El canto errante* (1907) show his powers in decline. His imagery is too superficially lush and exotic to be fully appreciated in the brown wastes of Castile; he is after all only a reflection of French poets, enchanting and delightful though the reflection often is.

Though *modernismo* itself lasted only for the space of ten years, its influence is obvious in JUAN RAMÓN JIMÉNEZ (1881–1958). His early poems in the collections published between 1903 and 1905, *Arias tristes*, *Jardines lejanos* and *Pastorales*, echo the work of the French symbolists, especially Verlaine, but they are less plainly imitated than those of Rubén Darío. They are written mainly in lines of eight syllables which is the traditional Spanish metre and they lack the French cadences which Rubén Darío had so skilfully transposed into Spanish. One of the best poems is *Nocturno:*

> *Es la media noche; paso*
> *por frente de la ciudad;*
> *la luna encantada duerme*
> *en el río de cristal.*
>
> *Oigo unas dulces campanas*
> *que no volveré a escuchar;*
> *las luces lejanas tiemblan;*
> *la brisa es primaveral.*
>
> (It is midnight; I pass by the front of the town; the fairy moon is sleeping in the crystal river. I hear the gentle sound of bells which I shall never hear again; the distant lights are shimmering; the breeze is the breeze of spring.)

Juan Ramón Jiménez was still strongly Spanish in outlook and he returned to the style of the old popular songs in his collection entitled *Baladas de primavera*. In doing so he probably extended considerable influence over the younger poets and later García Lorca was to adopt this method with great success. Juan Ramón Jiménez himself experimented with alexandrines in the French manner in his next collections *Elegía* and *La soledad sonora* (1908), giving a gently plaintive note combined with richness of expression:

Las antiguas arañas melodiosas temblaban
maravillosamente sobre las mustias flores ...
sus cristales, heridos por la luna, soñaban
guirnaldas temblorosas de pálidos colores ...

(The old sweet threads of gossamer were shimmering on the fading
flowers ... their brightness in the moonlight was like dreaming
garlands, pale and trembling.)

It was this richness of expression that led him to experiment still
further after 1916, discarding rhyme and fixed metres and concentrating
solely on striking, suggestive phrases. These strivings after pure poetry
—*la depuración*—make difficult reading and Juan Ramón Jiménez has
been criticised on the score of unintelligibility and extravagant epithets.
Nevertheless, these poems make a strong appeal to the intellect and the
reader can join with the poet in his search for the answers to the problems of the human mind:

¡Inteligencia, dame
el nombre exacto y tuyo,
y suyo, y mío de las cosas!

Later still his poetry tended to stray back to the traditional forms of
Spanish popular poetry while yet remaining highly elliptical in expression and often baffling in meaning. Since the last years of his life were
spent living abroad in Puerto Rico, it is difficult to gauge exactly his
place in Spanish literature. He was an individualist of an introspective
nature, but his influence on the Spanish poets of the 1920s and 1930s
was strong and his international reputation was sufficient to win him
the Nobel Prize for poetry in 1956. Perhaps somewhat ironically
almost his best known work is a book in prose, *Platero y yo* (1914),
which chronicles the life of an Andalusian donkey, the poet's almost
human companion. Such tales tend to be highly sentimental, but this is
delightful, witty and realistic and the prose is such that only a poet
could write.

Modernismo was not in fact connected with the aspirations of the
generation of '98 and this in itself may have accounted in part for its
rapid disappearance. A poet more closely associated with the aims of his
generation was ANTONIO MACHADO (1875–1939). Though born in
Seville he received most of his education in Madrid in the *Institución
Libre de Enseñanza* and he shared the ideals of the school's founder,
Francisco Giner de los Ríos, for the advancement of Spain intellectually
and morally. In his moving elegy to his old master, Machado strikes

the note of the urgency of the work to be done: *¡Yunques, sonad;
enmudeced, campanas!* (Anvils, ring! Be silent, bells!)

Antonio Machado identified himself wholly with Castile while his
brother, Manuel, also a poet, retained his typically Andalusian characteristics of living only for the day and enjoying life to the full. Antonio
became a teacher of French in the *Instituto* in Soria, high on the Castilian
steppes. Here he became passionately devoted to the empty, baked,
windswept countryside with its primitive villages and grim poverty
where men were ascetic by force of circumstance. Appropriately enough
his first book of poetry published in 1903 was entitled *Soledades;* it is a
collection of short poems, mostly bare and stark in style with assonance
in place of rhyme. Machado is fascinated by the beauty of the wide,
deserted Castilian landscape:

> *¡Chopos del camino blanco, álamos de la ribera,*
> *espuma de la montaña*
> *ante la azul lejanía,*
> *luz del día, claro dia!*
> *¡Hermosa tierra de España!*

> (Black poplars on the white road, poplars on the river bank,
> foam on the mountain top in the blue distance, the light of the
> clear, clear day! Beautiful land of Spain!)

He is also imbued with a resigned melancholy derived perhaps from
the contemplation of a countryside in decay. His preference is for the
soft beauty of the evening, the feeling of the swift passing of the exuberance of youth, the certainty of repose in death.

Antonio Machado knew moments of happiness in Soria for it was
there that in 1909 he married Leonor, a girl of sixteen whom he adored
and who died of consumption after only three years of married life.
This sudden end to his happiness was a crushing blow to Antonio
Machado and his next book of poems, *Campos de Castilla*, published in
the year of his wife's death, reveals his hopes of a new life that ended
only in sorrow. Not that he mentions Leonor, except for a passing
reference here and there; his love and his grief were too deep to be
expressed. The opening poems of this collection are mostly in alexandrines following medieval models and call passionately on Spain to
awake. In *Desde mi rincón* he conjures up a vision of Castile in the days
of her greatness and contrasts the modern Spain that idles and yawns.
But he sees hope not only for Spain, but for himself; in love, he wants
to live even if he has left his loving late:

Al olmo viejo, hendido por el rayo
y en su mitad podrido,
con las lluvias de abril y el sol de mayo,
algunas hojas verdes le han salido.

(On the old elm, cleft by lightning and half rotten, with the
rains of April and the sun in May, a few green leaves have
struggled forth.)

Machado's father had devoted much of his life to the study of popular
poetry and had founded a Spanish folklore society. It is not therefore
surprising that Antonio's poetry, although it has strong intellectual
appeal, is essentially popular in tone. The longest (and probably the
best) poem in *Campos de Castilla* is in ballad form, *La tierra de Alvar-
gonzález*, telling the story of two sons who murder their father to gain
his possessions. It is a pessimistic view of the hatred that greed engenders
and Castile is a land steeped in blood:

Páramo que cruza el lobo,
aullando a la luna clara,
de bosque a bosque: baldíos
llenos de peñas rodadas,
donde roída de buitres
brilla una osamenta blanca;
pobres campos solitarios
sin caminos ni posadas,
¡oh, pobres campos malditos,
pobres campos de mi patria!

(Desert the wolf crosses howling to the bright moon, going
from wood to wood; untilled fields filled with rocks rolled
down, where gnawed by vultures gleam white bones; poor
lonely fields without roads or inns, oh, poor accursed
fields, poor fields of my homeland!)

After his wife's death Machado moved to Baeza in northern Andalusia, but he was never at his ease there, missing the wilderness of
Castile, and in 1919 he returned to the land of his adoption, living in
Segovia. His poetic output had greatly dwindled though he remained
a master of style. His later poems are mostly brief, epigrams or popular
coplas. He is never tortured about the problems of life and death:

Fe empirista. Ni somos ni seremos.
Todo nuestro vivir es emprestado.
Nada trajímos; nada llevaremos.

(Empirical faith. We neither are nor shall be. All our
being is borrowed. We brought nothing; nothing shall
we take away.)

Even so he continued to have faith in youth and in the future of Spain and this faith was increased by the Civil War in which almost to the end he hoped for a Republican victory. In the bitterness of defeat he crossed the French frontier with hundreds of other refugees and in February 1939 he died in Collioure in the French Pyrenees, heartbroken at the thought of Spain helpless in the hands of dictators. One of the most vehement of his poems written during the Civil War was the fierce protest at the execution by the Nationalists of García Lorca:

> Se le vio caminando entre fusiles,
> por una calle larga,
> salir al campo frío,
> aun con estrellas, de la madrugada.
> Mataron a Federico
> cuando la luz asomaba.
> El pelotón de verdugos
> no osó mirarlo a la cara.
>
> Todos cerraron los ojos;
> rezaron; ¡ni Dios te salva!
> Muerto cayó Federico
> —sangre en la frente y plomo en las entrañas—
> Que fue en Granada el crimen
> sabed—¡pobre Granada!—en su Granada.

(He was seen walking along between the rifles down a long street, going out into the cold countryside still with the stars of early morning. They killed Federico when the light of day was peeping out. The squad of executioners dared not look him in the face. All closed their eyes; they prayed; not even God can save you! Federico fell dead—blood on his brow and lead in his guts —this crime was committed in Granada, you know—poor Granada!—in his Granada.)

Federico García Lorca

FEDERICO GARCÍA LORCA (1899–1936) is the Spanish poet of modern times who more than any other has captured the imagination of Spain and now of the whole world. His tragic death no doubt lends an air of romantic sentiment to his brief career, but his poetry and his plays have aroused fervent admiration everywhere. In spite of the immaturity of much of his work there is a colour and vigour in his poetry combined with a simplicity that blows like a fresh wind through the sophisticated drabness of life in modern cities. Lorca has developed a remarkable power of combining the traditional popular verse forms of Spain with an insistent appeal to the intellect; he is both popular and highbrow at the same time and his impact on the reader, no matter what his tastes, is immediate.

Born in Vaqueros near Granada, Lorca was influenced at an early age by the folk songs and ballads of the peasants. While studying law at Granada he became closely acquainted with the gypsies of the Albaicín quarter and steeped himself in their lore and traditions, which largely preserve the customs of Arab Spain. In 1919 he went to Madrid and lived at the *Residencia de Estudiantes* which was part of the *Institución Libre de Enseñanza* where he met Juan Ramón Jiménez and Antonio Machado and listened to lectures on philosophy by Ortega y Gasset and occasionally by Unamuno. These were the days before wireless and television, and in Granada especially people had to rely on themselves for their entertainment. Lorca's poems were recited at evening *tertulias* and gatherings in cafés long before they were published; his poetry is essentially intended for recitation and its appeal is first and foremost to the ear and not to the eye.

The first collection of poems published by Lorca was the *Libro de poemas* which appeared in 1921. Though they were praised by literary critics, some of whom had heard the poems recited by Lorca in his *obscura, cálida, turbia, inolvidable voz*, (dark, warm, passionate, unforgettable voice) the general public remained unaware of their existence. Many of the poems were inspired by the songs and games of children and Lorca early showed a preference for ballad form, using the traditional eight syllable line with assonance in the second and fourth lines of each stanza. Ballads were admirably suited to recital with guitar accompaniment and Lorca was an accomplished musician who studied and collected folk tunes in Andalusia. He was helped and encouraged in this work by his lifelong friend, the distinguished composer, Manuel de Falla.

It was not until 1927 that Lorca was able to publish his collection of *Canciones* which are original songs based on Andalusian folktunes. Here again the themes are often those of children's songs, for Lorca always kept something of the child's wonder and delight at the world. Describing Córdoba, Seville and Granada, the great cities of Andalusia, he says:

> Arbolé, arbolé
> Seco y verdé.
> La niña de bello rostro
> Está cogiendo aceituna;
> El viento, galán de torres,
> La prende por la cintura.

(Trees, trees dry and green. The child with the lovely face is picking olives; the wind, lover of towers, seizes her by the waist.)

This striking image of the wind, flirting with towers, is one that recurs in Lorca's poems, for he is fascinated by the power of the wind. He was by now developing his ability to create images of great splendour and vividness. He was a craftsman who worked hard on his style, spontaneous as it may appear. He certainly had inspiration—the Andalusians call it *duende* (impish spirit)—but he was very conscious of technique. He said: 'If it is true that I am a poet by the grace of God—or the Devil —it is also true that I am one by the grace of technique and effort, and of knowing exactly what a poem is.'

The advance in technique is clearly seen in the next collection, *Romancero gitano*, begun in 1924 and published in 1928. The imagery is more powerful than ever and springs from the memory of the intuitively poetical speech of countryfolk and also from reminders of Góngora's *conceptismo*, for instance, *los cuernos de la luna*, which is frequently repeated. Cynical critics maintain that nearly all Lorca's imagery was filched and point to examples in Horace and Sophocles as well as Góngora. Nothing is new no doubt, but Lorca uses his imagery with startling effect and aptness, as for example in the *Romance somnámbulo*:

> Sobre el rostro del aljibe
> se mecía la gitana.
> Verde carne, pelo verde,
> con ojos de fría plata.
> Un carámbano de luna
> la sostiene sobre el agua.
> La noche se puso íntima
> como una pequeña plaza.
> Guardias civiles borrachos
> en la puerta golpeaban.
> Verde que te quiero verde.
> Verde viento, verdes ramas.
> El barco sobre la mar
> y el caballo en la montaña.

(Over the surface of the pond the gypsy girl was rocking. Green skin, green hair, with eyes of cold silver. A ray of moonlight keeps her on the water. The night became intimate like a small market square. Drunken civil guards were beating on the door. Green, I love you green. Green wind, green branches. The ship on the sea and the horse on the mountainside.)

Green as the dominant colour of sleep-walking seems an image of miraculous aptness and, if one dare say so, of great originality even if it is true that a green light is invariably used on the stage for dream sequences or such unpleasant apparitions as the Rat King. Lorca is obsessed with colour in general; frequently it is blood red, especially in his more pessimistic poems, but green is the colour that appears most often for no particular reason, unless as has been vaguely suggested, it is the colour of Islam.

The *Romancero gitano* brought Lorca instant fame, not only in Spain, but in all Latin America. Yet he himself was not satisfied and felt that ballads were too popular in tone and too naive in form. Perhaps it was in the belief that he could write sophisticated poetry that he agreed to go to the United States for a year in 1929 to study at the University of Columbia. If this was his intention, he received a profound shock. Life in the United States horrified him; after the natural rhythm of life in rural Andalusia he found America and New York especially a 'mundane hubbub' in which the only human and sympathetic characters were the negroes. Only they still preserved the feelings and rhythms of life in its primitive and natural state. The collection of poems written about his stay in America, *Poeta en Nueva York* (published posthumously), contains verses without form, lacking any regular metre or rhyme, but staccato, harsh sounding, nightmarish like the continual whirling of life in a big city:

> ¡Ay Harlem disfrazada!
> ¡Ay Harlem, amenazada por un gentío de trajes sin cabeza!
> Me llega tu rumor,
> Me llega tu rumor atravesando troncos y ascensores,
> a través de láminas grises,
> donde flotan tus automóviles cubiertos de dientes,
> a través de los caballos muertos y los crímenes diminutos,
> a través de tu gran rey desesperado,
> cuyas barbas llegan al mar.

> (Oh Harlem in disguise! Oh, Harlem, threatened by a mob of headless clothes! Your throbbing comes to me, your throbbing comes to me through tree trunks and lifts, through grey strips where float your cars covered with teeth, through the dead horses and petty crimes, through your great king in despair, whose chin goes down to the sea.)

Some critics have hailed such poems as Lorca's greatest work, but in effect they are not the real Lorca who revels in the rhythms of Andalusia, complex and often savage, but patterned like life itself with spring, summer, autumn, and winter, birth, childhood, manhood and death,

García Lorca,

by Gregorio Prieto

not amorphous like the ceaseless turmoil of a modern city. Lorca always maintained that he wrote poetry so that people should like him:

> *Lo hago para que la gente me quiera; nada más que para que me quieran las gentes he hecho mi teatro y mis versos, y seguiré haciéndolos porque es preciso el amor de todos.*

> (I do it so that people will like me; it is only so that people will like me that I have written my plays and my poems and I shall go on doing it because one must be liked by all.)

Few could have loved the poet in New York, for he hated life.

Lorca escaped from New York and 'waltzed his way back to civilisation' via Cuba where he found the Latin way of life more to his liking in spite of the desperate poverty of the people. Back in Spain in 1930 he resumed writing in the traditional metres and published his *Poema del cante jondo* (composed nine years earlier). The Andalusian method of singing had always enthralled him and this was his contribution to this highly individualistic mode of song with its brief lines drawn out to great length by the singer who to the uninitiated would seem to be gargling. Yet there is a wealth of feeling expressed, rather like someone with an important message straining to get the words out; when at last they emerge, they come with passionate starkness:

> Amparo,
> ¡qué sola estás en tu casa
> vestida de blanca!
> Amparo, ·
> ¡y qué difícil decirte:
> yo te amo!

(Amparo, how lonely you are in your house, dressed in white! Amparo, and how difficult it is to tell you: I love you!)

Another poem of this period is the *Llanto por Ignacio Sánchez Mejías*, lamenting the death (August 1934) in the bull ring of his great friend, Sánchez Mejías, who was as noble in character as he was skilful with the sword. This poem represents possibly Lorca's best sustained work with its rich imagery, musical sounds and deeply felt sorrow:

> ¡Que no quiero verla!
> Dile a la luna que venga
> que no quiero ver la sangre
> de Ignacio sobre la arena.
> ¡Que no quiero verla!
> La luna de par en par.
> Caballo de nubes quietas,
> y la plaza gris del sueño
> con sauces en las barreras.
> ¡Que no quiero verla!
> Que mi recuerdo se quema.
> ¡Avisad a los jazmines
> con su blancura pequeña!
> ¡que no quiero verla!

(I don't want to see it! Tell the moon to come out because I don't want to see Ignacio's blood on sand. I don't want to see it! The moon is full. A horse of quiet clouds, and the bull ring grey with sleep with willows round the barriers. I don't want to see it! My memory is on fire. Tell the jasmine with its small white flowers that I don't want to see it!)

This is a youthful protest against the waste of death. Lorca had previously been too full of life to be horrified at death; he could cheerfully and boldly accept agnosticism and reject the hopeful doctrine of immortality which religion offers. But here was an example of the injustice of nature. Lorca believed that nature could never again shape such a man as Sánchez Mejías and yet it had snatched him away in the glory of his achievement.

Lorca's interests had been turning more towards the theatre and in the first flush of enthusiasm after the establishment of the Republic, he took a leading part in forming a student theatre group, *La Barraca*, which aimed at bringing the performance of classical plays like *Fuente Ovejuna*, *La vida es sueño*, *El burlador de Sevilla*, to the humblest peasant audiences. It was a noble ideal and despite the difficulties Lorca was again to experience the sensitivity of ordinary people for artistic expression. Here was a poetical revolution as great as the political one; this was poetry socialised. But then Spanish classical plays, like Shakespeare's, were always intended for a popular audience.

Lorca's first effort at drama had been a complete failure in 1920. *El maleficio de la mariposa* (The butterfly's spell) had been an effort at symbolism using insects for human beings as in his poem about the snail and the ants (*Los encuentros de un caracol aventurero*). In 1927 he had achieved moderate success with *Mariana Pineda*, the story of the execution in 1831 of a young girl because of her adherence to the liberal reaction against the tyranny of Fernando VII. Some members of the public applauded the play because they saw in it a protest against the dictatorship of General Primo de Rivera. In fact Lorca was preaching no political sermon; he had altered the normal historical portrait of Mariana Pineda and instead of depicting her dying for the liberal cause, he makes her sacrifice herself for the love of the liberal leader, Don Pedro, who callously leaves her to her fate. This altered conception of the heroine, though much criticised, greatly enhances the effect of the tragedy.

Mariana Pineda retains to a large extent the form of a ballad, beginning with a chorus of little girls singing the popular *romance* lamenting Mariana's death:

> *¡Oh qué día tan triste en Granada,*
> *que a las piedras hacía llorar*
> *al ver Marianita se muere*
> *en cadalso por no declarar!*

> (Oh what a sad day in Granada, which made even the stones weep to see Marianita die on the scaffold for not revealing information!)

The play is interspersed with ballads, some of which, like the description of the bullfight in Ronda, have no direct bearing on the plot; these ballads are almost like the songs inserted in a musical film and the spectator can sense that the recitation of a ballad is about to occur.

In *Mariana Pineda* Lorca has attempted, no doubt unconsciously, to fuse classical and romantic drama; the essential spirit of the play, as well as the verse metres with the predominance of *romances*, is based on the Golden Age dramas, while the theme of a beautiful girl going to her death for refusing to betray her friends or to yield to the amorous overtures of the wicked chief of police is typically romantic. Similarly the meeting of the conspirators (the weakest scene in the play) and the chorus of novice nuns might well belong to Italian romantic opera. Again there is an insistence on local colour which classical dramatists would have neglected. Lorca in his stage directions goes into considerable detail describing the costumes, scenery and lighting effects. In fact the reader is inclined to become irritated with the reiteration that the stage and the settings must look like an old print and to call each act an *Estampa* seems affected. Surely the director and actors can be left to do their own job and the reader's imagination is not wholly helpless. One sighs for Shakespeare's laconic stage directions, such as, 'The coast of Illyria' or 'A blasted heath'.

Mariana Pineda has been criticised in that it fails as a tragedy because the heroine makes little attempt to resist; she seems like a lamb resigned to the slaughter. This is not entirely true and the struggle in Mariana's mind forms an interesting study. She embroiders the liberal flag because she is devoted to the liberal leader, Don Pedro de Sotomayor; she is fully aware of her duty to her children as a widow and of the risks she is taking for Don Pedro. When confronted by the chief of police, Pedrosa, she begs him for mercy:

> *¡Tenga piedad de mí! si usted supiera!*
> *Y déjeme escapar. Yo guardaré*
> *su recuerdo en las niñas de mis ojos.*
> *¡Pedrosa, por mis hijos! . . .*
>
> (Have pity on me! If only you knew! And let me escape.
> I shall always keep your memory in my darling daughters.
> Pedrosa, for my children's sakes! . . .)

It is only when he embraces her amorously that she is physically repelled by him and pushes him away. Later when she is imprisoned in the convent awaiting death, she keeps hoping that her friends in Granada will do something to save her; she keeps asking Alegrito, the gardener's boy, for news of help from Granada:

> *¿Crees que van a dejar que muera*
> *la que tiene menos culpa?*

(Do you think that they are going to let die a person who
is least guilty?)

She asserts confidently that Don Pedro is coming, knowing full well
in her heart that he will not. She has no wish to die; she longs to live
for the sake of her children and her lover. But she is caught in the
cruellest circumstances. She cannot save herself as Pedrosa demands by
betraying the other conspirators; the punishment of lifelong shame for
herself and her children would be far worse than death. Mariana may
not be the type of Cornelian hero who dies manfully doing his duty and
scorning the easy road to safety. She is like a bird taken in a trap, but
it is her love or perhaps her weakness that has put her in such a position.

The best feature of *Mariana Pineda* is the poetry. Apart from the
various ballads which are all of the highest merit, the imagery is frequently brilliantly vivid and of great beauty, as for instance when in
the first act Mariana is anxiously waiting for darkness to fall:

> *¡Con qué trabajo tan grande*
> *deja la luz a Granada!*
> *Se enreda entre los cipreses*
> *O se esconde bajo el agua.*
> *¡Y esta noche que no llega!*
> *Noche temida y soñada;*
> *que me hieres ya de lejos*
> *con larguísimas espadas!*

(With what great difficulty the light leaves Granada!
It twines amid the cypresses or hides under the water. And
tonight that never comes! A night that is so feared and yet
longed for; which wounds me already from afar with long,
long swords!)

Or when Amparo remembers that her brother, Fernando, had described
the anxious Mariana as having in her eyes a constant winging of birds:

> *¡Ya me acuerdo! Dijo que en tus ojos*
> *Había un constante desfile de pájaros.*

This striking simile is immediately followed by two others less forceful
and a few lines later Mariana makes a somewhat laboured comparison
between dawn and a golden sunflower opening on the stem of night.
The imagery is at times overdone.

This striving after effect is apparent also in a number of rather
clumsily contrived situations; for example Mariana, when imprisoned

in the convent, on being told that there is a visitor for her, immediately thinks that it is Don Pedro and in a thoroughly feminine way wants to change her dress because the present one makes her look too pale. She arranges herself on a bench *en actitud amorosa*, but is crushingly disappointed that the visitor is Fernando; she then utters a series of exclama^t ory phrases worthy of any heroine of melodrama:

> *¡Pedro! ¿Dónde está Pedro?*
> *¡Dejadlo entrar, por Dios!*
> *¡Está abajo, en la puerta!*
> *¡Tiene que estar! ¡Que suba!*

This is only one of the several unconvincing incidents in the play where the author appears to strive too hard to create dramatic effect, just as an inexperienced ballet-dancer can be observed preparing herself with grim determination for some difficult manoeuvre. The top-class ballerina makes the whole dance flow smoothly from position to position without visible effort.

Lorca was not satisfied with *Mariana Pineda*, but in spite of its faults, which spring from inexperience, it remains a play of strong emotional appeal. He set out to experiment in new dramatic forms and attempted three farces in a style that was a mixture of the old Italian pantomime, a puppet show and a ballet. It was all part of the prevailing trend of the *deshumanización del arte* in an effort to break away from realism and from its offshoot, the somewhat trivial drawing room comedies of the period. The most successful of these three farces, written in prose, was *La zapatera prodigiosa*, produced in Madrid first in 1930 and in an extended form in 1935. It had the subtitle of *una farsa violenta* because the puppet-characters behave with a violence and lack of self-restraint usually denied to real people in any class of society. Lorca is thus enabled to discuss themes which the decorous theatre of his day normally glossed over. The farce deals with the problem of an old man who has married a young wife; the couple are totally incompatible and the situation is aggravated by the fact that the marriage is sterile. The wife longs for a child and this yearning makes her so shrewish towards her husband that he finally decides to run away. His absence makes the wife realise how fond she was of him and she builds on a dream picture of him as an ideal companion. The husband has similar feelings and returns disguised as a puppeteer. He gives a puppet show in his own house which his wife in his absence has turned into an inn in order to make a living for herself. After a long period of somewhat ponderous dramatic irony in which the Zapatera tells the puppeteer what a darling her husband is and how he has been driven away solely by backbiting neighbours, the Zapatero finally declares himself and the couple are reunited. The reconciliation is crowned by the half-serious, half-comic lamentations and insults uttered by the Zapatera whose final words are: 'How unfortunate I am with this husband God has given me!'

Obviously in a farce of this type realism is not to be expected any more than in a ballet such as *Coppelia*. The interest lies in the discussion of various topics and aspects of life. In *La zapatera prodigiosa* these range from a marriage between partners of different ages, sterility, the evils of gossip, the lecherous behaviour of males, to the question of the propriety of a woman managing a business of her own. Many facets of human behaviour are studied—how to treat a wife for instance. Should she be worshipped and indulged or is it better to act like the Alcalde, whose recipe is to beat his wife and squeeze her waist and whose four successive wives have died from this treatment, thus giving scope for further experiment? The farce contains much material which is thought-provoking so long as it is not taken too literally. The action moves at a rollicking pace, affording opportunities for interesting and suggestive ballet patterns as well. Yet the technique still appears jerky and disconnected, as in *Mariana Pineda*. The portrayal of various characteristics is not subtle enough. The Zapatera's maternal instincts gush forth as soon as she sees the Niño appear. Her tenderness for young things is shown by her concern for the lambs in a flock of sheep passing the window. Her fruitless search for happiness is symbolised by her frantic clutching at a butterfly that flutters round the room. Somehow all these suggestive details seem too obvious.

More mature is Lorca's trilogy of plays dealing with tragedy in simple country life, *Bodas de sangre* (1933), *Yerma* (1934), *La casa de Bernarda Alba* (1936). *Yerma* continues the theme of sterility in marriage: a young wife has no children while all round her the world is bursting with new life. *Bodas de sangre* and *La casa de Bernarda Alba* are both concerned with the obstacles that society places in the path of true love. In *Bodas de sangre* the obstacle is material interest: a girl has loved Leonardo for fifteen years, but she is compelled to marry a rich suitor. Just as the wedding is about to take place (in the presence of Leonardo who is now married to another woman), the lovers flee on horseback to a kind of dream forest. The thwarted bridegroom pursues them and in a savage fight in the cold moonlight of the forest the two men, rivals in love kill each other. Thus if true love had not been baulked in the first place, this tragedy would not have occurred nor indeed the numerous other deaths which this family feud occasions.

In *La casa de Bernarda Alba* love is barred by the puritanical outlook of the widowed mother who keeps her two daughters virtually imprisoned. To look at a man is a sin; Bernarda, the widow, urges the crowd outside the house tormenting a woman taken in adultery to kill without mercy. Such is the atmosphere in this Andalusian country house where there are seven women without a man. The youngest daughter, Adela, rebels against this tyranny and secretly meets her lover, Pepe el Romano, finally indulging in sexual intercourse with him in the shadows of the stableyard. Knowing that this rash act can bring nothing but misery Adela hangs herself. Her mother feels no grief at her death, only desperate concern to keep the matter secret for the honour of the family name. 'I do not wish to weep. Silence! She, the youngest daughter of Bernarda Alba, died a virgin. You hear me? Silence, I have said, silence!'

When Lorca was reading this play to his friends, he remarked on finishing each scene: 'Not a drop of poetry! Reality, realism!' Perhaps by this he meant that after all his experiments in the dehumanisation of art he was at last returning to the portrayal of life as it is. If this was so, he must have been deluding himself. He is above all others the poet of fantasy, a magician with words who conjures moods, feelings, impressions from the observation of tiny details, colours, sounds, wind, rain, light. No doubt there is always a basis of reality, a comment on life, but to expect realism from Lorca instead of poetry is like looking for Turner's *Fighting Temeraire* among the pages of *Jane's Fighting Ships*.

Benavente's conversation pieces

Lorca's plays provided a sharp contrast with those of a slightly earlier generation which had been dominated by the prolific output of JACINTO BENAVENTE (1868–1954). It is perhaps fashionable to decry his work as being polite trivialities, but in fact he too achieved something of a revolution in the theatre and richly deserved the Nobel Prize for literature awarded him in 1922. When Benavente began writing for the stage, he was faced in 1894 by a problem similar to that confronting Bernard Shaw. Madrid audiences were accustomed to harrowing melodramas full of romantic absurdities. Benavente set about altering the public's tastes by writing a series of conversation pieces with only the slenderest thread of plot, but with well-defined characters and witty dialogue in which a subtle irony is always to be found. They were nearly all concerned with the follies of upper-class society in Madrid, for Benavente declared that he felt it unfair to satirise the poor and the hungry. At first sight his plays appear to be mere frivolous dialogues, but underneath the apparent superficiality was an accurate observation of life coupled with an ability to pose a problem which could make people think at the same time as amusing them. The tiny *entremés*, *De pequeñas causas* (1908), is an excellent example of these methods. A minister has resigned from office, defending his principles, and nothing his colleagues can say will make him change his mind. His wife, however, has specially ordered a new Paris gown in which to attend a state dinner in honour of a Persian prince. The minister's resignation is withdrawn and the audience is left guessing who was right, the high principled minister or his practical wife whose know-ledge of political affairs is derived from her dressmaker.

Los intereses creados (1907) is apparently modelled on different lines, being an imitation of the Italian *Commedia dell' Arte* which flourished in the seventeenth and eighteenth centuries. It is in essence a glorified Punch and Judy show with the set characters of the old Italian farce: Leandro and Silvia the lovers, Crispín the bold and witty servant, Arlequín representing the arts, the braggart captain, Polichinela the miserly rich man who is dominated by his wife, herself a social climber, the venal lawyer, the faded courtesan (Doña Sirena) and the gullible innkeeper. Though in his preface Benavente declares them all to be mere puppets, many, if not all, of the characters are sharply outlined. Crispín is bold, resourceful, unscrupulous, though loyal to Leandro. The latter is weak and incapable of fending for himself for the most part, but when the test comes, he scorns to win Silvia by false pretences and amply demonstrates the basic idealism of his nature. Silvia, though she has but a small part to play, shows that she is a sensible and indepen-dent girl in the twentieth-century mould. She politely rejects parental direction in the choice of a husband: *Yo haré siempre lo que mi padre ordene, si a mi madre no le contraría y a mí no me disgusta.* (I will always do what my father orders, providing it would not upset my mother and not be against my own wishes.) She has no hesitation in leaving home when her father acts in a high-handed manner and she readily agrees to meet Leandro, although social convention would regard such a meeting as compromising. Thus Benavente anticipates Lorca's plea for the emancipation of women by almost thirty years.

The main problem posed in the play is whether idealism can exist without materialism. Leandro would be lost without his Crispín. They are in fact one person, just as Don Quijote and Sancho Panza are in reality one. In this way Benavente returns to the theme which has always fascinated Spaniards, and this may account for the phenomenal success of the play. But it is not merely a Spanish theme; it is a universal problem. Almost all the follies of life are satirised in the play—the intoxication of success when Crispín cries: *Sigamos con la conquista del mundo* makes him sound like an embryonic Napoleon or Hitler. The folly of trying to arrange marriages of convenience is severely castigated and snobbery is held to ridicule in the person of Señora Polichinela. The boastful Captain and Arlequín are willing sponsors, but the Captain for all his arrogant bragging is not a man of action and Arlequín reveals all the pride and jealousy of an undistinguished author. The grasping Doctor of Law is quite ready to falsify the whole lawsuit by inserting or omitting a comma. Scarcely any aspect of life is left without comment—it is self-interest that makes the world go round, though Benavente makes an exception in the shape of ideal love.

Benavente's own favourite play was *Señora Ama* (1908) in which he moved away from Madrid society to a village setting. The heroine is an exceptional type of woman divorced from reality—it would be difficult to imagine anyone of so heroic and saintly a nature. Perhaps this was why both public and critics preferred another play with a rural setting, *La malquerida* (1913). Though here the attempt to reproduce rustic speech is unconvincing, the play is well constructed, with each act ending at a climax in preparation for the final crisis. The play is a study of the problem of the presence of a stepdaughter (the unbeloved) in a family. Acacia is the daughter of Raimunda by a previous marriage and when she herself is engaged to be married, her fiancé is mysteriously murdered. It turns out that this murder has been inspired by the stepfather, Estéban, who is in love with Acacia and cannot bear to see her leave the house. Surprisingly it transpires that Acacia returns his love to the justifiable annoyance of Raimunda who reveals Estéban's guilt in the murder. Estéban tries to flee with Acacia, but Raimunda prevents him whereupon he fatally wounds her. Acacia then transfers her allegiance to her mother who prepares to meet death consoled by the knowledge of her daughter's preference for her. Any brief summary of the plot of a play gives a dangerously false impression, but it must be confessed that *La malquerida* verges on melodrama, so packed is it with improbable incidents and unreal characters. Benavente was a versatile dramatist and had a strong romantic vein in him as can be seen in his fairytale plays such as *La princesa sin corazón*. No doubt he wished to edge away from the conversation piece drama which he himself had created and taught his audience to enjoy.

Benavente is frequently criticised for his sentimentality and for his predilection for happy endings in order to please the theatre-going public. He admitted that he courted the audience:

> An author has the whole work in which to say what he feels and what he thinks; later, in the conclusion, seeing that life does not conclude anything, why not please the public? If this public, with or without concessions, had not been favourable to me from the start of my dramatic career, could I have continued to present plays? (*De sobremesa*, vol. 2, p. 176).

This is a weakness on Benavente's part and it limited his scope as a dramatist. Another fault is his tendency, like Bernard Shaw, to preach at his audience. Perhaps Benavente lacks the vigour and pungency of Shaw's wit, and his preaching can become tedious. Nevertheless, he is a dramatist of considerable stature and many of the plays in his vast output of dramatic works deserve serious study and due consideration in literary history.

The theatre after the Civil War

The triumph of Franco and the right wing in 1939 had the effect in the theatre of stifling experimental plays such as Lorca had attempted to create and of continuing the methods of Benavente with conventional comedies aimed at pleasing the public without ruffling any susceptibilities. Whereas Benavente usually has a comment to make on life, many playwrights after the Civil War set out merely to provide an escape from the misery of life at that period. Even ALEJANDRO CASONA (1903–65), who fled from Spain in 1937 and subsequently settled in Buenos Aires, was affected by the desire to escape from the realities of life. Casona, whose real name is Alejandro Rodríguez Álvarez, came from Besullo, a small village in the Asturias and after studying at the University of Murcia became an inspector of elementary education. Starting with short plays for children to act, Casona was able to extend his dramatic work after the Republic had been established in 1931 when he was given the task of creating a *Teatro del Pueblo* designed enthusiastically to bring the glories of Spanish drama to the uneducated masses. This post gave Casona the chance to gain recognition in the professional theatre and his play, *Nuestra Natacha* (1936), was a popular success, running for 1,340 performances. It is a tendentious play which pleads for new educational methods. Natacha who has spent some years in a reformatory in her youth returns to devote herself to the task of instituting teaching reforms and the moulding of character by creative rather than repressive means. Her new approach is highly successful, but the freedom she allows the children shocks her conservative superiors and she is forced to resign.

Such a plea for new thinking was very much to the taste of the eager intellectual reformers of the Republic, but they were anathema to the military dictatorship and Casona left Spain in February 1937 and has never returned. Exile seems to have removed from him the practical ambitions of a reformer and he yearns for beauty, kindness, love and peace in a dream world of fantasy, and much of his work is heavily larded with sentiment. Many of his ideas are of brilliant originality as in *Prohibido suicidarse en primavera* (Mexico 1937), which presents the picture of a sanatorium founded by Dr Ariel for curing would-be suicides. The whole atmosphere of the sanatorium is conducive to gloom, despair and melancholy and every means of committing suicide is readily available. If it was mere human cussedness that prevented suicide occurring in such surroundings, the play might be both credible and highly amusing, but the author insists on the beauties of nature, literature, art, music and meditations as therapy for tortured souls. The result is that a promising situation degenerates into lachrymose heart-searching with smiles of renewed hope shyly peeping through the tears.

The same degeneration is apparent in Casona's best known play *Los árboles mueren de pie* (Buenos Aires 1949). The first act is intriguing in its surrealist development. A modern business office is the centre of an organisation which works secretly to aid those in mental distress, a novel idea since as the Director declares: *De los males del cuerpo ya hay muchos que se ocupan.* (There are already many who busy themselves with ills of the body.) The operators who carry out this policy of mental assistance work like spies, bearing no name but only a number and their methods are whimsical in the extreme; men disguised as clergymen, conjurors, beggars, huntsmen, Norwegian sailors, all play their part in boosting the morale of the melancholy. After a bouncing, frolicsome opening, the second and third acts are disappointingly conventional. The Director aided by a girl patient turned assistant attempts to sustain the illusions of an elderly lady whose beloved grandson has turned out a ne'er-do-well. Her husband has been obliged to turn this wastrel out of the house and the wayward grandson has emigrated to Canada. The husband has then resorted to the subterfuge of forged letters asking for forgiveness and sending news of miraculous rehabilitation and a happy marriage in Canada. For a while his methods succeed in drawing *La Abuela* from her melancholy and despair until at last a genuine cable arrives from Canada announcing the grandson's impending return. *La Abuela* is overjoyed and begins making enthusiastic preparations for providing everything that her grandson liked when he was young. Meanwhile her husband hears that the ship in which the prodigal grandson was sailing has sunk with all hands. He dare not tell his wife this news for fear of breaking her heart and he enlists the aid of the moral welfare organisation.

The Director, Mauricio, and his new assistant, Isabel, agree to impersonate the grandson and his fictitious wife. Thanks to their brilliant acting and careful briefing the meeting with *La Abuela* is a triumphant success. Unfortunately unexpected things begin to happen. Isabel, who has never had a home of her own, falls under the spell of the tranquility of life in *La Abuela's* house and Mauricio, the brilliant, energetic helper of souls, falls in love with his patient Isabel. The bombshell explodes when the real grandson arrives suddenly, having taken a ship other than the one he had announced.

Cuando se lleva una vida como la mía nunca se viaja en el barco que se anuncia: ni con el nombre propio. ¡La policía suele ser tan curiosa!

(When you lead a life like mine, you never travel in the ship you announce: nor under your own name. The police are apt to be too inquisitive!)

The real grandson callously demands a large sum of money since apparently he is being blackmailed by his criminal associates. *La Abuela's* eyes are opened at last, or more accurately perhaps she stops pretending for one moment and brusquely tells her grandson to be gone. She then returns to her game of make-believe and the play ends with *La Abuela* bidding goodbye to Mauricio and Isabel still as if they were members of the family and giving them a recipe for a sickly home-made liqueur.

On the whole this complex plot is well managed, though it stretches credibility to breaking point. The characters tend to be dull, conventional types with the exception of *La Abuela* who provides the main interest of the play. She is shrewd and observant and has acquired a

knowledge of Canada and architecture in order to follow the supposed
career of her grandson. She allows herself to be deceived by Mauricio
because she wants to be deceived. Her love for her grandson, her joy at
his return, her preparations for his homecoming are merely methods of
drawing attention to herself. She must play the role of the loving
grandmother even though she knows full well it is only a pretence.
The return of the genuine grandson is as big a nuisance to her as it is an
embarrassment to her would-be helpers because she wants to escape
from the realities of life. On the other hand Mauricio, who operates in
a world of fantasy and fondly imagines that he can control reality, is
brought back to the limitations of human endeavour when he finds that
he has fallen in love with his ex-patient Isabel.

The dialogue of the play contains a few striking lines such as: *En el
verdadero amor no manda nadie, obedecen los dos* (With true love nobody
gives orders, both obey). The title itself is highly original; *La Abuela*,
when she knows the truth about her grandson, compares herself to a
tree: *Muerta por dentro, pero de pie. Como un árbol* (Dead within, but
still standing. Like a tree). In general, however, the style drags and the
wit is pedestrian with such jokes as: '*Hoy el inglés se ha convertido en un
idioma tan importante que hasta los norteamericanos van a tener que aprenderlo*'.
(Today English has become such an important language that even the
Americans are going to have to learn it.) Moreover, the tone is of such
sickening sentimentality that any audience would be driven to revolt,
it would seem. *La Abuela* answers her ne'er-do-well grandson's demand
for money with the words:

> *Conozco la cifra: acabo de oírtela a ti mismo; doscientos mil pesos vale la vida de la
> abuela. No, Mauricio, no vale tanto. Por una lágrima te la hubiera dado entera. Pero ya es
> tarde para llorar.*

> (I know the sum: I have just heard it from your own lips: 200,000 pesos is what
> Granny's life is worth. No, Mauricio, it is not worth that much. For a single tear I
> would have given it all to you.)

Nevertheless, audiences in many parts of the world greedily imbibe
this bittersweet concoction. The play ran for two years in Buenos Aires,
seven months in Rio de Janeiro, three months in Lisbon. As well as
scoring successes in Rome, Venice, Finland and Israel, it was received
with great acclaim in Germany where Else Heims came out of retirement to play the part of *La Abuela* and where critics in Stuttgart
eagerly greeted it as an antidote to existentialism. In Spain the play is
less well known either because Casona as an exile is still taboo or else
because as a race Spaniards do not incline to sentiment.

Nevertheless, Casona exerted considerable influence on contemporary dramatists. LÓPEZ RUBIO employs a similar mixture of fantasy and reality, cloaking serious problems with sophisticated wit, as in *La venda en los ojos* (1954), and ending the play on a note of restrained sadness— *realidad que no duele* (reality that does not hurt) as the dramatic critic Torrente Ballester expressed it. An even more marked resemblance to Casona is noticeable in the early comedies of RUIZ IRIARTE, especially in *El puente de los suicidas* (1944), but the atmosphere is more emphatically escapist and his *Tres comedias optimistas* frankly pander to the public's taste for happy endings. In the prologue he declares: *Lo que pide la sensibilidad del espectador inconscientemente, subconscientemente, es algo muy difícil de otorgarle: un poco de felicidad* (What the susceptibility of the audience requires unconsciously, subconsciously, is something very difficult to grant: a little happiness). Not for nothing have cynical critics dubbed the works of all three playwrights *el teatro de evasión*.

A similar sentimental flippancy is apparent in the plays of EDGAR NEVILLE (1899–1967) who flirts with serious problems in a gay and witty fashion. *El baile* (1952) had enormous success both in Spain and abroad. It contains only four characters and chronicles three stages in their lives from 1900 onwards; there seems little in the play but bright banter and gentle melancholy.

A more serious vein is to be found in the works of JOAQUÍN CALVO SOTELO (b. 1905). Trained as a lawyer, like so many intellectual Spaniards, he entered the government service in 1926 but fled to Chile in 1937 after his brother José, leader of the right wing opposition in the *Cortes*, had been shot by the police. Calvo Sotelo has travelled widely and there is more of an international flavour about his work than with most Spanish dramatists, as for example in *Criminal de guerra* (1951), which describes the dilemma of an American soldier in Germany torn between the dictates of military duty and loyalty to his German relatives. Perhaps he concentrates too much on problems of the present day so that in fifty years' time his plays may well appear out of date, but he is skilled in presenting controversial subjects and allowing his characters to discuss every aspect of them.

One of the most successful of his plays has been *La muralla* (1954), which ran for more than 5,000 performances in Spain and has been translated into English, French, German, Italian and Portuguese. The secret of its success lies probably in its highly credible plot and the rapidity with which the action develops. Jorge, a wealthy and respected

member of Madrid society, has had a heart attack. With the fear of
death upon him he reveals how he acquired the estate in Extremadura
which brings in all his wealth. During the Civil War in Badajoz he
connived at altering his godfather's will so that the estate was left to
him instead of his godfather's natural son Gervasio Quiroga. Now
Jorge wants to restore the property to its rightful owner (who is just
finishing a prison sentence for smuggling) in spite of the fact that this
restitution will leave Jorge's family in poverty. The reactions of his
family and friends form the main interest of the play. His wife, Cecilia,
at first agrees, but she is soon won over by the arguments of her
worldly and practical mother, Matilde, who, despite being a member
of a Committee for Moral Improvement, is determined not to allow
scruples of conscience to deprive her daughter of her fortune. Jorge's
daughter, Amalia, is engaged to the son of an up-and-coming politician,
Javier, who prudently sends his son to England when he finds that
Jorge is determined to give away his estate. Jorge's friend and secretary,
Alejandro, pays a special visit to Badajoz and destroys the last remaining
scrap of evidence of the forging of the will so resolute is he that Jorge
shall not ruin himself. All conspire against him, even Romualdo,
Jorge's old and trusted servant. Only a Galician priest (Calvo Sotelo was
born in La Coruña), a complete stranger, categorically declares that
restitution must be made. Jorge realises what a terrifying barrier (*una
muralla tremenda*) is being built up around him to prevent him from
doing his duty. He has summoned Quiroga from Badajoz, but his
family and friends prevent him from seeing the real heir; Jorge suffers a
second heart attack and dies calling on God to witness that he had tried
to surmount the barrier.

Such a situation appears very real in postwar conditions. It is easy to
imagine a young officer stooping to forgery to acquire an estate in time
of war when moral attitudes are lax and things are confused. It is easy
to understand that a man with such a load on his conscience would be
greatly perturbed when faced with the possibility of death. While the
audience will readily agree where his duty lies, they will also sympathise
with his family, who will be the innocent victims of a past crime in
which they had no part. It is a genuine dilemma which any member of
the audience can quickly appreciate. The weakness of the play is that
there is no hero, no character to admire, unless it be the Galician priest
who makes only a fleeting appearance. But he is a disinterested party and
it is comparatively easy for him to be high-minded. Even he, we learn,
is in Madrid to pull strings in government departments to hasten the

Stage setting for La Escelera by Buero Vallejo

completion of waterworks in Galicia so that some of his male parishioners can return to their homes in the village, where he can compel
their attendance at church. No one appears completely honest.

Jorge himself is not an attractive character. His sole motive for
restitution is his fear of the life hereafter: *Yo defenderé el más sagrado de
todos: mi derecho a salvarme* (I will defend the most sacred of all rights:
the right to save my soul). The audience cannot resist a sneaking
sympathy for his hypocritical, grasping, but energetic mother-in-law
who tells Jorge bluntly: *Tú lo que tienes es un miedo vulgar a los infiernos*
(The trouble with you is that you have a vulgar fear of hell). Though
much of the dialogue of the play is as apt and forceful as the line just
quoted, there is a tendency towards melodramatic expression, especially
as the climax is reached and a stage direction proclaims: *El dolor le
clava su diente infernal con redoblada fuerza* (Pain digs in its hellish tooth
with redoubled force). Despite this slightly contrived ending the
interest of the play is sustained to the last and the audience can disperse
still pondering what they would have done in similar circumstances.

Attempts have been made to wean the Spanish theatre-going public
from its taste for plays with a middle-class background and possibly the
most notable achievements in this direction have been made by
ANTONIO BUERO VALLEJO (b. 1916), who has tried to fuse realism with
symbolism as well as to introduce themes of permanent, universal

interest. His first play was *Historia de una escalera* (1949), in which the
action takes place on the staircase of a Madrid working-class tenement.
The characters' lives are studied over a period of thirty years and youthful hopes are seen transformed into the disillusion of old age. The
staircase itself stands as a symbol of the limitations of time and space
imposed on human beings who cannot break loose however hard they
try.

On similar lines is an even more successful play by Vallejo, *Hoy es
fiesta* (1956), in which the scene this time is set on the *azotea* (terrace roof)
of a Madrid apartment house. Most of the tenants are buoyed up by
hopes of winning money in a lottery draw and thereby bringing some
colour into their drab lives. Silverio, on the other hand, is absorbed by
the hope of obtaining forgiveness from his wife, Pilar, for a wrong
done to her many years before. Hope is the central theme of the play,
but hope is frustrated because Pilar dies before Silverio can make his
confession and receive her forgiveness. As the author expresses it:

> '*Hoy es fiesta*' intenta ser una tragedia acerca de la esperanza. O dicho de otro modo, una
> obra que procura esbozar el carácter tragico de la esperanza.

> (*Hoy es fiesta* sets out to be a tragedy about hope. Or in other words, a work which
> strives to outline the tragic character of hope.)

As a play it lacks form to a certain extent, resembling a series of sketches
or interludes which seem to bear little relation to one another. Only in
the third act is there any unity, when the hopes of material gain fuse
with the hope of spiritual comfort and end equally in forlorn disappointment.

The modern novel

The theatre in Spain since the Civil War has no doubt been handicapped
by the repressive censorship of the regime. Discussion of social questions
has been severely limited and tends to degenerate into frivolous
badinage about trifles. The novel has been similarly affected; there is
so much that cannot be said. Nevertheless, Spain had produced recently
several novelists of high promise and achievement. The first to burst
on the depressing scene after the Civil War was CAMILO JOSÉ CELA Y
TRULOCK (his mother was of English extraction). Born in 1916 Cela's
first novel was published in 1942 and created a sensation. *La familia de
Pascual Duarte* was not an account of brave deeds accomplished against

the Reds, but a plain, earthy, violent tale told in the first person in the picaresque tradition. It is the story of a peasant from Extremadura who is in prison condemned to death for a series of horrifying murders. Pascual Duarte is an ignorant, naïve person, who lives among poverty, superstition and cruelty and who is forced to live apart from people because he is incapable of making friendships; his only point of contact with other human beings is an overwhelming desire to destroy, which he can never restrain in spite of periods of remorse and repentance. The whole sordid story is told in pungent, straightforward prose describing impassively acts of horrific violence. The thesis of the novel, which however appears mainly descriptive, is that poverty, ignorance and superstition breed violence, cruelty and crime. Such was the influence of *La familia de Pascual Duarte* in Spain that it initiated a new school of novelists who labelled their movement *tremendismo* (gruesomeness) to rival the French existentialists. It was an ephemeral outburst condemned by Cela who contemptuously described its exponents as *novelistas de receta* (formula novelists).

Still in the picaresque tradition was Cela's next great success, this time a travel book, *Viaje a la Alcarria* (1948), which attempts to be entirely detached and subjective. It describes a journey undertaken by the author in the summer of 1947 tramping over the high, dry and dusty plateau of the Alcarria, a district some forty miles north-east of Madrid whose life has scarcely been touched by modernisation. To preserve complete detachment Cela dispenses with the first person and uses the somewhat tedious expression *El viajero* throughout. To a certain extent he succeeds and *Viaje a la Alcarria* reads more like a novel than a conventional travel book, but personal opinions cannot be excluded entirely and increasingly towards the end of the book the author obtrudes in the narrative with such phrases as: *El viajero piensa . . . el viajero cree . . .* Perhaps Cela would have done better to have invented a fictitious character with a name for his traveller.

The value of the book lies in the series of vivid descriptions like brilliant colour photographs which depict life as it is without glamourising it, but nonetheless extracting a hint of warmth and poetry from it. Cela's powers of observation are acute and his ability to select significant detail is uncanny. The description of his walk to the station in Madrid in the early morning at the start of his journey evokes all the squalor of a capital city when well-to-do, respectable citizens are asleep—the homeless beggars sleeping on the stone steps under the arches of the Post Office, the ragged boy poking a stick into the heaps of garbage, the dirty, scraggy, shorn sheep being driven to the slaughter-house, pathetically, pointlessly licking the asphalt of the roadway. The rest of the journey stands out with equal clarity; the reader really feels that he is tramping the dusty roads, stretching out for a sleep after lunch in the shade of an olive tree with thousands of insects buzzing all round him, or talking to muleteers, carters, *Guardias Civiles*, *alcaldes*, innkeepers, cripples, or jolting in a rickety overcrowded bus with three women passengers being sick, or looking over the relics of magnificent palaces of the sixteenth century, monasteries, churches, now dusty and decayed *como un bailarín rendido* (like a dancer exhausted). The whole of Spain, it seems, is contained in this small area, battered, dilapidated, often cruel, but dignified, resourceful, courageous.

In such a book, as in *Don Quijote* or *Lazarillo de Tormes*, there is a danger of repetition; one place is much like another and a traveller's reactions and observations tend to be similar. This weakness is noticeable especially towards the end of the *Viaje a la Alcarria*, but it is amply

Illustration from Viaje a la Alcarria. *Pastrana: Palacio de los Duques*

atoned for in the brilliance of the descriptive writing, which is in an easy, colloquial, but elegant style; it convinces by its simplicity and economy. *Comme il insiste peu*! said Sainte-Beuve of Stendhal and the same praise might be bestowed on Cela. The only embellishments of the book are short verses (not inserted until the 1954 edition) in traditional metres very much in the manner of Lorca. Some readers have found these verses irritating interruptions to the narrative, but in general they appear like whimsical pen and ink drawings which emphasise and enhance written descriptions as for instance when *El viajero* in Brihuega meets an old man, obviously poverty-stricken, but certainly not a beggar:

> *Un hidalgo derrotado*
> *se muere buscando pan.*
>
> *Tiene los ojos azules,*
> *muy antiguo el ademán,*
>
> *y camina los caminos*
> *con aire de capitán.*
>
> *Mira como una paloma,*
> *también como el gavilán,*
>
> *y es dulce con quienes piden*
> *y altivo con quienes dan.*
>
> *Por el cielo, un avefría*
> *se escapa del alcotán.*

> (A gentleman, down and out, is dying seeking bread. He has blue eyes and an old-fashioned manner, and he tramps the roads with the air of a Captain. His glance can be like a dove's as well as like a sparrowhawk's, and he is gentle with those who ask and haughty with those who give. Up in the sky, a lapwing escapes from the falcon!)

Cela's other most important literary work is the novel, *La colmena* (The Beehive), which was published abroad in 1951 because its stark reality made it dangerous to print in Spain. The idea is an original one; the scene opens in a low-class café and subsequently three days in the lives of each of the customers and staff are carefully detailed, tracing how they interact with one another or disappear from view, as the case may be. Cela described *La colmena* as *una novela reloj ... hecha de múltiples ruedas y piececitas que se precisan las unas con las otras para que aquello marche* (a novel like a watch ... made out of any amount of wheels and small pieces which fit one another so that the whole thing works). In Cela's view undoubtedly the mainspring of this watch is the sexual urge. No one can escape the influence of sex; it rules their lives. But *La colmena* is not a novel with a thesis; it sets out to portray reality and in this it is highly successful. It is left to the reader to draw what conclusions he chooses; the author scarcely gives a hint of his own opinions.

A highly individualistic writer whose novels reveal subtle psychological insight is MIGUEL DELIBES (b. 1920). As a professor of the *Historia de la cultura* in his native town of Valladolid, he has perhaps more time for contemplation and is less involved in feverish literary activities than writers who live in Madrid. There is a repose and a leisureliness in his novels uncommon in a restless age, moreover he normally concentrates his attention on a single character so that the psychological study is less diffuse than in a work like *La colmena*. His first novel, *La sombra del ciprés es alargada* (1947), shows a solemn attention to detail typical of the careful work of a university don. As a result the reader tends to feel that the author is working too hard and that the psychology and symbolism are a trifle self-conscious. The story is told by an orphan, Pedro, who is brought up by a tutor in a house in Ávila where all is gloom and pessimism. His tutor's philosophy appears to be that it is best not to have loved at all and therefore not to have lost. All ties of affection, indeed all ownership, inevitably involve the risk or certainty of loss; therefore it is advisable to have no affection, no possessions. Pedro's only friend and fellow pupil dies and the boy is convinced of the truth of his tutor's philosophy. Obsessed by the idea of death, Pedro determines to have no roots and no ties and enters the merchant navy hoping that this career will keep him apart from mankind and the anguish of broken affection (*el desasimiento*). Symbolism is offered wholesale to the reader. The cypress casts a long, dark shadow while the pine is open, rounded, sunny and sweet-smelling; some men are dark, sombre, pessimistic while others are open, gay and comfortable. Again, a ship in a bottle catches Pedro's eye and reminds him of the fact that his soul is imprisoned in the narrow confines of his body. What saves this ponderous book from tedium is the fluency and elegance of the style which conceal the stodginess of the subject matter.

Delibes continues his study of boyhood and of a single character in *El camino* (1950), which has won success not only in Spain, but in France, England, Germany, and the United States. The scene is laid, as in a novel by Pereda, in La Montaña, the hilly district south of Santander, a countryside which somewhat resembles Wales. Daniel, like many a Welsh boy, does not want to leave his native valley, but

Illustration from Viaje a la Alcarria. *The village of Cifuentes*

his father has ambitions to make him more than a village cheesemaker and intends to send him away to boarding school. Daniel is unhappy to be leaving his home, his friends and the valley, his mother is miserable at the thought of Daniel's absence, his father is annoyed that Daniel appears so ungrateful for the wonderful opportunity he is being offered at great expense to his parents. The obvious inference is: why follow a plan that makes everyone unhappy? Have parents the right to map out children's lives against their wishes?

The story is told in a series of episodes which move backwards and forwards in space and time as the eleven-year-old Daniel lies awake, thinking, on his last night before leaving home. Such a method of narration might result in confusion, but in fact the episodes are skilfully handled and present a delightful variety of incidents, pathetic or humorous—some even grotesque and verging on caricature. The evident danger of a book of childhood adventures is sentiment and nostalgia and *El camino* does not altogether escape this danger, but the setting and the characters are so real and so clearly defined that the occasional tinge of sentiment does not obtrude. Though the title, *El camino*, is symbolical of life's road ahead for Daniel as planned by his father, the reader is not sated with symbolism as in *La sombra del ciprés;* the events

Illustrations from El Camino

Molledo: Image of
Nuestra Señora del Camino

Donkeys tethered near the village letterbox at Molledo

and the characters pass their message without comment from the author and the reader is at liberty to extract as much or as little food for thought as he pleases.

Delibes has again explored the father and son relationship in *Mi idolatrado hijo Sisí* (1953). Cecilio Rubes is a prosperous businessman in a large provincial town where he is a merchant in *materiales higiénicos*. As a person he is selfish, vain, pompous and stupid, inordinately proud of his invention of a specially shaped bath for the stouter figure. His only son, whom naturally he names after himself, is spoilt, pampered and cosseted, while his wife, Adela, is constantly rebuked and humiliated. Father and son always band together against the mother and bully her ceaselessly. When the Civil War breaks out, young Cecilio is found a safe job by his father well behind the lines, but nonetheless being away from his father gives the lad a chance of making a man of himself. Just as he is beginning to develop, he is killed in an air raid and at the news of this tragedy his father collapses completely into a pathetic, empty husk of a man with only the special bath (which nobody has bought) as a symbol of his useless life. The novel achieves a high degree of reality with its sharply outlined characters. Though it is slow-moving, with long descriptive passages, it is never dull, since Delibes skilfully contrives to describe Cecilio both from inside and outside, to show what the world looks like to him and also what he looks like to the world.

The individual element in Delibes's work is even more strongly evident in *Diario de un cazador* (1955), which is the personal narrative of a porter (*bedel*) in a secondary school who has a passion for shooting game. He is a quarrelsome grumbler with no purpose in life except when he is on the moor with his dogs in pursuit of hares, quail and partridges. It is a highly suggestive story of a life unfulfilled and is told in the episodic, laconic style of *El camino* with little description and no philosophising.

La hoja roja (1959) is by contrast a study in two lives thrown together by chance. *El viejo Eloy* is an elderly widower who lives alone in a small apartment looked after by *La Desi*, an ugly, ignorant village girl who has come to town to find work. Eloy recalls constantly in the vague repetitive way of old age his memories of married life in the town and his work in the council sanitation department while *La Desi* remembers her childhood in the country. Both characters seem to sense that life holds no hope for them in the future. Again the father and son relationship enters the narrative for Eloy goes to visit his successful son and his daughter-in-law in Madrid and is treated by them with monstrous inhumanity.

Delibes has the quality of observing universal characteristics whereas Cela can be said to more of a *costumbrista* intent only on painting the Spanish scene. Delibes can be compared more with Balzac, who burrowed deep into the human heart in presenting *La comédie humaine* and not merely *La comédie française*. It is true that all Delibes's works are concerned with detailed descriptions of Spanish life, especially *Las ratas* (1962) which deals with the struggle for existence in the harsh climate of central Castile. *El nini* is the child of an incestuous marriage and is strangely imbued with wisdom and knowledge of country life beyond his years. He lives in a cave with *El tío Ratero* and a dog; all three go out to catch huge water rats which they sell as food to the villagers. The provincial governor decides to turn them out of their cave and acting through the village *alcalde* serves an eviction order on them. The people of the village live like animals under constant threat from without, from officious governors, grasping landlords, wind and snow in winter, burning sun in summer. Whether or not Delibes intended the implication, the novel seems a powerful plea for human beings not making a hard life harder for one another.

Delibes is much taken up with technical devices in novel writing; symbolism is one which occurs in almost all his books, repetition of a refrain is another used to underline the fading memory of *El Eloy*, the dating of episodes by newspaper cuttings in *Mi idolatrado hijo Sisí*, the division of the villagers' year in *Las ratas* according to the festivals of outlandish saints—*El tiempo continuaba áspero por Santa María Cleofé* (the weather continued bitter over St Mary Cleophas' Day). Once the reader becomes aware of these devices he is apt to feel annoyed rather as one becomes irritated or amused when an orator's mannerisms suddenly obtrude. But Delibes is a skilled craftsman with a deep knowledge of human nature and a splendid ability for descriptive writing. The indications are that Delibes will find a place among Spain's greatest novelists.

The remarkable exuberance of literature in Spain since 1898 has continued despite political and material disasters and is by no means ended. It is especially noteworthy that during more than a quarter of a century of dictatorship literary activity has not been suppressed or dimmed, despite a rigid censorship. Probably the answer lies in the enormous driving force of Spanish individuality which cannot altogether be silenced, though it is true that the denial of free expression is a serious handicap for writers with a comment to make on life. A certain tense reticence can certainly be noticed in the novels of Cela or Delibes and in the plays of Calvo Sotelo, but the impetus of literary tradition has played a great part in keeping Spanish literature alert and alive. It withered in the eighteenth century because writers sought inspiration from abroad. In the twentieth century writers have constantly had in mind the traditional focus of Spanish culture, not only of the Golden Age, but also of the Middle Ages too. In helping to foster this reverence for native culture no man has had greater influence than DON RAMÓN MENÉNDEZ PIDAL (b. 1869), a medieval scholar of distinction and an enlightened director of the *Real Academia*.

Part 3
Arts, architecture and music

Chapter 11
Architecture

It has been said that 'Spanish art is alluvial', meaning that each flood of invasion or entry of foreign influence has left its overlay. The successive floods have been numerous—the Greek and Phoenician traders, the Romans, the Visigoths, the Moors, the medieval French monastic orders, the Germans and Flemings in the fifteenth century, the French Bourbons in the eighteenth century and finally the northern tourists in the 1960s. All these waves of foreign influence have left their mark on Spanish architecture, and to trace its development is a matter of the utmost complexity. The successive overlays make it impossible for the ordinary visitor successfully to sort his impressions into neat architectural categories, but at least he can comfort himself that nowhere else in Europe, perhaps in the world, can he see such a variety of trends and styles.

Roman architecture

Remains of pre-Roman buildings survive in many parts of Spain, but mostly in places remote from tourist routes. One easily accessible town, Tarragona (sixty miles south-west of Barcelona) bears traces of walls of gigantic size where remnants of doorways seem large enough for giraffes. These walls built probably at the time of the Greek settlements in Spain (c. 600 B.C.) lie beneath part of the extensive Roman fortifications which stretched for some forty-two miles round the city when it was at the height of its importance in the Augustan era (c. 28 B.C.). The many fine Roman buildings in the city were later used as stone quarries and half the present buildings in the older part of Tarragona

LEFT   *The Roman Bridge at Alcántara*

can boast stones cut by masons in Roman times and many of these bear
Latin inscriptions.

The best Roman remains in Spain exist in a place where the ravages
of war were less often experienced. Mérida in south-west Spain was
the Roman city of Augusta Emerita and capital of Lusitania, rated as
the ninth city of the Empire, of greater importance than Athens.
Though conquered by the Moors in 713 and recaptured by the Christians in 1228, its Roman buildings escaped wholesale devastation. The
bridge over the Guadiana, 866 yards long and built about 95 B.C.,
survives almost intact and the theatre and amphitheatre still demonstrate
their beauty and the skill of their designers and builders. Another
Roman bridge, farther north in the province of Cáceres on the Portuguese border, must have aroused the admiration of the Moors who gave
it the name of Alcántara (Arabic simply for 'the bridge') and left it to
continue its useful work for future generations. It is one of the earliest
monuments on which the architect, Julius Lacer, has left his name and
the date of construction (105 A.D.) inscribed proudly on the structure:
Pontem perpetui mansurum in saecula munda fecit divina nobilis arte Lacer.
He had every reason to be proud because his superbly proportioned
bridge, with much of its original pavement intact, is still in use, towering 130 feet above the Tagus with the two central of its six arches each
having a span of some 100 feet. The Moors damaged it in 1214 and in
1809 General Mayne destroyed one of the arches, which remained
broken until 1860. Despite clumsy restoration then and previously, the
bridge remains, as Lacer claimed, a permanent memorial to the architectural genius of the Romans.

The arrival of the Visigoths in Spain about 415 did not mean an
invasion by complete barbarians, for they had sampled civilisation in
various parts of Europe and the Middle East. Their artistic ability is
proved by the jewels of the votive crowns found in 1858 in a secret
store at Guarrazar near Toledo and showing unmistakable influence of
Persian design. Remains of Visigothic buildings are mostly confined to
small fragments such as those in the church of San Cristo de la Luz in
Toledo, but there are in isolated parts of Spain, particularly in the north
where the Visigoths had found refuge from the Moorish invaders, a
few churches for which Visigothic origin is claimed. Mostly they are
plain and stark with a little ornamentation in debased Roman style.
Often Roman capitals and columns have been filched from nearby
ruins, but one curious feature of these churches is the existence of the
horseshoe arch of the round type in which the arch often forms almost

three-quarters of a circle. Some of these may be seen in the church of San Juan de Baños near Palencia; completely restored in recent times, it is believed to date from the middle of the seventh century and contains, so it is claimed, the dedication inscribed by the Visigothic King Recceswinth. The church was built before the Arab invasion and therefore the horseshoe arch was not an imitation of Moorish architecture. Some historians claim that the Visigoths in Spain invented this particular form, but this is most unlikely and influence from Persia or possibly from India must be presumed.

The Moors as builders

By the time of their invasion of Spain in 711 the Moors had achieved little in the way of building and had evolved no definite architectural style. In their conquests they made use of local builders and pillaged Roman ruins for their materials. This they did when building the great Mosque at Córdoba (begun in 786) for almost all the six hundred or more columns have been stolen from previous buildings, with the result that often the capitals do not fit or have been made to do so by clumsy modifications. It is above the columns that the true Moorish style is demonstrated in the horseshoe arches of alternating red and white stones and in the splendid *mihrab* or niche indicating the direction of Mecca. This consists of a profusely decorated octagonal chamber with a roof of a single block of marble thirteen feet in diameter carved in the shape of a shell. In spite of the manifold alterations made to convert the mosque into a cathedral, and the sixteenth-century insertion of a Gothic choir, the mosque at Córdoba is one of the most interesting relics of the splendour of Arab civilisation in Spain.

Moorish architecture spread its influence far and wide over the peninsula, for the *Mozárabes* (Christians living under Moorish rule) learnt the methods of their masters and by the ninth century many of them had moved to the north where the Christians were then rallying strongly. Their capital had been Oviedo where five churches built about this period still survive in part. Perhaps the most interesting of these is San Miguel de Lillo on the Monte Naranco overlooking the city. It is completely vaulted in stone, perhaps as a precaution against Norman pirates who found timber-roofed churches easy to destroy. Like the other churches of this period in the neighbourhood the arches are round and not horseshoe in shape, but much Byzantine ivory work reveals undoubted influence from the Middle East, probably as a

ABOVE *The Roman Theatre, Mérida*

BELOW *The Mosque at Córdoba*

result of travellers along the Mediterranean route. Another church at Naranco, Santa María, has a Mozarabic altar dating from about 850 when the *Mozárabes* were becoming increasingly active in the north. For the next two hundred years their style dominated ecclesiastical architecture. The dozen or more surviving Mozarabic churches are mostly in inaccessible places in northern Spain where the tide of wars over the centuries least affected them. The chief feature of their style is the use of the horseshoe arch (which must this time have been imitated from the Moors), projecting eaves carried on stone brackets and often domes fluted in a curious pattern as in the monastery of San Miguel de Escalada between León and Palencia, founded by monks from Córdoba in 913. Features of the previous Christian architectural designs, such as barrel vaulting, pierced stone slab windows known as *ajimez* and stone screens, were also incorporated in Mozarabic churches. An example of one of these, as well as some Romanesque capitals on the columns, is also to be seen in San Miguel de Escalada. These capitals foreshadow the next phase in Spanish architecture, when influence from south France caused considerable imitation of characteristics of Roman buildings.

The greatest of Romanesque buildings in Spain is possibly the cathedral at Santiago de Compostela (begun in 1078), though the Baroque additions and alterations in the seventeenth and eighteenth centuries mask its main features. The general plan is so similar to the cathedral of Saint Sernin in Toulouse that it must be presumed that the architect was a Frenchman. The interior at least is still plainly Romanesque with its round arches and lofty vaulted ceiling made to look even higher in the gloom caused by the lack of a clerestory, which is normal in Spanish cathedrals since the strong sunlight is usually kept at bay. The splendid Pórtico de la Gloria at the west end of the cathedral was added by the architect MESTER MATEO (identified as a Frenchman, Mathieu) in 1188 and, though there are later embellishments, displays a fine range of medieval statuary in which the Spanish liking for coloured figures is already becoming apparent. A cast of this portico is in the Victoria and Albert Museum in London.

The cathedral at Ávila is partly Romanesque, as are the city walls of which the cathedral apse forms an integral part. The fortifications date in the main from this period, though much use was made of earlier material and there is an unmistakably Moorish look about the pointed stones that form the crenellations. Moorish architecture had been developing simultaneously with Christian architecture, and of the many

Moorish buildings of this period to survive, the Giralda tower (1184–96) of Seville cathedral is the best example. Built of brick with walls eight feet thick, it is lit by a series of windows with graceful arches whose capitals are richly decorated with brick arabesque patterns called *ajaracas*. The ascent of the tower is up a gentle slope wide enough for two horsemen to ride abreast and no visitor need fear anything worse than weariness if he chooses to climb the twenty-eight landings to the platform where the Moorish work ends and the steeple of 1568 completes the tower.

Contemporary with the Giralda tower is the Alcázar in Seville (*al-kasr* is the Arabic for citadel). The Caliph at Córdoba had by the eleventh century lost his hold over Moorish Spain and the chieftains at Seville declared their independence. They embellished their fortress palace with columns and other materials brought from Az-Zahara near Córdoba and still to be seen in the Dormitorio de los Reyes Moros. After the capture of Seville from the Moors in 1248 the Alcázar became the palace of the Christian kings and was further embellished, especially by Pedro I *el Cruel* (between the years 1364 and 1379 approximately). The work was done by Moorish craftsmen living under Christian rule, known as *Mudéjares*, the counterpart of the *Mozárabes*. Later additions, and particularly the clumsy restorations in the nineteenth century, have made the Alcázar look debased in comparison with the Alhambra at Granada.

The Alhambra (Arabic *al-hambra*, the red, a name whose significance is at once apparent to the visitor) dates in the main from the thirteenth and fourteenth centuries, because Granada did not really assume importance as a Moorish centre until after the recapture of Córdoba in 1236. The lightness and delicacy of the design of the courtyards is remarkable in comparison with massive Christian buildings of the same period. In fact the fragility of its construction makes one marvel that so much of the palace has survived, especially in view of the long period of neglect between 1700 and 1830. As in the Alcázar at Seville there is a profusion of decoration in stalactite form; these 'stalactites' were originally used as structural features to balance the complex thrusts of a dome, but later they became mere decorations. In the Alhambra they form ornamentation of the lightest and gayest type that perfectly matches the slender pillars of the halls and courtyards. The palace in its magnificent situation on the hill dominating the city and with a distant view of the snows of the Sierra Nevada is one of the wonders of the world.

Walls of Ávila

The Gothic cathedrals

The reconquest of large tracts of territory from the Moors gave a
powerful impetus to ecclesiastical building in the thirteenth century.
The influence of the Cistercian monks who replaced the Cluniacs as the
dominating monastic order brought to Spain the Gothic style of the
northern French cathedrals and the pointed arch was generally substituted for the rounded Romanesque arches. The three great Spanish
cathedrals of this period are those at Burgos, Toledo and León, begun
in 1221, 1227 and ?1240 respectively. Toledo cathedral is second in size
only to that of Seville, being some 371 feet long, 187 feet wide and with
vaulting 100 feet above the floor level. Only the great height impresses
the visitor at first because the Spanish habit of placing the choir in the
nave surrounded by massive screens and Cyclopean brass grills, not to
mention the clutter of florid *bric-á-brac* collected over the centuries,
masks the vastness of the interior and hides the plain, austere arches and
columns of the French Gothic style as practised by the Cistercians. León
cathedral is on a smaller scale, though almost equal in height, and it has
much more lightness of design than the stalwart pillars of Toledo.
Indeed the design was too light to be durable and the building had to be
completely restored in the late nineteenth century, but the exterior,
apart from the fifteenth-century tower at the south-west end, presents
much the same appearance as its original form and closely resembles the
cathedrals at Amiens and Rheims. By contrast Burgos has been totally
transformed externally by the addition of the western towers of rich
design by HANS OF COLOGNE (1442–58) and the octagonal lantern tower

(1567), which give the cathedral a somewhat toothy or tattered appearance. The interior suffers from the usual florid Spanish ornamentation aggravated by Renaissance decorations in stone on the columns and arches, and it is difficult to detect underneath all these trappings the sturdy design of a French three-aisled cathedral. Much more appealing to the eye is the uncluttered stonework of the nearby Cistercian convent of Las Huelgas of similar date.

The fourteenth century saw a great upsurge in the power and prosperity of Aragon, which included Catalonia. A series of fine cathedrals at Barcelona, Gerona, Pamplona (in Navarre) and Palma (in Majorca) reveal a style that is subtly different. Some of the architects were foreign, but a Spaniard from the Balearic Islands, JAIME FABRE, did much

The Alcázar, Seville. The Hall of the Ambassadors

to develop the Catalan style, which is characterised by exceptionally wide naves with vaulted stone roofs since the aim was to produce large churches for congregational use. The width of the nave at Gerona is 73 feet, about twice that of Westminster Abbey, and the wide vault above is carried at a height of 111 feet, loftier in fact than at Toledo.

The geometrical vaulting in the Catalan cathedrals is somewhat akin to the style of German churches, and in fact long before the accession of the Habsburgs to the Spanish throne groups of German and Flemish architects settled in Spain—Hans of Cologne who worked at Burgos and the whole family of architects and sculptors from Brussels, the Van den Eykens, known in Spain as the EGAS; they were closely associated with Toledo. Another Fleming, JUAN GUAS, was the chief architect of the fine late Gothic church in Toledo, San Juan de los Reyes, begun in 1476 by the Catholic monarchs after their victory over the Portuguese and originally intended to house their own tombs. The style is florid but well proportioned, and the cloister is one of the most visually harmonious buildings in Spain. The church is decorated with the device of Fernando and Isabel, a Gordian knot to denote the unity of Spain and a sheaf of arrows symbolising the crusade against the Moors, insignia which are to be found on a host of buildings of this period throughout Spain. What is so confusing is that at this very moment of the triumphant campaign against the infidels, Christian churches, including San Juan de los Reyes, display a profusion of Moorish decoration. It is this intermingling of styles in Spanish architecture that positively obstructs classification, but at the same time gives a really Spanish flavour to buildings inspired by foreign models or designed by alien architects. The great cathedral at Seville typifies this strange but harmonious mixture. Begun in 1402 and not completed until about a century later, it incorporates Moorish elements in the Giralda tower, the Puerta del Perdón and the Patio de los Naranjos, but in other respects is similar in plan to Milan cathedral which rivals it in size.

With the coming of Italian influence in the late fifteenth and early sixteenth centuries Spanish architecture, complex at best, enters its most baffling phase. The Gothic style still held the field to a large extent, but the Renaissance forms from Italy, often by way of France, became increasingly prominent, as for instance in Carlos V's unfinished palace at Granada for which he pulled down a section of the Alhambra. Although it seems like a grey carbuncle among the Moorish buildings, it typifies the Renaissance revival of interest in Roman architecture; it was one of the earliest such buildings in Spain, begun in 1526 under the

The Transparente, Toledo Cathedral

ABOVE   *The Escorial*

BELOW   *The Post Office, Madrid*

direction of PEDRO MACHUCA who had studied in Rome. The cathedrals at Granada (1520), Jaén (1532), Málaga (1538) all reveal Renaissance influence, which is in the main characterised by restraint, but the greatest achievement of this form of architecture is the monastery and palace of the Escorial (1563–84). Shaped unconventionally like a grill to symbolise the martyrdom of St Lawrence, to whom it is dedicated, its exterior is plain to the extent of grimness. The great church is austerely classical, somewhat resembling Wren's St Paul's, and it is a relief to be able to gauge the proportions of the building without the normal obstructive jumble. Only the reredos (98 feet high) by Giacomo Trezzo of Milan (1588) gives the impression of grandiose magnificence in ornamentation.

The Plateresque style

Not all Spanish Renaissance architecture is so easily defined, for architects in Spain carelessly or whimsically mixed Roman with Gothic, often adding Moorish detail for good measure. The Lonja (Exchange) at Zaragoza (1541) has Gothic vaulting springing from Ionic columns, and at Salamanca Gothic vaults are similarly superimposed on Roman

Palace of Carlos V, Alhambra   RIGHT   *Madrid, Memorial to Cervantes*

pilasters. This jumbled style is loosely known as Plateresque, since it is thought to have derived from a German *platero* (silversmith), Enrique de Arfe who settled in Spain early in the sixteenth century and exercised considerable influence on ENRIQUE DE EGAS, who had one of the largest practices as an architect in Spain. Plateresque was in fact more a pattern of decoration than a basic architectural style. Examples of it abound throughout Spain from the sculptured portal of the Hospital Real (1507–11) at Santiago de Compostela, designed by Enrique de Egas, to the Ayuntamiento (Town Hall) at Seville, built about 1527 to the plans of Diego de Riano, with a profusion of Renaissance ornament very unlike the Italian. The portal of Salamanca University is a fine example of Plateresque decoration with its medallions and myriad statues and carvings of surprising variety, including one of a skull and a frog to find which visitors are often invited to stake a bet. For those who wish to make money from their visit to Salamanca it is convenient to know that this particular carving is on the first pilaster to the right. The façade of the Colegio de San Ildefonso in Alcalá de Henares is likewise decorated richly in Plateresque fashion and here too can be seen the open loggias which Plateresque architects favoured especially on the upper storeys where a secluded promenade was afforded. In fact Plateresque architecture is particularly suited to sumptuous aristocratic houses in a period of splendour.

Decoration of the Baroque period

With the vogue for lavish decoration widespread in Spain, the advent of Renaissance Baroque forms was eagerly welcomed early in the seventeenth century. Moreover the Baroque style accorded well with the grandiose but decadent pomp of Spanish court life of the period. At best the Baroque style reveals exuberant invention and vital energy; at worst it exudes vulgarity and bad taste. The architect most closely associated with Baroque in Spain was JOSÉ CHURRIGUERA (1665–1723) and though the most flamboyant excesses are usually known as Churrigueresque, his work was in fact reasonably restrained. Examples of his work are to be found in the façade of the Ayuntamiento at Madrid and in many buildings at Salamanca, particularly the Colegio de Calatrava (1717) where restraint seems to have been thrown to the winds. The Royal Palace at Madrid (1738–64) is Baroque in design, but it is decorous and not in the least flamboyant. The palaces at Aranjuez (enlarged 1712) and La Granja (1721–23) are slightly more

Gaudi's Church of the Holy Family at Barcelona

elaborate in decoration, especially as regards statuary, more noticeable
perhaps because there is a general air of neglect. A less probable site for
Baroque fantasies is the Tobacco Factory at Seville (1728–57), a vast
building 202 by 160 yards, the scene of Don José's fateful encounter with
Carmen in Bizet's opera and now more prosaically occupied by the
faculties of law and science of Seville University.

Possibly the outstanding achievement of Baroque architecture in
Spain is El Obradoiro (1738), the western façade of the cathedral of
Santiago de Compostela by FERNANDO CASAS Y NOVOA. The plethora of
stone ornaments include a hunting scene in which angels are mingled for

reasons unknown, but the general effect is striking and harmonious. Equally striking, but barbaric and vulgar, is the Transparente (1732) behind the altar in Toledo cathedral where a cluster of clouds, rays of sunshine, scrolls, brackets, capitals, balusters in marble and bronze are grouped, lit by a highly decorated hole pierced in the Gothic vaulting. The intention was to portray the glory of heaven lighting the shrine beneath, but the effect, though admittedly impressive, is one of tawdry sentiment.

The Bourbon kings, with instinctive French taste, wished to impose a more severely classical style on Spanish architecture, but the Baroque urge was strong and eventually they had to establish academies to compel Spanish architects to follow the more restrained trend. An example of this *academismo* is the Museo del Prado begun in 1785 by JUAN DE VILLANUEVA, but not completed until 1830. Here again desire for decoration has not been entirely suppressed as it has, for instance, in the New Buildings at Magdalen College, Oxford. It was not in the nature of Spaniards to do so; in their ordinary life they may be austere and frugal, but any great work such as a new building demands and receives an outburst of furious energy which in many instances does not last until the building is completed. A modern example of this is the church of the Holy Family at Barcelona with its four lattice-work towers. Begun in 1884 to plans by Gaudi it is still unfinished; the architect is long since dead (1926) and the models for its construction were mostly burnt in 1936.

The nineteenth and twentieth centuries

The architecture of the nineteenth century is a jumble that defies classification. Most of the buildings of any importance are in Madrid or Barcelona, for other cities in Spain slumbered into shabbiness during the period and there was until very recently little large-scale building except for railway stations and bullrings, neither of which are normally visited for their architectural beauty. The Panteón in Madrid with its memorials to nineteenth-century Spanish worthies (some of the statues by Benlliure are excellent) is faintly Romanesque in style. The Bolsa (Stock Exchange) is Renaissance, as is the Banco de España, which is spacious, massive and solid with heavy brass ornaments and grills. The Post Office beggars description, with its highly decorated towers that have earned it the nickname of *Nuestra Señora de las Comunicaciones*. Its interior, with its huge expanse of marble floors and staircases, has the grandiose pomp of a Renaissance cathedral. Curiously, the sale of stamps, possibly the most useful service in a Post Office, is relegated to a small crypt reminiscent of the Royal Tombhouse at the Escorial.

On the whole public buildings of the twentieth century, particularly those (and they form the great majority) erected since the Civil War, are conservative in design and many huge blocks of flats are well proportioned with pleasing red brick exteriors. How well they will last is debatable because traditional solidity seems to have deserted the Spanish building industry. To stay in a modern flat in a large block demands the use of earplugs or sleeping pills since the noise of neighbours, which in Spain is considerable, is plainly to be heard day and night through wafer-thin partitions or doors that never fit and always creak on their hinges. Similar shoddiness is apparent in the rash of building all round the eastern and southern coastlines of Spain, where tourists from all northern European countries pullulate during the spring and summer months. Weird buildings of all categories abound from imitation Moorish to starkly futuristic. It is too early to pass judgment on these products of hasty native and foreign planning and investment. From a cursory glance at their construction it would appear that they will not endure long enough for their details to be included in architectural history. Probably the most durable architectural achievement in modern Spain is the Basílica del Valle de los Caídos (1942–56) near the Escorial, for this great church is hollowed out of the mountainside. It is impressive, though perhaps theatrical, and the huge cross (492 feet high) has only a stone facing to cover the prosaic concrete inside.

Chapter 12
Painting

As with architecture, Spanish painting has been constantly open to foreign influence. Most of the great painters lived or studied abroad at some time, many of the masterpieces painted in Spain were the work of foreigners settled there; yet Spanish art has qualities that stamp it as essentially national. Perhaps its most brilliant achievements have been in representational painting; Spanish artists have tended away from personal comment and symbolism. Only three artists in the history of Spanish painting stand out as highly imaginative, El Greco, Goya and Picasso. El Greco was a Cretan, Picasso has spent almost all his working life abroad, only Goya was entirely Spanish (though his old age was spent in France) and he was a phenomenon without parallel. Spanish painters have always sought to depict what they see with strict, literal truthfulness and this desire often inhibits the use of symbolism. The Spanish temperament is for the most part intensely reserved, with deep emotions kept in check and only occasionally bursting forth. Spanish painting is frequently dramatic, but it is usually reserved, dignified, and restrained, and until recent times, the colours have often been sombre and dim in a country where daylight is intense and brilliant.

The caves of Altamira

The earliest Spanish paintings were faithful representations of animals depicted on the roofs of caves such as that at Altamira near Santander. Here the pictures of bison, deer, wild boar are astonishingly lifelike and vigorous even though they are painted on the rough stone roof using only black and red as colours. Compared with other cave art, the paintings are some of the most dynamic and colourful to have been discovered. With reason the French archaeologist Déchelette described

LEFT *St. George and the Dragon. Details from the retablo attributed to Marsal de Sax*

A cave painting at Cogul

the cave as 'the Sistine chapel of prehistoric art' and for many years experts considered the paintings too good to be genuine. Discovered in 1879 it was not until the very end of the century, when other similar caves were found in France, that these paintings were recognised as being some twelve to fifteen thousand years old. Other caves in various parts of Spain contain samples of prehistoric art, not so perfect as at Altamira, but still striking. The deer hunt in the Cueva de los Caballos at Castellón, though primitive in technique, is full of action and represents men as well as animals, not isolated pictures as at Altamira, but grouped in energetic poses. The same early attempts at composition are to be seen at Cogull near Lérida. Here the animals appear more domesticated, for close to them are men unarmed and women with full bosoms wearing skirts to mid-calf.

The dominance of Aragon and Valencia

Spanish painting owes little to Moorish influence, though Mozarabic work is well represented in miniature manuscript illustration. The relics of ninth-century church mural decoration tend to reflect Roman or Byzantine styles. In the church of San Julián de los Prados (*c.* 830) at Oviedo there is an elaborate scheme of fresco decoration, much decayed, but capable of fairly exact reconstruction because the lines of the drawings are engraved on the walls. The theme is a repetitive series of porches which surround smaller pictures of buildings with draperies above them. The inspiration may have come from a Roman theatre and the frescoes

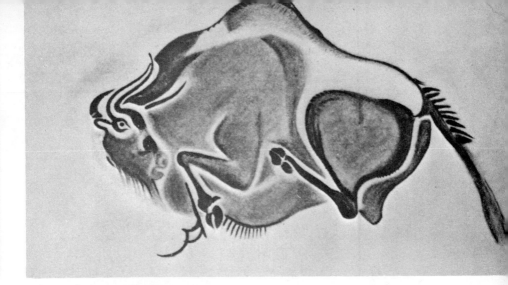

Bison in the cave at Altamira

form a late example of the type of ornamentation common in Roman palaces. Other interesting church paintings are to be found in the Asturias and in León, notably the church of San Isidoro (1149) which contains narrative pictures of the Bible story. The most active area for painting in the Middle Ages was Catalonia, where the influence of Italy was strongest. Nevertheless, while contemporary Italian painters were mostly continuing the Byzantine style, Catalan artists were relying much more on personal observation. FERRER BASSA (?1285–1348) achieved much important work for the kings of Aragon and though his paintings reflect the style of Sienese artists there is more realistic observation of detail in them. The frescoes in the monastery of Pedralbes reveal close imitation of the style of Siena in the Coronation of the Virgin, and a more naturalistic rendering of the Arrest of Christ in the Garden. St Peter, a headstrong, forceful character, is cutting off Malchus's ear with exceptional vigour, and this secondary incident catches the eye and draws attention away from the central figure of Christ.

Catalan supremacy in painting gave way in the fifteenth century to artists in Valencia who were influenced by Flemish methods. In 1427 Jan Van Eyck visited Valencia with an embassy and spent almost a year in Spain. Three years later LUIS DALMÁU, *pintor de casa del senyor Rey*, was given a hundred gold florins for a journey to Flanders to study painting, and his *Virgen de los Concelleres* in the museum at Barcelona demonstrates what he had learnt. The Virgin and Child are surrounded by five Barcelona councillors who had commissioned the

Mural at the Monastery of Santa María de Pedralbes, by Ferrer Bassa

painting and who appear far more Flemish than Mediterranean. The angels, the architecture, the countryside, the folds of the garments, are all exactly copied from Flemish models, especially from the *retablo* in the church of Saint Bavon in Ghent. Flemish styles were particularly suitable for decorating *retablos* and these were much in demand during the spate of ecclesiastical building in the fifteenth century. The many panels enabled artists to paint scenes of energetic action or detailed narrative without having to overcome the manifold difficulties of a large painting. An excellent example of the Spanish *retablo* is in the Victoria and Albert Museum in London and depicts, appropriately enough, the deeds and martyrdom of St George. It was commissioned for the church of San Jorge in Valencia in the early years of the fifteenth century and shows St George assisting a king of Aragon in a fierce battle against the Moors, possibly the victory of El Puig by Jaime I in 1237. The scene is admirably lively and animated. Other panels in the *retablo* show in gory detail the saint's tortures and martyrdom;

attributed to ANDRÉS MARSAL DE SAX, who in a Valencian document of 1396 is described as *pintor alamany*, these paintings, even in the context of the violence of medieval life, have a preoccupation with the gruesome which seems to appeal to the Spanish eye.

Another Valencian painter of this period was JAIME BAÇO (?1410–61), called JACOMART. The son of a tailor, he became court painter to Alfonso V of Aragon and later to Juan II; in their service he spent much time in Italy and anticipates in Spain many features of Italian Renaissance painting. He was probably of northern French extraction and therefore the Flemish style was likely to be well known to him. His studio at Valencia was a centre of artistic activity with many pupils and apprentices. His *retablo* dedicated to San Martín, now in the bishop's palace at Segorbe, north-west of Valencia, contains much delicate painting, especially in the gentle expression of the saint's features. In general Jacomart was too much of an international painter to have had a permanent influence on the development of Spanish painting. More Spanish in tone was the work of JAIME HUGUET (d. 1492), a native of Tarragona, who was painting actively between 1448 and 1487. His success in Barcelona was enormous and the various City Guilds besieged him with commissions so that he was obliged to delegate much of his work to assistants and apprentices. This is the reason for the wide differences in quality in the various paintings attributed to him. This effect can be seen in the *retablo* for the Cofradía de los Blanqueros (Guild of Tanners) commissioned in 1463 and not completed until twenty years later (it is now in the Museo de Barcelona). Probably only one panel is entirely by the hand of Huguet himself and this depicts the consecration of St Augustine as bishop. In spite of the profusion of decoration in gold and embroidery on the ecclesiastical robes the heads of the bishop and clergy are magnificently observed, finely drawn and full of character. Huguet more than any of his contemporaries managed to present realistic figures taken from life, while continuing with the rich decoration of glittering armour and sumptuous robes in the style of the Flemish painters.

By the end of the fifteenth century, with the Moors finally defeated, schools of painting began to flourish in all parts of Spain—the brothers GALLEGO in Salamanca, PEDRO BERRUGUETE in Toledo and Ávila, ANTONIO and DIEGO SÁNCHEZ in Seville (the *Road to Calvary* in the Fitzwilliam Museum at Cambridge is a fine specimen of their work), BARTOLOMÉ BERMEJO in Córdoba. All these painters relied to a large extent on Italian or Flemish models for their inspiration; there was

Virgen de los Concelleres, by Luis Dalmau, Museo d'Arte, Barcelona

perhaps a preference for the style of Flanders and the Netherlands since it displayed more realism and materialism and suited the Spanish taste for literal representation of things seen. No claim can be made for a genuinely Spanish style until the appearance of LUIS DE MORALES (1517–86) from Badajoz in distant Extremadura. He followed the Italian style in many respects, but his emaciated figures of Christ crucified, the features distorted with pain and grief, form a model for later Spanish paintings and sculptures, and Morales achieved great popularity.

Both Carlos V and Philip II appointed foreigners as court painters. Carlos V chose Titian who never visited Spain, but whose influence is plainly to be seen in Spanish court portraits of the sixteenth century, particularly in the work of JUAN FERNÁNDEZ NAVARRETE (1526–79), known as EL MUDO because of an illness which had rendered him dumb from childhood. He was busily engaged from 1569 in executing paintings for the Escorial where some of his best works are to be seen, for example *La Sagrada Familia* in which Navarrete was gravely censured for including a cat and a dog in the foreground; relating a religious scene to everyday life was in fact one more manifestation of the Spanish desire for literal representation. Philip II selected a Fleming for his court painter, Anthony Mor, from whom ALONSO SÁNCHEZ COELLO (?1513–90) learnt his craft. Coello's portrait of the Infanta Doña Catalina (in the Prado) is beautifully drawn, entirely objective and somewhat severe in the true Spanish fashion.

El Greco

After the good—but conventional—work done by native Spanish painters it was a foreigner who gave art in Spain the benefit of his startling originality. DOMENICO THEOTOCOPOULI (1541–1614), called EL GRECO, left his native Crete to study painting in Venice, where art was flourishing under such master painters as Titian, Tintoretto, Paul Veronese. From Venice he went to Rome in 1570, but his paintings found little favour there, though they caused much comment. His outspoken views likewise gained him no friends; he strongly criticised the frescoes of Michelangelo whom later he dubbed as a 'nice man who did not know how to paint'. It is rumoured that El Greco had to leave Rome because of his unpopularity, and in 1577 he arrived in Spain, where he settled at Toledo. Three years later he received a commission from Philip II to paint the *Martyrdom of St Maurice and the Christian Legion* for the church of the Escorial. The picture was never hung there because its unusual composition, attenuated figures, violent contrasts and harsh colours made it too unorthodox for the King's liking.

Though he lost the royal patronage, El Greco had many admirers and friends and there was no lack of commissions for him in Toledo, where he remained until his death. *The Burial of Count Orgaz* was painted there in 1586 for the church of Santo Tomé in which it still hangs. The subject is based on the miraculous apparition in this very church in the fourteenth century of the two patron saints, St Augustine and St Stephen, who lowered the Señor de Orgaz into his grave. In the lower half of the picture the burial is being witnessed by a group of Toledan gentlemen, of whom one is said to be a self-portrait of the artist. All these mourners are extremely vivid and each is taking due part in the solemn, miraculous ceremony while on the right a priest (his surplice is a masterpiece of painting) is looking up to heaven where the soul of the Count is being received into Glory by Christ the Judge.

ABOVE *Detail from Burial of the Conde de Orgaz, by El Greco*

RIGHT *Franciscan Friar, by Zurbarán*

The two halves of the picture form a remarkable contrast; the lower is naturalistic, straightforward, though superlatively vital and expressive; the upper half is strongly imaginative and symbolic. It is true that it retains some of the qualities of medieval Byzantine work (the Count's soul is represented by a naked, childlike figure), but the choice of colour is so novel, the grouping is so original, that it is plain that El Greco was exploring fresh fields in painting. Here was a man who saw visions, striving to convey his spiritual experiences in what he painted; yet despite all the distortions, the elongated figures, the unusual colours, in his later pictures El Greco gives his message by representing life as observed. *The Burial of Count Orgaz* achieved considerable success in Toledo and there, if not at the Escorial, his work was highly appreciated. Commissions came from many parts of Spain; some of his pictures even found their way to Spanish America. His influence on Spanish art was profound; it was he who gave the impetus to the great surge of painting in the seventeenth century. He is a figure like Góngora in literature,

a startling innovator, unappreciated by the unimaginative, but powerfully suggestive and influencing without the beholder realising it.
Technically he was richly inventive, and was indeed responsible for a
new 'vision', in which the sun was replaced by the subtler light of the
moon, in which things and people were lit from behind, in which
darkness was used in a positive way.

As with Góngora in poetry, the immediate development from El
Greco was a reaction against his style. FRANCISCO RIBALTA (1551–1628)
was strongly influenced by Italian forms; his paintings, however, reveal
a certain sentimentality, a debased form of El Greco's desire for painting
to be expressive and not merely representational. Ribalta's *Christ
bearing the Cross* in the National Gallery in London shows this tendency
towards sentimentality and also has the strong effects of light and shade
which El Greco had exploited so skilfully. Ribalta's pupil, JUSEPE DE
RIBERA (1589–1652), spent most of his working life in Naples, but
remained obstinately Spanish in outlook and technique. His use of
light and shade is also noteworthy. His subjects were often torture and
martyrdom, yet he always retains his Spanish dignity, as may be seen
in his *Christ on the Cross* (Museo de Vitoria) or *St Andrew holding his
Cross* (Prado) in which St Andrew is depicted as an emaciated old man,
sorrowful but superbly dignified. The contrast between light and shade
is particularly strong in *St James the Greater* (Prado), which also shows
some of Ribalta's tendency towards sentimentality.

FRANCISCO ZURBARÁN (1598–1662) was perhaps the first painter in
Spain who consciously sought to be an impressionist, not in the technical sense, but in the sense that he was concerned with impressions rather
than with objective reality. Though he was strictly truthful in painting
what he saw (it was said that he never painted any object without
having it in front of him), he was always trying to convey the impression of a scene or experience beyond the actual literal representation. He
seems intent on extracting the utmost beauty and feeling from the
subject and scene chosen. In his painting of a *Franciscan friar at prayer*
(National Gallery, London) the beauty lies in the fervour of the clasped
hands and the dramatic emergence of the figure from the dark background, suggesting the light and hope that prayer gives in the darkness
of despair. The same drama is apparent in *Christ on the Cross* (Valdés
Collection, Bilbao), but here the figure is in infinite pain and sorrow
and seems to be sinking into darkness. Not all Zurbarán's work is
successful, for he was caught up in a freakish craze to paint portraits of
fashionable ladies of the day as saints; even the handsome Santa Catalina

in the Prado resembles a stage figure in her sumptuous clothes rather than a religious picture.

Velázquez

The great painter of the court at this time was DIEGO RODRÍGUEZ DE SILVA VELÁZQUEZ (1599–1660). Born in Seville, he received an admirable artistic education from Francisco de Herrera and more particularly from Francisco Pacheco, whose daughter he married and who taught him much of the theoretical aspect of painting. Velázquez from the beginning strove to attain mastery in conveying faithfully what he saw, and his early sketches and paintings known as *bodegones* are of homely subjects—kitchen scenes with meat, game, utensils and peasant figures. The people in them are full of character and splendidly observed, as in the scene of the *Old woman frying eggs* (Cook Collection, Richmond). An early portrait also reveals his power of characterisation. Nothing could be more pensive, courageous and determined than the expression on the face of Sor Francisca Jerónima de la Fuente, who at the age of sixty-five set out for Manila to found a new convent. Perhaps the best of these *bodegones* is the *Waterseller of Seville* (Duke of Wellington's Collection, Apsley House, London), where the use of light and shade is extremely skilful and the figures have real dignity and importance.

Seville was too provincial for a young painter of such promise and Pacheco urged Velázquez to undertake the journey to Madrid to seek a post at court. The first visit was made in 1622, when Velázquez painted the striking portrait of Góngora (Boston Art Gallery, U.S.A.). Its success encouraged him to return to Madrid in 1623. Here he was fortunate in being recommended to the new *valido*, the Conde-Duque de Olivares, himself a *Sevillano*, and soon he was commissioned to paint a portrait of King Philip IV. This was an immediate success and Velázquez was appointed court painter, a post he held until his death. Free from monetary anxieties and forbidden to undertake commissions other than from the King, Velázquez was able to study his craft throughout his career; his paintings were his own creations and not the work of apprentices as so often happened in the studios of busy painters. This is perhaps one of the reasons why his technique and achievements were so far in advance of those of his contemporaries.

It is said that Velázquez was endowed with the best eyesight that any artist ever possessed and this enabled him to set down what he observed with exceptional fidelity. He was a slow and painstaking worker, and

ABOVE *Los borrachos, by Velázquez*

RIGHT *The Waterseller of Seville, by Velázquez*

BELOW *Detail from Las Meninas, by Velázquez*

this very capacity for painstaking observation may be the cause of a certain lack of selectivity in his pictures; he tends to present so many persons and objects of equal visual importance that the normal eye cannot assimilate them all and is confused. This tendency is evident in *Los borrachos* (The drunkards) in the Prado; it was Velázquez's first attempt at a mythological painting and its real title should be the Triumph of Bacchus, but Bacchus is represented by a semi-naked country lad quite unlike a god, while four bibulous villagers are drinking themselves into a rare good humour. The portrayal of the villagers is masterly; each figure exudes rustic conviviality and each face oozes alcohol. But the composition is such that the viewer is in the position of an officer inspecting a line of troops, passing from one to the next without being able to seize an impression of the scene as a whole. Velázquez had not as yet realised that the eye notices only what it is focused on and that a picture must do nothing to distract the eye from the main focus. In portraits this difficulty scarcely arises, and Velázquez was already an acknowledged master of portraiture, but the lack of arrangement in composite pictures was evident and may have prompted Rubens, who visited Madrid in 1628, to advise Velázquez to make the journey to Italy to complete his artistic apprenticeship. Philip IV grudgingly gave leave and Velázquez set out in 1629 for Italy, where he spent eighteen months visiting all the great artistic centres, Verona, Venice, Bologna, Rome, Naples. It was in Italy that he painted the picture entitled *The Forge of Vulcan* (Prado) which demonstrates a definite advance in composition. The forge is manned by accurately observed peasant types, among whom is Vulcan himself; here again it is difficult to focus the eye on any one person or object, so faithfully have they all been depicted, but the light tends to draw attention to the somewhat feeble figure of Apollo giving the news of Venus's infidelity. It is clear in this picture that Velázquez was on the way to solving his technical problems.

Velázquez made a second visit to Italy in 1648, this time on an official mission to buy paintings and sculptures with which to decorate a new gallery in the Alcázar in Madrid. His work on his return shows him as the real master of his craft, especially in the two great pictures, *Las hilanderas* (The Spinners) and *Las meninas* (The Maids of Honour), both in the Prado. Here the composition cannot be faulted, with interest both in the foreground and in the background of the paintings and not merely a line of figures as in *Los borrachos*. *Las meninas* has a story to tell, namely the difficulties encountered in attempting to amuse a naughty little Infanta Margarita while her parents are posing for their portrait; the foreground figures of the maids of honour, the dwarfs, the dog and the princess herself are brilliantly grouped with the main lighting projected on them. Velázquez himself appears a shadowy figure standing before his easel while at the far end of the spacious room a door opens onto a sunlit corridor where a palace official is mounting some stairs. The King and Queen are seen reflected in the mirror, small blurred figures who, one feels, will soon exercise parental authority in telling their daughter to behave. The whole picture is a triumph of painting in three dimensions and in managing the interplay of light and shade. The device of the mirror appears in an early painting of Velázquez before he left Seville, *Christ in the house of Martha and Mary*, and it occurs again in the *Rokeby Venus* (both in the National Gallery, London); in both these paintings the use of the reflections in the mirror is highly expressive.

Velázquez brought his skill in representational art to a pitch of perfection that none of his contemporaries attained, but because he worked in isolation as court painter he imparted his knowledge to no one. As a result he had no successor, though many attempted to imitate him. It is true that he advised and encouraged ESTEBAN MURILLO (1618–82), another *Sevillano*, who visited him in Madrid in 1642. Like Velázquez in certain of his pictures, Murillo was able to find beauty in low life and many of his peasant paintings are delightful: for example the *Flower girl* and the *Two peasant boys* (both in the Dulwich Art Gallery, London), and the *Boy drinking* (National Gallery, London). Two more, *Girls selling fruit* and the *Melon eaters* (Pinakothek, Munich), besides containing excellent grouping and delicate effects of light and shade, give a hint of humour, a quality almost entirely lacking in Spanish art. There is tenderness too, an understanding of people's feelings as in the picture of the *Women at the window* (National Gallery, Washington); here one girl is peeping round the shutter, half hiding her face with her shawl in the timid Spanish–Moorish fashion, the other, more brazen, is leaning out of the window watching the scene below with frank interest, but with an expression of wistful regret at not being able to take part herself. Perhaps this tenderness veers at times towards sentimentality, especially in Murillo's religious paintings, such as the *Apparition of the Virgin to St Bernard* (Prado) or the *Betrothal of the Virgin Mary* (Wallace Collection, London). Most of these religious paintings were executed for convents in Seville and it is understandable that sweetness and gentleness should be the prevailing theme. Even here some of the subjects seem more closely related to everyday life than was usual with religious paintings, as if Murillo was seeking to relate biblical scenes to common experiences. Perhaps here (as in the Dutch art of his time) were the first gropings after democracy similar to the picaresque novel in literature.

The end of the seventeenth century in Spain was a period of bankruptcy, financially and morally, and this was mirrored in the artistic activity of the country, including the painting. In the eighteenth century the gaps were filled by an invasion of foreign artists under the Bourbons. Tiepolo accomplished much elegant work particularly in the Royal Palace at Madrid, but not unnaturally it was the French school that had most impact. LUIS MENÉNDEZ was known as the Spanish Chardin while LUIS PARET, a brilliant draughtsman with a disturbing wit behind his elegance, earned the title of the Spanish Watteau. French influence is plain to see in the early work of FRANCISCO GOYA (1746–1828) whose designs for tapestries are in the style of Fragonard, but behind such innocent and decorative scenes as *Blind Man's Buff* or *the Swing* there is a strong hint of cynical impudence that declares that here was a painter who would be no slavish imitator of French elegant artificiality.

Goya

A native of Aragon, Goya did not visit Madrid until he was nearly twenty and his career as a painter developed slowly. His early paintings submitted to the Spanish Academy of Fine Arts received scant attention and in 1771 Goya decided to make a journey at his own expense to Italy, where he gained a second prize for a picture submitted to the Parma Academy. This was his first real success, but such an individualist was he that the more official recognition he received, the greater freedom he allowed himself in his methods. His first opportunity in Spain came with his appointment to the Royal Tapestry Factory through the influence of his brother-in-law, Francisco Bayeu, a well known painter of the time. Accepted by the Academy in 1780, Goya was nominated *Pintor del Rey* in 1786 and on the accession of Carlos IV he was given the more intimate title of *Pintor de Cámara*. His portraits of the royal family are almost without exception ribald and derisive and it is a mystery how they were received so enthusiastically by the sitters. The only explanation is that their attention was caught and fixed by the glorious colour and detail of the robes and decorations and

was diverted from the pettiness and viciousness of the facial expressions. His private sitters received little mercy either and the striking portrait (1805) of Doña Isabel Cobos de Porcel (National Gallery, London) reveals both her sensual nature and her beauty. Doña Antonia Zárate, painted in ?1805 (Beit Collection, London), was a leading actress of the day and she has indeed a composed dignity, but the slight, almost imperceptible twist to the mouth suggests cruelty and intolerance. Goya could indeed paint sympathetic portraits of people of whom he approved, as for example the fine portrait of the poet, Menéndez Valdés or of the Duke of Wellington who comes out well although neither sitter nor artist found each other congenial company. Perhaps Goya's most sensitive portrait is that of the Condesa de Chinchón (Collection of the Duque de Sueca, Madrid); he had painted her when she was a child and now in 1800 she was at the age of twenty-one the wife of the odious Godoy and pregnant too. The gentle sadness of a girl forced by her station in life into an unhappy marriage is plain in the bewildered, uncomprehending expression in the eyes.

Goya had revolutionised court painting by the truth as well as the insolence of his brush and he revolutionised religious mural decoration in the church of San Antonio de la Florida (now his memorial) in Madrid. These frescoes represent the miracle of St Anthony, but the onlookers are the population of Madrid in Goya's day with the *majos* and *majas* and ragged little urchins climbing up on the balcony rails to get a better view. Goya's representation of *El dos de Mayo* is not the heroic conception of a patriotic struggle so familiar in the poems of the day, but a bloody, savage, nauseating battle between soldiers and civilians. There is nothing dignified or heroic about his *El tres de Mayo*, only a violent, furious vengeance by the French on terrified Spanish citizens. His pictures of incidents in popular life are equally truthful, for example the *Waterseller* and the *Knife-grinder*, which are sympathetic, but quite devoid of sentimentality. In everything that Goya painted with the exception possibly of some early pot-boilers there is complete artistic integrity.

In 1792 Goya had become deaf as a result of an illness and to occupy his mind during convalescence he painted a series of small satirical sketches in which he gave full rein to his imagination in a way impossible in normal commissioned works. One of these small canvases depicted a scene of a fight in a madhouse and the whole series is a foretaste of the violently satirical etchings published in 1798 under the title of *Caprichos*. It has now been shown that most of the *Caprichos*

RIGHT *Isabel de Porcel, by Goya*

The Swing, by Goya

are connected with topical events or scenes from current literature and are not therefore so grotesque and fanciful as was formerly supposed. Many are nonetheless terrifying as is also the series of *Disasters of war*, masterpieces of aquatint done during the *Guerra de la Independencia*, recording some of the horrors he had witnessed. Evidence of a distorted mind is confirmed in the so-called Black Paintings with which Goya decorated the walls of the country house, the *Quinta del sordo* (Deaf man's house), which he rented shortly after suffering a serious illness. This series includes the bestial picture, painted aptly enough for the dining-room, of Saturn devouring his children. Goya could still paint fine portraits, as for example the one of Don Ramón Satué (?1823), a liberal-minded clergyman in whose house Goya took refuge after the suppression of the liberal regime in 1823. Out of sympathy with the tyrannical rule of Fernando VII whose portrait he had so often painted with such insolence, Goya went into voluntary exile in Bordeaux where he continued to paint and draw with undiminished energy. Besides doing portraits of his friends and experimenting with miniatures on ivory, he engraved a splendid series of *Bulls of Bordeaux* in the recently invented process of lithography. Possibly the most original of all Spanish painters, Goya had innumerable imitators, but there was none to compare with him or to carry his original technique a step further.

Painting in the nineteenth century

Spanish painting in the nineteenth century reflects many styles and trends from abroad, romanticism as in the *Paisaje de el Escorial* by VAN HALEN, neoclassicism as in the *Death of Viriatus* by MADRAZO, impressionism as in *Paisaje urbano* by ROSALES. The work was extremely varied and much of it was of a high order, especially the paintings of MARIANO FORTUNY (1838–74), whose picture *La vicaría* (The vestry) created a sensation in 1868, not only in Spain, but in Paris as well. It is only a small picture, but it depicts the signing of the register in a Spanish church with its massive grills and ponderous decorations all painted in great detail. The poses of the figures (with the exception of the old parish priest) are a shade too theatrical, but the picture is clear in colour and sparkling with gaiety and reminiscent of a scene from the *Barber of Seville*. This style represents a reaction against the drama of romanticism and the pomposity of neoclassicism and consciously imitates the gay lightness of the period of Louis XV. It has all the sparkle of an early Goya, but the social comment is lacking; it is merely a brilliant and charming ballet scene. Painted in the same year in Rome was a picture by EDUARDO ROSALES (1836–73) of a nude. This picture represents something new in Spanish painting with its simplicity of colouring and impressionistic pose. More orthodox was his portrait (1871) of the young Condesa de Santovenia; it is indeed a handsome picture and carries on the Spanish tradition of clearcut contrasts of light and shade.

ABOVE   *Detail from* La Vicaría, *by Fortuny*

RIGHT   *Desnudo, by Rosales*

Similar in type was the work of JOAQUÍN SOROLLA (1863–1923) whose huge mural paintings executed in 1911 for the Hispanic Society of America depict peasant scenes from various parts of Spain with great vigour and liveliness and are flooded with the clear light of the Peninsula. The *Campesinos Leoneses* have much of the same quality of peasant realism as in *Los borrachos* by Velázquez, but many of the other scenes, such as the wedding procession in Valencia (Sorolla's native province) are too theatrical in pose to be plausible. Less impressive, but more interesting are his portraits of intellectual celebrities of the generation of '98 and that of Pío Baroja (also belonging to the Hispanic Society in New York) is intensely suggestive of this small man from the Basque provinces brimming with energy and vitality.

One of the most original painters of the late nineteenth century was FRANCISCO GIMENO whose work was entirely neglected in his time and is very little known now. His paintings are rich in colour and have a certain dramatic tension and feeling without romantic sentiment. One of the most delightful is *El niño y el perro* (1891, Sala Collection,

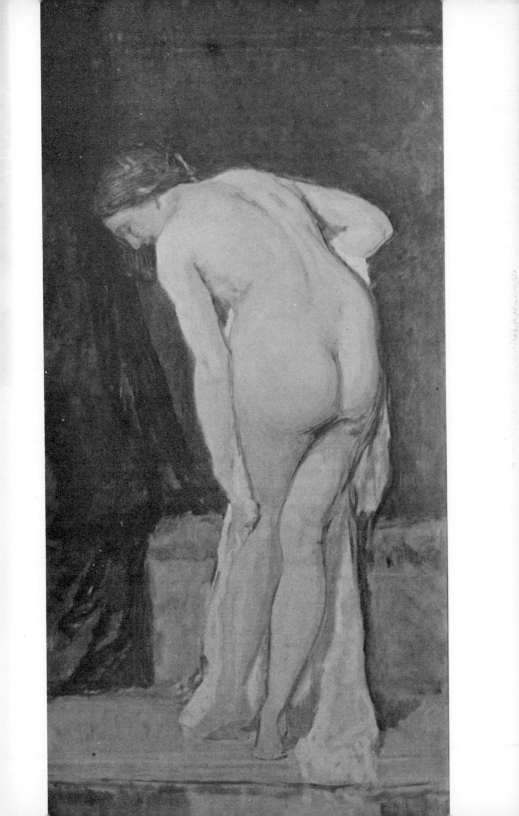

Wedding Procession, by Sorolla

Barcelona); it shows a mongrel dog faithfully guarding a child who has been left imprisoned in its chair and whose baleful glance suggests that this neglect is greatly resented. Such a subject might be unbearably sentimental, but in this instance there is complete realism in the squalor of rumpled clothes, castaway toys, ruffled feelings. Much more thea-

trical in style are the paintings of IGNACIO ZULOAGA (1870–1945) who
has been compared with Sargent as a portrait painter. He continues the
tradition of Velázquez with vigorous design and alternations of light,
but there is perhaps a crudeness in the colour that almost amounts to
carelessness. His portrait of Unamuno (Hispanic Society of America) is
similar to a portrait of a seventeenth century writer, but the face is
lacking in both the sensitivity and animation that characterised
Unamuno.

Picasso and modern Spanish painters

The twentieth century has seen a great revival of Spanish painting,
though many of the great painters have studied, worked or lived
abroad. The scene has long been dominated by PABLO PICASSO (b. 1881).
Born at Málaga, Picasso did much of his early work in Barcelona.
After a failure to establish an art journal called *Arte Joven* in Madrid he
returned to Barcelona, but shortly afterwards (1904) settled in Paris,
where he became friends with the leading painters of the period, both
young and old. Just before settling in Paris Picasso had produced the
works of his 'blue' period, so called because of the general colour tone,
as exemplified in his *Child with a Pigeon* (1901), now frequently repro-
duced on English Christmas cards, and his *Two figures with bowed heads*
(1904) where the blue tones tend to suggest quiet resignation. There
followed the 'pink' period in Paris when Picasso was interested especially in circus scenes which he observed in the *Cirque Médrano*. *Harlequin
and his family with a monkey* (1905) is a transitional example with pink
tones ousting the blue. Quite naturalistic, it expresses the hardness of
life in a circus, for both Harlequin and his wife seem tired and emaciated;
weariness has overcome even the monkey, only the baby, as is the way
with the very young, has bounce and life. More representative of the
'pink' period is the *Two female nudes* (1906), but this picture again shows
transition (Picasso has always been a great experimentalist) to the
'negro' period, inspired perhaps by the exhibits in the Ethnological
Museum in Paris. The 'negro' period is characterised by strong lines,
graceful curves and above all sombre colouring, as in the *Three seated
figures* (1907–8) where the blues, greens, browns all seem to melt into
one rich, dark tone.

As with the literary men of the period, artists showed a strong reaction to plain realism; negro art was never purely naturalistic and rarely
intended to be merely ornamental. It was trying to convey a meaning

ABOVE   *Head of a Man with a Cigar, by Gris*

LEFT   *Woman and Birds in front of the Sun, by Miro*

by the building up of plain shapes in severe colours. In this way it contributed to Cubism, which attempts to convey its meaning by building up geometrical shapes. It was Cézanne who advised that nature should be viewed in terms of cubes, cones and cylinders. Picasso and his friends, particularly JUAN GRIS (1887–1927), a native of Madrid who had come to Paris in 1906, took this advice very seriously and began to tackle the problems of creating pictures out of geometrical shapes. Many of the results were strikingly successful. Picasso's *Seated woman* (1909, Penrose Collection, London) is brilliantly executed; the lines of the face suggest firmness and an almost disapproving expression mixed with weariness. In the same collection the *Girl with the mandolin* (1910) gives a fine idea of the player's concentration with a firm left hand pressing the frets while the right hand is plucking with the greatest delicacy. In some ways Gris almost surpassed Picasso in Cubist painting and his *Portrait of Maurice Raynal* (1911) is a masterpiece, depicting a person of brilliant intelligence with a penetrating gaze, though purists might object that the portrait is not entirely geometrical in build-up and therefore not truly Cubist. The colours of these Cubist paintings were restrained, grey and brown predominating, and not unnaturally there was a reaction before long in favour of vivid, almost garish colours as in Picasso's *Schoolgirl* (1919, Douglas Cooper Collection, Nîmes), where the raw tones and square shapes almost suggest a playing card.

The Cubist movement lost impetus after the first world war and Picasso, sure of his techniques, painted in so many styles, including neoclassicism, that it is pointless to try and place his works in categories. He had always been able to paint admirable naturalistic portraits, such as that of Max Jakob (1915) and his *Seated Harlequin* (1923, Kunstmuseum, Basle) which are as discreet and charming as the most orthodox could desire. At the same time he was influenced by surrealism, a word first mentioned in the programme for Massine's ballet *Parade* (1917) for which Picasso had designed the sets and costumes. What exactly surrealism amounts to has always been difficult to determine, but clearly it springs partly from an interest in visions which are deep down in the mind suggested possibly by the writings of Freud. It was by no means the first time that such manifestations had appeared; some of the weirder drawings of Blake and Goya attempt to explore in this direction, while Coleridge and De Quincey deliberately resorted to drugs to be able to record on paper impressions of the dreams so induced. Picasso's work between 1925 and 1927 is full of distorted and

Apparition of Face and Fruit Dish on a Beach, by Dali

turbulent figures, but he was never as deeply absorbed in surrealism as his compatriots SALVADOR DALI (b. 1904) and JOAN MIRO (b. 1893), both leaders of surrealism and founders of the movement.

Picasso returned to an expressive form of painting when the Civil War broke out in 1936. He went back to Spain as a supporter of the Republicans and was made Director of the Prado, whose pictures he later helped to safeguard. His painting of the obliteration of Guernica by German bomber aircraft is a terrifying picture, but even more poignant is his *Weeping woman* (1937, Penrose Collection, London), where the emotional agony is suggested by the harsh colours, and sorrow by the sharp angles of the facial expression. On Franco's victory Picasso returned to France, where he spent the whole period of the second world war unmolested by the Germans. After the war he publicly proclaimed himself to be a Communist and this coupled with his work for the Republicans makes his name taboo in Spain while the

The child with the dove, by Picasso

Franco regime lasts. Yet without question he is Spain's most original and most accomplished painter of this century and his versatility is remarkable; he has cultivated with success every form of painting from Cubism to still life. His use of paper gummed on a canvas (*papiers collés*) to form shapes of heads and figures is masterly; he has written surrealist poetry, cast bronze statues, invented new lithographical processes. His genius is colossal and like Goya his integrity as an artist is complete. Barred at present from his own country, he has deservedly won the world's acclaim because of his mastery of his entire craft; unlike many modern artists he has taken the trouble to perfect his technique without ever dulling his inventive inspiration.

Salvador Dali, who spent several years in the United States, is also a painter with a highly developed technique, but with a much more restricted range than Picasso. His *Apparition of face and fruit-dish on a beach* (1938, Wadsworth Athenaeum, Hartford, U.S.A.) is beautifully drawn and painted in great detail with various objects serving several purposes, for example the fruit-dish forms a part of the girl's features, her eyes are shells on the beach, a distant mountain forms a dog's head, his collar is a railway viaduct, his back is the fruit on the dish, his back legs are sand dunes. One is tempted at first to treat it as a puzzle picture such as appears in Christmas annuals, but there is more to it than that. It represents the confusion of the dream world whose impressions are often more real than impressions of the actual world. Most people can recall experiences of fevered dreams with vivid colours, incongruous objects and a strange medley of figures. Dali recreates a nightmare scene in his *Giraffe aflame* (1935, Kunstmuseum, Basle); here in the background is a giraffe with its mane ablaze, outlined against a dramatic dark blue sky while in the foreground are two shadowy human figures. The larger of these appears to be groping forward though the back is supported by a kind of clothes prop and the breast and left leg form a chest of drawers. It has the poignant and dramatic quality of a dream, and indeed Dali is one of the artists of the twentieth century who most often experiences and explores the reality of dreams and visions.

By contrast the themes of Joan Miro seem at first sight easier to understand, perhaps because he gives a precise title—sometimes misleading—to each surrealist picture. He lives and works in his native Catalonia, but he has travelled widely and in 1947 he executed a huge thirty-foot mural for the Terrace Plaza Hotel, Cincinnati. Working in a vast studio at Barcelona he had declared in 1938 that he considered easel painting petty in its aims, but perhaps at times his style seems a little thin for large-scale paintings. He has been described as having had his development arrested at an infantile stage, and certainly it would be true to say that he paints like a child, uninhibited and unrestrained by intellectually imposed visual rules and concepts—as can be seen in his *Circus* (1934) where the colours are gay and the design lively, but the whole effect childlike. He is a painter who has to be approached solely through the appreciation or form and colour; otherwise his paintings evoke puzzled resentment or derision. Whatever his rating a hundred years hence may be, his work has achieved considerable success and been bought by galleries in many parts of the world.

Chapter 13
Music and dancing

Spanish music today has achieved world-wide popularity and spurious imitations of it were fashionable throughout Europe in the nineteenth century, especially after the success of *Carmen* (1875) by the French composer Bizet who had never even visited Spain. Indeed in Spain itself in the last century there was a vogue for bogus Spanish music composed largely by foreigners, but also the influence of Italian opera in musical circles was extremely strong. Perhaps it is for these reasons that practically no one can name a Spanish composer who was working before the very end of the nineteenth century. Spain's musical history up to modern times is virtually unknown, although it can be traced with certainty back to the sixth century, when music first became prominent in church liturgy.

Religious music

The earliest centre of religious musical activity in Spain was at Seville where two brothers, SAN LEANDRO (d. 599) and SAN ISIDORO, both successively archbishops of the city, established a firm musical tradition in the church services. San Leandro had visited Constantinople where he had studied with St Gregory the Great, the founder of music in the Roman liturgy and he is specifically referred to as a composer of many melodies—*multa dulci sono composuit*. San Isidoro was the author of a textbook on the theory of music in which among other things he describes the musical instruments then in use. Toledo being the seat of Visigothic government was perhaps even more influential than Seville as a centre for church music; here three other saints—Eugenio, Ildefonso and Julián—achieved notable work in composing and co-ordinating various forms of chants for hymns and psalms. Secular songs

LEFT *The Monastery at Montserrat*

that may have been written by SAN EUGENIO (d. 652) are preserved in a Visigothic document (ninth or tenth century) known as the *Códice de Azagra*. Among the collection of songs are two laments for the death (*c.* 652) of King Chindaswinth and of his wife Queen Reciberga; the Latin words are known to have been written by San Eugenio, who was archbishop of Toledo at the time, and the accompanying melodies may have been by his hand too. Unfortunately the musical notation used (Visigothic *neumes*) gives no indication of alterations in pitch and no satisfactory modern transcription of the melodies has been achieved. However, it is known that Spanish church music at this time had strong popular appeal and the congregation took considerable part in the services, interpolating *Amens* at the end of each phrase of the Lord's Prayer and chanting a response of *Deus miserere* between prayers in the Lenten liturgy. Church music in Spain was well developed in the seventh century and possibly reached its highest point just before the Moorish invasion of 711.

Moorish music

The Koran ordered Mohammedans to shun wine and music, but after rich and powerful caliphates had been established with luxurious courts, these ascetic ordinances were frequently neglected. The Moors in Spain were no exception and they may have introduced the lute and other instruments. ZIRYAB was a noted Moorish musician at the court of Abd al-Rahman II (822–852) and he was credited with adding a fifth string to the lute. He had eight sons and two daughters all of whom were musicians and they together with his numerous pupils helped to disseminate Arab music throughout Muslim Spain. The Arab music theorist, AL-FARABI (872–950), compiled a treatise which was translated into Latin and was assiduously studied by Christian musicians. Indeed Christian kings in Spain had Moorish musicians at their courts while in Moorish occupied territory Christians were permitted to continue their church services unmolested.

Alfonso el Sabio encourages music

One of the Christian kings who employed Moorish musicians was Alfonso X *el Sabio* (1221–84) and the collection of his *Cantigas* gives a fascinating picture of the cult of music in medieval Spain. The collection of more than 400 songs in praise of the Virgin is contained in a

Guitarras moriscas, detail from MS. of the Cantigas of Alfonso X

manuscript in the Escorial (there are three other versions) and its illuminations give an idea of the varied musical instruments of the day; it also indicates the method of composing and rehearsing the songs. The instruments include triangular psalteries, lutes, two forms of guitar (the *guitarra latina* has sides that curve in, the *guitarra morisca* is oval-shaped), a viol played with a bow, bells, flutes, horns, castanets, even a hurdy-gurdy. All told, more than seventy musicians are depicted with various forms of instruments. The compositions were directed by the King personally, for he is seated in the centre with scribes on his left writing at his bidding. On his right *trovadores* are concerned with the melodies, for in medieval times they were the composers, and on the extreme right and left are instrumentalists evidently waiting for the song to be rehearsed. Other illuminations show the *cantigas* being performed with all the musicians facing a statue of the Virgin Mary. Six musicians, sitting on a bench, are playing various instruments while a viol player stands behind them. Next to him three people are dancing, holding hands. Strangely enough nobody seems to be singing, but the dancers may have sung as they danced or the picture may represent a dance at the conclusion of the song. Fortunately the *Cantigas* are written in a clear form of musical notation which, though it presents difficulties in transcription, has left the melodies safe for posterity.

The *Cantigas* are written in the Galician dialect and Santiago de Compostela was a flourishing centre of music in the middle ages. In the cathedral is preserved a twelfth-century manuscript, the Codex Calixtinus, containing the text and music of Latin hymns sung by pilgrims to the shrine of St James. It provides an early example of melodies set for more than one voice at the same time. Pilgrims on the way to Compostela were entertained by *juglares*, professional entertainers, musicians, mummers and acrobats. Many of the *Cantares de gesta* were sung, it is thought, by *juglares* to entertain and instruct the pilgrims on their long journeys. Another important centre of music for pilgrims was the monastery of Montserrat near Barcelona, believed to be the site of the Holy Grail (the cup used by Christ at the Last Supper in which Joseph of Arimathaea was said to have caught his blood). Today the monastery has only fragments of the original buildings surviving, but contains a flourishing school of church music and an extensive library of early manuscript music. In the Middle Ages the monks used to compose music for singing and dancing to amuse pilgrims. Of these songs the most important collection is the *Cants dels Romens* preserved with their melodies in the fourteenth-century *Llibre Vermell*. The words are partly in Catalan and partly in Latin and three of the songs are in canon form for two or three voices. Another is entitled the *Ballada dels goytxs de nostra dona en vulgar cathalan a ball redon* (Ballad of the joys of Our Lady in popular Catalan, with a round dance). The first part of the ballad is in Catalan and recounts the seven joys of Our Lady. It seems clear that this was a popular Catalan folk tune suitable for a round dance like the modern *sardana* in which all the dancers hold hands. To this is added a second part in Latin, *Ave Maria*, with a more solemn chant to remind the pilgrims that their journey was not wholly a secular jaunt.

Secular songs

The fifteenth century saw a great increase in secular songs, partly owing to the Renaissance and partly owing to the more settled state of the country after the union of Castile and Aragon in 1479, for the nobles now had time to patronise the arts instead of being constantly engaged in war. One such patron was the Duque de Alba at whose castle near Salamanca JUAN DEL ENCINA (*c.* 1468–*c.* 1529) was court musician and poet. An important collection of songs, the *Cancionero del palacio* (discovered in 1870) may have been made specially for the Duke's household because out of 550 songs seventy five are by Juan del Encina. Some of the songs are now missing, but all that survive appear to date from the end of the fifteenth century or beginning of the sixteenth and it is possible that Juan del Encina, who was with the Alba household from about 1490 to 1498, started the collection which was continued by his successor. Most of the words of the songs are in Castilian, but there are some in Portuguese, Basque, French and Italian and many are composed for three or four voices. The majority are *villancicos* which are properly any kind of peasant songs, though latterly the term has been reserved for Christmas carols. The *villancico* normally began with a *cabeza* (refrain) and each six line stanza elaborated the theme of the *cabeza*. Many of the *villancicos* are clearly genuine folk tunes, but even those composed by court musicians tend to have a rustic simplicity combined with a strong rhythm, for the *villancico* was designed for dancing as well as to be sung. Many other forms of song are included in the *Cancionero del palacio*, serious, comic, bawdy or tragic. The laments were called *endechas* and the Spaniards share with the Scots the ability to compose laments which are exquisitely moving. Love songs also abound and many of them have charming simplicity and freshness; some of the very best were composed by JUAN VÁZQUEZ who published two collections in 1551 and 1560 which include the delightful *De los álamos vengo, madre* incorporated by Manuel de Falla in his harpsichord concerto (1926).

The other major song form at this period was the *romance* which usually recited stirring historical deeds, though it was adapted to many other themes. It enjoyed great popularity among all classes and collections of ballads proliferated. Unfortunately it was not usual to print the tunes alongside the words and only comparatively few melodies have survived in collections definitely intended for performers, such as the *Cancionero del palacio*. The ballad melody required a single period of thirty-two notes to fit the couplets of sixteen syllable lines and as such it was repeated throughout the recitation of the *romance* which might amount to several hundred lines. Repetition of a theme rarely worries the uneducated, but grates on sophisticated ears. The *romance* was therefore extensively pruned by courtly poets who altered the sixteen syllable line couplets to stanzas of four lines each of eight syllables. This allowed more elasticity and the musical treatment could be much more varied.

Popularity of the guitar

The popularity of the *romance* may account for the importance of the guitar as a musical instrument in Spain. Long musical recitations were not suitable for accompaniment by several instruments and the guitar was ideal for the purpose, capable of backing the singer's voice with a series of chords when *rasgueado* (strummed), which was the popular method and not too difficult for the player. The guitar was also capable of great variation and subtlety when *punteado* (plucked) and was therefore suitable too for accomplished courtly musicians who in their eagerness for virtuosity added a fifth, sixth or even seventh string. The guitar under these circumstances becomes an exceedingly complex instrument with a wide range of performance and very difficult to play, though never as difficult as the lute and much more versatile. The guitar was called the *Vihuela de mano* to distinguish it from the *vihuela de arco* played with a bow* and in the sixteenth century several manuals were written for instruction in mastering the instrument. These are often known as tablature books, because the tunes are written in parallel lines indicating the place of the finger on the various frets numbered 1 to 10 with 0 for an open string. The most notable of these tablature books is by LUIS MILÁN (*c.* 1500–*c.* 1562), a native of Valencia of noble family whose musical gifts found favour in many courts. The *Libro de vihuela de mano intitulado El Maestro* (1535) gives careful instructions for tuning and playing the guitar in order to help those eager to acquire this fashionable accomplishment, although Milán claims that he himself was entirely self-taught. The book also contains numerous pieces for the guitar including *villancicos*, *tientos* (preludes) and *pavanes* (courtly dances), all graded according to the difficulties presented in playing them.

The variety possible with music composed for the guitar is shown in another manual, *Los seys libros del Delphín de música*, published in 1638 by LUIS DE NARVÁEZ who became *maestro de vihuela* to Philip II and was such an accomplished player that he could improvise on the guitar four part variations to any piece of four-part music set before him. These variations (*diferencias*) Narváez extended to no less than twenty-one for the *Romance del Conde Claros* and his skill served as an inspiration to Spanish guitarists during the sixteenth century; their favourite theme was a tune which Narváez had used, *Guárdame las vacas*, which became

---

* *Vihuela, viola* etc. stem from Vulgar Latin *vitula*. The classical Latin word *fiducula*, gives the German *fiedel* and English *fiddle*.

so well known that an English version exists (1600): 'I pre-thee keepe
my kine for me'. Another *consumado tañedor* (expert player) of the
period was MIGUEL DE FUENLLANA who, blind from birth, was so
skilful, it is said, that he could play a guitar that was not even tuned.
His tablature book, *Orphénica lyra* (Seville 1554), contains a large number of original compositions.

The guitar was not the only instrument to prosper in Spain in the
sixteenth century for there was a strong school of organists, headed by
the blind musician ANTONIO DE CABEZÓN (1510–66), who was for a long
time in the service of Philip II and who may have accompanied him on
one of his visits to England. Cabezón has often been called the Spanish
Bach and contemporary accounts speak enthusiastically of his mastery
of the organ. His compositions which survive were published in 1578
by his son, who warns that they represent only 'crumbs fallen from the
table', since they are pieces for the instruction of his pupils and do not
indicate his own prowess. Nevertheless, these *tientos* and *diferencias*
reveal a remarkable power of invention and a complete knowledge of
counterpoint as practised at the time and have rewarded the patience
of scholars who have unravelled the problems of the notation used to
record them. There were a number of outstanding church musicians,
but several of them spent most of their working life in Rome and
qualify perhaps more for a place in Italian musical history. The best
known of these were CRISTÓBAL MORALES (1500–53) and TOMÁS LUIS
DE VICTORIA (*c.* 1548–1611). Morales by virtue of many admirable
motets, such as *Jacob mourning his two sons*, earned the title of *luz de
España en música* from Juan Bermudo, the great Spanish music theorist
of the sixteenth century.

Victoria

Victoria is probably the greatest of all Spanish composers, but since he
spent almost thirty years of his active working life in Rome and in fact
succeeded Palestrina as choir master at the Roman Seminary (1571),
his music is usually classified as belonging to the Italian school. Victoria
is always described in Latin documents as *abulensis*, which implies that
he was a native of Ávila where it is possible that he knew Santa Teresa,
for she mentions his brother Augustín in one of her books of *Fundaciones*. Victoria went to Rome in 1565 to become a member of the
Collegio Germanico, which had been founded in 1552 by Ignacio

Loyola for the training of German priests to combat Lutheranism. Victoria was clearly intending to become a priest himself, but he postponed taking orders temporarily to become a chapel-master. In 1572 he published a book of thirty-three motets which include the well-known O *quam gloriosum*, the expressive and beautiful O *vos omnes* and one for Holy Week, *Vere languores nostros*, in a pathetic and moving style. It has been said that these motets bear such a strong resemblance to those of Palestrina as to be mistaken for his work, but Victoria's music has a passionate intensity that Palestrina himself imitated in some of his own motets published in 1584.

In 1575 Victoria was ordained priest, but continued his work as chapel-master in the Collegio Germanico which had lately been re-founded (1573) by Pope Gregory XIII. Victoria had composed an eight part psalm, *Super flumina Babylonis*, for the solemn service of refoundation at which it was sung by two choirs. Somewhat mysteriously he left the college in 1578 probably to take up an an appointment as chaplain to Philip II's sister, the widowed Empress María, but he cannot have been continuously a member of her suite because he stayed on in Rome and published several more collections of musical works before finally returning to Spain in 1594. There in 1600 he published in Madrid yet another miscellaneous collection of masses, psalms, magnificats, hymns and motets evidently for performance in the chapel of the *Descalzas reales* (Royal barefooted nuns). This was the convent in Madrid to which the Empress María and her daughter had retired and Victoria remained in their service. The Empress died on 1 March 1603 and Victoria composed as a tribute to her memory what has been termed the 'greatest triumph of his genius', the *Officium defunctorum* (published 1605). It is a requiem mass for six voices with an additional motet of great beauty *Versa est in luctum*. The whole work is a masterpiece, with impressive harmonies, but touchingly simple and sincere.

The Empress had left Victoria a pension which enabled him to live in comfort and he continued as organist in the chapel of the *Descalzas reales*, though he relinquished the post of chapel-master. His work as a composer was done and he published no more music. His religious compositions (181 in all) form a splendid part of the music of the Church. If they are based on the Italian style, it is heartening to find here and there Spanish traditional melodies skilfully blended, as for instance in the Latin hymn *Vexilia regis* (1585) which forms part of an extensive composition for Holy Week possibly destined for performance in Spain.

The development of musical drama

Another important musical development of the sixteenth century was the inclusion of song in theatrical performances. Juan del Encina had inserted *villancicos* in his tedious *Églogas* and this arrangement was continued by his imitators, notably Gil Vicente. Lope de Rueda, the great itinerant actor, used to sing a prologue to his pieces, accompanying himself on the guitar. A great many of the dramas of Lope de Vega and other Golden Age playwrights were interspersed with songs in the same way as those of Shakespeare were. In 1629 Philip IV was entertained to a 'pastoral eclogue', *La selva sin amor* (The forest without love) written by Lope de Vega, who in the dedication speaks of the performance being sung (*que se representó cantada*). He goes on to say: 'The instruments occupied the front part of the theatre, without being seen, and to their accompaniment the actors sang the lines; all the emotions, such as surprise, sorrow, love, anger, being expressed by the composition of the music itself.' The eclogue is 700 lines in length and all in one act in the usual pastoral convention. No music has survived for it, but with some truth it may be called the first Spanish opera.

Soon afterwards another type of musical play began to develop and has persisted to this day, though in greatly altered form. It was named the *zarzuela* because it was intended for performance in the Zarzuela Palace not far from Madrid. An early example of the *zarzuela*, though performed in the Retiro Palace because the court had suddenly transferred to Madrid, was Calderón's *El laurel de Apolo* (1658). Though still concerned with shepherds and shepherdesses, gods and goddesses, a popular note is introduced in the shape of a *seguidilla*, that is a country song and dance, and the *zarzuela* has ever since retained this popular character. The music has unfortunately been lost, as with another play by Calderón, *La púrpura de la rosa* (1660), written to celebrate the marriage of the Infanta María Teresa to Louis XIV. The prologue (*loa*) states that the play *habrá de ser toda música* and the objection that the Spanish temperament would not tolerate an entire *comedia* sung is dismissed by maintaining that *La púrpura de la rosa* was not a *comedia*, but only an entertainment in one act. Evidently the public in Spain was not yet prepared for full length opera, but it was growing accustomed to the taste, for later in the same year Calderón wrote a libretto in three acts. By a fortunate chance the music for the first act was discovered in 1926 in the library of the Duque de Alba's residence at Madrid and the score was published in 1933. The composer was JUAN HIDALGO, the harpist of the Capilla Real, and the melodies of the opera are extremely expressive and reveal a strong popular influence, already apparent in earlier Spanish solo songs. Hidalgo also anticipates Wagner to a certain extent by introducing a kind of *leitmotif* in the theme of Aurora's lament which recurs throughout the act.

Spanish musical plays enjoyed great popularity throughout the seventeenth century, with more than a hundred native composers at work, but with the advent of the Bourbon kings in 1700 Spanish music fell almost at a blow before the invasion of Italian performers and composers. From 1737 to 1759 the renowned Italian male soprano, Farinelli, was engaged at a huge salary to sing the same four songs every night to dispel the chronic melancholia of King Philip V. In 1729 Domenico Scarlatti came to Madrid and remained there except for one visit to Naples until his death in 1757. Much of his music is influenced by the rhythms of popular Spanish songs, so much so that his Sonata No. 263 has acquired the name of *Bourrée d'Aranjuez*. Scarlatti's compositions belong properly to the history of Italian music, but his influence on Spanish composers right up to the present day has always been marked. One of his pupils was PADRE ANTONIO SOLER (1729–83), organist and choirmaster of the Escorial and composer of much music for the organ and harpsichord. His charming sonatas (twenty-seven were printed in London in 1752) are little known today except in arrangements by his modern editor, JOAQUÍN NÍN (1879–1949). The neglect of them in England is all the more reprehensible since a copy of them exists in the Fitzwilliam Museum at Cambridge with a note by Lord Richard Fitzwilliam (1745–1816) saying: 'The original of these harpsichord lessons was given to me by Father Soler at the Escorial, 14th February, 1772; Father Soler had been instructed by Scarlatti.'

Another Italian composer who spent nearly all the latter part of his life in Spain was LUIGI BOCCHERINI (1743–1805) who wrote among other compositions three quintets for strings and guitar and a Spanish ballet for performance in Vienna and Moscow in 1775. The four movements are larghetto, minuet-andantino, allegretto and contredanse, and the Spanish atmosphere is suggested by pizzicato strings and syncopated passages. It was indeed a hybrid style which became normal for music in the theatre in Spain during the eighteenth century. The *zarzuela* continued to present themes from Greek mythology and most of the arias were in the Italian style, though a few *seguidillas* and *villancicos* were incorporated in the rustic or pastoral scenes. This tendency is evident in a *zarzuela* dating from about 1700, *Veneno es de amor la envidia* by SEBASTIÁN DURÓN, then choirmaster of the Capilla Real. Durón, it seems, had a greater gift for theatre music than for church music and the story goes that after King Philip V had listened to an indifferent performance in the Chapel Royal he asked Durón why his conducting was always more successful in the theatre than in church. Durón replied: 'Your majesty, in the theatre it is the devil who leads the performers whereas in the Chapel Royal it is only myself.'

JOSÉ DE NEBRA (1688–1768) was such a prolific composer that he earned the title of the Lope de Vega of Spanish music. Among his many compositions for the stage was a setting of Calderón's *La vida es sueño* and a large number of *zarzuelas*. Fashionable taste compelled him to adhere to mythological subjects for the libretti, but he was not above parodying Italian mannerisms. In *Aquiles en Troya* (1747) two comic characters sing *seguidillas* beneath the walls of Troy and thus determinedly maintain the popular element that the *zarzuela* had contained almost since its inception. Nevertheless, it was not until 1768 that a writer dared completely to flout convention and produce a *zarzuela* on a contemporary theme, sentimental and romantic as it may be. Ramón de la Cruz wrote *Las segadoras de Vallecas* which deals with the story of a wealthy young landowner who falls in love with a pretty member of a band of reapers engaged to gather his harvest. Fortunately she turns out to be in reality of good family, because a musical comedy cannot afford to offend all preconceived ideas. This *zarzuela* with music by ANTONIO RODRÍGUEZ DE HITA (d. 1787) was new in conception and turned public attention away from legendary heroes and implausible shepherds. Its success encouraged the author and composer to produce in 1769 a similar but more striking work, *Las labradoras de Murcia*, which portrays the life of silkworkers in Murcia. The principal scene is one in which a thunderstorm threatens and the workers, believing firmly in the local superstition that the noise of thunder will kill silkworms, arrive with their guitars and perform a *jota*, that is a swift and noisy song and dance, to exclude the sounds of the storm. The orchestra provides admirably descriptive background thunder while the performers on the stage give an artistic rendering of folk music. This *zarzuela* is in a way a masterpiece which unfortunately has been forgotten and since the full score exists in the Biblioteca Municipal in Madrid an opportunity exists for an enterprising musicologist to revive a piece in which words and music combine so happily.

In spite of Ramón de la Cruz's innovations the popularity of the *zarzuela* waned in the late eighteenth century not only because Italian opera under extensive royal patronage continued to thrive, but also because of the rise of a kind of miniature musical comedy known as a *tonadilla*. Originally this was a short song attached to an *entremés* or *sainete*, performed between the acts of a longer play because the Spanish theatre audience cannot bear to be kept waiting in inactivity. Such songs gave an opportunity for gay social satire similar to that of the *sainetes* and also an escape from the stilted Italian style. Soon *tonadillas* combined action with singing and also included dancing; over two thousand such works can be found in the Biblioteca Municipal in Madrid on every kind of subject, allegorical, historical, biographical, but the favourite theme is contemporary satire portraying the ordinary working population of Madrid and especially the violent dandies and their girls, the *majos* who bear a remarkable resemblance to the swaggering and destructive teenage bands that have appeared in the 1960s in England and other European countries. One of the best known *tonadilleros* was MANUEL GARCÍA (1775–1832) who, besides being a leading opera singer, was for a time assistant conductor in the Teatro de la Cruz in Madrid. One of his *tonadillas*, *El criado fingido*, contained a folksong in a syncopated rhythm known as a *polo* and inspired part of the prelude to the fourth act of Bizet's *Carmen*. In fact the music of the *tonadillas* was genuinely based on Spanish folk-music, representing a complete breakaway from Italian forms and as such inspired composers in many parts of Europe, not least Rossini (and later Liszt) who eagerly took up Spanish themes, while musical activity in Spain itself was largely stifled by Fernando VII's exile of all liberal intellectuals. During this period the *tonadilla* disappeared from the Madrid stage, since satire was dangerous, and when after Fernando's death in 1833 liberalism returned to Spain, its place was taken by a revival of the *zarzuela*. To such a low ebb had composition fallen in Spain that this national theatrical style was in fact regenerated by an Italian, Basilio Basili, in 1839 with the production of *El novio y el concierto*. This reaction against Italian music by an Italian was hailed as a novelty and achieved an instant popularity which has never since dwindled.

The *zarzuela* received splendid impetus from a composer of distinction, FRANCISCO ASENJO BARBIERI (1823–94) whose wide experience enabled him to bring extremely colourful popular Spanish music to the stage. He had played the clarinet in military bands, theatre orchestras, and with street musicians, and was for a time conductor of a touring opera troupe whose finances were so precarious that he often had to make his way back to Madrid on foot, earning the price of a meal singing and playing the mandolin. Hence he was steeped in authentic Spanish folk-music and not merely in imitations. His skilful presentation of the genuine elements of the national musical tradition inspired native composers like Albéniz and Falla to eschew foreign forms. His best *zarzuelas* have almost the zest of a picture by Goya, who indeed appears as a character in one of them, *Pan y toros* (1864); here the scene in which the president of the bullring is elected is particularly vigorous with a march and chorus accompanied by guitars and mandolins on the stage.

A Spanish opera

With the *zarzuela* so popular it seemed that an authentic Spanish opera could not be far off. So far there had never been a successful opera in Spain, though a Spanish composer working abroad, MARTÍN Y SOLER (b. 1756), had briefly outshone Mozart in Vienna with his opera *Una cosa rara* (1786). Mozart includes one of the tunes from it in the selection of popular airs played by the orchestra at Don Giovanni's final supper party, but though the tune is gay and jaunty, it appears thin and insignificant alongside Mozart's own *Non più andrai*. Hopes were pinned on Barbieri to write a Spanish grand opera, but he excused himself on the grounds that he could never find 'an author with whom I could come to an understanding'. It was left to a composer inferior to Barbieri to score a moderate success in the field of serious opera. TOMÁS BRETÓN (1850–1923) was a pupil of Arrieta, one of the foremost exponents of the Italian style in Spain, but although Bretón studied for a year in Italy at the expense of the Spanish government, he came out strongly in favour of national music. 'Italianism chokes and degrades our art', he declared in a militant speech to the Real Academia. His first operatic triumph was his five act opera, *Los amantes de Teruel* (1889), based on the play by Hartzenbusch, which was received with acclamation in Madrid and Barcelona and with polite interest in Vienna and Prague. An even greater triumph was his three act opera, *La Dolores*, produced in 1895 for sixty-three consecutive performances in Madrid to be followed by similar successes in South America. Unfortunately Bretón's music has lost its appeal and his operas are rarely heard today, but his ideal of nationalism in music had a significant effect on his contemporaries and FELIPE PEDRELL (1841–1922) worked unceasingly in

the cause of regenerating Spanish music with the goal of national grand
opera as his ultimate aim. In his dramatic trilogy, *Los Pirineos*, he tried
to recreate Spanish music so that it reflected not only folk-songs, but
also the genius and masterpieces of 'the great centuries of art'. In
attempting to achieve this he borrowed from popular music and from
the works of sixteenth century composers such as Tomás de Santa
María and these borrowings are not fully merged into the work, which
bears a slightly patchwork appearance. More successful is *La Celestina*
(1904), but here again much admirable material for the singers is scarcely
matched in the orchestral parts. Nevertheless, it was acclaimed as the
Spanish *Tristan und Isolde* and Pedrell was hailed as the Wagner of
Spain; but Pedrell lacked Wagner's musical genius, although he equalled
him in fervent devotion to national themes. It is on his research into the
history of Spanish music that Pedrell's fame chiefly rests and it was his
teaching and guidance that inspired a group of young Spanish composers whose work has made the late nineteenth and early twentieth
century the greatest epoch in Spanish music.

Albéniz and Granados

Two of Pedrell's pupils, Albéniz and Granados, with their compositions
for the piano, made genuine Spanish music as famous internationally
as the imitation variety that Bizet had so successfully propagated.
ISAAC MANUEL FRANCISCO ALBÉNIZ (1860–1909) had a remarkably
adventurous career up to the age of twenty, showing a precocity that
only Mozart could rival. His first piano concert was given at the age
of four and his application to join the Paris Conservatoire at the age of
seven was rejected solely on the grounds of his tender age, because, so
the story goes, after passing the entrance examination, he had the
misfortune to break a mirror playing with a ball. At the age of eight
Albéniz ran away from home and embarked on a concert tour alone
throughout northern Spain. Not long afterwards on a similar jaunt to
Andalusia he stowed away on the steamer, *España*, bound for Puerto
Rico. He was put ashore at Buenos Aires where he lived as he could
like a classic Spanish *pícaro*. However, he managed to contrive a concert
tour and ended up in Cuba at the age of thirteen in comparative
affluence. Here he met his father who tried to bring him back to the
family fold, but finally let him go on his wanderings, impressed by the
money the boy had made. Albéniz went to New York and was soon
penniless; after working as a docker for a time, he made a name for

Isaac Albéniz

himself as a trick pianist, standing with his back to the piano and playing
with the backs of his fingers. By these inelegant methods he collected
enough money to return to Europe, calling at Liverpool and London
where he played with considerable success. After studying in Brussels
and receiving lessons from Liszt in Germany he again toured Europe
and America, this time as a respectable and respected virtuoso.

It was in 1883 that Albéniz began to be interested in Spanish national music under the guidance of Pedrell and he gradually assumed the role of a composer of serious music rather than that of a musical freak. He was, however, tempted by a financial offer from an English millionaire banker, Francis Money Coutts, who had pretensions as a dramatic author and proposed a large annual income if Albéniz would compose music for these plays (and for no other). Albéniz duly made what he called his 'pact with Faust' and some insipid productions followed on English pseudo-historical themes, chief of which was *Henry Clifford* (1895). Albéniz managed to persuade his patron to choose a Spanish subject and the following year *Pepita Jiménez* emerged with more success. But since Valera's novel was written mostly in letter form, Coutts's meagre talents were strained in dramatising the struggle between love human and divine. The libretto was clumsy and the music contained variegated passages with themes taken from several European nations. Moreover, Albéniz was never master of orchestral music and the score is more suitable for the piano.

After 1892 Albéniz had begun to concentrate on composition for the piano and in spite of being greatly influenced by musicians of the Parisian school, Bordes, D'Indy and Dukas, it was from Andalusia that he drew his inspiration (though he himself was a native of Catalonia). Though his piano compositions are reckoned in hundreds, it is for his suite *Iberia* that he is chiefly remembered. Published in four books between 1906 and 1909, the suite consists of twelve movements, almost all evoking some place in Andalusia, though one 'impression' entitled *Lavapiés* attempts to depict life in the popular quarter of Madrid. This in fact is probably the least successful because of its elaboration and complexity. Much of Albéniz's work is needlessly difficult to play, but the music is full of deep feeling and colour and extremely diverse in character and rhythm. Almost all the popular music of Andalusia finds a place in the suite, the gay *Sevillanas*, the amazing semi-oriental *cante jondo*, the *saetas* or laments of Holy Week, *fandangos, coplas, jotas, bulerías*, are all superbly interwoven among the various impressions of Andalusian towns, Seville, Granada, Málaga, Almería, Cádiz, Ronda. The piece entitled *Triana* (referring to the crowded suburb of Seville south of the river Guadalquivir) is played probably most often of all on account of its attractive melodies and vigorous rhythms of the *paso doble* and *marcha torera*, and it has been compared with Liszt's *Hungarian Rhapsodies*. Equally effective is another impression of Seville, *Eritaña*, the name of a famous inn on the outskirts of the city. Of this Debussy wrote: 'Never has music achieved such diverse, such colourful impressions: one's eyes close, as though dazzled by beholding such a wealth of imagery.'

ENRIQUE GRANADOS (1867–1916) in contrast to Albéniz hated travelling, especially by sea and persistently refused all invitations to visit America until at last he was persuaded to attend the first performance in New York of his opera *Goyescas*. On his way home he and his wife lost their lives when the steamship *Sussex* was torpedoed by a German submarine. Like Albéniz, Granados was a Catalan, but he was attracted to Madrid not Andalusia, and the Madrid he chose to depict was the bustling, arrogant life of the city in the time of Goya when the upper and lower classes seemed to merge in exuberant festivities. But Granados for all his passion for Goya neglects the satire and fierce human commentary of the artist's work and concentrates on the gay and charming picture of life represented by Goya's early paintings and the tapestries in the Escorial. His music has classical composure tinged with the sentiment and pathos which at the end of the eighteenth century foreshadowed the coming of romanticism. It is not so truly representative of Spain as Albéniz's work, for it does not evoke the life of the people; it represents a slightly idealised picture of a kind of life that no longer existed in Madrid, and it has been described as escapist music. There may be some truth in this criticism, but the music of Granados is full of charm, rich in colour and with subtle rhythms. His most important work for the piano is the *Goyescas*, a series of six pieces published in two volumes between 1912 and 1914. Bearing the subtitle of *Los majos enamorados*, the pieces depict the complicated business of love-making in Spain. The first piece is *Los requiebros*, referring to the elaborate compliments that gallants pay to ladies in the preliminary skirmishes of wooing. The second *Goyesca* is the *Coloquio en la reja* when the two lovers talk decorously in the evening through the window grill and the suitor serenades his lover with guitar accompaniment which is represented by the piano part in the bass. After *El fandango del candil* (Dance of the Lamp), the lovers have a passionate interview in which they reproach one another while the nightingale sings (*Quejas o la maja y el ruiseñor*). Jealousy provokes a duel between two suitors and one young gallant is mortally wounded (*El amor y la muerte*). The suite ends with a kind of epilogue in the form of a serenade by the ghost of the dead suitor (*Serenata del espectro*). A seventh piece written later has now become attached to the suite as an introduction named *El pelele* (The Dummy) based on Goya's picture of the *majas* gaily tossing up a man of straw, indicating how lightly women play with men's affections.

The theme connecting this series of piano pieces was made into a libretto by Fernando Periquet and Granados adapted the music for an opera which was to have been performed in Paris in 1914. Cancelled by the outbreak of war the work was eventually performed at the Metropolitan Opera House, New York, on 28 January 1916, and was received with acclaim by the critics for its genuine Spanish atmosphere (of which no doubt they were indifferent judges) and also for the 'haunting power' of the music. It was performed five times, but has been neglected ever since. Characteristically the extract from it most frequently performed at concerts is the orchestral intermezzo hastily composed by Granados shortly before the first performance in order to allow time for a change of scenery.

Albéniz and Granados were both Catalans, although they were neither directly interested in the music of their native province and in Catalonia at the end of the nineteenth century there was a remarkable wealth of musical talent. JAIME PAHISSA (b. 1880) was a successful operatic composer with his romantic Catalan drama *La Princesa Margarida* (1906); he also wrote many orchestral works of which *El camí*, a symphonic poem, is the best known. There were a host of other Catalan composers of considerable distinction who have not, however, won an international reputation, but the chief glory of Catalan music is the 'cellist PABLO CASALS (b. 1876) who besides being acknowledged complete master of his instrument did splendid work in popularising classical music in Spain by founding an orchestra and a concert association for the working classes. Like so many composers, writers and artists he has chosen to live in exile since the fall of the Republic in 1939. Other regions besides Catalonia produced first-rate musicians. PABLO DE SARASATE (1844–1908) came from Navarre and astounded the world by his virtuosity on the violin, being spoken of in the same breath as Paganini; in addition he was a composer of no mean merit for his instrument. He executed the most difficult bravura passages with the utmost ease and nonchalance and his manner on the concert platform was dignified and graceful, as shown in the portrait of him by Whistler. The Basque Provinces were also well represented musically; the foremost of their composers was JOSÉ MARÍA USANDIZAGA (1887–1915) whose best known work was the highly successful opera *Las Golondrinas* (1914) with a plot telling of love and jealousy in a circus troupe. His purely Basque music such as *Umerzurtza* (The orphan) for soprano, tenor, chorus and orchestra is possibly more interesting, but since he had studied in Paris at the Schola Cantorum, there is always a slight French flavour about his music which is vaguely reminiscent of César Franck.

Madrid itself could boast of a highly popular composer, CONRADO DEL CAMPO (1879–1953), who was a fervent romantic. His one act opera *El final de Don Álvaro* (1910) depicts the tragic and stormy end to the life of Rivas's hero. Like Granados he has evoked the gay, ebullient life of the late eighteenth century in Madrid in *El lavapiés* (1919), but his best known works are a series of string quartets, *Caprichos románticos*, inspired by Bécquer's *Rimas*. By contrast a composer from Alicante, OSCAR ESPLÁ (b. 1881), has shown a greater tendency to experiment although he bases much of his music on the folk-songs of the Levante. Being by profession a civil engineer and also by inclination a philosopher, he was naturally interested in the structure of musical composition and he evolved a scale of his own devising, C, D flat, E flat, E, F, G flat, A flat, B flat, but this experiment, interesting as it is, has not produced much harmonic variety and Esplá's music tends to be monotonous. His work best known in the international field is *Don Quijote velando las armas* (1927) which was originally intended for a small orchestra, but was recast for a full orchestra with additional percussion.

More famous abroad was an Andalusian musician, JOAQUÍN TURINA (1882–1949), who in many ways was an indifferent composer; he achieved little in the style of César Franck until Albéniz persuaded him to cultivate the form of Andalusian music. Such is the power and fascination of this type of music that Turina's work quickly gained widespread popularity in spite of a certain lack of invention. He wrote charming pieces for the piano; the suite *Sevilla, Tres danzas andaluzas, Mujeres de España*, is widely known for its picturesque qualities. His *Canto a Sevilla* for soprano and orchestra and his *Danzas fantásticas* have also received performances in many countries.

Manuel de Falla

It was from Andalusia that the greatest modern Spanish composer originated, MANUEL DE FALLA (1876–1946). Born in Cádiz, Falla was brought up in a musical family and at the age of eleven took part with his mother in a performance of Haydn's *Seven last words of Our Saviour* which had originally been composed especially for one of the churches at Cádiz. It was after listening to a series of concerts in the Museo de Bellas Artes in Cádiz that Falla determined to devote his life to music and as a first step towards this aim he began to study under the celebrated pianist José Trago at the Madrid Conservatoire. His ambition lay not in the direction of being a concert pianist but a composer and, in order to achieve fame and at the same time to earn money, Falla attempted two *zarzuelas* which were utter failures. Such a disappointment might have discouraged him for ever, but fortunately he came under the influence of Felipe Pedrell, who more than any other man had been the guide and mentor to all the great Spanish composers of the modern era. As with so many others Pedrell convinced his pupil that inspiration should be sought from the folk-music of Spain and in 1905 Falla won a prize given by the Academia de Bellas Artes with his two act opera *La vida breve*, to which he gave an Andalusian setting.

This success enabled him to establish himself as a piano teacher and he earned sufficient money to undertake a journey to Paris which he had long yearned to visit. He went to stay for a week and remained seven years, making friends with most of the leading musicians there, including Dukas, Ravel and Debussy who were admirers of Spanish music. In Paris he acquired not a cosmopolitan outlook on music, but rather a firm technique of orchestration. Moreover, his devotion to Spanish folk-music was confirmed and strengthened by the friendship he made in Paris with Isaac Albéniz, who offered much stimulating advice. In 1909 Falla began to compose some evocative nocturnes for piano and orchestra on lines similar to Albéniz's *Iberia* suite, entitled *Noches en los jardines de España*. This work is not in reality a piano concerto, for the piano is an integral part of the orchestra rather than being complementary to it. All the charm and rhythmic power of Spanish folk-music is to be found in the *Noches* together with an underlying melancholy that is essentially part of the Spanish character. Falla revealed his mastery of blending popular with academic music in his *Siete canciones populares españolas* (1914), where he presents folk-tunes with accompaniments of such subtlety that like the poetry of García Lorca (whom later he was to influence greatly) the music offers a combined appeal to popular taste and intellectual interest.

On the outbreak of the first world war Falla returned to Spain where he produced a ballet, *El amor brujo*, especially for the famous dancer Pastora Imperio, who had begged him for a ballet in which she could not only dance but sing as well. Its theme is the exorcising of the ghost

Falla, by Picasso

of a dead lover who intervenes in the courtship of Candelas and Carmelo and the music, though hastily composed, is dramatic and effective; no actual folk-tunes have been used, but Falla has exactly captured the spirit of *Cante jondo* in the vocal sections, particularly in the *Canción del amor dolido* which has all the passionate melancholy of the most moving *saetas* heard in Holy Week. The dances are also outstandingly effective; the Dance of Terror is a powerful evocation of the emotion of fear and the Ritual Fire Dance which Candelas performs at midnight to exorcise evil spirits is primitively savage and forceful. First produced in 1915 at the Teatro Lara in Madrid, it did not begin to achieve popularity as a ballet until after 1925 and particularly after its performance in 1928 by Antonia Mercé, better known as *La Argentina*.

Falla's next work was also a ballet, *El Corregidor y la Molinera*, which was first performed in 1917. It was then largely rewritten and produced in London in 1919 by Diaghilev with choreography by Leonide Massine under the title of Alarcón's novel on which it was based, *The Three-Cornered Hat*. With the added attraction of décor by Picasso, the ballet was an immediate success and has since gained an international reputation, being especially popular in Russia where no doubt its theme of the virtuous peasant couple triumphing over the lecherous Corregidor appealed to good Party members. Again there is a basis of folk-music, but only a few snatches from actual folk-tunes. The rhythms are unmistakably Andalusian, though a *jota* from Navarre is included because the miller's wife came from Estella.

Falla was showing signs of drawing away from Andalusian inspiration alone and was finding a more universal application for his creative ability, though still remaining Spanish in essentials. His puppet opera, *El retablo de Maese Pedro*, was intended for a private performance in the marionette theatre belonging to the Princesse de Polignac in Paris where it was first performed in 1923. It was a complex production because it depicts the puppet show given before Don Quijote by Maese Pedro recounting the ballad of Don Gayferos and Melisendra pursued by the Moors. There are therefore two sets of marionettes, Don Quijote, Maese Pedro and the Boy who tells the story of the smaller puppets in the show. The production is further complicated by the fact that Don Quijote, believing the Moorish marionettes to be real infidels, hews them in pieces with his sword. The staging of such a performance in a commercial theatre achieved little success until the three main characters were played not by marionettes but by singers, an experiment first made at Bristol in 1924. The music was scored for a small orchestra

Jota de Cadavedo

of some twenty-five players, but Falla with these modest resources
achieves a great variety of effects. Above all he has created the impression of music of the Golden Age and the opera gives a faithful image of
a contemporary setting of an incident from Cervantes's novel.

This sense of historical forms of music is also revealed in Falla's
Concerto (1923–26) for harpsichord, violin, cello, clarinet, oboe and
flute. Again there are reminders of folk-tunes, particularly the theme
taken from the *villancico*, *De los álamos vengo, madre* by Juan Vázquez,
which appears in the first movement. Equally there are reminders of
Scarlatti's style, yet much of the music is austerely modern. The
Concerto is short, taking only about ten minutes to play, with three
movements, Allegro, Lento and Vivace. The effect of spaciousness and
sonority achieved in this work with its limited number of instruments
is quite remarkable. The blend of ancient and modern once more
makes the comparison inevitable between Falla's music and Lorca's
poetry. Falla is Scarlatti reincarnated and yet in no sense an imitation,
because all Falla's individuality and modern idiom are retained. Lorca
echoes Góngora, but is still characteristic of the twentieth century.

Falla in fact composed a setting for Góngora's poem, *Soneto a
Córdoba*, in 1927 on the occasion of the tercentenary of the poet's

death. The song has a harp accompaniment which is reminiscent of the work of sixteenth-century *vihuelistas*, strong, sonorous and rich in tone and it is unfortunate that this work has been much neglected by singers and harpists. This composition virtually marks the end of Falla's active career as a creative artist. He had never been a facile composer and had always taken the greatest care to polish his music before its performance. He had retired to a cottage near the Alhambra in Granada and from here he frequently organised festivals of *Cante jondo*, but his work as a composer had slowed down. He was engaged on a *magnum opus* in the shape of a setting for a Catalan poem by Jacinto Verdaguer named *La Atlántida*, which deals with the legend of the lost continent of Atlantis and how hearing of it inspired Columbus to set out westward in search of new land. Progress was slow, understandably enough because Falla had been obliged first to learn Catalan in order to read the poem since he scorned to use the Castilian version for his setting. Work was further interrupted by the Civil War and in common with so many other intellectuals Falla went into voluntary exile, taking up residence in Alta Gracia de Córdoba in Argentina where he died in 1946 with *La Atlántida* still unfinished. Falla's body was transported back to Spain and buried with considerable pomp in Cádiz cathedral. The incomplete score of *La Atlántida* was entrusted to one of Falla's pupils, Ernesto Halffter, so that it could be finished and performed in 1956 when the city of Cádiz celebrated the 3,000th anniversary of its foundation. Unfortunately the finished score was not forthcoming and the work remains shrouded in mystery, except that it is said that the Prologue and Part III are fairly complete with full orchestration by Falla, but that Parts I and II are only in outline form. Portions of *La Atlántida* were performed for the first time in public at Barcelona on 24 November 1961, and the style proved to be notably different from that of Falla's earlier work, resembling, especially in the choral passages, the austere grandeur of sixteenth-century Spanish music.

Music since the Civil War

ERNESTO HALFFTER (b. 1905) is of German extraction, but strangely enough the only musical encouragement he received was from his Spanish maternal grandmother who gave him a liking for Italian opera; at the age of sixteen he had already composed two operas in the Italian style. Such precocious gifts attracted the attention of Manuel de Falla who accepted the boy as a private pupil. He taught Ernesto Halffter not only to appreciate Spanish national music, but also to acquire a sound and disciplined technique of composition rather than to exploit his facility. At twenty Ernesto wrote a four-act opera, *La muerte de Carmen*, which follows Mérimée's story more closely than the libretto that Bizet used and whose music is authentically Spanish though on similar lines to that of Bizet. It was intended for a French screen version of *Carmen*, and the vast score was greatly reduced for the purpose of the film. In 1934 he was appointed Director of the Madrid Conservatoire, but the Civil War caused him to leave Spain and he settled in Portugal where he composed possibly his best work, the *Portuguese Rhapsody* (1939) for piano and orchestra.

The Halffters are a musical family: Ernesto's brother, RODOLFO HALFFTER (b. 1900) has also achieved fame as a composer, especially with his ballet, *Don Lindo de Almería* (1936). Though he has a deep knowledge of Spanish folk-music, his style of composition is more academic than his brother's and there is a strong resemblance in his works to Schönberg and Stravinsky. He was closely associated with the Republican government's musical activities and like his brother had to leave the country in 1939; since General Franco's victory he has lived in Mexico, where he continues to compose music based mainly on Spanish themes.

The nephew of these two brothers, CRISTÓBAL HALFFTER (b. 1930) is an active composer in Madrid and has written a ballet, *Saeta* (1955), performed by the Marqués de Cueva's company, and a solemn mass for mixed chorus with orchestral or organ accompaniment, the *Misa Ducal* (1956), commissioned by the Duque de Alba and first performed at his residence in Madrid. Apart from a strong Catalan school of composers, FEDERICO MOMPOU (b. 1893), XAVIER BASSOLS (b. 1912) and NARCISO BONET (b. 1933), almost all contemporary Spanish composers are living abroad. The most significant of them perhaps is JULIÁN BAUTISTA (b. 1901), a member of a group of composers almost all of whom were dispersed by the Civil War. Bautista emigrated to Argentina, but has composed many works on Spanish themes. His *Tres ciudades* (1938) concerns three Andalusian towns, Málaga with a tragic lament (*Malagueña*), Córdoba with a nocturne (*Barrio de Córdoba*) and finally Seville with a passionate, sensual dance (*Baile*). As in Lorca's poems the traditional folk elements are integrated into the musical structure. A similar mixture of peasant simplicity and modern sophistication is to be found in his *Catro poemas galegos*, evoking reminders of the great deeds of Spain's past, such as the defence of La Coruña organised by María Pita against Sir Francis Drake, or Bishop Adaulfo of Santiago who proved his innocence by fighting a wild bull in the ring. On similar heroic lines, but with modern sophistication in the use of dissonance and irregular rhythms, is the *Romance del Rey Rodrigo* (1956), a choral work based on the ballads which tell the story of King Rodrigo's betrayal to the Moors by Count Julián.

Other composers living abroad whose ties with Spain are far more tenuous have written music on Spanish traditional themes, notably JOAQUÍN NIN-CULMELL (b. 1908) who in 1958 wrote a score for a ballet on the Don Juan legend and CARLOS SURIÑACH (b. 1915) who, though like Nin-Culmell is a citizen of the United States, has composed a large number of works in the Andalusian style, chiefly in *flamenco* form. One wonders whether the popularity of Spanish music is not somewhat exploited in the modern world where people surrounded with the comforts of central heating and frozen, precooked food are inclined to yearn for primitive passion and rhythmic power for their musical diet. In satisfying this craving Spanish folk-music has made a unique contribution and even had there been no Spanish composers of the stature of Albéniz and Granados and Falla, the music of Spain would still have made a fascinating subject for study.

Folk-music

Spanish folk-music is completely different from that of any other European nation; Spain, because of its geographical position, has largely been cut off from the main stream of European culture and has been subject to widespread influence from the Middle East. This influence was naturally strongest in Andalusia where not only was Moorish culture dominant for many centuries, but also large numbers of gypsies settled in the fifteenth century. Hebraic influence has also been added to the brew, but the basic ingredient of Spanish music was the adoption by the Visigoths before the Moors arrived of the Byzantine style of chanting church services. The most striking result of this curious mixture is the *cante jondo* (or *hondo*) of Andalusia; it is called 'deep song' by many English writers because of the intensity of feeling expressed, but the name may derive from the Hebrew *Jom Tor*, meaning a feast day. There is indeed a resemblance to the chanting of Jewish services in synagogues, but the strongest influence is probably Byzantine. The melody of the *cante jondo* is usually contained within the compass of the sixth, but the singer's voice moves through a series of extremely small gradations, much less than a semi-tone, so that there are available many more than the normal nine notes of a sixth. This sliding of the voice with subtle changes of volume is further elaborated by an extensive use of embellishments, such as apoggiatura, so that the final version of the melody is richly decorated. This enables a *copla* (a stanza of four lines) to represent a full length song with guitar accompaniment, when the words, though they may contain a striking image, are often somewhat pedestrian. Such a song depends for its effect almost entirely on the singer and presents great difficulty in performance. It is almost impossible for someone not brought up to this style of singing to interpret *cante jondo* effectively; it is fascinating to hear Spanish maids washing up over an English sink spontaneously singing *cante jondo* while the rain beats a cheerless accompaniment on the window pane. Folk-music is deeply ingrained in Spaniards and until very recently has successfully resisted the onslaughts of jazz. Now with the extension of wireless and television programmes some withdrawal is noticeable and shops even in quite small towns are full of records of American or Liverpudlian origin, but national feeling is still strong and indigenous forms of music still persist just as pipe music has by no means been ousted from Scotland.

Like much Scottish music Andalusian songs are in the form of laments; *playeras*, *soleás* and *saetas* are all songs expressing deep feelings of sorrow. The *soleá* is a song of loneliness on the part of someone cut off by the death of sweetheart or father or mother. The *saeta* is the passionate lament sung unaccompanied before the figure of Christ scourged or crucified which is carried in the religious processions of Holy Week. The gaiety associated with Andalusia is normally reserved for *flamenco* songs and dances, which are of more recent origin than the *cante jondo*. *Flamenco* means Flemish, but was merely the nationality ignorantly attributed by common people to the gypsies who had infiltrated into Spain from the north. There is an infinite variety of these songs, many of them being named after the towns in which they are popular, *granadinas*, *malagueñas*, *rondeñas*, *sevillanas*. The predominant rhythm is 3/4 or 3/8 time and all are lively as are the dances for which they form the accompaniment. These dances are not of gypsy origin, but form part of the folk-lore of the whole of Andalusia. For the most part they are not community dances, but are danced by one or two performers, though the onlookers take an important part by clapping the complex rhythms and encouraging the dancers with shouts of; ¡*Olé!* and other forms of *jaleo*. The rhythm is also emphasised by the

ABOVE *Easter procession*

BELOW *El Jaleo by Sargent*

dancers snapping their fingers (*pito*), since castanets are not used in true *flamenco* dancing and by the continuous tapping of the feet (*zapateado*) which is especially favoured by male dancers as a sign of dominant virility. This is best displayed in the *farruca* in which the woman, if she appears at all, plays only a minor role. The man dances at furious speed, tapping out the rhythm, turning, leaping, throwing himself full length to the ground and jumping to his feet again. Suddenly in the midst of this welter of movement he will come to a sudden dramatic halt which by contrast emphasises the astonishing rapidity of the rest of the dance.

Spanish Dancing

The woman *flamenco* dancer comes into her own with the *tango* which is only vaguely related rhythmically to the ballroom version. In the *tango* the woman stamps the rhythm with her heels (*taconeo*) and twirls a round flat *sombrero* in her hands when she is not wearing it on her head. A similar dance for a woman is the *garrotín*, distinguished by a fluttering arm action, but the gayest is the *alegría* in which the dancer makes full use of the long-trained skirt *a volantes* in sudden turns while snapping her fingers to provide a cross rhythm with the guitars and the clapping of the onlookers. *Flamenco* dancing is a noisy procedure and the uninitiated find it difficult to tolerate more than a limited quantity at a time, but the dances, when well performed, are powerful, rhythmical and controlled, though hinting at extreme passion and violence of feeling. The energy of the male dancer in his tight-fitting trousers, cummerbund, short open jacket and round flat *sombrero* is extraordinary.

Although music differs widely in the various provinces, there are many obvious similarities since most of the folk-songs were based on the chanting in the churches and on the Moorish influence which extended almost throughout the peninsula. The guitar often gives way as an accompaniment to rustic flutes and small drums or tambourines or in Galicia to a bagpipe (*gaita gallega*). In Castile songs are marked by asymmetrical patterns of notes and a dominant cadence, and are hard to sing except by those accustomed to such music from childhood. Especially difficult to master is the end of many songs, *canciones de ronda* (serenades by night to sweethearts or friends), when the singer gives a sharp, shrill cry followed by others in a descending scale of irregular intervals. This disconcerting whinny is also to be found in the Basque Provinces and is believed to be of Celtic origin.

Types of guitars

In Castile the *bolero* is danced and originates from Cádiz where it was invented about 1780 by SEBASTIÁN CEREZO. It spread quickly from Cádiz after Spain had been discovered in the nineteenth century by travellers such as Richard Ford and Théophile Gautier. Its name derives from the verb *volar* (to fly) and it is a dance which gives plenty of scope for the performers to display their virtuosity. The dance is divided into three parts; the first is the *paseo* in which the performers merely walk round, as in many other varieties of Spanish dancing, with a fine mixture of grace and pride. In the second part individual dancers show off their skill with leaps, pirouettes and entrechats (*cuartas*) accompanied all the time by the chatter of castanets. The final part is called the *bien parado* (lit. well stopped) because the dancers suddenly cease all movement at the end of a musical phrase and adopt striking attitudes which evoke applause from the audience and cries of *bien parado*.

Another well-known dance linked with folk-music is the *jota* which, though popular in many parts of Spain, is to be found in its most characteristic form in Aragon. The music is in lively triple time and the dance is equally rapid, demanding much energy and physical endurance. Like so many Spanish dances which remind one of the display dances of birds, the theme of the *jota* is basically one of courtship. It is danced by couples, the man in black breeches and waistcoat with brightly coloured headgear and sash and the woman in a full peasant skirt of plain colour with a black shawl wrapped around her bosom and shoulders as if she were in danger of catching cold. The dancers face each other with arms above their heads, vigorously clacking their castanets in time with the guitars and *bandurrias* (a variation of the mandolin) which accompany the dance. At times the woman sits on the ground while the man whirls and pirouettes around her; at other times the couple both kneel and, as it were, dance on their knees. Again the speed of the dance is emphasised by the sudden stops and the adoption of a pose that is proud and challenging with head drawn back and one arm curved above it. Then abruptly the dance continues at a furious pace, but always with exquisite grace. The Valencian *jota* is similar, but the women's costumes of softly embroidered silk give it a less austere and primitive aspect.

Another gentler and less passionate dance is the Catalan *sardana* which calls for no feats of virtuosity or complex dancing technique; it is in fact a communal round dance, popular in the Middle Ages in many countries and much in favour in the seventeenth century among the aristocracy. The name originates from the province of Cerdagne in the Pyrenees, partly French and partly Spanish and the word is first found at the end of the sixteenth century. Though the type of dance is of very ancient origin, the *sardana* in its present form is really the work of JOSEP VENTURA (1817–75) and MIQUEL PARDAS (1818–72). Pep Ventura devoted his life to collecting popular dance tunes of Catalonia and composing fresh ones in the traditional style. He also altered and extended the accompaniment to the *sardana* by a group of musicians known as a *cobla* which now usually consists of four brass and four woodwind instruments; the master of ceremonies who announces the start of the dance also beats time on the *tambouri* attached to his elbow at the same time playing a tiny, three-holed pipe. The dance is basically simple, consisting of two steps to the left and two to the right with the men and women holding hands in a circle. The dance is divided into two parts, the first sad and slow in which the steps are described as *curts* (short steps) and the second part is gay and quick with the steps called *llargs* (long steps), though in fact this means that four steps are taken as opposed to two. A *sardana* appears simplicity itself, but as in an eightsome reel appearances are deceptive and the dancers have to pay strict

ABOVE   *Día de Vascongadas*

BELOW   *The Pilar Oro Ballet*

Dancers at Badajoz

attention to the music in order to end up in the right place. The modern arrangement of the *sardana* was established definitely by Miquel Pardas, a well-known dancer, in his book *Método per apendre a ballar sardanas llargas* (1850). The *sardana* is especially picturesque because of the brightly coloured costumes of the dancers; the women wear flowered skirts and tight black bodices over white blouses while the men wear black breeches and waistcoats with scarlet caps and sashes and kingfisher blue stockings.

The Basques also have a communal dance, but it is characteristically energetic and vigorous and as a result the male element predominates. The dance is complex, consisting of as many as eight figures of which the central figure is the *desafío* (challenge). Here the line of dancers divides and the *aurresku* (leader) and his opposite number, the *atzescu* (rear man) try to outdo each other in leaps and pirouettes. Gradually the two rows of dancers draw together until they are only some three yards apart and the *desafío* ends with an extra lofty leap. At other times the dancers form a single line holding hands, with the *aurresku* and *atzescu* displaying their skill and energy at opposite ends of the file. Another well-known Basque dance is the *ezpata-dantza* (sword dance) which again contains many features of the mime; one man represents a corpse and the other dancers prepare to avenge his death. Though Basque dances are passionate indeed, they are not sensuous like the Andalusian dances; the movements are more relaxed and less stylised and the foreigner can find relief in the greatly reduced amount of noise.

The region of the Asturias has a communal round dance known as the *danza prima* whose origins are believed to date from pre-Christian times. It is danced to the accompaniment of two singers who chant a lengthy ballad of complex love affairs and at the end of each of the many verses the dancers join in with a refrain. It must be admitted that there is a certain monotony in both ballad and dance, as with *Sir Roger de Coverley*, but the spectacle is gay and festive, particularly as the women's costumes are among the prettiest in Spain—skirts of blue or red with a glimpse of plentiful white petticoats beneath, white blouses and caps and black aprons.

Perhaps the most heartening feature of Spanish peasant music and dancing is that it is still to a large extent spontaneous and natural; in spite of increasing commercialism, singing and dancing are still practised by the ordinary people of Spain and are by no means confined to professionals. Certainly for variety and interest Spanish traditional singing and dancing are scarcely matched in any other country in the world. It is strange that the Spaniards have no word with which to describe their festival customs and are obliged to have recourse to the somewhat insipid English term of *el folk-lore*.

The main roads hum with lorries ... but many of the old streets of Castile remain unchanged

Epilogue

In 1936, soon after the rebellion against the Republican government had been firmly launched, Unamuno, the leading Spanish philosopher of the day, at a public meeting in Salamanca attended by Señora Franco coldly curbed the enthusiasm of Nationalist propaganda by remarking: *Venceréis, pero no convenceréis* (You will win, but you will not convince). It is now nearly thirty years since Franco won and it is interesting to speculate whether he has convinced the Spanish people of the justness of his cause and of his subsequent rule.

Outwardly things have improved enormously and in particular in the last ten years in which the tourist trade has set almost all the coastal towns booming, not to mention many other places of exceptional interest such as Segovia, Ávila, Toledo, Salamanca, Seville, Granada. In almost every Spanish town near the main tourist routes the shops are filled with consumer goods undreamed of ten years ago—gas stoves, electric cookers, washing machines, gramophones, television sets. Madrid and other cities are crammed with cars so that driving through their streets is a severe test. The main roads hum with lorries and cars; roadhouses, petrol stations, wayside cafés have sprung up like mushrooms and huge cardboard bulls, bottles and general advertising blurbs bespatter the bare hills and fields beside the road. The old-fashioned Hispanophile feels depressed as he gazes at these recent excrescences, watches the tractors ploughing the vineyards and threads his way through the huge American bulldozers, graders and rollers engaged on roadworks which a few years ago would have been accomplished by gangs with picks and baskets. He may recall that in 1955 he drove his car down the dry bed of a river to bathe on a deserted beach between Málaga and Motril and that now he would find the same beach crowded with foreign holidaymakers careering round in speedboats with water-skiers in tow while on the nearby headland a rash of smart but shoddy villas has erupted, housing well-to-do loafers from every country in western Europe. He may shudder in Granada when he looks up towards the Sierra Nevada where every hilltop seems to bear an electric pylon, and he will remember that the Spanish propaganda magazine *Es* boasts with pride that the previous year has seen the erection of 150,000 more pylons. Taking an evening stroll in the handsome *paseo* at Málaga, the ageing Hispanophile will note with dismay that on benches in shady nooks young men and maidens are locked in unabashed embraces in defiance of the ancient laws of courtship in Spain. He will see girls and boys holding hands and smoking cigarettes, the girls as brazenly as the men; even lads of ten or twelve can be observed puffing conscientiously, though without evident enjoyment, at cigarettes which ten years ago their fathers could never have afforded.

These things may seem trivialities, but it is impossible not to have the impression that Spain is rapidly being spoilt. There are brighter sides to the picture. The younger generation in Spain looks sleek and prosperous; indeed at a glance one would say that the girls are too fat. The grocer in the village by the once deserted beach now has a refrigerated counter; he sells Coca Cola by the ton, Omo and Vim and every known form of modern detergent to aid washing in water that is still derived from one village fountain. On Sunday he drives out in his smart car among the wealthy villas and then indulges in some underwater fishing in the clear sea among the rocks, armed with goggles, breathing tube and submarine guns. Pylons may besmirch the hills, but almost every village enjoys electric light and power with all the blessings, real and dubious, that they confer. Only the old people still look pinched, wrinkled and haggard as though life has been unbearably hard, but somehow they seem to have a dignity, friendliness and willingness to oblige that is sometimes lacking in the brash, confident and pushing younger generation.

The old, traditional poverty-stricken Spain is not hard to find, if that is what the traveller wishes to see; he has only to venture off the main Madrid road to the right or left to find himself in age-old, crumbling villages where the harvest is being threshed in the most primitive fashion. He will be disturbed to think how cruelly hard life must be in the villages of the barren uplands of Castile or Extremadura where, it is estimated, the average peasant's yearly income does not exceed £70. There is still plenty of opportunity for the cultivation of those Spanish virtues of frugality, perseverance, endurance and resignation.

The old traditional, poverty-stricken Spain is not hard to find; the younger generation—perhaps symbolised by El Cordobés?—looks sleek and prosperous

If the peasant is bound by the physical need to keep himself and his family alive, the town dweller equally lacks freedom economically and politically. Salaries are generally too low for comfortable living; a university professor may have to undertake the responsibility of being headmaster of a private school as well in order to make a living, and so find himself without any leisure at all. Worst of all he finds himself limited in self-expression and in the material he can use for teaching. The expression of unorthodox views is likely to cost him his jobs and perforce the family man has to conform. It is this lack of freedom of thought and expression that has kept so many of Spain's leading intellectuals in self-imposed exile. There are signs of some relaxation of the censorship of ideas. For the first time since 1939 the Press was freed from censorship by a law promulgated in 1965 and rubber-stamped in 1966 by the obedient, appointed *Cortes*, but even this freedom is more theoretical than practical because any paper that published unorthodox articles could be prosecuted under the manifold subversion laws or else find its labour withdrawn by the government controlled Syndicates and its raw materials withheld for no reason given. Everything in Spain depends on being *enchufado* (plugged in), that is to say having the right contacts. A conscript (military service for two years is compulsory) can escape the worst rigours of barrack life if he is well *enchufado*. The services anyway are top-heavy with officers because influence can still find soft jobs. It is almost nauseating to sit in the entrance hall of a luxury hotel like the Miramar at Málaga and watch officers and officials waiting humbly for hours, decked out in their best uniforms or suits, to shake hands with some influential minister who is staying there on holiday. Such patronage and toadying exist in any country, but one feels that knowing the right people matters more in Spain than elsewhere and for that very reason the right people may not be in the top positions. Almost everything in Spain now seems shoddy—buildings, roads, manufactured goods; anything modern is cheapjack, as if the man in charge does not know his job. This was not always so, for in general there is a tradition of solidity in construction and still humble craftsmen, like the inlay cabinet makers of Granada or the embroideresses of Majorca and the Canaries, produce exquisite work at tragically low prices.

All the second-rate service in industry, education, medicine, science, is by no means all the fault of the Franco regime. It has not on the whole been a rule of tyranny, but one of paternalism. Franco has tried to make all Spaniards conform to wholesome laws for their own benefit, an

The peasant of the old villages is bound by the physical need to keep himself and his family alive . . . but the modern holiday resorts are frequented by Spaniards as well as foreign tourists.

almost superhuman task in Spain. He has organised social insurance, a national health service, security of employment and a host of other benefits which are real enough, though they may seem inadequate in comparison with those enjoyed by the affluent society in Britain. By and large the lot of the ordinary Spaniard of the middle and working classes is infinitely better now than before 1936, but there is also something lost. The real intoxication of the early months of the Republic in 1931 was the freedom to say what one liked; there was immense enthusiasm on the part of intellectuals to share the treasures of Spanish thought, scholarship and art with the uneducated masses. But under the Republic there was chaos; the Spaniard has little social discipline and extremists were soon to the fore. Under the Franco regime there has been order and discipline which at times have been repressive and harsh. Conditions are still far from good or else why would thousands of Spaniards leave their enchanting land to seek humble domestic posts in France, England, Germany, Switzerland or elsewhere?

What does the future hold? The hope of almost all thinking Spaniards is that continuity can best be maintained by the restoration of the monarchy. There are two sons of Alfonso XIII still living, Don Jaime, who suffered from haemophilia and renounced his claim to the throne for reasons of ill health, and Don Juan, who lives in Portugal and who refused to do a deal with Franco, maintaining that he must be restored in his own right or not at all. However, he has allowed his son, Don Juan Carlos, to be educated in Spain. Don Juan Carlos has married into the Greek royal family and now all seems to be set that after Franco's death he will be the rallying point for Spain's traditional loyalty to the monarchy. Under a restored and perhaps more enlightened monarchy the present paternal rule may continue to hold Spain in peace and growing prosperity. Franco has concentrated on the family as the focal point of Spanish social structure and in this he has undoubtedly been right. In Spain the family is a real unit; the young are supremely well cared for and the old are rarely forgotten and left to fend for themselves. It is from the family that a strict code of behaviour emanates. Many who have employed Spanish servants in England must have marvelled alike at their obstinacy and honesty, their natural dignity in spite of the humble surroundings from which they come. It is from their families that they learned their virtues rather than from the Church, for on the whole the Church exerts little influence on ordinary people in Spain. Churches are largely deserted except for elderly women and regular attendance at mass is the exception rather than the rule. A

Spaniard, it is said, goes to church to be baptised, confirmed, married and buried; at other times there is an attitude of indifference, though the Church is still influential in politics and education. If the power of family loyalty can still be maintained, hopes for a peaceful future of Spain with gradually increasing liberalism run high. Unfortunately the forces of disruption are likely to gather only too readily. Apart from latent anarchism, communism or republicanism there is still a strong urge for separatism in the northern provinces and in the Basque country in particular there are a number of adherents to the utterly lost cause of Carlism. It may be that after General Franco's death there will be an explosion throughout Spain.

It is to be hoped that Spain has not sold its soul to Mammon in the shape of the currency that the foreign tourist brings. Certainly the Spaniards obstinately continue their way of life amid the multitude of foreigners who in order to do their shopping have to pick their way amid a herd of goats and buy their bread straight from the panniers of a donkey. The Spaniards are a great nation, rich in thought, literature, art and music, dignified, courageous, uncomplaining. Their faults lie in their inability to get on with each other; only in an emergency, especially when fighting a common enemy, can they unite. At other times they are overwhelming individualists; they have to quarrel with each other and no form of apology is admissible in Spain. A Spaniard in his own eyes must always be right; he must also in his own estimation always be engaged on some work of transcendental importance. To build a road right up the Sierra Nevada captures his imagination and he achieves his object in the face of fantastic difficulties. To maintain such a road is beyond his capacity and so the road peters out into a stony track just where it begins to be most interesting. However, Spain is different, just as Ireland is unique; both are nations that will cut off their noses to spite their faces. As such they have a fascination because the remainder of the western world cannot comprehend them. Spain, like Ireland, has scenic beauty that beggars description and this adds greatly to its charm, but the real interest lies in the fact that the Spaniards have developed their own intensely individual personality and culture unheedful of what the rest of the world may think.

Appendix: Spanish verse metres

1. The Spanish system of versification is based on the number of syllables in a line (*verso*). The syllabic count is reckoned to the last accented syllable, plus one more, e.g.

> *¿Por qué volvéis a la memoria mía*
> 1   2 3 4 5 6 7 8 9 1011
> *tristes recuerdos del placer perdido*
> 1 2 3 4 5 6   78 9 1011

2. When reckoning the syllables account must be taken of the running together of vowels (*sinalefa*). The rules for *sinalefa* are:

(*a*) Two identical vowels are merged into one sound.

(*b*) A weak and a strong vowel adjacent form a diphthong with stress on the strong vowel.

(*c*) When two strong vowels are adjacent the first elides.

(*d*) *Sinalefa* does not take place if an o or u stands between a, e, i, e.g. *pariente o amigo;* nor if the middle syllable is a distinct syllabic group, e.g. *me cuida y ama.*

(*e*) H does not normally prevent *sinalefa* taking place.

Note. These rules are not invariably observed by poets and are only a general guide.

> *a aumentar la ansiedad y la agonía*
> 1 2 3   4 5 6 7   891011
> *de este desierto corazón herido?*
>   1 2 3 4 5 6 7 8 91011
> *¡Ay! que de aquellas horas de alegría*
> 1   2   3 4 5 67   891011
> *le quedó al corazón sólo un gemido*
> 1 2 3 456   78   9 1011

> *Espronceda: Canto a Teresa*

Poetry imitated from the Italian forms from the beginning of the sixteenth century is mostly regular in metre, e.g. *sonetos, odas, liras, églogas.* Earlier poetry and much modern verse are often highly irregular in syllabification.

3. Verse may be without rhyme (*versos sueltos*, blank verse), usually only found in eleven-syllable lines: or it may have assonance, i.e. similarity of vowels in the last word of the line, or it may rhyme: masculine (*aguda*) when the final syllable rhymes, feminine (*llana*) when two syllables rhyme, proparoxytone (*esdrújula*) when three syllables rhyme; *rima perfecta* occurs when the last word rhymes from the accented syllable onwards.

4. *Verse forms*

The most important are:

   (*a*) Eight-syllable lines

   Romances: usually rhyming, but in the older ballads assonance was normal. Also the lines consisted of two sections each of eight syllables.

   Redondillas: lines of 7 or 8 syllables, four lines to a stanza rhyming abba.

   In the drama of the Golden Age *romances* are used for recounting narratives, *redondillas* for conversational exchanges.

   Quintillas. five-line stanzas in *rima perfecta* used in lyric verse in the Golden Age.

   Décimas: ten-line stanzas rhyming abbaccddcc, much used by Calderón (1600–81) in lyrical speeches.

   (*b*) Eleven-syllable lines

   Mostly used in poems in the Italian style. The caesura is after the seventh syllable, often forming a half line and giving flexibility to the verse.

   Liras: five-line stanzas of 7, 11, 7, 7, 11 syllable lines and rhyming ababb.

   Silvas: alternate lines of 7 and 11 syllables with a free rhyming scheme and sometimes a free arrangement of the length of lines. Rather a shapeless verse form, but its flexibility is useful in songs; also used to express lofty emotions in Calderón's dramas.

   Tercetos: stanzas of three lines with linking rhyme scheme, aba—bcb—cdc, ending usually with a final stanza of four lines. Good for expressing continuous thought in verse, e.g. satires. Not used for lyrical verse.

   Sonetos: fourteen lines (8 + 6). *Octava* has two rhymes abbaabba and the *sextilla* has three, cdecde. The *soneto* is used for heroic poetry and to mark the entrance of a heroic character in drama. It is more suitable for single poems usually epigrammatic in form. *Octavas* and *sextillas* are frequently used on their own outside the sonnet form. The *octava* rhymes ababab cc and the *sextilla* consisting of alternate seven- and eleven-syllable lines rhymes ababcc.

(c) Six-syllable lines are often used for *endechas* (laments) in rhyming eight-line stanzas.

(d) Twelve-syllable lines
   Coplas de arte mayor: eight-line stanzas rhyming abbaacca. Used in heroic poems up to the end of the fifteenth century.

Lines of four syllables, five syllables, nine syllables, ten syllables, fourteen syllables (*alejandrinos*) and sixteen syllables are also found, but are less common.

5. *Dating a poem*

(a) Study the metrical arrangement.
   Viejos romances: probably fifteenth century, but they have often been imitated especially by romantics.
   Italianate forms: probably sixteenth or seventeenth century, i.e. sonnets, odes, eclogues, etc.
   Irregular arrangements: probably romantic or modern.

(b) Study spelling and syntax. Forms like *desto, dello, haber* or *tener* not later than sixteenth century.

(c) Study allusions in the text: e.g. *Dos de Mayo* probably early nineteenth century. Religious and mystical poems mostly sixteenth century. Poems with extravagant, flowery phraseology probably by Góngora or his imitators in the sixteenth century. Dramatic and highly sentimental poems are likely to be of the romantic period. Modern poems are mostly short and strive after sound effects rather than a clear expression of thought.

   Lope de Vega in his *Arte nuevo de hacer comedias* (1609) defines the use of verse forms as follows:

> *Las décimas son buenas para quejas;*
> *El soneto está bien en los que aguardan;*
> *Las relaciones piden los romances,*
> *Aunque en octavas lucen por extremo;*
> *Son los tercetos para cosas graves,*
> *Y para las de amor las redoudillas.*

Further reading

Part 1: The Land and its History
Chapter 1
BORROW, GEORGE. *The Bible in Spain*. London 1842, many editions since.
BORROW, G. *Gypsies of Spain*, 1841, and many reprints since.
BRENAN, G. *The face of Spain*. London 1950.
—— *The Spanish labyrinth*. London 1943.
—— *South from Granada*, 1957.
BRODRICK, A. H. *Pillars of Hercules: the Iberian Scene*. London 1950.
COLES, S. F. A. *Spain everlasting*. London 1945.
DIXON, R. A. N. *Spanish rhapsody*. London 1955.
FAIRMAN, C. *Another Spain*. London 1952.
FORD, RICHARD. *A handbook for travellers in Spain*. 1st edition. London 1845, reprinted 1966.
—— *Gatherings from Spain*. London 1846, reissued many times since.
HAVELOCK ELLIS. *The soul of Spain*. London 1926.
HELM, M. *Spring in Spain*. London 1953.
HÜRLIMANN, N. *Spain*. London 1954. Excellent illustrations.
MacARTHUR, D. W. *Auto nomad in Spain*. London 1953.
MORTON, H. V. *A stranger in Spain*. London 1955.
MUIRHEADS BLUE GUIDES. *Northern Spain* (2nd ed.), 1958. *Southern Spain* (2nd ed.), 1964.
OGRIZEK, D. *Spain and Portugal*. New York 1953. Colour pictures.
PRITCHETT V. S. *The Spanish Temper*. London 1954.
REYNOLDS, J. *Fabulous Spain*. London 1955.
SITWELL, S. *Spain*. London 1950.
STARKIE, W. *Spanish raggle taggle*. London 1934.
—— *The Road to Santiago*, 1957.
TOMLINSON, H. M. *South to Cadiz*. London 1934.
TREND, J. B. *Spain from the South*. London 1928.
—— *The Civilization of Spain* (2nd ed.), 1967.
TSCHIFFELY, A. F. *Round and about Spain*. London 1952.

Chapter 2
ALTAMIRA, RAFAEL. *A history of Spanish civilisation*. London 1930.
—— *Manual de historia española*. Madrid 1934.
ATKINSON, W. C. *Spain. A brief history*. London 1934.

BERTRAND, LOUIS and PETRIE, SIR CHARLES. *The history of Spain*. London 1952.

CARPENTER, R. *The Greeks in Spain*. Bryn Mawr, Penn. 1925.

CASTRO, A. *The Structure of Spanish History*, 1954.

DIXON, P. *The Iberians in Spain*. Oxford 1940.

DOZY, R. *Spanish Islam*, 1913.

HUME, M. A. S. *The Spanish people*. London 1901.

IRVING, WASHINGTON. *Chronicle of the conquest of Granada*, new edn. London 1910.

—— *Legends of the conquest of Spain*. London 1836.

MENÉNDEZ-PIDAL, R. *The Cid and his Spain* (*La España del Cid*), trans. H. Sunderland. London 1934.

MONTGOMERY-WATT, W. *A History of Islamic Spain*, Edinburgh 1965.

PEERS, E. A. ed. *Spain. A companion to Spanish Studies*, 4th edn. London 1948.

PRESCOTT, W. H. *The history of Ferdinand and Isabella*. London 1842.

RUSSELL, P. E. *The English Intervention in Spain and Portugal in the time of Edward III and Richard II*, London 1955.

SUTHERLAND, C. H. V. *The Romans in Spain 217 B.C.–A.D. 117*. London 1939.

TREND, J. B. *The language and history of Spain*. Cambridge 1953.

Chapter 3

AGUADO BLEYE, S. *Manual de historia de España*. Bilbao 1927–8.

AZORÍN. *An hour of Spain between 1560 and 1590*. London 1930.

BERTRAND, LOUIS. *Philippe II, une ténébreuse affaire*. Paris 1929.

—— *Philippe II à l'Escorial*. Paris 1928.

BLACK, J. B. *The Reign of Elizabeth*. Oxford 1936.

BRATLI, C. J. B. *Philippe II, roi d'Espagne*. Paris 1912.

CHAYTOR, H. J. *History of Aragon and Catalonia*. London 1933.

ELLIOTT, J. H. *Imperial Spain 1469–1716*. London 1963.

EYRE, E. *European Civilisation, its origin and development*, Vols. 3, 4, 5. Oxford 1935–7.

FROUDE, J. A. *The Spanish story of the Armada*. London 1898.

GEYL, P. *The Revolt of the Netherlands 1555–1609*. London 1932.

HAMILTON, EARL J. *American treasure and the price revolution in Spain*. Cambridge, Mass. 1934, reprinted 1965.

HARING, C. J. *Trade and navigation between Spain and the Indies in the time of the Hapsburgs*. Harvard Economic Studies, Cambridge, Mass. 1918.

KAMEN, M. *The Spanish Inquisition*, 1965.

KIRKPATRICK, F. A. *The Spanish Conquistadores*. London 1946.

LEA, H. C. *A history of the Inquisition in Spain*. 4 vols. New York 1906–7.

LYNCH, J. *Spain under the Hapsburgs*, Vol. I, 1964.

MARAÑÓN, G. *Antonio Pérez*. London 1954.

MATTINGLY, G. *The defeat of the Spanish Armada*. London 1959.

MERRIMAN, R. B. *The rise of the Spanish Empire in the Old World and the New*. New York, reprinted 1962.

MERTON, R. *Cardinal Ximenes*. London 1934.

PARRY, J. H. *The Spanish Seaborne Empire*, 1966.

RENIER, G. *William of Orange*. New York 1933.

SEAVER, H. J. *The great revolt in Castille*. London 1928; also Cambridge, Mass.

TREVOR DAVIES, R. *The golden century in Spain 1501–1621*, 4th ed. London 1958.

TURBERVILLE, A. S. *The Spanish Inquisition*. London 1932.

VAN DYKE, P. *Ignatius Loyala, the founder of the Jesuits*. New York 1926.

Chapter 4
ARTOLA, M. *Los afrancesados*. Madrid 1953.
BUCKLE, H. T. *History of civilisation in England*, Vol. 2. London 1903.
CÁNOVAS DEL CASTILLO, A. *Historia de la decadencia española*. Madrid 1911.
COXE, W. *Memoirs of the Kings of Spain of the House of Bourbon*. London 1813.
DUNLOP, J. C. *Memoirs of Spain during the reigns of Philip IV and Charles II*. Edinburgh 1843.
ELLIOTT, J. H. *The revolt of the Catalans*. Cambridge 1963.
FANSHAWE, ANNE. ed. B. Marshall. *Memoirs, 1600–1672*. London 1905.
HERR, R. *The eighteenth-century revolution in Spain*. London 1958.
HUME, M. A. S. *The Court of Philip IV*, reprinted London 1927.
—— *Spain: its greatness and decay, 1479–1788*, 3rd ed. Cambridge 1913.
MARAÑÓN, G. *El conde-duque de Olivares*, 3rd ed. Madrid 1952.
NADA, J. *Carlos the bewitched*. London 1962.
SARRAILH, J. *L'Espagne éclairée de la seconde moitié du XVIIIe siecle*. Paris 1954.
TREVOR DAVIES, R. *Spain in decline*. London 1961.

Chapter 5
BOLLOTEN, B. *The Grand Camouflage*, reprinted 1968.
BORKENAU, F. *The Spanish Cockpit*, 1937, reprinted 1963.
BRUGERA, F. G. *Histoire contemporaine d'Espagne*. Paris 1953.
CARR, R. *Spain 1808–1939*. Oxford 1966.
CLARKE, H. BUTLER. *Modern Spain 1815–1898*. Cambridge 1906.
CROZIER, B. *Franco, a Biographical History*. London 1967.
FERNÁNDEZ ALMAGRO, M. *Historia del reinado de Alfonso XIII*. Barcelona 1933.
—— *Historia política de la España contemporánea*. Madrid 1956.
GALDÓS, B. PÉREZ. *Episodios nacionales*. Madrid 1872–1912. 46 novels on nineteenth century history.
HENNESSY, C. A. M. *The Federal Republic in Spain*, 1962.
HILLS, G. *Franco, the Man and his Nation*. London 1967.
HOLT, E. *The Carlist Wars in Spain*, 1967.
HUME, M. A. S. *Modern Spain 1788–1898*, 2nd ed. London 1906.
HUMPHREYS, R. A. *Liberation in Latin America*. London 1952.
JACKSON, G. *The Spanish Republic and the Civil War*, 1965.
KIERNAN, V. G. *The Revolution of 1854 in Spanish History*, 1965.
MADARIAGA, S. DE. *Spain*. London 1946.
OLIVAR BERTRAND, R. *Prim*. Barcelona 1951.
OLIVEIRA, A. R. *Politics, economics and men of modern Spain 1808–1946*. London 1946.
OMAN, SIR CHARLES. *History of the Peninsular War*. 7 Vols. Oxford 1902–30.
OYARZÚN, R. *Historia del carlismo*, 2nd ed. Madrid 1944.
PAYNE, S. *Falange*, 1962.
—— *Politics and the Military in Modern Spain*, London 1968.
ROBERTSON, W. S. *Rise of the Latin American republics*. London 1918.
SECO SERRANO, C. *Historia de la España moderna*. Barcelona 1962.
THOMAS, HUGH. *The Spanish Civil War*. London 1961.
TREND, J. B. *The origins of modern Spain*. Cambridge 1934.
WELLER, J. *Wellington in the Peninsula*, 1962.

Part 2: Literature

BELL, A. F. G. *Castilian literature.* Oxford 1938.

BRENAN, G. *The literature of the Spanish people.* Cambridge 1951.

COHEN, J. M. ed. *Penguin book of Spanish verse—with translations,* rev. ed. London 1960.

ENTWISTLE, W. J. *The Spanish Language.* London 1936.

FITZMAURICE-KELLY, J. *A new history of Spanish literature.* Oxford 1926.

—— ed. *Oxford book of Spanish verse,* rev. J. B. Trend. Oxford 1949.

MENÉNDEZ Y PELAYO, M. *Historia de las ideas estéticas en España,* new edn. 6 vols. Madrid 1941.

MÉRIMÉE, E. and MORLEY, S. G. *A history of Spanish literature.* New York 1930.

ROMERA-NAVARRO, M. *Historia de la literatura española.* Boston 1928.

——, ed. *Antología de la literatura española.* Boston 1933.

TICKNOR, G. *History of Spanish literature,* 6th ed. 3 Vols. Boston 1891.

VALBUENA PRAT, A. *Historia de la literatura española,* new edn., 3 Vols. Barcelona 1950.

Chapter 6

CRAWFORD, J. P. W. *Spanish drama before Lope de Vega.* Philadelphia 1922.

ENTWISTLE, W. J. *European Balladry.* Oxford 1939.

FITZMAURICE-KELLY, J. *Chapters on Spanish literature.* London 1908.

MENÉNDEZ-PIDAL, R. *Poesía árabe y poesía europea.* Madrid 1938.

—— *Poesía juglaresca y juglares.* Madrid 1924.

MORLEY, S. G. *Spanish ballads.* New York 1911.

PUYOL Y ALONSO, J. *El Arcipreste de Hita, estudio crítico.* Madrid 1906.

ROSE, R. S. and BACON, L. *The Lay of the Cid—a verse translation.* Berkeley, Cal. 1919.

SIMPSON, L. B., translator. *La Celestina.* University of California 1955.

TREND, J. B. *Alfonso the Sage and other essays.* London 1926.

Chapter 7

ARMESTO, SAID. *La leyenda de Don Juan.* Madrid 1908.

BELL, A. F. G. *Luis de León.* Oxford 1925.

CHAYTOR, H. J. *Dramatic theory in Spain.* Cambridge 1925.

CHURTON, E. *Góngora: a historical and critical essay on the times of Philip III and IV.* 2 Vols. London 1862.

ENTWISTLE, W. J. *Cervantes.* Oxford 1940.

FITZMAURICE-KELLY, J. *Lope de Vega and Spanish drama.* Oxford 1902.

GÓNGORA, LUIS DE. *The Solitudes (Soledades),* trans. E. M. Wilson. Cambridge 1965.

KENISTON, E. *Garcilaso de la Vega, a critical study of his life and works.* New York 1922.

MADARIAGA, S. DE. *Don Quixote.* London 1934.

MORENO BAEZ, E. *Guzmán de Alfarache.* Madrid 1948.

PARKER, A. A. *The allegorical drama of Calderón.* Oxford 1943.

—— *Literature and the Delinquent,* Edinburgh 1967.

PEERS, E. A. *Studies of the Spanish mystics.* New York 1927.

—— *St Teresa of Jesus.* London 1953.

RENNERT, V. *The Spanish stage in the time of Lope de Vega.* New York 1909.

SHERGOLD, N. D. *A History of the Spanish Stage,* 1967.

Chapter 8

COTARELO Y MORI, E. *Iriarte y su época.* Madrid 1897.

—— *Don Ramón de la Cruz y sus obras.* Madrid 1899.

CUETO, L. A. (MARQUÉS DE VALMAR). *Historia crítica de la poesía castellana en el siglo XVIII.* Madrid 1893.

JUDERÍAS, J. *Don Gaspar Melchor de Jovellanos.* Madrid 1913.

MARTÍNEZ RUBIO, J. *Moratín.* Valencia 1893.

PARDO BAZÁN, E. *Examen crítico de las obras del P. Maestro Feijóo.* Madrid 1877.

PELLISSIER, R. E. *The neo-classic movement in Spain during the XVIII century.* California 1918.

PIÑEYRO, E. *Manuel José Quintana.* Madrid 1892.

Chapter 9

ALARCÓN, P. A. DE. '*Historia de mis libros*', in his *Obras completas.* Madrid 1899.

ANDRADE COELLA, A. *La Condesa Emilia Pardo Bazán.* Quito 1922.

AZORÍN. *Rivas y Larra, razón social del romanticismo.* Madrid 1926.

BARJA, CÉSAR. *Rosalía de Castro.* New York 1923.

—— *Libros y autores modernos.* New York 1924.

BELL, A. F. G. *Contemporary Spanish literature.* New York 1923.

BLANCO GARCÍA, F. *La literatura española en el siglo XIX,* 2nd edn. Madrid 1909–12.

CASCALES Y MUÑOZ, J. *Don José de Espronceda: su época, su vida y sus obras.* Madrid 1914.

GONZÁLEZ BLANCO, A. *Historia de la novela en España desde el romanticismo hasta nuestros días.* Madrid 1909.

HILTON, R. *Campoamor, Spain and the World.* Toronto 1940.

LÓPEZ NÚÑEZ, J. *Bécquer: biografía anecdótica.* Madrid 1915.

MCCLELLAND, I. L. *The origins of the Romantic Movement in Spain.* Liverpool 1937.

MONTERO, J. *Pereda.* Madrid 1919.

NAVAS, CONDE DE LAS. *Don Juan Valera: apuntes del natural.* Madrid 1905.

PEERS, E. A. *A history of the Romantic Movement in Spain.* 2 Vols. Cambridge 1940.

—— *Rivas and Romanticism in Spain.* Liverpool 1923.

WALTON, L. B. *Pérez Galdós and the Spanish novel of the nineteenth century.* London 1928.

Chapter 10

AZORÍN. *Clásicos y modernos.* Madrid 1919.

BALBONTÍN, J. A. *Three Spanish Poets.* London 1961.

BAREA, A. *Lorca, the poet and his people.* London 1944.

BLANCO-FOMBONA, R. *El modernismo y los poetas modernos.* Madrid 1929.

CANSINOS-ASSÉNS, R. *La nueva literatura.* Madrid 1917.

DÍEZ CANEDO, E. *Juan Ramón Jiménez y su obra.* Mexico 1924.

DURAN, M., ed. *Lorca: a collection of critical essays.* New York 1962.

GONZÁLEZ BLANCO, A. *Los contemporáneos.* Paris 1906–8.

ROMERA NAVARRO, M. *Miguel de Unamuno.* Madrid 1928.

STARKIE, WALTER. *Jacinto Benavente.* Oxford 1924.

VALBUENA PRAT, A. *La poesía española contemporánea.* Madrid 1930.

—— *Historia del teatro español.* Barcelona 1956.

Part 3: Arts, Architecture and Music

Chapter 11

BEVAN, B. *History of Spanish architecture.* London 1938.

BYNE, A. and STAPLEY, M. *Spanish architecture of the sixteenth century.* New York 1917.

—— *Provincial houses in Spain.* New York 1925.

BYNE, M. S. *Forgotten shrines of Spain.* London 1926.

FLETCHER, SIR BANISTER. *A history of architecture on the comparative method.* London 1945.

GADE, J. A. *Cathedrals of Spain.* London 1911.

HARTLEY, C. G. *The cathedrals of southern Spain.* London 1913.

HARVEY, J. *The Cathedrals of Spain,* 1957.

KING, G. G. *Pre-Romanesque churches of Spain.* Bryn Mawr, Penn. 1924.

KUBLER, G. and SORIA, M. *Art and Architecture in Spain and Portugal and their American Dominions,* 1500–1800, 1964.

LEES-MILNE, J. *Baroque in Spain and Portugal,* 1960.

MAYER, A. L. *El estilo gótico en España.* Madrid 1929.

PALOL, P. DE and HIRMER, M. *Early Medieval Art in Spain.* London 1867.

PORTER, A. KINGSLEY. *Spanish Romanesque Sculpture,* Paris 1928.

STREET, G. E. *Some account of Gothic architecture in Spain.* London 1865, new edn. 1914.

TYLER, R. *Spain, a study of her life and arts,* 1913.

WHITEHILL, W. M. *Spanish Romanesque architecture of the eleventh century.* Oxford 1941.

WHITTLESEY, A. *Renaissance architecture of central and northern Spain.* New York 1920.

Chapter 12

Arte y decoración en España. 12 Vols. Barcelona 1917–28.

BERNETE Y MORET, A. DE. *The School of Madrid,* 2nd ed. London 1911.

CALVERT, A. F. *Sculpture in Spain.* London 1912.

—— *Goya.* London 1908.

FROTHERINGHAM, A. W. *Spanish Glass,* 1964.

GAYA NUÑO, J. A. *La pintura española del medio siglo.* Barcelona 1952.

GOLDSCHEIDER, L. *El Greco, paintings, drawings and sculptures.* London 1954.

GUDIOL, J. *The arts of Spain.* London 1964.

HAGEN, O. F. L. *Patterns and principles of Spanish art.* Madison, U.S.A. 1943.

HARTLEY, C. G. *A record of Spanish painting.* London 1904.

KING, G. G. *Heart of Spain.* Cambridge, Mass. 1941.

LAFUENTE FERRARI, E. *Historia de la pintura española.* Madrid 1953.

MAYER, A. L. *La pintura española.* Barcelona 1926.

ORTEGA Y GASSET, J. *Velázquez.* London 1954.

PELLICER, C. *Picasso antes de Picasso.* Barcelona 1946.

POST, C. R. *A history of Spanish painting,* 8 Vols. Cambridge, Mass. 1930–41.

SITWELL, S. *Southern Baroque art.* new ed. London 1951.

TEMPLE, A. G. *Modern Spanish painting.* London 1908.

Chapter 13

ARMSTRONG, L. *Dances of Spain.* London 1950.

CHASE, G. *The Music of Spain,* 2nd ed. New York 1959.

HAGUE, E. *Latin American music, past and present.* Santa Ana, Cal. 1934.

PEDRELL, F. *Cancionero musical popular español,* 4 Vols. Valls 1918–22.

—— *Diccionario biográfico y bibliográfico de músicos y escritores de música españoles* (incomplete). Barcelona 1897.

SCHINDLER, K. *Folk-music and poetry of Spain and Portugal.* New York 1941.

TREND, J. B. *Manuel de Falla and Spanish Music.* New York 1929.

—— *The music of Spanish history to 1600.* Oxford 1926.

VAN VECHTEN, C. *The music of Spain.* New York 1918.

Index